White Women, Rape, and

the Power of Race in Virginia,

1900–1960

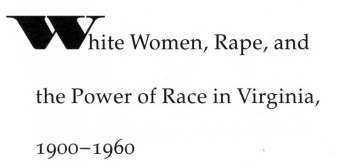

White Women, Rape, and

the Power of Race in Virginia,

1900–1960

Lisa Lindquist Dorr

THE UNIVERSITY OF NORTH CAROLINA PRESS
CHAPEL HILL AND LONDON

The paper in this book meets the guidelines for
permanence and durability of the Committee on Production
Guidelines for Book Longevity of the Council on Library
Resources.

Library of Congress Cataloging-in-Publication Data
Dorr, Lisa Lindquist.
White women, rape, and the power of race in Virginia, 1900–1960 /
Lisa Lindquist Dorr.
     p. cm.
Includes bibliographical references (p.   ) and index.
ISBN 0-8078-2841-6 (alk. paper)
ISBN 0-8078-5514-6 (pbk.: alk. paper)
     1. Rape—Virginia—History—20th century. 2. Virginia—Race
relations—History—20th century. I. Title.
HV6568.V8 D67   2004
364.14'32'08996073075509041—dc22
2003017452

cloth   08 07 06 05 04   5 4 3 2 1
paper   08 07 06 05 04   5 4 3 2 1

CONTENTS

ACKNOWLEDGMENTS

In the time between conceiving a dissertation project and seeing it come to fruition as a book, one accumulates numerous debts along the way. It seems only fitting that the final piece of the project is to acknowledge those debts, both intellectual and material. The *Journal of Southern History*, *IRIS: A Journal for Women*, and the New York University Press previously published portions of this work as articles, and I appreciate the permission to reprint them here. A Yalden-Thompson Research Grant from the University of Virginia Society of Fellows and a Littleton-Griswold Research Grant from the American Historical Association helped defray the costs of traveling from courthouse to courthouse around Virginia and to the Library of Virginia in Richmond. A dissertation fellowship from the Carter G. Woodson Institute for African and Afro-American Studies enabled me to spend two years writing the dissertation. Far more beneficial than the money, however, was the community of scholars gathered at the institute itself. Their insights and criticisms have immeasurably improved my thinking and my writing, and I continue to value their friendships. I thank especially Rolland Murray, Adrian Gaskins, Joe Hellweg, Greta de Jong, Natasha Gray, Phillip Troutman, Rosanne Adderley, Ian Strachan, Dylan Penningroth, Robert Vinson, and Patricia Krus.

Academic work, despite its reputation for isolation, nonetheless is only possible with the cooperation of a good many people. I would like to thank the county clerks in Virginia's courthouses for their help in locating information about my cases, even though the cases in which I was interested were, by their accounts, from the ancient past. I appreciated their good humor in the face of a driver of a purple car with Michigan plates who wanted to know about black-on-white rape. Robert Y. Clay, Minor T. Weisiger, and Jennifer Davis McDaid at the Library of Virginia were also invaluable. Minor Weisiger pointed me to the clemency files, without which this project would not have been nearly so interesting. Jennifer McDaid, once I had moved to Alabama, helped me clear up some confusion about citation information. Chris McKiernan, an old friend, also completed some last minute research for me at the Fairfax County Courthouse, when I was unable to return to Virginia. All their efforts made my work easier.

I have been blessed by wise counsel throughout my academic life. Ann J. Lane, my adviser at the University of Virginia, deserves special thanks. Her words of wisdom have encouraged not only myself but my friends and colleagues across the country as well. She is the kind of professor I would like to be. Grace Elizabeth Hale proved to be not only an astute and brilliant critic but also a dear friend. Reginald Butler, director of the Woodson Institute, and Cindy Aron lent their keen eyes to the project at critical stages. Alfred Brophy at the University of Alabama Law School gave the final manuscript a careful and lawyerly read. Laura Edwards's comments were invaluable as I worked to transform the manuscript from dissertation to book, as did those of the second anonymous reviewer for UNC Press. I thank them for their time, attention, and insights. I would also like to thank my colleagues here at the University of Alabama's history department. I did not saddle any of them with the manuscript, but they have created a wonderful atmosphere in which to work. Not many departments are so congenial, and I am grateful for their friendships and their professional advice.

Finally, I would like to thank my family. They have offered me unending encouragement and support when my spirits flagged, always reminding me of the value of my chosen profession. My parents, George and Mary Lindquist, and my grandmother, Cora Nederlanden Lindquist, also came through when our finances got tight. Greg deserves a special thanks, as colleague, friend, and husband. I know of few academic couples for whom intellectual pursuits are a true partnership. He has been my best and most faithful critic, and much of what is good in this book grew from his gentle prodding. His confidence has never wavered. And last, I want to thank Fiona and Sophie, my precious girls, whose bright faces keep everything in perspective.

Messin' White Women, Snake Lyin' Tales

Black-on-White Rape in Virginia

On a cool, spring day in March 1931, two white women hitched a ride on a freight train in Alabama in the hopes of finding work in a neighboring state. When authorities stopped the train some time later, both women, fearing arrest for violating the Mann Act, which prohibited transporting even willing women across state lines for illicit purposes, told police that they had been raped by nine black men who were also scattered along the train.[1] Their accusation caused a furor, and a mob that gathered to lynch the men dispersed only with promises of a speedy trial. Despite little evidence of rape, the men were convicted based on the women's testimony and sentenced to death. As the case meandered through four separate trials and two supreme court decisions, local whites continued to support the women's charges, even though one recanted her claim of rape after the second trial. Allegations eventually surfaced that the women were no paragons of virtue. Both had occasionally resorted to prostitution to support themselves and apparently had engaged in sexual relations with unmarried white men in the days before they made their accusations. Nevertheless, in an early articulation of what would come to be rape shield laws, which, in the 1970s, attempted to protect against attacks on the character of a rape victim, white southerners argued that the two women's sordid sexual past should have no bearing on the case. As one spectator told a reporter, the victim "might be a fallen woman, but by God she is a white woman."[2] Though the nine accused men eventually won their freedom, the Scottsboro case, as it came to be known, has become the paradigm for all black-on-white rape cases in the twentieth century, in which the accuser's whiteness overrode any consideration of her gender, sexual history, or class status. As one song about the case insisted, "Messin' white women / Snake lyin' tale / Dat hang and burn / And jail wit' no bail."[3] This case seemingly proved the power of the "rape myth": that white southerners accepted all white women's accounts of rape when they accused black men, thereby instigating a united effort to seek revenge. The myth insisted that black men were driven to assault white women and that, as a deterrent, "black beast rapists" should pay with their lives, even if white women's charges were little more than "snake lyin' tales."

The Scottsboro, Alabama, case, however, was exceptional in a number of respects and created more controversy than the rape myth would suggest. For one, it motivated a national movement to free the accused men. It also spurred heated confrontations between the NAACP and the Communist Party. Few cases received the national and international press coverage that the Scottsboro trials received. Few resulted in any Supreme Court rulings on due process; two such decisions grew out of the Scottsboro case. Even the claims of rape by the two women generated more controversy than the rape myth would suggest. Many scholars are familiar with the pronouncements of William W. Callahan, the presiding judge over the third series of trials of the Scottsboro men. He instructed the jury that no white woman, regardless of her class or sexual history, would consent to sexual relations with black men, "whether she be the most despised, ignorant and abandoned woman of the community, or the spotless virgin and daughter of a prominent home of luxury and learning."[4] Fewer recall the willingness of his predecessor in the second trial to question the victims' characters. After the jury returned guilty verdicts, Judge James E. Horton Jr. threw out the verdicts, writing, "History, sacred and profane, and the common experience of mankind teach us that women of the character shown in this case are prone for selfish reasons to make false accusation both of rape and insult upon the slightest provocation, or even without provocation for ulterior purposes. . . . The tendency on the part of the women shows they are predisposed to make false accusations upon any occasion whereby their selfish ends may be gained."[5] Judge Horton raised the traditional suspicions about the motives behind rape victims' accusations. In his analysis, the compromised characters of the victims superseded the explosive issue of race. Indeed, many of his fellow white southerners, both in Alabama and elsewhere, shared his distrust of those "messin' white women."[6]

As another prominent 1931 case from Virginia illustrates, white southerners did consider issues other than race when they confronted white women's accusations against black men.[7] Two and a half months before the two women made their charges in Scottsboro, Dorothy Skaggs, a white woman married to an enlisted sailor, allegedly left her home in Portsmouth, Virginia, to go to a guitar lesson. She later testified in court that, while walking along the street, she was struck on the head, dragged into an alley, and raped by a black man. William Harper was subsequently arrested and identified by the victim; after a beating by police, he confessed to the assault.[8] Harper's trial proceeded predictably, and he was convicted and sentenced to death. When the defense revealed new evidence, however, the Norfolk court quickly granted him a new trial. At the second trial, Harper produced six white witnesses who testified that on the night in question, Dorothy Skaggs was not on her way to a guitar lesson but was at a roadhouse across state lines in North Carolina, drinking and dancing with a man who was not her husband. Harper was quickly acquitted, but the case was not over. Dorothy Skaggs and a white woman who had corroborated her story of rape were brought to trial on charges of perjury. Both were initially convicted and sentenced to five years in prison. Eventually, however, both women were granted new trials and were subsequently acquitted.

The original case against Harper followed the expected trajectory of black-on-white rape cases. Harper's confession was the result of police brutality, and police apparently did little to question Dorothy Skaggs's accusations. But when presented with evidence contradicting Skaggs's account of rape, the judge ordered a new trial. Newspaper coverage quickly questioned her innocence, publishing allegations that she used drugs and had previously cheated on her husband, a sailor away at sea.[9] Whites in Norfolk ultimately had no difficulty believing that a white woman, especially one of Dorothy Skaggs's apparent reputation and character, would use a false charge of rape to get herself out of a tight situation. After all, she faced prosecution under the same Mann Act provisions as did the two white women in the Scottsboro case; she voluntarily crossed the border into North Carolina with a man who was not her husband for presumably illicit purposes. An editorial in a Richmond newspaper asked whether the unquestioned acceptance of white women's charges of rape resulted in justice for the men they accused, especially when those men were black:

> How many instances have there been when, with counsel and court less careful, the tragedy that was diverted in this instance, has been played out to the end? How often have frightened, undefended Negroes confessed to crimes they never committed? How many times have they been railroaded to prison or to the electric chair because bad women wanted to cover up their own misdeeds? The questions are disquieting. Here in Virginia . . . a woman may accuse a man of rape, and with the consent of the court, may make a deposition and not appear in court against him. Accusation has almost been tantamount to conviction.[10]

Clearly, the newspaper suggested, no rape victim's accusation should escape careful scrutiny.

The conclusions of the second Norfolk jury, the willingness of the court to charge Skaggs with perjury, and the editorial in the Richmond paper notwithstanding, Virginia was not a bastion of racial equality in the courtroom. Despite being anomalous in its lack of mob violence, Virginians nonetheless voiced the familiar rhetoric about the danger black men represented to white women and the need to maintain white supremacy. The Scottsboro case and the Harper/Skaggs case together, however, suggest that white women's accusations of rape could elicit a range of responses in the legal system. Consider several other cases also tried in Virginia at about the same time. In 1930, Raymond Alsberry received a sentence of twelve years in prison after being accused of attempting to rape a twenty-six-year-old white woman. Jacob Duncan, in 1927, received an eighteen-year sentence for raping a white girl who was not more than fourteen at the time. In 1928, Harold Taylor's four-year sentence for attempted rape of a white woman was overturned after the court ruled the verdict improper. Taylor pleaded guilty to assault and battery and received a twelve-month sentence and was fined $250. In 1931, Frank Ross was acquitted on an attempted rape charge with no fanfare when his white employer provided him with an alibi.[11] All these cases indicate that white southerners, perhaps especially the white elites who controlled the legal process, considered factors other than the racial composition of the case when they determined what constituted "justice" for accused black men. Indeed, their deliberations over white women's charges and black men's fates illuminate a great deal about social relations in the segregated South.

The numerous cases that passed through the legal system without excessive media attention, without the participation of civil rights groups, without appeals to higher courts, and without apparent mob action provide a better means of examining southern attitudes toward all kinds of interracial relationships. These cases reveal a complex collection of interracial interactions and alliances that often existed in contradiction to white southerners' rhetoric about the need to protect and defend white women. A close examination of 288 cases of black-on-white rape in Virginia reveals the balancing act required to maintain intertwined race, class, and gender hierarchies. Although these cases demonstrate that being accused of an assault by a white woman placed a black man in considerable jeopardy, they also show that extreme punishment was not inevitable.[12] Seventeen of the 288 accused black men (6 percent) were killed through extralegal violence.[13] Approximately 230, or 87 percent, of the 271 men not lynched were convicted of some crime, ranging from rape and murder to robbery, assault and battery, and even "annoying a white woman."[14] Of those 230 convicted men, fifty (22 percent) were executed. Nevertheless, most black men escaped with their lives, and many with comparatively minor sentences. While 48 (21 percent of the 230 convicted men) received the maximum prison sentences allowed under Virginia law, the majority (133, or 58 percent) received lesser sentences. Fifty-two convicted men (23 percent of the 230 convicted men) received sentences of five years or less.[15] Thirty-five men (13 percent) were acquitted or saw the charges against them dismissed. Finally, Virginia governors granted many convicted men conditional pardons long before they completed their sentences.[16]

Looking back through time, it is not possible to determine exactly what occurred between the accused black men and the white women who named them as assailants. Though legal trials ostensibly sought to ascertain "The Truth," in reality they functioned as ritualistic spectacles that diffused the furor usually awakened by the alleged assault. Trials themselves were public performances in which white juries usually, though not always, acted out their role as the protectors of white women, adhering to a script of sexual and racial ideologies made familiar through southern rhetoric.[17] Most accused black men were convicted, but they were not necessarily guilty. The verdict of the jury merely indicated which side's version of events better adhered to accepted social realities and expectations. Once the jury returned its verdict, back-stage maneuverings in appeals or clemency petitions allowed white legal authorities to weigh the need to punish black men with the need simultaneously to reassert related class and gender hierarchies.[18] Their decisions rendered judgments upon related issues: the white woman's behavior as victim and her or her family's reputation for abiding by accepted social norms; the previous good reputation, age, or mental ability of her alleged assailant and his ability to use his relationships with other whites to win leniency; and even whites' perceptions of the defendant's desire to subvert the racial hierarchy. Many of the actions for which black men faced capital charges would not have placed a white man in legal jeopardy, underscoring the power of white legal authorities to police both consensual and forced interracial sexual relationships. Simultaneously, however, clemency files also contained considerable criticism of the failure of some whites to behave as a "superior" race should.

Cases of black-on-white rape both fed and grew out of white fears. White Virginians, like other white southerners, believed that blacks were reverting to savagery, that black men were driven biologically to desire white women and to fulfill those desires by force.[19] Most horrifying, whites convinced themselves that by stealing sexual relations with white women, black men were attempting to seize the patriarchal privileges and social power that southern society gave white men. For whites, responding to black men's alleged assaults was both a means of racial control and a way to assert white supremacy. To many white Virginians, however, automatic extralegal violence represented a crude tool of white power. Avoiding a lynching and conducting a legal trial, in their eyes, proved the superiority of white civilization. Only the most civilized of men could sublimate their primitive urge for retribution in favor of the rational and objective rule of law. Although legal authorities willingly used the potential for mob violence to influence a case, they also acknowledged that black men did not always represent a sexual danger to white women. Some black men might commit violent crimes against white women, some might even express sexual desires for white women, but not all of these actions were preludes to rape. Making these sorts of distinctions allowed whites to judge not only black men's supposed propensity toward sexual violence but also women's own anxieties toward strange black men.

White women's accusations of rape also brought struggles for power among whites, both women and men, to the fore. The rape myth, based on white women's role as the symbolic guardians of white purity and virtue, gave white women considerable ability to accuse black men of rape and demand that white men provide protection through revenge. This power theoretically resided in the hands of all white women, regardless of their character or social status, and thus gave all white women, no matter how untrustworthy, virtually dictatorial power over white men's actions. Fickle, weak women, however, could be manipulated. Allegations that disreputable men's wives or daughters had been raped could become a means for men to assert their own white privilege, or to settle scores with black men. Black-on-white rape cases thus could buttress the racial hierarchy, but they also leveled class and gender hierarchies that were equally important to the southern social order. Despite the rhetoric of white solidarity, not all whites were equal, and not all white women were worthy of protection. Whites' varied responses to charges of black-on-white rape balanced these interests over the course of the legal process and conceded that not all whites were superior to all blacks and that all rape victims, even white women accusing black men, merited suspicion and scrutiny when they levied their charges.

Whites did not always weigh these competing considerations simultaneously or even openly, however. Most black men were convicted, representing tangible proof of white men's rhetorical duty to protect all white women. Whites usually upheld white solidarity in decisions about guilt or innocence and then, in considerations of pardon, raised concerns about the defendant's or the victim's character or their place in the community. White elites, in the person of legal officials, law enforcement officers, or state authorities, often sought to "correct" justice years after the jury returned its verdict. The variety of white responses to black men's assaults flies in the face of accepted scholarly and popular conclusions about black-on-white rape: that all black men faced death for even the most ludicrous charges made by scheming white women. This assumption grew out of the tangled history of race in America.

White fears of the black beast rapist have a long history in the South, but they are not timeless. Indeed, they reflect a particular historical context. In the antebellum South, communities tolerated sexual relations between white women and black men as long as those involved in them did not blur the relationship between race and slavery, usually through the birth of a "black" child to a white woman. In the late nineteenth century, in the midst of whites' efforts to reassert control over their former slaves and over southern society in general, sexual relations between white women and black men became politicized. After Reconstruction, whites conflated black men's desires for white women with their desire for political rights as men, thus creating the rape myth.[20] By the twentieth century, the rape myth was at its height, and it structured most white southerners' beliefs about the consequences of allowing interaction between white women and black men. The rhetoric about black men's propensity to rape and the corresponding need for white men to protect white women flourished both in debates about black men's civil and political rights and in discussions about new freedoms and opportunities for white women. The rape myth thus enforced white women's subordination to white men and the social, economic, and political power of whites over blacks.[21] Historians assumed that this rhetoric determined how white southerners responded to any and all allegations that a black man assaulted a white woman, and they found considerable proof in the wave of lynchings that plagued the South in the late nineteenth century and well into the twentieth.

There is no doubt that lynchings served as a means of social, economic, and political control of African Americans and represent some of the most egregious instances of injustice and brutality in American history. Lynching controlled African Americans through fear and united whites across class and gender lines. Lynching also became a catalyst for civil rights activism among African American men and women and brought the true nature of southern race relations to the attention of the rest of America. Only occasionally, however, did these extralegal murders result in federal intervention.[22] Many white southerners sought to justify extralegal violence by claiming it was a necessary means of deterring black rapists, and lynching unsurprisingly became the primary vehicle for discussions of sexual relations between white women and black men in the twentieth-century South. Despite the fact that most lynchings did not grow out of charges of sexual assault, northern critics accepted southerners' favorite explanation for the necessity of mob justice. Historians did so as well, taking white southerners at their word that they were compelled to respond to all charges of rape with, at best, barely contained violence. The development of the rape myth and the explosion in extralegal violence together help account for the widespread belief that all black men accused of assaulting white women paid with their lives.[23] Nevertheless, our focusing solely on lynching and infamous cases of interracial rape that represent some of the worst miscarriages of justice may obscure more than it reveals about the relationship among race, gender, sexuality, and power in the South. Though charges of black-on-white rape could explode into mob violence, even in Virginia, in most cases, they did not. The rhetoric white southerners used to condemn black men's supposed propensity to rape white women did not necessarily reflect all of the ways in which whites understood interactions between white women and African American men.

The prevalence of the rape myth in the South, the endless reiterations of the dangers black men represented to white women, and the extent of extralegal violence all played important roles in creating common understandings about the likely outcome of any interaction between a white woman and a black man. More important, the historical echoes of both the rape myth and lynching continued to resonate because they reflected African Americans' legitimate sense of racial injustice that pervaded the court system and American society in general. Black-on-white rape cases became the cipher for blacks' inability to achieve justice and equality throughout the twentieth century. They came to express something true about the South—the reality of racial injustice, discrimination, persecution, and exploitation—though the individual cases in and of themselves might not always have accurately reflected that larger truth.[24]

But it is not enough merely to point out that black men occasionally, even usually, escaped with their lives and thus what we thought we "knew" about black-on-white rape may be incorrect. There remains a gulf between the pervasive rhetoric about "black beast rapists" and whites' responses to what, in their eyes, was the most egregious of racial transgressions that requires explanation. White southerners were not insincere when they denounced black men as rapists. White southerners, even those in Virginia who eschewed lynching, earnestly believed that black men's assaults on white women represented attacks on the racial hierarchy and on white civilization in general. At the same time, these cases involved real people who had reputations and relationships in Virginia communities. The reality of southern life, the inevitable and continual interactions between blacks and whites, and the troublesome behavior of some whites and some women all had to be considered when cases came to the attention of the courts and the community. White southerners' need to achieve equilibrium among the mandates of segregation, white patriarchy, and all kinds of personal interactions created the gap between rhetoric and reality. Not every accused black man who previously "knew his place" immediately transmogrified into the stereotypical black beast rapist. Not every white woman who made an accusation was a paragon of white female virtue. White testimony could be mistaken or defy credibility. Despite their support for the ideological construct of the rape myth, some whites viewed the black tenant they had known for years as more honorable and trustworthy than the lewd, poor, disreputable, or perhaps just hysterical and anxious white woman who accused him. Interracial relations under segregation were more fluid than the rules of racial interaction would imply, and indeed they had to be if segregation as an institution were to survive. Under close scrutiny, this seemingly straightforward social system becomes enormously complex.

White Virginians' willingness to impose varied sentences, to reconsider the relative severity of a given crime, and to grant pardon to convicted black men provided them the flexibility necessary to maintain segregation as a malleable system of racial and social control. It allowed white Virginians to adjust the rules of racial separation to fit the specific needs of their own communities.[25] If, by contrast, segregation had upheld impermeable boundaries and had been enforced by rigid rules that insisted that any racial transgression provoke an invariably violent response, it would have been too brittle to survive. Communities could excuse any private crossracial relationship that blurred the racial hierarchy as long as the public behavior of whites and blacks and men and women continued to conform to segregation's rules. A system of racial relations in which some transgressions of racial boundaries could be forgiven, ignored, or erased was a more flexible, and therefore more durable, mode of control. The threat of lynching struck fear in the hearts of all blacks. Significantly, however, lynching's power to uphold segregation and to control those who lived under its mandate arose from its very arbitrariness. Not every violation of the rules of racial etiquette, including those prohibiting sexual relations between white women and black men, resulted in an execution by a mob. Who paid for racial transgressions with their lives and who did not was largely random.[26] At the same time, the ability of white elites to show mercy to accused black men through the legal system could be a powerful means of control over the black community, as well as a means of reassuring whites that southern society was just.[27]

This flexibility of response and the varieties of punishment black men received allowed southern whites to incorporate and consider the multifarious forms of racial interaction that continued despite segregation's attempt to enforce racial separation. The combination of the threat of extralegal violence and the legal system's ability, through granting mercy, to acknowledge and neutralize the power of marginalized whites—especially white women—to accuse blacks of crimes with impunity created a complicated and subtle means of social control. It patrolled interracial boundaries and simultaneously upheld the patriarchal power of white males and the class distinctions among all whites that remained despite the frantic insistence that all whites were superior to all blacks. Unsurprisingly as a result, some of these cases led to conflict among whites about who controlled the ultimate fate of African Americans.

It is possible to analyze the social implications of cases of black-on-white rape and to examine how white responses to those cases illuminate the workings of southern society. It is not possible, however, to determine what precisely happened between victim and assailant. Most white southerners accepted, at least initially, that black men who faced charges of rape were guilty because that assumption accorded with their beliefs about both black men's innately savage, criminal nature and the sexual allure of white women. Certainly their assumptions reflected their cultural concerns rather than the literal truth, and black men were punished accordingly. Racial bias accompanied every case throughout the legal process, but it did not always manifest itself in predictable ways. And, as we must question white southerners' assumptions that all black men were guilty, we cannot assume that black men were always innocent. It is unlikely that *all* white women made false accusations. It is equally unlikely that because assaulting white women carried such certain and grave consequences, no black man would be so foolish or suicidal to attempt it. It is unreasonable to assume that black men as a group were able to refrain entirely from sexual violence. Black men, such as Eldridge Cleaver, have even admitted that very thing and attributed political meaning to it.[28] Consequently, though it is clear that some white women "cried rape," it is equally clear that not all white women lied when they accused black men.[29]

Most scholars would agree that the historical treatment of black-on-white rape cases has an important place in our understanding of race relations in the South. But it should have an equally prominent place in our understanding of the prosecution of rape. Many white women who accused black men of rape faced the same distrust and suspicion that confronted women who raised charges of sexual assault by white men. Although white women in these cases escaped scrutiny into their sexual history or reputation at trial, when testifying offered them some limited opportunity to challenge insinuations about their character, these questions about their reputation frequently surfaced in considerations of pardon, when their voices were entirely absent. Not only did some women bring their assaults on themselves, some whites seemed to believe, but some white women's characters were already so compromised that their having been violated did not represent a threat to the social order. They were not sheltered under the mantle of white womanhood with its attendant promise of protection. White men's discussions about a victim's complicity in her violation indicates that whites believed that certain kinds of women, and potentially all women, were untrustworthy, either because they were irrational or because they were deceitful. Though the accusing women's whiteness conveyed privilege and their white femaleness endowed them with an exalted symbolic role, the fact that they were women also made them vulnerable to violent men, both white and black. That the legal system erected barriers to justice for African American men should not blind us to the difficulties that patriarchy created for women, white and black, as well. In fact, both women and black men were subject to the same system of power.

Although these conclusions are drawn from as comprehensive a collection of cases as possible, they surely are not based on every case of black-on-white assault that occurred in Virginia between 1900 and 1960. There is no easy way to gather criminal case records. Virginia maintains no compendium of rape cases. Virginia prisons do hold records of the crimes of which inmates were convicted, but these records have several important drawbacks for this study.[30] Though they indicate the race of convicted rapists, they do not include the race of the victim. Equally important, lists of rapists from prison records would not include men who were charged but acquitted of rape or were acquitted of rape but convicted of other lesser crimes such as assault, battery, or "peeping," or convicted of more serious charges such as murder. Consequently, the 288 cases that comprise this study have come from a variety of sources.

The *Richmond Times-Dispatch* consistently reported cases that occurred throughout the state of Virginia. Virginia's black newspapers also ran stories on rape cases, especially white-on-black cases in the 1940s and 1950s. In both sources, there were many instances in which women reported they had been assaulted but for which police never arrested a suspect. If a newspaper named a suspect, I proceeded to the courthouse where the case was tried. Each courthouse in Virginia determines its own procedure for maintaining criminal case files under broad state guidelines that mandate that criminal records only need to be kept for a certain number of years. Some courthouses kept both the order books and the case files for all cases in their jurisdiction. Some of these case files still contain evidence such as hair samples and photos of the victim's injuries, or descriptions of testimony. In other files, however, only the summonses for witnesses and jury members remain. Several courthouses have kept only the minimum of records, generally the order books recording the formal legal procedures and the jury's verdict. Others have lost or disposed of them entirely. Where possible, I have supplemented legal sources with local news reports of both assaults and trials. The clemency files located in the papers of Virginia's governors also contain numerous cases of black-on-white rape. These proved to be the richest source, as legal officials often candidly revealed their honest opinions about the case, the defendant, the victim, and the jury's verdict. Other cases came to my attention through the NAACP files on microfilm.

The resulting 288 cases of black-on-white rape in which the assailant was identified thus represent a significant percentage of the cases for the period under study, but my analysis avoids several admittedly important and interesting questions. Because I examined approximately eight months of pardon papers for each year of the study, estimates of the percentage of convicted men who either petitioned for pardon or received pardon are impossible to make. Similarly, because I confined my attention to pardon papers for cases of rape or attempted rape or for defendants already included in my list of cases, my study does not include pardons granted to men convicted of other crimes against white women such as robbery or simple assault. The difficulty in ascertaining the extent to which convicted men were released early is further complicated by Virginia's legal procedures. Before 1942, decisions about the early release of convicted offenders resided solely in the hands of Virginia's governors, in the form of pardons or conditional pardons. After 1942, when Virginia established its parole board, parole became another form of early release. Unfortunately, the records of the parole board are not available to scholars without the written permission of the convicted men. Consequently, though many men, in addition to those included in this study, were likely released on parole, their numbers, or the factors affecting the parole board's decisions, are not included in my analysis. The nature of legal record keeping in Virginia, moreover, makes it difficult to draw comparisons of black men's treatment in the legal system to white men's. Culling Virginia's newspapers, clemency records, and courthouse files for cases of white men accused of rape would necessitate the research efforts sufficient for a second book. I do not attempt such a comparison here. Accounts of white men's cases in the Richmond papers suggest that many, if not most, white men who faced trial either were acquitted or received minimal prison terms. The clemency papers indicate that convicted white men occasionally received more severe sentences, but that was usually when they were convicted of raping a daughter, step-daughter, or other female relative. As yet, however, there is no comprehensive study of rape in the South in the twentieth century and thus no way to put my findings in comparative perspective. Finally, although the prosecution of rape after World War II receives separate attention in this book, I am less concerned with the issue of change over time. Though my approach challenges accepted periodizations of the twentieth-century South, the themes I address in the following chapters remain remarkably consistent throughout the period under study.

Black-on-white rape cases expose the paradoxes that existed at the heart of southern society. These cases reveal the tension between civilization and savagery, between the desire for orderly and predictable racial boundaries and the relationships that crossed both race and gender lines, between the inequality among whites despite white supremacy and the rhetoric implying iron-clad white solidarity, and between the dignity of blacks and a system that insisted they were inferior to all whites. Black-on-white rape so inflamed the white population precisely because it revealed the fissures in segregation. Whites' responses to individual cases attest to the need among whites both to control blacks and to convince themselves that the legal system provided something like genuine justice. Ultimately, these cases show us how race, class, and gender interacted in southern communities and illuminate the distribution of power across the full spectrum of society. In the practice of protection, white southerners sought to order a complicated social reality into easy categories of black and white, despite the contradictions embedded within it. Cases of black-on-white rape simultaneously supported and undermined segregation because they revealed the agency of white women and African Americans in their attempts to pursue their own forms of justice. Historians are well familiar with how white southerners talked about black-on-white rape; this study examines their actions when allegations of assault surfaced. These cases reveal how all Virginians negotiated and contested the distribution of power in southern society and underscore the difficulties white men faced in trying to exert effective control over the entire uncooperative lot.

CHAPTER 1

A Deadly Menace to the Very Framework of Society Itself

White Violence and the Legal System

In 1912, newspapers around Virginia reported that a young white widow named Bertha Ferguson had been attacked and raped. Within hours, police had apprehended Alfred Wright, an eighteen-year-old black man. When police brought Wright to Ferguson, she identified him as her assailant and he was charged with the crime. Despite Wright's claims of innocence, the sheriff announced that the evidence against him was "complete."[1] Two days later, Wright's case went to trial and the jury heard testimony for most of the day. Despite the efforts of Wright's attorney to win mercy based on his youth, Wright was quickly convicted and sentenced to death. Wright's trial was reportedly "the speediest trial and conviction that ever took place in the State," the jury having deliberated only fifteen minutes before returning its guilty verdict to the expectant crowd.

To many white Virginians reading about the case, the trial represented a victory of order over lawlessness. Newspapers reported that tempers of the community were "stirred to the highest pitch of excitement" at news of the crime. Feeding on white southerners' apparent appetite for extralegal retribution against black men, initial media accounts of the case focused not on the crime but on the reaction it produced among local whites. "Appomatox [sic] Jail Heavily Guarded," read one headline. Only underneath, in smaller print, did it state that the jail was guarded to prevent the lynching of a black man accused of assaulting a white woman.[2] The promise of a speedy trial, however, had prevented the mob from taking the law into its own hands. Once the trial began, news reports emphasized the court's commitment to due process. According to reports in the Richmond papers, Wright's attorney, Duncan Drysdale, "put up a magnificent defense" and made an "excellent argument for the life of his client." Hearing the verdict and the jury's imposition of the death penalty, "the community was entirely satisfied," content to let Wright await his execution in Richmond.[3]

A closer look at Wright's trial, however, reveals that whites in Appomattox did not entirely abandon extralegal violence in favor of the rule of law. The threat of violence permeated the trial and largely directed the jury's verdict and sentence. In his request for an appeal, Drysdale called public opinion "bitterly inflamed and incensed against the accused" and pointed out that no one in the community questioned whether the crime had been committed or whether Wright was the guilty party. Drysdale noted that Wright had been heavily guarded from the moment he was arrested to prevent a lynching. The night before the trial, the sheriff, hearing of a plot to storm the jail, had moved Wright to a schoolhouse on the outskirts of town. The specter of violence accompanied Wright into court. Drysdale reported that the courtroom was "crowded with an audience composed exclusively of citizens of the county, that frequent mutterings could be heard while counsel was making this motion [to change the location of the trial], and that at said moment [authorities] found it necessary to have the prisoner guarded by four men armed with rifles and shot guns, loaded with gunpowder and leaden bullets, ready for instant action."[4] Moreover, Drysdale continued, the official responsible for ensuring Wright's safety at trial "publicly stated in open court . . . that if [defense motions for a continuance and a change of venue] were granted, he could not answer for the safety of the prisoner, meaning thereby, that in the event [the motions were] granted, he was apprehensive that the prisoner would be taken by the people from the custody of the officials and lynched."[5] Only an immediate trial in Appomattox would satisfy local whites and prevent Wright's punishment at the hands of a mob. Indeed, outraged members of the white community invaded the courtroom to ensure enforcement of their will.

For Alfred Wright, there was little meaningful distinction between mob action and the legal process. The angry whites who threatened violence in the courtroom and the legal officials who tried Wright's case ultimately worked together to ensure that Wright paid for the rape of Bertha Ferguson with his life. Duncan Drysdale appealed Wright's conviction on the grounds that the presence of the mob in the courtroom made it impossible for Wright to receive a fair trial, but his efforts were derailed by the judge's ability to render the collaboration between the mob and the legal system invisible. The judge insisted that "the [court] has never seen a more peaceable and orderly crowd in the courtroom," despite news reports during the trial that there was a plot within the courtroom itself to lynch Wright if he was not sentenced to death.[6] In a terse opinion, the Virginia Supreme Court upheld Wright's conviction and sentence, arguing that members of the defense presented no evidence other than their own affidavits about the sentiments of the courtroom spectators, nor did they provide evidence that, given time, Duncan Drysdale could have proved his client's innocence.[7] In short, even if Wright's trial lacked important elements of due process, he was guilty and deserved no better. Alfred Wright was executed in May 1913, two months after the court issued its ruling.

In many respects, Alfred Wright's experience with the legal system represented white Virginians' preferred method of responding to black men's crimes against white women. Although his trial and execution amounted to a "legal lynching," where court procedure was a thinly veiled substitute for mob violence, white Virginians could nonetheless claim that Wright's fate came at the hands of judicial authorities rather than a mob. White Virginians trusted their legal system to police the boundaries of racial interaction, and they prided themselves on avoiding the lawlessness that plagued states farther south. Between 1880 and 1930, Georgia lynched 460 people, 441 (96 percent) of whom were black. Virginia, by contrast, lynched 86 people, 70 (81 percent) of whom were black.[8] Virginia's success at avoiding mob violence and bringing accused black men to trial, however, did not mean that racial prejudice and white hostility did not influence court procedure. Legal trials did not represent white Virginians' rejection of extralegal violence in the enforcement of white supremacy. Instead, the potential for violence was woven into the legal process. The threat of violence became a tool used by the legal establishment to assure the white community that black men would receive severe punishment when accused of crimes against white women. The relative paucity of lynchings in Virginia, despite the violent deaths of eighty-six people at the hands of mobs, did not indicate that Virginia was less prone to the racial violence that characterized southern states. It merely represented the degree to which lynching and legal trials worked hand in hand to protect the racial hierarchy. Both forms of retribution interacted along a continuum of social and racial control.

Convictions and severe sentences warned the black community about the limits of white racial toleration and the penalty blacks could expect for violating the rules of racial interaction. For Virginia's legal establishment, "allowing the law to take its course" provided a better means than did vigilante violence of controlling the complex web of racial, class, and gender relationships that formed the basis of the social order. Criminal trials allowed the white community to participate in punishing errant black men while they simultaneously limited that participation. Trials also provided a clearly visible ritual enactment that defused and diffused the hysteria provoked by allegations of black-on-white assault. Trials, with their orderly procedures and seemingly color-blind legal protections, re-assured whites that accused black men deserved their ultimate fate. While lynchings and trials could have the same end result—the death of a black man—trials allowed whites to convince themselves that black men re-ceived the same justice accorded to white defendants. Court procedures, like vigilante violence, enacted the white community's will; unlike vig-ilante violence, legal proceedings created the fiction of a moral and egali-tarian dispensation of justice.

Despite efforts by the legal system to guard black men from overt due-process violations, trials for charges of black-on-white rape resulted in predictable convictions. Black men accused of assaulting white women rarely escaped punishment precisely because white Virginians saw the crime of black-on-white rape as a direct attack on white civilization and on a social order founded upon white supremacy, and they guarded against it accordingly. George J. Hundley, the judge in Alfred Wright's case, made explicit the connection between the literal rape of white women and the figurative rape of white civilization when he rejected Wright's motions for a continuance to allow his attorney time to prepare for trial. The judge, in an unusual move, included his entire decision in the record of the court. He agreed that the time between the commission of the crime and Wright's arraignment and trial had been very short, and he conceded that he was usually very lenient regarding requests for continuance. But Wright's case, he argued, was different: "The offense charged is of a peculiarly heinous nature. By common consent it is regarded as the worst crime in all the catalogue denounced by our laws. No other crime so excites, alarms and arouses our people. It not only violates the laws of God and Man, but owing to the peculiar conditions prevailing in this our land, it is a deadly menace to the very framework of society itself."[9]

Although Hundley's decision was rendered in the courtroom, it nonetheless justified the collaboration of violence and legal procedure by emphasizing whites' perception of the larger meaning of black-on-white rape. Bertha Ferguson's rape was not one of the "worst crimes" because it represented a fate worse than death for her personally. It was one of the worst because the very act of a black man taking sexual relations with white women by force attacked the heart of white patriarchal civilization. Black men's sexual violence fouled the highest and most sacred symbol of white supremacy—frail, white women dependent on white men for protection. It also represented an attempt to seize white men's racial and patriarchal prerogatives—symbolized by their sole sexual access to white women—that placed white men at the top of the southern social order. In white eyes, black men, in assaulting white women, upended society by laying claim to the white masculinity on which civilization was founded.[10]

White responses to charges of black-on-white rape thus represented whites in defense of a social order based on interlocking, and mutually reinforcing, gender, racial, and class hierarchies, which helps explain the inflammatory nature of the crime. Allegations of black-on-white rape, however, also set in sharp relief paradoxes at the heart of southern society. Southern whites claimed to represent the highest achievement of civilization, yet they nevertheless encouraged the barbarity of lynching. White civilization existed at the intersection of civility and aggression, of white women's protection and mob violence. That contradiction, even in the eyes of legal authorities, frequently required justice not only to maintain racial and gender hierarchies but also to co-opt whites' desire for violence into the legal system itself.

Whites in Virginia made no secret of their belief in the superiority not only of their culture but of their evolutionary development as well.[11] White men's vaunted masculinity reached its apex in its ability to subvert their thirst for vengeance through the legal system. At the same time, white men earned their right to dominate both inferior women and inferior races because of their capacity for both restraint and aggression. Legal trials of black men accused of assaulting women, like that of Alfred Wright, however, did not merely represent the triumph of lawful order and restraint over lawless violence. They also demonstrated the ability of court procedure to absorb the violence of outraged whites. White savagery and white control were not antithetical but complementary.

The potential for violence was a palpable and necessary presence in Virginia courtrooms. It assured whites that their thirst for vengeance and retribution against blacks would be carried out in a way that satisfied white manhood's primitive need for aggression and the simultaneous need to demonstrate the superiority of civilization made possible by white men's power and dominance. Self-restraint, a quirky relic of a receding Victorian past, however, no longer needed to be located in the individual. Instead, white men in Virginia exerted controlled vengeance through the legal system. White men remained civilized because the court enacted their primitive desires for revenge, and indeed folded the threat and desire for violence into the legal process.[12]

The seeming lack of civility of mob violence was contained and incorporated into the law as a tool of racial control. Treating extralegal violence and the rule of law as complementary and indeed collaborative, rather than contradictory, resolved the seeming paradox of civilized men engaging in barbarous acts of violence and torture. Whites' thirst for revenge and retribution, and the desire of local whites to participate in black men's punishment when they were accused of sexual crimes by white women, became part of the legal process, expressed in the mutterings of court spectators and the verdicts and sentences of white juries. This pairing of violence and law seemingly united all whites against all blacks and gave all white men a role and a stake in enforcing the racial hierarchy. Both law and vigilante violence worked hand in hand in support of white civilization.

The South, including Virginia, however, was not free to create its own definition of white civilization and of the relationship between violence and order. White southern understandings of vigilante justice existed in the context of the nation's increasing distaste for lynching as a form of retributive justice. Over the course of the twentieth century, it became increasingly untenable for white southerners to argue that lynching was part of white superiority or was anything other than a particularly brutal and barbaric form of murder. White Virginians came to this conclusion earlier than did most other southern states. Though the number of lynchings decreased in the twentieth century, the role of violence in the legal process did not. It only became less visible, routinized and subordinated to the grim ritual of courtroom procedure.

Most white Virginians would have agreed that a swift trial, a conviction, and an execution were the surest deterrents to mob violence. White Virginians shared with other southerners the belief that black men's proclivity to rape white women represented the most severe challenge to white supremacy. Black men's desires for white men's patriarchal prerogatives, as exemplified by their supposed desire for white women, necessitated strict separation of the races, enforced by the laws of segregation. Invoking the rhetoric of white women's need for protection became a standard white response not only to allegations of black-on-white rape but also to many alleged violations of racial etiquette. As one Virginian put it, "The writer of this believes (as every true Virginian must believe) in the language of the Bible: 'A life for a life'; and the revised version 'a life for the honor of a noble woman.' "[13] When allegations of assault surfaced, this rhetoric initiated an impressive public spectacle, performed in the media and in local gossip and ritualized in either a lynching or a criminal courtroom, and perhaps finally in the electric chair. Whites used these spectacles to return errant black men to their "place" and to warn other African Americans, and white women as well, about the consequences of misbehavior. This public exhibition punished black men who failed to abide by mandates of racial separation while it reaffirmed appropriate relationships across race and gender lines for the rest of the community. Whites' beliefs about the sexual purity of white women, their equation of black men's supposedly violent sexual desires with a challenge to white power, and their need to suppress challenges to the racial hierarchy virtually guaranteed that black men accused of any sort of assault on a white woman would be convicted at trial.[14]

Punishing black men through the legal system did not deprive the white public of participating in the maintenance of racial boundaries. Legal trials theoretically prevented outraged whites from exacting extralegal punishment and assured them that their desires would continue to shape the legal process. That black men faced trials rather than lynch mobs does not mean that they received justice. Racial prejudice permeated the legal process at every step. Although law enforcement officials took actions to ensure that black men survived to face a jury, their whisking accused men out of town when rumors of gathering mobs surfaced and pushing for speedy trials to avert mob violence often deprived defendants adequate time to prepare their cases, as Alfred Wright learned. Moreover, law enforcement often used the threat of mob violence and other coercive methods to force confessions. Court-appointed lawyers did not always give their unpopular clients their best efforts. Consequently, there is no way to determine whether black men were indeed guilty of the crimes of which they were accused and convicted. The legal system capitalized on Virginia's reputation for avoiding lynching and on the ever-present possibility of mob violence to guard the state's power to punish blacks. At the same time, it carried out the will of the larger white community, with seemingly little concern for ascertaining guilt.[15] Allegations of black-on-white crimes provided a powerful opportunity for the white community as a whole to use the courts to reinforce community standards determining appropriate relations across race and gender lines.[16]

By the twentieth century, fears of black men's sexual desires occupied an exaggerated place in the white southern psyche that belied their recent origins.[17] Few white southerners doubted that the separation of white women from black men was a critical and time-honored foundation of an increasingly segregated southern social order.[18] The power of white southerners' inflamed rhetoric is most apparent in lynchings—the brutal killing, usually of African Americans, by white mobs. Southerners justified resorting to mob violence, despite its horror, by insisting that swift, brutal retribution was the only means of curbing black men's violent desires for white women, and thus protecting white society. Punishing accused black men by lynching rather than through criminal trials also spared victimized white women the additional trauma of reliving their ordeal through their testimony. James K. Vardaman, governor of Mississippi, threatened that "every Negro in the state will be lynched" in order to protect white supremacy. John Temple Graves, a well-known newspaper publisher in Atlanta, "sought to communicate the imminent peril facing every white female in the South." Citing the inadequacy of legal procedure to curb black men's criminal tendencies, he compared the lynch mob to an "engine of vengeance, monstrous, lawless, deplorable," but he also called it the "chief defense of women."[19] Few southerners approached the zeal of Rebecca Latimer Felton, a contributor to the *Atlanta Journal* and later the first woman appointed to the U.S. Senate. In an address to the State Agricultural Society of Georgia in 1897, she gained national attention for exclaiming, "If it takes lynching to protect women's dearest possession from drunken, ravening human beasts, then I say lynch a thousand a week if it becomes necessary."[20] Despite the clamor of whites who shared Felton's views, most black men who were lynched were not charged with crimes against white women. Murder, often of a white employer, formed the most common pretext for lynching.[21] Nevertheless, Felton's provocative rhetoric illustrates the power of using alleged crimes against white women as justifications for lynching and racial oppression. This justification relied on a paternalistic and racist logic that northerners, who often shared southern prejudices, found difficult to counter.[22]

Not all southerners resorted to lynching as a form of racial control with the same frequency. Georgia and Mississippi outranked other southern states for the number of lynchings within their borders. Virginia, by contrast, lynched fewer individuals than any other southern state. Few historians dispute that lynching became a method of racial control, as well as a means for uniting whites across class lines. Recent scholarship argues that lynching, rather than being a remnant of the backwards South, was modern. Lynching underwent its modernization as it moved from "simple," retributive vigilante justice to a highly stylized, culturally encoded public spectacle. Indeed, associating civilization with control allowed whites to claim an extreme if grotesque form of higher development. The ability to torture slowly and deliberately a human being to death, in this twisted logic, proved the superiority of southern whites, because they could resist inflicting violence passionately and emotionally. Thus, there was no contradiction between the crowd's brutal act of murder and its description in the newspapers as orderly and purposeful.[23] The rhetoric and ritual that surrounded lynching expressed white attitudes about the desirability of white women, the supposedly inviolable yet vulnerable separation of whites and blacks, and whites' ambivalence about committing violence in the name of civilization, even as it reflected whites' fears that African Americans were not content with their subordinate position. In the minds of white southerners, not only did assaults against white women represent black men's rejection of racial subordination, it signaled their desire to share in patriarchy, in effect, their laying claim to manhood with the same privileges as white men over women both white and black.

The rhetoric accompanying Virginia's lynchings insisted that protecting white women by immediately punishing black men ultimately preserved white civilization. Coverage of William Page's lynching in Northumberland County in August 1917 openly asserted that protecting white womanhood lay at the heart of white Virginians' notions of white masculinity and the social order. According to the newspapers, Captain Truitt, father of one of Page's alleged victims, was "a staunch old Virginian, who places the safety of his womenfolk first and the majesty of the Commonwealth second." A mob led by Truitt took Page first to his family to say good-bye and then into the local African American community, where they hanged him from a tree outside the schoolyard. Three hours elapsed between the alleged assault and Page's death.[24] Newspapers presented the lynching as the inevitable result of Page's criminal actions. The *Richmond Times-Dispatch* assured whites that the local African American population supported the mob's actions. "When [African American community leaders] found there was no question of the guilt of Page, they lent their full influence toward quieting their people."[25]

Page's death occurred before the legal system could institute proceedings against him. Nevertheless, his fate traced a tangled connection between mob justice and legal justice. The newspaper speculated that Page was lynched because whites feared the legal system's punishment might prove to be inadequate. A similar assault in the area two years earlier had resulted in a prison term for the convicted black assailant. "The mob that gathered had this in mind, and believing that only a prison sentence awaited Page resolved to stamp such outrages out completely, and to make of Page an example that would prevent any crimes for a long time to come."[26] Although officials would argue otherwise nine years after Page's death, coverage of this lynching suggested that juries could not always be counted on to impose the community's conception of appropriate punishment, even though the jury itself was drawn from the community. The possibility of unpopular sentences provided justification for lynching as a method of racial control. Whether or not Page's lynching achieved the desired deterrent effect, it had a predictable conclusion. After an investigation, authorities determined that he had died at the hands of "parties unknown." The court's determination absolved the white community of using murder to promote order and rendered invisible the barbarity necessary to commit such an act. All whites, thus, remained civilized.

The composition of the mob that killed James Jordan in 1925 further indicates that lynching responded to the desire of the white community for swift, sure, and extreme punishment. Accused of raping a young white mother in her home, Jordan was arrested after a former employer recognized him from a sketch circulated by police. That evening, a mob of an estimated 500 people broke into the jail where he was being held. He was taken to a vacant lot, where he was hanged from a tree, his body riddled with bullets, and then set aflame. Local support for vigilante justice was apparently widespread. Officials reported that Jordan's death was not the work of an isolated band of rabble. "Everybody in the county seemed to have been there," the commonwealth's attorney commented to the press. According to authorities, "the circumstances of the attack had aroused an indignation throughout the county that could not be controlled when it became known the perpetrator of the crime had confessed,"; the lynching was an uncomfortable confluence of savagery and civilization. Although officials conceded that they did not support resorting to mob violence and planned to mount a "rigid" investigation, members of the mob never faced charges, thereby ensuring that "everybody in the county" maintained their white civility.[27]

Individual white Virginians, with tacit community approval, also occasionally took the law into their own hands. The following cases, rarely included in most tallies of lynchings, reinforce the claim that white Virginians' tolerated extralegal violence to a considerable extent. Adam Howard was killed in 1912 by Aubrey Bowie, the father of the young girl to whom Howard allegedly made "improper approaches." A grand jury refused to indict Bowie for Howard's murder.[28] In a similar case nine years later, news reports in Danville, Virginia, blamed Harry Davis for causing his own death. When Davis entered a white woman's home apparently intending to rape her and threatened her with death if she did not cooperate, she screamed and ran to the home of her neighbor, Willie Cranford. Later that evening, Cranford shot Davis in the chest with a shotgun after he found Davis peering into the white woman's door. Danville's mayor ruled that Cranford's actions constituted justifiable homicide.[29] The willingness of the legal system to excuse such actions, as it did when it failed to prosecute whites who participated in lynchings, demonstrates how extralegal violence and the legal system ultimately served the same ends—to restore civilization on white terms.

Virginians never condoned lynching as the only possible response to crimes against white women, merely as a justifiable one when a lynching occurred. They frequently turned to the courts, and a modern, public spectacle of trial and execution, to contain the threat black men posed to white women. The same year that Page was lynched, six black men faced trial for similar offenses. In 1925, when James Jordan died at the hands of a mob, thirteen other accused black men had their cases tried in court. To some white southerners, the influence of violent mobs in court did not represent disorder but rather a progressive complement to law enforcement, as commentary on the case of Henry Smith shows. Catherine Powell, an elderly widow, identified Henry Smith as the man who assaulted her in August 1908. News of the assault outraged whites, but Smith's crime alone did not cause white violence. In an unrelated incident, a white police officer was shot and killed by a black man. The *Virginian-Pilot* reported that the news of the killing of the city's oldest "bluecoat" "threw the entire city," which had barely recovered from the "intense strain" caused by the news of Powell's assault, "into a turbulent sea of agitation, the like of which has not been seen here in years."[30] And in florid prose, the newspaper breathlessly described a riot. By evening, the city government had called in troops, who restored order. Several days later, a mob, armed with a rope reportedly carried by a black man, appeared at the jail and unsuccessfully attempted to avenge the assault on Powell. Smith was soon convicted and sentenced to death.[31] Smith's execution inaugurated a new spectacle of retributive justice: he had the dubious distinction of being the first criminal in Virginia to be executed by electric chair.[32]

The arrest and trial of Henry Smith occurred within days of the riot in Springfield, Illinois, that provided the catalyst for the founding of the NAACP. An article comparing the two mob episodes appeared in the *Independent* soon after, making a distinction between the southern civility of the Virginia mob and the aggression displayed by whites in Illinois. The author, W. A. Woodbridge, called the mob action in Portsmouth an example of "meditated vengeance . . . against the individual who had committed the crime for which he knew he must die, if not at the hands of the mob, then by law." The Springfield riot, by contrast, involved the "bitter cruel relentless causeless hounding of innocent, helpless people simply because they are colored." Whites in Portsmouth, in his view, did not engage in random violence against the entire black community but instead legitimately targeted criminals. In Springfield, northern white rioters targeted victims solely because of the color of their skin. Comparing the two events, he transposed the image of extralegal violence against blacks from white southerners to white northerners. Woodbridge portrayed limited and quickly controlled mob action, like that in Portsmouth, as a rational, if impulsive, complement to law enforcement.[33] Mobs, by threatening to take the law into their own hands, ensured the punishment of presumably guilty black men. Woodbridge, of course, made the dubious assumption, one likely shared by most whites, that most targets of mobs deserved their fate. At the same time, he implied, mobs ensured public support for jury verdicts. Orderly mobs inserted the public into a legal process that could otherwise return unpredictable resolutions. The potential for mob violence and the desire to maintain the facade of civilization mandated convictions and severe punishment, and eliminated the possibility that white dissatisfaction over sentences would lead to subsequent lynchings.

Even though white Virginians resorted to lynching several times after Woodbridge penned his article, they nonetheless seemed largely to agree with his argument that mob action and the legal process could work together. In print and in action, they began to distance themselves from lynching.[34] Over the course of the twentieth century, though mobs lynched fewer men, the specter of the mob and the potential for mob violence continued to cast its shadow over the legal system. Virginia's response to

black-on-white crime represented a "managed" expression of racial outrage. As a border state, Virginia was at the crossroads of New South
boosterism, reactionary agrarianism, and the progressive liberalism of the
North. Its reputation as a "progressive" state mandated a less extreme
approach in its handling of race relations and racial conflict. Although
lynchings occurred within Virginia's borders, legal authorities, law enforcement officials, and state institutions enforced a different spectacle that
used a courtroom trial to punish black men accused of crimes against
white women. This spectacle placed Virginia in the vanguard of the New
South and provided a means by which Virginia elites could use carefully
orchestrated, meticulously managed modes of racial control to preserve
traditional hierarchies of race, gender, and class without overt violence.

Scholars have noted that Virginia's strong executive branch, sensitivity
to criticism from outsiders, and toleration for a limited degree of black
independence and mobility helped dampen white Virginians enthusiasm
for lynching.[35] Two related developments also contributed to Virginia's
relative reluctance to resort to extralegal violence. Beginning early in the
century, white elites became enamored with the "science" of eugenics—
the idea that the human race could be improved and that social problems
caused by poverty, crime, vice, disease, and mental weakness could be
eliminated by limiting the reproduction of those deemed by experts to be
defective, socially inadequate, or generally "unfit." In Virginia, these ideas
led to the passage of three eugenically minded pieces of legislation in the
1920s: the Racial Integrity Act, which strengthened prohibitions against
marriages between whites and nonwhites; a law allowing the compulsory
sterilization of the "unfit"; and the Massenburg Public Assemblage Act,
which mandated racial segregation at all public venues. These laws did
not specifically target blacks, but they expressed the desires of elite Virginians to manage racial problems and class tensions and to simultaneously
promote civilization through "rational" and "humane" social engineer-
ing. Eugenicists adopted several strategies to promote their vision of a
healthy society, including encouraging advantageous procreation among
the "fit" and, through sterilization, preventing the birth of those who,
because of their heredity, might later become burdens on society. They
also advocated segregating unhealthy or inferior people from mainstream
society by institutionalizing the mentally disabled and promoting racial
separation through Jim Crow. Through these measures, eugenics propo-
nents sought to solve social problems before they appeared.[36]

The idea of using science to solve the "problem" of black beast rapists
appeared as early as 1893. In an article in the *Virginia Medical Monthly*, two

prominent physicians, one the head of the American Medical Association practicing in Richmond and the other practicing in Chicago, discussed the advantages of using castration to control black men who raped white women. Not only would castration cure their sexual urges, their emasculation would serve as a warning to other black men not to repeat their crimes.[37] Virginia only rarely sterilized men convicted of rape, but eugenicists believed that limiting the reproduction of all types of social defectives would prevent the next generation of criminals.[38] Virginia elites, because of the "promise" of eugenics, saw science as the best vehicle for promoting a peaceful social order and stable race relations. The violence and barbarity of lynching was unnecessary.

Lynching offended Virginia elites in another way. Virginia had no discernible populist movement; it was run by a Democratic machine for most of the early part of the twentieth century. As with eugenics, elites viewed top-down political management as an essential element of the state's social order. Mob violence challenged the social hierarchy because it represented an illegitimate form of popular power. At their core, mobs threatened elites' ability to make decisions over the fate of accused criminals and to judge when and how black-on-white crimes violated the racial order. Vigilante justice ultimately expropriated elite control over racial, gender, and class hierarchies and threatened to replace order with disorder. Consequently, state and local authorities made great efforts, though not always successful, to thwart angry mobs and determine black men's fates in a court of law. Despite the desire of elites to maintain control over the process of punishment, they acknowledged the need to bow to popular white will. Angry whites filled the galleries of courtrooms, and local white men formed the juries that decided the verdicts and the sentences. In a cynical assessment of the attitudes of white Virginians, Oliver Hill, a prominent black attorney in the state, commented, "We don't need to lynch the niggers. We can try them and then hang them."[39] Significantly, however, that whites were allowed to determine the trial outcome did not indicate that elites always accepted those judgments. Once juries returned their verdicts, legal officials used quiet behind-the-scenes maneuvers to adjust black men's sentences to conform to their ideas of justice. Criminal trials, then, allowed for popular participation in the punishment of accused black men but did so in a forum that preserved white elites' power to act as the final arbiters of black men's fates.

Coverage of lynching and mob gatherings in the white press illustrated Virginians growing distaste for mob action. As the coverage of William Page's lynching shows, white newspapers were clearly reluctant to celebrate lynching but, in stark contrast to the African American press, were unwilling to condemn it entirely either. Over time, whites began to see lynching not as an unfortunate but necessary chore but rather as an embarrassment. Officials increasingly interpreted extralegal violence as the product of ignorant whites' irrational unwillingness to let the "law take its course." To newspaper editors and legal officials, the presence of mobs around Virginia's courthouses blemished Virginia's reputation for law and order, at a time when Virginia was attempting to align itself with a national economy and culture. Violence represented a backward response to crime; legal trials were part of a progressive system that effectively protected established racial hierarchies. These arguments gained credence, and by 1930, lynchings had officially ended in Virginia. The white community in general, however, seemed less convinced that courts were reliable vehicles for punishing black men. The shadow of incipient mobs and the talk of public outrage that permeated coverage of cases wending through the legal system testify to the continuing power of white public will in official responses to crimes against white women.

The potential conflict between elite attitudes toward mob violence and white popular opinion regarding the need for immediate punishment is apparent in coverage of the 1926 lynching of Raymond Byrd, the last officially acknowledged lynching in the state of Virginia. Most Virginia newspapers condemned the actions of the mob. The *Richmond News-Leader*, for example, argued that "it was not the 'Virginia way' to put on masks, to hide individual identity in a mob, to hang some wretch in the dark of the moon, and then to slink away in blood guiltiness," likening lynchings carried out at the hands of unknown parties to cowardice.[40] The *Roanoke Times* condemned lynching as "vicious" and pointed out that it was so inefficient a means of assuring "proper punishment for crimes committed by Negroes upon white women that no effort should be spared to bring to book those who ride roughshod over forms of law in order to take summary vengeance upon someone suspected of the offense."[41] Editorial opinion insisted that the legal system represented the most effective means of controlling errant blacks. Punishment at the hands of white juries was virtually assured, and placing decisions regarding sentences in juries' hands shielded Virginia from the glare of hostile national publicity generated by lynchings.

Though the question of the effectiveness of the legal system to punish black men suspected of rape was evident in most debates about lynching at this time, it was irrelevant in Byrd's case. Byrd met his death at the hands of a mob because his alleged victims refused to appear in court to accuse him of a crime. Constrained by a legal system that required the claim of victimization from a white woman, the courts had no power over Byrd, even though the white community felt certain he had engaged in sexual relations with two, and perhaps three, of the white daughters of his employer. The white community stepped into the void created by legal procedure and punished Raymond Byrd, but the case had important ramifications. In response to the state's embarrassment over Byrd's lynching, Governor Harry Byrd (no relation) eventually signed antilynching legislation into law in 1928.[42]

Virginia's antilynching legislation met with mixed success. It won praise from other states throughout the country, but it resulted in the prosecution of only three people. It did, however, effectively deflect attention away from the white community's role in preserving racial boundaries. Despite its passage, white Virginians do not appear to have given up extralegal justice entirely. Shadrack Thompson in 1932 attempted to elude a posse and was later found hanging from a tree. Similarly, in 1935, Nelson Pendleton, who also fled armed vigilantes, was reportedly found dead in an orchard by members of the posse. In both cases, Virginia's whites avoided national opprobrium because officials ruled the men's deaths as suicides.[43] The *Richmond Planet* called for authorities to rule that lynching was the cause of both deaths: "Better to face the ugly fact, accept the disgrace and enforce the Byrd law than to attempt to evade the issue by setting forth this unbelievable suicide defense."[44] Authorities did not do so, protecting Virginia's law-and-order reputation while condoning occasional lynchings through inaction. As long as white vigilantes executed their quarry without attracting attention, and as long as they avoided the carnivalesque spectacle lynchings that generated national condemnation, extralegal violence could continue without official interference.

In general, whites responded to charges of black-on-white rape by allowing the legal system to fulfill the desires of the white community to punish black assailants.[45] Public trials still showed African Americans the cost of violating racial boundaries, but they united white outrage with the legal system, encouraging whites to give official legitimation to the management of racial relations. News reports still frequently mentioned "high feeling" in communities where alleged assaults occurred, but state authorities, law enforcement officials, and legal officials effectively channeled white outrage into the legal process.

Virginia's criminal code allowed black and white defendants to be treated differently even when they faced identical charges. Before 1866, Virginia law mandated more severe punishments for African Americans accused of serious crimes. Rape statutes, for example, mandated the death penalty for slaves and free blacks, while whites were imprisoned anywhere from ten to twenty years.[46] After the South's defeat in the Civil War, the federal government forced southern states to revise their criminal codes to remove unconstitutional racial disparities in sentencing. Rather than remove the provision mandating capital punishment for slaves or free blacks, the Virginia legislature made rape a capital crime for all offenders, regardless of race, but also allowed for terms of imprisonment ranging from ten to twenty years. The punishments for rape remained largely unchanged until the 1970s, save for the following exceptions: in 1887, the General Assembly reduced the minimum prison term from ten years to five, and in 1924, it increased the maximum prison term for both rape and attempted rape to life in prison.

Virginia's criminal code made little distinction between rape and attempted rape in terms of punishment. In 1894, the Virginia General Assembly made the crime of attempted rape a capital offense. Opinions by Virginia jurists suggest that many Virginians believed there was little difference in the social and physical trauma associated with rape and attempted rape. Henry Hart, a black man convicted in 1921 of the attempted rape of a white woman, appealed to the Virginia Supreme Court, arguing that the death penalty was excessive punishment for an attempted crime. The opinion upholding his conviction and sentence disagreed: "It is a matter of history of the State, and of common knowledge among its people, that the crime of attempted rape is well-nigh, if not altogether, as heinous as the consummated offense of rape. It is well known that public indignation is as much aroused by the one offense as by the other."[47] The Court went on to assert that such extreme penalties were necessary to deter the outraged citizenry from resorting to extralegal measures.

The statements made by the Virginia Supreme Court in Henry Hart's case indirectly reinforced the racialized character of rape. Only rarely did Virginians display outrage when white women accused white men of rape; they assumed rape to be the almost-exclusive crime of black men. In the South, as elsewhere in the nation, people were vehement in their denunciations of rape as a heinous offense. But the general unwillingness to convict white men accused of the crime suggests that they believed true instances of rape by white men to be exceedingly rare.[48] Despite efforts to remove racial disparities in sentencing, the laws regarding the punishment of men accused of sexual assaults were only race-neutral on their face. Virginia statutes did not offer guidance on which rape cases merited capital punishment and which warranted only a prison sentence, and, as with all crimes, they placed the power to determine sentencing not in the hands of the judge but in the hands of emissaries of the white community, the jury.[49] This statutory sleight of hand allowed juries, composed of white men, to impose different sentences depending on the races of both the defendant and the victim.[50] Racial disparities in punishment occurred for all categories of crimes, but especially for rape and attempted rape. While Virginia executed fifty-four men convicted of rape or attempted rape between 1908 and 1965, *not one* of them was white. Black men convicted of rape or attempted rape received the most severe punishments allowed by law.[51]

Placing sentencing in the hands of jurors made such decisions the result not merely of the legal process but also of community beliefs about the seriousness of the assault. The men who formed the juries that tried these cases were products of the communities in which the assaults occurred. Once these jurors returned their verdict, they had to return to those communities. Their verdicts, and the sentences they imposed, likely reflected local ideas of what constituted justice. While there is no direct evidence from Virginia that this was true, statements from the white jurors involved in the infamous Scottsboro, Alabama, trials support the contention that jurors consciously aligned their verdicts and sentences with their understanding of prevailing white opinion. The foreman of the jury in Haywood Patterson's third trial explained that the decision to sentence Patterson to seventy-five years in prison was a "compromise" verdict. Despite the jurors' belief that Patterson was innocent, they believed that a conviction was necessary to allow them to return to live in their community with their honor intact. Consequently, they convicted Patterson and sentenced him to a prison term rather than death.[52]

Steeped in a culture that viewed the sexual assault of white women by black men as a heinous crime against white supremacy, white juries hardly represented neutral arbiters of black men's fates. Commonly held social presumptions predisposed the white men sitting on juries to view any sexual contact between white women and black men as rape and most contact between black men and white women as carrying a sexual threat. The threat of lynching, the reports of high feeling in communities, and the rhetoric about the purity of white womanhood were common threads in cases of black-on-white rape in Virginia. This familiar script of alleged black violence and white response did not disappear once the accused faced a jury. Jurors brought it with them into the courtroom and measured the prosecution's case against their preconceived notions of black men's supposed tendency to rape white women. Violations of defendants' due-process rights played a lesser role in verdicts than did the cultural heritage and beliefs about black men and rape that jurors brought with them into the jury box.[53]

Although Virginia's court system virtually guaranteed that whites controlled the dispensation of justice, mob action remained an ever-present possibility. State officials offered local authorities a variety of methods to help prevent mob violence and to ensure a trial when a black man was arrested for an assault on a white woman. Accused black men were held in distant jails for safekeeping in the hopes that a geographical barrier between mob and defendant would discourage vigilante violence. For example, word of the arrest of Archer Ellis in 1912 in Charles City County caused "popular excitement [to run] high and indignant citizens heard rumors of lynching." He was moved to the Richmond jail for safekeeping.[54] Jesse Carter's 1925 arrest for rape in Prince Edward County also incited high feeling, and outraged citizens surrounded the building in which he was being held and questioned. Carter was moved to an undisclosed location and held safely until his trial.[55] Taking such precautions, whether because of rumors of a developing mob or of the appearance of crowds around a jail, often successfully thwarted violence. A mob seeking Joe Gibbs, for example, dispersed after learning that he was no longer held in the jail they had surrounded.[56] Even if there were no evidence of mob activity or expressions of outrage in the community, officials often took precautions to protect the prisoner anyway. When William Nelson was arrested for attempting to rape a white woman walking in a field, "officials stated that no trouble was anticipated but precautionary measures have been taken."[57] Measures such as moving accused black men out of the community demonstrated authorities' determination to maintain control over white responses to black men's crimes.

Official efforts to prevent mob violence, however, did not insulate criminal trials from the influence of white rage. As Alfred Wright's trial attests, the threat of violence shaped the course of the trial and the jury's verdict. In the rush to prosecute a defendant and contain the mob, the nature of the crime often dictated the outcome of the trial. Defendants themselves, perhaps better than anyone, recognized the precarious position they occupied, as communities often responded to reports of attacks with outrage. Defense attorneys often tried to avoid the potential danger to their clients by invoking the salacious nature of the crime and the passions it aroused as justifications for moving the trial to a different county, where white public opinion was less likely to influence the jury's verdict. Lee Archer was accused of raping Cora Whitehurst in 1913, and his lawyer followed this strategy; in doing so, he described the atmosphere that surrounded many charges of black-on-white rape:

> The crime with which [Lee Archer] is charged, but which he denies, is a serious one and one which, by reason of its nature, is calculated to, and does inflame public sentiment in the community in which it was committed to a high degree; knowledge of said crime and the sentiment aroused thereby spreads quickly and grows in intensity as it spreads; whereas on the day of the alleged crime there was scarcely any notoriety in the neighborhood, yet on the following day the sentiment was such that several parties were being organized for the purpose of lynching [Lee Archer]. These rumors were so well defined and apparently so well founded on fact, that the judge of this court, of his own motion, ordered [Archer] to be brought to the Norfolk City jail for safekeeping.[58]

Archer's attorney continued that removing Archer to the Norfolk jail nearby only increased the fury of the public, making it impossible to find a jury that was not already prejudiced against him. These remarks suggest that white outrage was contextual; it remained confined only to whites in the community in which the assault occurred. Local juries could not separate their personal feelings about local crimes from the legal process. Whites outside of the community would be less likely to be infected with high feeling and thus were capable of rendering a more just verdict. Ironically, Archer's lawyer criticized legal officials for moving Archer to another jail, arguing it contributed to local belief in his guilt.[59]

Distancing prisoners from angry mobs was one method of preventing extralegal violence. A speedy trial and conviction was another. Court officials brought the accused men to trial as quickly as possible, thus removing any delay that might provide an opportunity for mass action. Speedy trials, however, also ensured that outrage among prospective jurors, who were usually drawn from the community in which the alleged crime occurred, had no opportunity to dissipate. Arthur Neale, for example, was indicted the day after his alleged assault of a twelve-year-old white girl, and he waited only two days for his trial. He was convicted and sentenced to death after a trial lasting one day. There were no reported threats against him because the community was "satisfied" with his rapid trial and punishment.[60] In 1932, Sam Pannell was tried and convicted of rape and attempted murder only nine days after the alleged assault. The speed of Sam Pannell's trial is particularly noteworthy because Pannell's brother

George was acquitted of the crime several days before Sam was even arrested.[61] Near-instantaneous trials encouraged verdicts that accorded with white community desires. They also left defense attorneys with little time to prepare their cases. Often, these men could offer little more than pleas for mercy to counter the popular desire for severe punishment.

The governor's office also mandated the use of the state militia to maintain order during trials of alleged rapists, as the case of Tom Coles shows. In 1915, Georgia Royster, a fifteen-year-old schoolgirl told police that on her way home from school, a black man had dragged her into the woods and raped her. Tom Coles was arrested and taken to Petersburg to prevent "summary vengeance." His alleged accomplice, Richard Carter, was arrested and incarcerated in Danville. White citizens of Mecklenburg, where the crime occurred, stormed a train from Danville, thinking that Carter was returning to Mecklenburg to face trial. After the attempt to lynch Carter, officials became increasingly concerned about rumors of a plan to storm the Petersburg jail and lynch Coles. No mob appeared, but at Coles's trial one month later, state militia troops accompanied Coles from Petersburg to the Mecklenburg courthouse and stood guard outside while the trial took place. The meaning of their presence could hardly have been lost on Coles's jury. The troops provided a continual reminder to the jury of the punishment local whites expected Coles to receive. He was convicted, sentenced to death, and executed.[62] Interestingly, Carter was released without being charged because Georgia Royster, the victim, testified that he had not raped her; he had merely stood guard while Coles assaulted her. Despite the community outrage and attempted lynching, Carter was never punished for his participation in the crime.[63]

That the state intervened to prevent mob violence does not necessarily imply that, given the opportunity, most communities would have lynched black men. Newspaper commentary suggests that many whites in Virginia feared rumors of lynchings would reflect a lack of local support for the rule of law and Virginians' inability to balance aggression with civilization. Especially in rural areas, rumors that outrage would lead to violence suggested that rural whites were less civilized. Most whites resented the implication that they lacked the self-control of "more refined" urban whites. When John Henry Williams, in rural Nottoway County, attempted to flee a posse that believed he assaulted a white schoolgirl, Richmond newspapers reported that a mob had surrounded the jail in which they believed Williams was being held. After Williams was moved to Richmond, the people of Nottoway County were reportedly "aggrieved that the charges [of mob action] should have been published in the press reflecting upon them. Nottoway citizens stand for law and order, and expect to see the law is upheld."[64] Avoiding mob violence became a badge of honor for local communities awaiting the trials of black men accused of assaulting white women. Fauquier County prided itself on the uneventful capture of a black man accused of attempted rape in 1920. Scoffing at reports appearing in "distant [that is, urban] papers . . . describing great excitement, hundreds of angry citizens, [and] a 'man-hunt'" to catch Andrew Fields, the local newspaper reported, "There was not a sign of disorder, excitement or general commotion. Nine-tenths of those in town . . . slept quietly without knowing anything had happened."[65]

The case of William H. Burgess illustrates how trials of black men became important public relations opportunities for white Virginians who supported law and order. Trials allowed rural whites in Virginia to separate themselves from the charges of lawlessness and savagery directed at other southern states and to insist that they, too, represented the progress and promise of white civilization. White Virginians used the absence of lynching to congratulate themselves for their forbearance, insisting that refraining from vigilante action required manly fortitude. Burgess was arrested and tried in 1917 for attempting to rape two white women on two separate occasions in rural Fairfax County. The *Fairfax Herald*, the local newspaper that covered the case, criticized papers in Washington, D.C., for their reports that a lynching was inevitable. The paper insisted that there was no excitement over Burgess's case, largely because the accused had been apprehended before any word of the assaults reached the public.[66] Legal officials who kept the white community ignorant of an arrest ultimately deserved credit for preventing the lynching.

Some white Virginians contested lynching's relationship to white notions of masculinity. Burgess faced trial the same year as William Page's lynching, at which time protecting white women was central to white masculine notions of honor. Another component of masculinity, however, was control. Some white men feared Burgess would be lynched, and they encouraged his removal from the community. But their "hysterical" actions did not represent the opinion of the larger white community of men who channeled their anger into the courts. The Fairfax paper commented that "the Washington papers made it appear that intense excitement prevailed here, with threats of a speedy lynching, and these false rumors, in conjunction with the hysteria of a few old ladies of the masculine gender culminated in the unnecessary removal of the prisoner to Richmond for safekeeping."[67] Real men did not lynch because real men did not need to resort to extralegal violence. They restrained their passion in favor of reason and the rule of law. Burgess's conviction and death sentence amply demonstrated the effectiveness of this attitude. White men's emotion found its outlet in the electric chair. Once Burgess had been convicted and sentenced to death, the judge in the case thanked the local community "for preserving the good name of Fairfax."[68] The newspaper expressed similar sentiments, saying, "It is a matter of great satisfaction to every thinking person in Fairfax that no attempt was made to harm Burgess, in spite of the brutality of the crime, and the friends and relatives of the ladies in the case deserve credit for their self control under circumstances that were enough to cause them to take the law into their own hands."[69] Though acknowledging the temptation that such outrages might produce, Fairfax nevertheless took pride in its reliance on the legal process. It considered reports of threatened lynching by a neighboring community to be an affront to its reputation and dignity. Like most southerners at the time, they believed that the temptation to take the law into one's own hand was strong and that restraint represented civilized fortitude and virtue.

Even after juries returned their verdicts, the potential for violence continued to influence black men's treatment in the legal system. Legal officials occasionally justified denying convicted men conditional pardon by arguing it would reward the white community for its restraint. Walter Bowen, for example, was convicted of raping a seven-year-old white girl in 1916, and he received a sentence of eleven years. Four years after Bowen's incarceration, the governor received a petition requesting his pardon signed by five "representing citizens of his community."[70] Governor Westmoreland Davis wrote the commonwealth's attorney asking his opinion regarding the petition. Mr. McCorkle, who tried Bowen, refused to recommend Bowen's release. He was explicit in his reasoning and based it on his concern for law and order. "Considering the serious nature of the offense, and the strain that such an offense places upon the people in any community to withhold taking the law into their own hands," he opined, "I feel that it would be a grave mistake to grant a pardon to this prisoner. I feel confident that you will agree with me that the restrain[t] and self-control exercised by the people of this county should be rewarded, and like conduct on their part in the future encouraged, by permitting the verdict of the jury to stand."[71] Governor Davis refused Bowen's petition, as did his successor in 1923. He completed his prison sentence, an apparent reward for the community that refrained from lynching him.

The potential for violence shaped every step of the legal process from where authorities held arrested men to decisions about pardon and early release. Authorities even used the possibility of future violence to influence jury deliberations. Authorities prosecuting black men accused of assaulting white women explicitly alluded to recently dispersed mobs, to angry spectators in the courtroom, and even to the furor sure to follow crimes not yet committed. Allusions to violence became tools to encourage guilty verdicts and severe sentences. Legal officials suggested to jurors that if they did not sentence black men to death, lynching would be the inevitable community response the next time a white woman made allegations of assault, as Henry Perman's case in 1925 shows. In his closing statement to the jury at Perman's trial, the prosecuting attorney said, "There has never been a lynching in Norfolk County and God forbid there ever will be. Be courageous, for if a crime like this goes unpunished, we cannot tell what the consequences will be. . . . If you would deter rapists, let them know it means death." Despite being instructed by the judge to disregard the prosecutor's statement, Perman's jury did what was expected of them: they sentenced him to death.[72] Authorities were aware that unpopular verdicts and sentences jeopardized the rule of law in future cases. Juries, too, were ever mindful that their verdicts should accurately reflect white public opinion, as local whites ceded power to the legal system only because they trusted it to carry out their will. Newspaper editorials reinforced this view. As coverage of the Byrd lynching shows, many whites viewed lynching as unnecessary because the courts could be relied upon to dispense white ideas of justice. Preventing future lynchings provided juries with a powerful motivation for sentencing black men to death.

The possibility of violence cast a shadow over the investigations into allegations of assault as well. In their questioning of black suspects, police used the threat of violence to coerce confessions out of black men and to silence their claims of innocence, fulfilling W. A. Woodbridge's vision of the mob as a tool of law enforcement. Robert Williams's case provides an apt example. In 1920, Annie Ross, a Swedish masseuse working in Lynchburg, Virginia, told police that she had been raped while she was walking home from a movie. Police arrested Robert Williams when they determined the soles of his shoes matched prints left at the scene of the crime.[73] Ross, however, could not identify Williams as her assailant. In fact, she would later insist that he was not the man.[74] Usually, the alleged victim's failure to identify the suspect as her assailant prompted law enforcement officials to release him. Instead, police and court officials tried Williams for the crime because he confessed to police. Despite Ross's refusal to participate in Williams's trial, a jury convicted him and sentenced him to death.

Before his scheduled execution, however, Williams appealed to the governor to commute his sentence, arguing that his confession was a desperate lie extorted from him by force. According to Williams's petition for commutation, one week after his arrest a mob attempted to break into the jail where he was being held. Hearing of the plan in advance, police officials removed Williams from the jail.[75] But the police used the mob as leverage to obtain his confession. According to Williams's affidavit, the officers took him into a dark alley, repeating at every step that "the mob is coming to get you and we have taken you out here for safe keeping." When the alley reached a dead end, an officer told him, "I hear the mob coming now and we shall have to leave you here and flee for our lives unless you say that you committed the crime, and if you will say that you committed the crime we can save you from that angry mob." To save his life, Williams told the officers, "I did it," though he gave them no other statement or any details of the crime. The jury convicted Williams because of his "confession."[76] Despite the pleas of forty-six people, including eight clergymen from black and white churches, that Williams's sentence be commuted, as well as a statement from another witness testifying to Williams's alibi, the governor declined to intervene and Williams was executed three months after Annie Ross reported her attack. Williams's case attests to the common goals of mobs and law enforcement officials. Legal officials discouraged mob violence, but they were nonetheless willing to use the threat of mob violence when necessary to achieve their desired result. Their actions sent a message to African Americans that there was no distinction between the legal system and the mob.

It is difficult to determine how frequently police used violence, both threatened and actual, to obtain statements from black men. Newspapers frequently reported when police obtained black men's confessions, but they never questioned the validity of those confessions. Convicted black men, however, often attributed their confessions to police violence when they petitioned Virginia governors for clemency. Anderson Finch, who was convicted of attempted rape in 1903, insisted police brutality drove him to implicate both himself and another black man, Doc Bacon, in a crime against the wife of Bacon's employer. Finch allegedly told the prosecuting attorney before his execution that while he was being questioned, authorities "had a rope about his neck and threatened to hang him if he did not tell them who had committed this crime; that to save his life he told them that Doc Bacon did it while he watched."[77] The governor refused to commute Doc Bacon's death sentence despite Finch's statement and the fact that the victim, Bacon's employer, refused to testify against him.

The lawyer for Henry Palmer, who was accused of raping and murdering a white woman in 1929, also argued that Palmer's confession should be disregarded. The defense unsuccessfully requested that the judge instruct the jury that a confession obtained "by motives of hope or reward, or by fear of injury excited by a person in authority" was "never admissible as evidence." Apparently, while Palmer was being questioned by six officers, "Leon Nowitzky, detective, upon arresting the accused . . . struck him a severe blow and blackened and injured his left eye and caused him to fear the detective."[78] In another incident twelve years after Palmer's execution, law enforcement officials used the threat of violence to obtain a confession from fifteen-year-old Joseph Mickens, who was accused of raping a young white mother in 1941. Mickens, a minor, told the court that approximately ten law enforcement officials questioned him at once, and though the officers did not "beat him or even slap him," they did persist in questioning him for several hours, "first one then another and in groups; that he got so tired sitting up there in the chair until he would doze and then catch himself."[79] On the witness stand, Mickens claimed that the officer's methods were threatening. They had also placed a noose on the table and told him that "he was drawing the rope tighter and tighter around his own neck, pointing to the rope and telling him he had better talk."[80] Law enforcement officers and legal officials demonstrated to African Americans that white authorities could forestall lynchings but they would nonetheless use violence and coercion within the legal system to obtain convictions, regardless of black men's guilt or innocence.

Newspapers rarely published suspects' allegations that they had confessed only after violent police coercion. Occasionally, news reports noted that an accused assailant received the "third degree," but generally the press assumed, as did the public, that harsh interrogation methods were necessary to overcome black men's innate tendency to lie, and that black men confessed to assaulting white women because they were guilty. Confessions, no matter how they were obtained, as Robert Williams discovered, made the prosecutor's job easy, even if the alleged victim said that the defendant had not committed the crime. Once black men were arrested and charged with rape, criminal procedure worked against them. Confessions obtained through coercion were only one of an arsenal of weapons legal officials used against black men accused of assaulting white women.

Southern courts, especially in cases that did not elicit northern condemnation, offered the appearance of due process, though that did not guarantee that trials were fair or their outcomes just. Objective standards of justice required the willingness of white court officials to challenge both white public opinion and the tenets of white supremacy, which provided the framework for punishing black men for alleged crimes. This was especially true for the white men who acted as counsel for accused black men. Most black men accused of raping white women in Virginia received legal counsel. Sometimes, black men's families had the means, either on their own or with the help of local community supporters, to hire competent legal assistance. In 1925, for example, Lee Ernest Bell's family wrote to a sister in Ohio asking for money to pay the $500 retainer for Bell's attorney. Bell's sister took it upon herself to notify the NAACP of his case.[81] It is unclear who ultimately paid for Richard Daniel Brown's attorney, though the judge postponed the trial date until his family secured counsel.[82] Judges also routinely appointed members of the local bar to defend black men accused of assaults against white women and ordered state compensation for their services. The judge in William Gee's case in 1926 appointed an African American attorney to represent him in his trial for the rape of an elderly Confederate widow.[83] John Wade's appointed lawyer was paid $25, a common amount, for defending Wade against charges of attempted rape and robbery in 1923. Wade fared well with his lawyer's representation. Although he was convicted of attempted robbery, he received a sentence of only two years in prison.[84] Concern for at least appearing to protect the legal rights of defendants was part of Virginia's efforts to promote progressive control of racial interaction.

Despite the apparent intent of the Virginia legal system to provide all its accused citizens with legal counsel, it was occasionally unsuccessful. Local attorneys, fearful of incurring the wrath of potential white clients, were often reluctant to act as counsel for black men accused of assaulting white women. Extant records rarely contain concrete evidence of white attorneys' efforts to avoid taking accused black men as clients, and few attorneys expressed their unwillingness to act as counsel to black men in statements made to the court. Most avoided taking on black men's cases in more subtle but no less telling ways. Their actions effectively deprived black men of legal counsel, as happened in the case of John Lewis Rollins and his cousin, George Matthews. The two men were accused in 1915 of breaking into the home of a white widow and attempting to rape her and her daughter. Both men allegedly confessed, and each claimed that the other initiated the crime. Both were quickly convicted of rape and attempted rape, sentenced to death, and executed. Neither man, however, had counsel at trial. According to the newspaper, "The prisoners had no counsel, and while the court desired to appoint counsel for them, all of the attorneys who were not engaged in the case had left town."[85] Though the newspaper report did not say it, the nature of the crime and the furor it created in the community obviously discouraged local attorneys from representing the defendants. Rather than confront the judge with their reluctance, they all quietly made themselves unavailable. Rollins's and Matthews's executions came, then, as no surprise.[86]

The presence of defense counsel, on the other hand, was rarely an impediment to conviction. White juries were usually eager to convict black men regardless of the arguments of the defense. Having a lawyer by one's side in court did not guarantee a vigorous defense either. Many white lawyers in twentieth-century Virginia were probably no less reluctant than those considering the Matthews and Rollins case in 1915, but they did not express their discontent by leaving town. Court records make definitive proof elusive, but it is likely that some appointed attorneys sought to protect their local reputations by doing as little as possible for their unpopular clients. With black men safely convicted and severely punished, appointed attorneys could argue to the white community that they had been forced by the local judge to provide a defense but that they largely stood by to see "justice done." The distinct lack of motions made by defense counsel on their client's behalf is perhaps indicative of this approach. Judge J. Lawrence Campbell, for example, apparently sought to ensure competent counsel for Will Finney, who was charged with raping his employer's young daughter in 1908, by appointing Judge John P. Lee as his counsel. At Finney's trial, it appears that Lee made no motions in his client's defense. Finney was judged not guilty of rape but guilty of attempted rape and sentenced to death. His sentence was commuted to life in prison after a concerted campaign by legal officials convinced the governor that Finney was mentally disabled. Though Judge Campbell, the prosecuting attorney, the sheriff, and community members petitioned on Finney's behalf, his counsel, Lee, the man who should have had the most intimate acquaintance with Finney's mental abilities, was not among them.[87]

If the number of motions to overturn verdicts provides any indication, however, most appointed attorneys made some effort to defend their clients. In many cases, defense counsel objected to the indictment, or, more frequently, motioned to overturn the jury's verdict as contrary to the law and evidence. Judges rarely granted these motions and usually did not even schedule court time to hear attorney's arguments for or against them. At many trials, defense attorneys also expressed a desire to appeal the jury's verdict. Judges routinely postponed sentences, especially executions, to allow attorneys time to prepare their appeals. In many cases, however, either no appeal was ever filed, or the supreme court quickly decided not to hear the case. The fact that a lawyer obtained the time from the trial judge to prepare the appeal does not necessarily mean that the lawyer continued, or was able to continue, to defend his client or that the defendant had the financial wherewithal to appeal his conviction, however. Solomon Douglas's effort to appeal his 1921 assault conviction, for example, foundered when he could not afford to transcribe the record of his trial.[88] Regardless of their willingness to take on black men as clients, defense attorneys faced burdens beyond the likelihood of conviction.

Whether or not accused black men's attorneys took their responsibilities seriously, the very nature of the cases made achieving a fair and complete trial extraordinarily difficult. Communities were overwhelmingly willing to judge any accused black man guilty, especially after he had been identified by the alleged victim as her assailant. Defense attorneys occasionally claimed that whites' desire for conviction made any attempts to investigate the crime impossible. In 1941, Charlie Brown's attorney, W. L. Parker, clearly articulated the difficulties he faced in a letter to Governor Price requesting the commutation of Brown's death sentence. Brown had been charged with raping a white woman, and he apparently confessed to beating her and trying to kill her as well.[89] He was convicted and sentenced to death. His attorney argued that Brown had not received a fair trial. His motions to move the trial to a neutral county had been overruled, and the trial occurred while twenty-five state troopers stood guard with "riot guns and tear gas equipment." He also insisted that evidence in Brown's favor could not be uncovered because "no one would talk to me at all, and while no one actually threatened me, I was nevertheless, the recipient of several messages that if I tried to do anything to help the 'nigger,' I would get something that I would not 'like.' "[90] Even the most well intentioned efforts on the part of an attorney were no guarantee that he could mount a vigorous and complete defense for his client. White public opinion, even when not expressed through crowds surrounding jails and in courtrooms, nonetheless found ways to ensure a verdict to its liking.

Public outrage not only made it difficult for defense attorneys to investigate their clients' cases, it determined the power of the evidence prosecutors presented against accused black men. Attorneys and even legal officials admitted that attitudes about sexual relations between white women and black men predisposed jurors to accept the prosecutions' accounts of crimes and that black men were convicted on mere shreds of evidence.

Ernest McKnight was convicted in 1909 in Fairfax County of attempted rape and sentenced to eight years in prison. R. R. Farr, his attorney, tried to have him released. After his initial arguments failed, Farr pleaded for McKnight's release because he was dying of tuberculosis. McKnight, he insisted, "was sentenced on the very slimmest kind of evidence, evidence that would never have secured the conviction of a white man. . . . The case made out against him by the commonwealth was very slight, they not . proving that he touched or attempted to touch the girl against whom he was charged with committing the offense for which he was convicted." Governor Mann refused to extend pardon because McKnight's tuberculosis was a threat to public health.[91]

Flimsy evidence sustained the convictions of black men accused of assaulting white women largely because of whites' exaggerated beliefs about the severity of the crime. In the early twentieth century, governors occasionally refused to make decisions about pardon in rape cases if the race of the victim was not explicitly stated. Indeed, if they were unsure, governors specifically requested the race of the victim, underscoring the centrality of race in their deliberations, as well as in whites' perception of the crime. When James White petitioned the governor for a conditional pardon in 1910 for his attempted rape conviction in 1901, the governor's secretary wrote the prosecuting attorney asking the victim's race. At the bottom of the attorney's letter, the clerk scrawled, "Mrs. Somma says Mrs. Meyer [the victim] is her sister-in-law and is white." White's petition was refused.[92] James Bond's 1917 request for conditional pardon was also rejected, perhaps partially because of the response the governor received when he asked "whether or not his crime was committed on a white woman." It was.[93] And while some governors claimed to have a color-blind policy not to pardon *any* men convicted of rape or attempted rape, others were explicit that their policy was not race neutral. Governor Swanson, in his deliberations over whether to extend a conditional pardon to John Roberson, a drunken man who stumbled into the wrong house, stated his policy forthrightly: "I have determined not to interfere executive clemency in any case where a colored man is convicted of rape or attempted rape on a white woman, and in any case of rape I am extremely particular and require the strongest reasons before I interfere with the verdict of the jury and the judgment of the court."[94] Despite his statement, he pardoned Roberson well before he completed his sentence and, for varying reasons, made exceptions to his stated policy in other black-on-white rape cases as well. Though he gave rhetorical primacy to the importance of race in rape cases, his actions indicate that other factors could outweigh it.

That white assumptions about black rapists played a central role in black men's convictions was no secret. On several occasions, judges instructed juries that they could not be influenced by the issue of race. In John Anderson's 1938 trial for rape, the judge specifically warned the jurors that "in arriving at their verdict they cannot and shall not permit themselves to be influenced by the fact that the defendant is a colored man and the prosecutrix a white woman." Despite the efforts of the judge to remove race from the case, Anderson was convicted, sentenced to death, and executed.[95] The same instruction was given, verbatim, by the judge to the jury in the 1948 trial of Richard Daniel Brown.[96] He, too, was convicted, although he received a sentence of life in prison. Brown's and Anderson's juries were largely instructed to do the impossible. Jury verdicts usually supported prevailing stereotypes about black men's sexual intentions toward white women. They also speak to a common understanding that the motivations for mob violence were little different from what motivated white juries to convict and punish accused black men. Regardless of whether or not a judge had any intention of protecting black defendants' legal rights, the line between vigilante violence and criminal justice often blurred.

White rhetoric accompanying allegations of assault, the threats of violence, the appearance of angry crowds, and finally the trial and conviction were all part of the same performance. Each represented an aspect of a process through which the white community enforced its behavioral norms on African Americans and protected white women. The methods of law enforcement officials and white mobs appeared at odds, but their goals were the same. All were the means to control the racial hierarchy by punishing black men who allegedly committed racial transgressions. Black men's criminal trials for rape in Virginia were progressive, modern spectacles, encoded with cultural meaning. They exerted social control over observers and participants of all genders, classes, and races by unifying elite and popular efforts to punish blacks. In Virginia, mobs resorted to murder only rarely, but the ever-present potential for mob violence and the fact that jurors drawn from the white community were responsible for determining the sentences of convicted black men guaranteed that the punishments black men received would reflect the will of the white community. The mob and that legal system could effectively work together to avenge black men's crimes against white women. With these two forces working in tandem, whites balanced the need for civilized order and the rule of law with their violent desires for revenge and retribution. The legal process effectively masked white desires for violence, and efforts to ensure elements of due process promoted the appearance of the rule of law. Able to refrain from lynching and present an image of fairness at trial, whites assured themselves of the superiority not only of their civilization but also of the methods they used to uphold and defend it.

Trials were powerful reenactments of appropriate relations both within segregated society and between individuals. But the cooperation between outraged whites and the legal system also obscured the tensions that lurked beneath the surface of these seemingly predictable trials. Most black men accused of crimes against white women were convicted, but they were convicted of a variety of offenses. Even black men convicted of the same crimes received disparate punishments, and most convicted black men were not sentenced to death. More important, many black men did not serve their full sentences. The process of punishing black men, then, was considerably less predictable than conviction rates and the presence of mobs would suggest. Whites and blacks, men and women, continually contested the legal process. Criminal trials embodied whites' common desire to control blacks, but debates about how to maintain that control also spoke to divisions in the white community. Not all whites viewed white civilization in the same way, and, significantly, not all whites were equally civilized. At the same time, the way in which different whites responded to cases of black-on-white rape suggests that despite whites' propensity to call all black men rapists, the homogeneity of black defendants was not so absolute. The following pages explore when, how, and why different groups disputed the seemingly rigid ritual of punishing black men. Their arguments, counterarguments, and forms of leverage over the legal process uncover a far more racially interactive society than the rules of segregation would imply. Whites and blacks and men and women engaged in a wide variety of social, work-related, familial, and sexual relationships. White men took seriously their duty to protect white women but not always to the same degree in every situation. African Americans, in turn, resisted whites' characterization of black men as uncivilized rapists at every turn.

The tensions beneath the surface demonstrate how assumptions about the mythical black beast rapist came into conflict. Trials of black men accused of assaulting white women, and the considerations of their sentences made later by legal elites in Richmond, were far more contested and contingent than the conviction rates suggest. As the next chapter argues, the white community, the legal system, and the executive branch did not always agree on how or when a black man's actions toward a white woman threatened the social order. They did not even agree on when the racial script of black-on-white rape should be invoked to shore up white supremacy. Not every form of contact between white women and black men represented a sexual or societal threat. In Alfred Wright's case, which began the chapter, Appomattox legal officials and the community agreed on the nature of his crime and the price he should pay. White solidarity was not so evident in every case.

CHAPTER 2

Shadow and Act

White Women's Fears and Black Men's Intentions

In August of 1939, a Richmond police officer came upon seventeen-year-old Ruby Hogan crying on a city street shortly after four in the morning. She told the officer that she had been raped by three black men while George Shinault, her white companion, had watched. After she was taken to the hospital, three black men, Tom William Johnson, Arthur Lee Harvey, and Robert William Miller were arrested, along with George Shinault. Shinault was convicted of two counts of contributing to the moral delinquency of a minor and sentenced to eighteen months in prison and fined $750. Each of the three black men, however, was only required to post a $500 bond. Hogan herself was held on a delinquency charge and placed under the care of the Children's Bureau of the State Department of Public Welfare.[1]

The newspapers following the case reported that testimony at trial was rife with "conflict and confusion." When arrested, all three black men admitted to having intercourse with Hogan, a clear violation of appropriate racial behavior. Ruby Hogan, however, was no paragon of white virtue. Her actions that evening violated the rules concerning not only racial interaction but proper female behavior as well. At trial, the black men asserted that Hogan had danced with other black men at a nearby hotel bar and also had sexual relations with Shinault. Hogan, they argued, was little more than a prostitute, accepting fifty cents and a bottle of corn liquor from the three black men in exchange for sexual relations. Nevertheless, at trial, the black men testified that they had become frightened and left before sexual relations took place. Other testimony described Hogan herself as being "tight," a euphemism for drunk, on the night in question. Shinault, the white man, chose to corroborate the story of the black men, denying that Hogan had been raped. Hinting that whatever happened between Ruby Hogan and the men was consensual, he testified that he left the garage with Hogan and the three black men still inside, making no effort to determine what transpired among them.

The case was not tried before a jury, and the opinion of the judge, though holding all parties in some measure responsible, placed the majority of the blame on George Shinault. Judge Ingram presented his opinion without comment, but the punishments he imposed indicated his concern. Shinault had taken a young white woman out, allowed her to get drunk and to dance with black men, led her to a garage for a "petting party," and then permitted three black men to join them. He received the most substantial punishment of anyone involved, eighteen months in prison and a $750 fine. Although the judge ruled that Shinault had failed in his duty as a white man to protect a white woman, the sentence he imposed hardly represented protection either. The court did not cloak Ruby Hogan in chivalry and did not invoke her status as a white woman. Indeed, the three men Hogan accused of rape escaped with comparatively minor punishments. The court did not view Hogan, the alleged victim, as blameless, either. It turned her over to the authorities as a juvenile delinquent in need of supervision and reform. The black men, Ingram's judgments implied, had only taken advantage of a situation created by the moral failings of low-class whites.[2]

The *Richmond Afro-American*'s headline after the trial triumphantly announced, "Charges of Attack Flop."[3] Only the races of the participants merited public interest in what would otherwise have been a mundane morals case. Regardless of whether Hogan had been a willing participant to what had occurred that night, once she charged the three black men with rape, she immediately ceded the power her status as a white woman provided to the legal system. After levying the charges, white men judged the merits of her case within the framework of collective preconceptions about race and gender norms. Their decisions determined whether the case involved the incendiary issue of black-on-white rape. Ruby Hogan's case, they decided, did not. She had been out late drinking, dancing, and petting with both white and black men. Her apparent moral turpitude mitigated the severity of her charges. It was not a case of black-on-white rape, and any sexual relations that occurred moved from being illegal to being illicit, from rape, a felony, to fornication, which was rarely prosecuted. Her accused assailants were men "not of good fame" exploiting morally bankrupt whites rather than "black beast rapists" who preyed on an innocent white woman.

As Hogan's experience shows, white southerners were not always ready to leap to the defense of a white woman who claimed she had been assaulted by a black man, nor did they interpret all interactions between white women and black men as sexual assault. Not every instance of contact between white women and black men provoked southerners' heated rhetoric about black beast rapists, which characterized the rape myth in the South; not every case proceeded predictably from accusation to conviction to incarceration or execution, according to the familiar racial script of protecting white womanhood. Even if the public, in news accounts, did initially lash out in outraged protest over allegations of assault, whites nevertheless differentiated among cases. Not all assaults by black men against white women were equally threatening; not all involved equally serious violations of white prerogatives and racial supremacy. Whites chose to invoke the black beast rapist and imperiled white womanhood in some cases and not in others, and they occasionally changed their minds about whether the rape myth applied at all.

The willingness of whites to differentiate between cases of interracial assault and rape grew, in part, from contradictions inherent in the system of segregation. The goal of segregation was to keep the races apart, with whites always occupying superior space. Segregation in theory created clear, easily determined lines between whites and blacks and elucidated clear rules regarding racial interaction. Segregation, as it was lived and experienced, was far less tidy. Despite legal efforts to ensure racial separation and despite a complex set of rules of etiquette that theoretically structured every encounter between whites and blacks, the activities of daily life created situations that did not neatly fall within those prescribed rules. The inevitable interactions created tensions that often resulted in confusion and mistrust, not the stable predictability that whites envisioned and desired.[4] This particular insecurity lead to misunderstandings, sometimes with tragic consequences, especially in rural areas, where residents were accustomed to familiar and predictable encounters with people they knew either personally or by reputation.

Steeped in a culture that tended to frame any interaction between white women and black men within the discourse of violence, white women often became frightened around black men, especially those whom they did not know or knew only slightly. Public thoroughfares, lonesome country roads, even white women's own doorsteps and front yards provided considerable space for ambiguous or mistaken interactions. In this ambiguous social milieu, white southerners, especially the white males who made up the legal system, interpreted some assaults as threats to the racial order while dismissing others. Whites' determination that not every individual act of violence toward white women carried the same danger of sexual assault becomes clear in the varied charges levied against black men, the widely disparate sentences they received when convicted, and the willingness of legal authorities and governors to pardon convicted black men.

Uncovering the distinctions white Virginians made in these cases requires looking beyond jury verdicts. Juries applied racially determined standards of justice and convicted accused men largely because they were black. They convicted most black men of some crime, usually rape, attempted rape, assault, or robbery. Legal officials, when offering their recommendations regarding executive clemency, freely admitted that black men were convicted for crimes on evidence that would never have sustained a guilty verdict for a white man. Consequently, conviction rates alone merely indicate that white Virginians accepted pervasive beliefs about black men's criminal tendencies toward white women. And they reveal far less about white Virginians' beliefs regarding acceptable interactions between white women and black men. But a close analysis of whites' descriptions of black men's actions, which may or may not have been accurate, as well as the charges officials chose to bring against accused black men, reveals that whites did not force every interchange between white women and black men into the framework of sexual violence. No theoretical argument can account for the vagaries in every case, and the precise criteria influencing officials' decisions are difficult to determine. Nevertheless, even using whites' own perceptions of interactions, which would privilege white women's accounts over those of black men, legal officials looked beyond racial shibboleths to decide black men's fate. This chapter explores some of the factors that may have influenced their judgments.

Historical discussions of black-on-white rape, and of lynching as well, have suggested that black men could be convicted of rape or attempted rape after the most incidental contact. Scattered cases of lynchings and rape support this contention, as black men occasionally paid with their lives for innocent or accidental contact with white women.[5] Historians bolster this conclusion by pointing to the ideology of segregation that constructed white women as the iconographic embodiment of white supremacy and racial purity. They occupied an exalted, untouchable position in southern culture and came to represent the South itself. According to this ideology, because white women were responsible for maintaining racial purity, white southerners saw violations of white women's bodies and their personal space as an assault upon the racial hierarchy and the social order.[6] No impudent invasion of white women's person or space by a black man could be tolerated by white men. In many ways, this theoretical construct justified the racial separation mandated by segregation laws. Well aware of white women's rhetorical position, black men learned to tread carefully around white women, lest they be accused of an unintentional racial trespass.

White women, in turn, learned to fear black men. White racial ideology taught white women that black men desired them and might resort to rape to satisfy their desires.[7] Newspaper reports of assaults by black men against white women heightened these fears. Most white women did not experience assault themselves, but these stories reminded white women that they could potentially be the target of a black man's assault at any time and in any place, even in their own homes. The slightest contact with a black man or strange behavior by black men could set off deeply ingrained alarms in white women, as southern social custom trained white women to interpret such actions as sexual threats.

Officials faced the sensitive task of weeding out accusations made by particularly anxious white women whose nervousness was a function of their environment and their supposedly natural tendency toward weakness and vulnerability. Some accusations could result from misunderstanding rather than criminal intent. Where an assault occurred could play a role in whether officials believed that the actions of the black men in question were in fact harmful in intent or that they were merely interpreted as such by fearful and irrational women. Black men's actions in urban areas took on a wider range of meanings because urban dwellers were more accustomed to encountering strangers whose motives were unclear. Black men reported in the media as having "attacked" white women on city streets might face lesser charges of robbery or assault, as the anonymity of urban life made more room for interpreting black men's behavior in different ways. Rural courts, operating in small, more intimate communities were less tolerant of ambiguous social encounters between white women and black men and were more likely to interpret black men's actions as carrying a threat not only to a specific white woman but to white supremacy in general. The location of an assault was not the only factor judges, juries, and state officials had to weigh in shepherding cases through the legal system, nor did it alone determine whether a black man's actions signaled intent to rape. Nevertheless, its consideration underscores the fact that charges of black-on-white rape did not always follow a predictable course and that black men's actions were not interpreted uniformly.

Officials used other factors to analyze charges of assault. The nature of a black man's actions and whether he clearly demonstrated sexual intent and a willingness to use force also influenced perceptions of the severity of an assault. Under Virginia law, rape convictions required evidence that the assailant desired sexual relations *and* that he used force in an effort to accomplish sexual penetration. Juries often determined that the evidence failed to demonstrate one or the other element. Many actions by accused men had little to do with sexual intercourse, and the courts had to determine which actions implied an intent to rape. Similarly, juries faced cases in which black men did little more than express sexual desire for white women. Those expressions, though seeming to confirm white men's worst fears, ultimately appear to have been less threatening to the social order. In white eyes, such expressions confirmed that black men found white women desirable, and thus may have affirmed the logic of a segregated social order based on racial hierarchy, which placed white women in an exalted position.

The rules of evidence, however, constrained legal actions. Although Virginia law placed decisions about guilt and sentencing in the hands of white jurors, who could use their own racial prejudices to determine their verdicts, white community opinion was not hegemonic. The rules of evidence determined the admissibility of confessions or the reliability of bloodhounds tracking suspects from the crime scene. Judges warned juries that confessions obtained by force were unreliable and that bloodhounds could err. Judges instructed juries about the criminal elements required for a conviction of rape or attempted rape, but they also might encourage the jury to consider convicting the defendant of a nonsexual crime such as assault. Juries retained the ultimate power to interpret the evidence brought before them and to decide whether interactions between white women and black men constituted rape, the most serious violation of the racial order. Juries, however, even given the option of convicting men of rape or attempted rape, did not invariably assume that all African American men intended to rape the women who accused them and should thus pay with their lives.

Pardon petitions contained descriptions and interpretations of the actions that resulted in black men's arrests and convictions and often included legal officials' reevaluation of the seriousness of those actions. A petition frequently included the defendant's own account of events, as well as statements by judges and state officials regarding the meaning of a jury's verdict. A jury's vote to convict an accused black man did not necessarily indicate its absolute belief in his guilt. Correspondence between defense attorneys, governors, and prosecuting attorneys in pardon requests regularly acknowledged that a larger message undergirded a jury's sentence. White authorities believed that if the evidence of sexual assault was clear and convincing, beyond a reasonable doubt, juries would invariably sentence accused black men to death. That comparatively few men actually faced execution (only 50 of 230 convicted men) suggests that a great number of juries maintained some doubt as to the guilt of the assailant or the validity of a charge but voted for conviction anyway. Reasonable doubt, then, saved black men from the death penalty but usually not from conviction.

Rather than viewing prison sentences that were shorter than the statutory maximum solely as expressions of the jury's mercy—a mercy that most white southerners would believe was misplaced—legal officials attributed them to the weakness of the prosecution's case. In other words, a sentence other than death indicated the jury's doubt about the validity of the charge, and such doubt often later justified black men's pardon. Charles Wilson, for example, petitioned the governor for a conditional pardon in 1915, after serving eleven years of a twenty-year sentence. Manly H. Barnes, the prosecuting attorney who wrote on Wilson's behalf, stated that the victim "was not of the best reputation." He went on to say, "It is clear to me now that the jury was not fully satisfied that a rape had been committed; if they had[,] the death penalty would have been imposed, I think, without a doubt." Wilson's petition was granted.[8] In Walter Jones's case, the judge identified the jury's doubt more precisely. Jones was convicted of both rape and attempted rape in Lynchburg in 1906. The jury sentenced him to twenty years in prison. Responding to Jones's 1919 petition for release, Judge Frank P. Christian wrote, "At his trial I had considerable doubt as to his identity having been proved. In fact, this was reflected in the verdict of the jury as he was charged with the rape of a white woman." He, too, recommended that Jones be released; the governor complied.[9] Both Wilson and Jones were convicted during the nadir of race relations in the South and America. Their pardons years after conviction suggest the relative cooling of racial tensions both in the localities where the crimes occurred and nationally. They also indicate that even at the height of racial tensions, not all black men were sentenced to death for crimes against white women.

Arguments about latent reasonable doubt in the minds of juries suggest that juries convicted black men largely because they were accused of assaulting white women, regardless of the evidence against them. Walter Moore's attorney, R. W. Kime, made the jury's doubt the centerpiece of Moore's petition for release. Moore was charged with the rape of a sixty-four-year-old white widow. She testified that he appeared at her door one evening claiming he had a letter for her. When she let him in, he raped her.[10] Convicted of rape in 1914, Moore was sentenced to eighteen years in prison. He petitioned for conditional pardon in 1920. Kime insisted that the jurors' sentence reflected their doubt, and he asserted that the conviction resulted not from the evidence but from the races of assailant and victim: "In defending the prisoner, I told the jury that if they believed he was guilty of the offense, they ought to give him the death penalty; but I knew they would not do so because they did have such a doubt. Moreover, I told them that if they convicted the boy they would convict him on the fact that he was a negro boy and that the woman was a white woman; for otherwise if both were white or both were black they would undoubtedly acquit him."[11] The governor denied Moore's petition in 1920 but, citing doubts as to whether he was indeed the guilty party, granted it in 1924.[12]

White legal officials' statements inferring doubts on the part of the jury bolstered requests for pardon that involved other factors, such as the character of the victim. In pointing out that the jury's unwillingness to inflict the death penalty indicated its doubts as to the defendant's guilt, legal officials could grant pardons that might otherwise have raised the ire of the white community. If a segment of the white population already harbored doubt about a black man's guilt, early release from prison would be a reasonable course of action, despite white beliefs about the threat black-on-white rape posed to the racial order.

Any pardon petition, however, required legal officials to draw conclusions about intent from descriptions of black men's actions. It was, of course, impossible to determine what actually occurred between white women and black men, as the descriptions of events varied between

newspaper accounts, evidence at trial, and the recollections of legal officials years later. Newspapers might use excessively graphic accounts to
boost readership, which could influence the white community's understanding of a given crime. Prosecutors might emphasize the horror of an
assault in an attempt to bolster their cases, justify conviction, or discourage pardon. Courts acknowledged different motivations behind black
men's actions, but newspaper reports were less nuanced in their descriptions of assaults. Almost invariably, especially in the early part of the
period under study, news reports characterized black-on-white crimes
as "attacks" on women—always assumed to be white unless otherwise
noted—which left plenty of room for white readers to infer a sexual motivation. Newspapers rarely used the term "rape" to denote sexual assaults,
instead referring to them as "criminal assaults" or "criminal attacks." Few
readers, however, missed the implications of the alternate terminology.[13]
The verb "attack" itself was a conveniently vague term; it could signify
assault, attempted assault, attempted rape, rape, or even robbery. The
headline "Negroes Attack Woman in Street" surely tapped into white
fears of black men. The article accompanying the headline, however, reported a purse-snatching.[14] Other reports of assaults did not deliberately
suggest that a sexual attack took place, but they often emphasized white
women as particular targets of interracial violence. The headline "Holds
up Woman at Pistol's Point" was not inappropriate placed above an article
reporting a crime against a white woman, but it was misleading. Mrs.
Decosta, the victim in this case, had been walking on the street at midnight
with an escort when they were both mugged by a "negro highwayman."
The headline of the article reporting the crime implied she alone was the
victim.[15] Misleading headlines caught readers' attention, and they also
played on fears of white women's vulnerability to black men, especially
unfamiliar ones, on city streets. Headlines reminded the white community that any interaction between a black man and a white woman could
result in violence. The blurred distinctions between rape and robbery in
the media suggested that in the white public's view, only a fine line existed
between attacks targeting women's property and those targeting their
bodies.

These blurred distinctions become especially obvious in cases that occurred in urban areas. Public streets provided fertile space for social misunderstandings across racial and gender lines, misunderstandings that
underscore the enormous complexities inherent in a segregated society. It
was impossible to divide public areas neatly into black and white spaces.
Despite segregated restrooms, entrances to buildings, waiting rooms, and

railroad cars, streets and other public spaces remained gray areas, shared by both whites and blacks. Consequently, the nature of interactions between black men and white women occurring on public streets was often ambiguous. White southerners developed strict racial codes to govern interactions in these gray areas, but the rules of behavior could not structure every encounter. Generally, southern whites expected blacks to defer to them in the use of sidewalks and streets. Black men and women who failed to defer to whites could be immediately branded as insolent, and accusations of insolence could erupt into violence. The process of maintaining boundaries between white and black space and between appropriate and inappropriate contact, especially between black men and white women, was not as simple as labeling every form of contact inappropriate and every inappropriate contact as rape or attempted rape.

In urban areas where blacks and whites who did not know each other passed frequently on the streets, anonymity could make white women feel vulnerable and cause misunderstandings about black men's actions. Urban courts facing these situations often convicted black men of less serious charges, such as assault. The statistics for convictions of nonsexual crimes such as assault, assault and battery, or robbery in cases originally reported in the media as "attacks" on white women bear this out. Of the thirty-two black men convicted for violent interactions with white women that trials determined did not include an intent to commit rape, twenty-one occurred in urban areas.[16] Urban authorities acknowledged the ambiguity of interactions between strangers and did not always interpret those actions within the framework of black men's supposed propensity to rape white women.

Most of the cases involving charges of assault by a black man against a white woman became opportunities for whites, both in the press and the legal system, to redefine what constituted legitimate interaction across race and gender lines. Every black man who touched the body of a white woman could not be judged a rapist. Despite white southerners' best efforts, interracial contact, whether it was innocent or not, was bound to occur, especially in crowded urban areas. In determining the line between acceptable interaction and criminal contact, courts were able to work within the realities of dynamic, modern, civilized social space. Courts allowed accidental contact to escape severe punishment and gave the benefit of the doubt to black men who appeared to "know their place." In white minds, this flexibility lent a certain credibility and civility to efforts to enforce segregation.

In September 1916, Danville residents read that two white women had been assaulted by two black men. The women told police that as they walked along the street in the evening, two black men accosted them, grabbed their dresses at the throat, and then fled aboard a trolley.[17] Though the news accounts speculated that robbery had been the motive, police charged two men, Tim Brooks and Linwood Womack, with attempted rape. The two men, however, gave a different account of the incident. They insisted that they had merely been running to catch the streetcar when they accidentally brushed against the two women.[18] After being released on bail, an unusual move in cases of assaults against white women, both men agreed to plead guilty to simple assault. They each received a sentence of six months in jail and were fined $250. The women's instinctive reaction to being jostled attests to the unease white women felt around black men they did not know. Feeling vulnerable on a darkened city street in the evening, they interpreted the black men's actions according to the familiar script of black-on-white assault. But white legal officials did not validate their insecurity by insisting Womack and Brooks face trial for attempted rape. The court's decision to allow the men to plead to a lesser charge and the sentence the court imposed suggests that the court accepted the two men's version of events. The court acknowledged the ambiguity and misunderstanding surrounding public interactions between white women and black men and accepted an alternative explanation of black men's motives. At the same time, however, Brooks and Womack received punishment for terrifying the white women and violating their personal space.

Courts also acknowledged that publicity surrounding assaults shaped white women's interpretation of black men's actions, as the case of William Dance in 1927 shows. The nature of Dance's contact with the white woman who accused him was ambiguous, but it is likely she interpreted his actions as an attempted rape by associating them with another recent case. William Dance's "assault" occurred shortly after a similar incident involving William Nelson. In August 1927, a young married woman named Mabel Cole reported being assaulted as she was walking home from her job at the Tubize Silk plant in Hopewell, Virginia, and local papers closely followed the case.[19] Cole identified William Nelson as her assailant; he was found guilty of attempted rape one week after the assault, sentenced to death, and executed in November 1927.[20] Two weeks after Nelson's trial concluded, a sixteen-year-old woman named Lillian Nobles was walking toward her home near the Tubize Silk plant in the evening when she encountered William Dance on the street. She became frightened and screamed.[21] Apparently, Dance was doing little more than walking toward a white woman he did not know, but Nobles interpreted Dance's actions as menacing. He was arrested and charged with attempted rape, though there was never any physical contact between them.[22]

The court was not so quick to condemn William Dance. In early October, he was indicted for a felony, but he never faced trial. In June, seven months after his arrest, the commonwealth's attorney decided to dismiss the charges against him and he was set free.[23] The court offered no reason for dismissing the charges, but they may have concluded that Nobles became frightened and screamed only because Dance's actions seemed threatening in light of the recent assault in the same area. The court's actions reveal a willingness to approach some white women's accounts of assault with skepticism and to interpret such charges in a context not entirely ruled by white fears of black men's assaults. Of course, the decision did not absolve Dance entirely; court officials allowed him to languish in jail for seven months before they released him. Either in deference to public opinion or from an unwillingness to discount entirely the word of a white woman, the court delayed its decision. Without the benefit of trial, Dance served a sentence that was typical for a conviction of simple assault.

The courts' decisions in these cases reflect the complex relationship between white social custom and cultural attitudes about race and legal procedure. White outrage alone did not determine their actions, which had to adhere to legal procedure and reflect, at least to a degree, the ideals of justice. The cases of Brooks, Womack, and Dance demonstrate the Virginia courts' willingness to interpret contact between white women and black men as part of the incidental jostling that was bound to happen on busy public thoroughfares. Significantly, however, black men went to jail for causing women to fear that racial boundaries were in jeopardy, thereby granting a degree of legitimacy to white women's fears.

Even in urban cases in which black men's actions involving white women were clearly criminal, officials did not always conclude that they were motivated by sexual intent. The *Richmond Times-Dispatch*, for example, reported in 1910 that a black man attacked a woman in her home. Junius Robinson, the "Negro" in question, however, had merely stolen her pocketbook after a struggle. He was convicted of assault and battery and sentenced to twelve months in jail and fined one cent.[24] In 1921, Mr. Dickerson, a white man, found his employee, William Harrison, armed with a pistol, hiding under his bed. The *Richmond Times-Dispatch* implied a more ominous encounter with the headline "Negro Caught Under Bed of Woman." Mrs. Dickerson also slept in the bed under which Harrison hid, but she was not present when her husband discovered him. Harrison was charged with burglary, not attempted rape, and he received a sentence of nine years in prison.[25]

Even heightened racial tensions did not force white authorities to interpret all crimes by black men as sexual in nature. Albert Swinson, who was charged in 1924 in Richmond, reportedly tried to enter a white woman's home armed with a pistol. A jury found him guilty of attempted robbery and sentenced him to four years in prison.[26] The relative leniency of the charge, however, is more striking given the context in which it occurred. Albert Swinson attempted to rob Katie Clark during the same week in which seven other white Richmond women claimed they had been assaulted by black men. The headline announcing Swinson's arrest read: "Police Report More Attacks by Negro Men."[27] Though local police and the newspapers did not publicly speculate that these crimes were connected, the *Richmond Times-Dispatch* created an atmosphere of crisis by reporting all seven attacks in a single article. Despite the rash of assaults, the court did not automatically conclude that Swinson intended to rape his victim.

Rural courts were less likely to interpret black men's actions toward women as nonsexual. Innocuous contact between unacquainted rural white women and black men easily acquired sinister overtones, and local court officials were more likely to affirm the woman's interpretation of black men's actions. The case of William Thomas in 1927 in Madison County, a rural area northwest of Richmond, provides an apt example. According to the testimony of Dora Hudson Clore, the local schoolteacher, she had been alone in the schoolhouse in the evening when Thomas entered and asked her for a bit of bread. He then allegedly grabbed her by the throat. She broke away and ran to a nearby store for help. A Madison County jury convicted Thomas of attempted rape and sentenced him to death.

As Thomas awaited his execution, the African American newspaper the *Richmond Planet* printed an interview with him, along with a plea to the governor to commute his sentence. The article argued that Thomas was merely reaching for a crust of bread, not Clore's throat, before Clore ran for help and claimed he assaulted her. Despite this alternate version of events offered in the black press, the governor declined to intervene on his behalf and Thomas paid with his life.

Thomas's case also illustrates the complexities of segregation. Dora Hudson Clore was a young, married schoolteacher alone in the schoolhouse in the early evening. William Thomas was a stranger in Madison

County, described as an itinerant hobo. No one in Madison County knew him by name or reputation and thus they had no prior knowledge by which to measure his motives when he encountered Clore alone. It is impossible to know whether his request for food was genuine or merely a ploy, much less whether he intended to force intercourse when he allegedly moved to choke her. Had Clore known Thomas, she might have been more willing to believe that all he wanted was bread. Instead, finding herself alone with a strange black man, she took no chances. The jury accepted her account and legitimized her fear. Because of Thomas's status as a stranger in a rural community accustomed to familiarity among its residents, Clore's interpretation of their encounter prevailed.[28]

Ambiguous encounters between strangers underscore the failure of segregation to separate blacks and whites in southern public space completely and predictably. Conflicts involving white women's bodies and their presence in public space went beyond fears of sexual violence; they were part of larger conflicts between whites and blacks over who had primary right to occupy social space.[29]

The Williams / Tucker case, in which a white man and a black man fought over a white woman's right to a public sidewalk in Lynchburg in 1910, illustrates well how white women's bodies became a site on which men of both races struggled for racial advantage. The headline in the *Richmond Times-Dispatch* reporting the incident between Williams and Tucker read, "Insolent Negro Cuts a Woman," emphasizing a conflict between a black man and a white woman. The article that followed described an altercation between Albert Williams (erroneously named David Bradley in the article), Wilson Tucker, and Tucker's wife. While walking down a Lynchburg sidewalk, the couple came upon two black men. One "passed around" the white pair, but Albert Williams jostled Mrs. Tucker as he passed. "When Tucker grabbed the negro and asked what he was about," the article continued, "the negro struck him and cursed him. Tucker quickly got out his knife and slashed the negro as he [Williams] was stabbing his wife." This struggle was not solely about the use of the sidewalk. It was at heart a larger conflict over white superiority and privilege. Tucker and Williams battled over the racial hierarchy and deference that centered on unequal access to public space. Both Tucker and Williams were arrested and indicted for malicious cutting, suggesting at least the appearance of equal justice. Both stood trial on the same day before nearly identical juries. The jury acquitted Tucker, the white man who supposedly avenged the honor of his wife's body and right to public space. Williams, who resisted his subordinate racial position, was found guilty of assault and battery and sentenced to thirty days in jail and fined $25.[30]

In their test of wills, Tucker was backed by the power of the state, the legal system, and white culture, but not unequivocally. Both men faced indictment on the same charge. Significantly, however, Williams stabbed a white woman, the wife of the man with whom he was in conflict, to assert his rights. Although the news report defined the conflict primarily as a violation of a white woman, the court did not. The court viewed the altercation as between the men. Tucker's wife played no role in court whatsoever. As Williams's minor sentence demonstrates, the stabbing of a white woman by a black man was only slightly more serious than a white man's stabbing of a black man. Williams's eventual conviction undoubtedly stemmed from his race, since most members of the all-white jury likely saw Williams at fault for not yielding the sidewalk to the Tuckers' white privilege.

The Lynchburg jury, by convicting only Williams, legitimated the Tuckers' right to the sidewalk. But white women did not always receive unqualified right to occupy any space they chose. Decisions in cases involving episodes of physical violence between white women and black men reflected beliefs about acceptable interactions between white women and black men not only in public spaces but in private as well. The case of Junius Booker, for example, involved a white woman's spatial transgression. Virginia Rutherford, the mother of six children, was allegedly beaten by her husband in June 1910. Fearing her husband, she sought refuge at the home of her black neighbors, the Bookers. Mrs. Booker tried to discourage Rutherford from staying with them, but Junius Booker, her husband, made her welcome. By seeking refuge with the Bookers, Rutherford violated cultural precepts of where and from whom white women should seek protection.

Rutherford spent one night at the Booker home without incident. During the second evening, Junius Booker "began to act queerly." Soon thereafter, he attacked Rutherford, shaking her, throwing her against the door, and biting her nose, nearly severing it from her face. Mrs. Booker summoned the police, who arrived to find Rutherford unconscious. In the police officers' account of the incident, both Mrs. Booker and the neighbors attributed Booker's violent outburst to intoxication, and the *Richmond Times-Dispatch* speculated that Rutherford had brought whiskey with her when she sought refuge in the Booker home. Mrs. Booker later revealed that three years prior to her husband's assault on Rutherford, he had been arrested for an assault on an eighty-year-old white woman. For that offense, he was judged insane and incarcerated at Central State Hospital. "He is said to be always in a right frame of mind except when he is drinking," the article noted.[31]

Despite Rutherford's possible whiskey consumption, and despite the allusion made by the paper that she had previously appeared in police court and that authorities were on the verge of removing her six children from her care, the headline, "Negro Attacks White Woman," and the article itself placed the case within the framework of a crazed black man assaulting a white woman. Rutherford was described as a "white woman fighting with all her strength against the maniacal negro." Calling the assault an attempted murder, the paper reported that "the neighborhood [was] much excited." According to the reporter, however, Rutherford gave no explanation for why she chose to spend the night in the home of a black man.[32]

And this indeed was the quandary. According to southern mythology, Booker's assault was the logical outcome of a white woman placing herself on intimate social terms with a black man, especially if she was seeking sanctuary from a white man. Reports of Rutherford's consumption of alcohol and rumors of her unfitness as a mother made explicit her complicity in the attack. Mrs. Booker had warned her she should not stay, so Rutherford was partly responsible for the assault. Yet the paper's reinforcement of her status as a white woman and Booker as a black man complicated her responsibility. As a woman of low character, she was complicit; as a white woman, she was a victim. The newspaper reports presented Rutherford's beating as a warning to other white women: black men could offer them no protection; indeed, white men, to whom, presumably, Rutherford should have gone initially to escape her white husband's violence, were the only source of protection.

Familiarity lessened the likelihood of misunderstandings between white women and black men, but it also might make white women less worthy of protection. Rutherford clearly was acquainted with the Bookers; she knew them well enough to see their home as a refuge from her husband. It is also clear that it was common knowledge in the neighborhood that Booker could become violent when drunk. One might argue that if Rutherford knew this, she should have looked elsewhere for sanctuary. Yet she already defied the mandates of segregation and ideologies about racial identity. She and her husband lived in a mixed neighborhood, and her husband failed to act as a chivalrous protector. Her fitness as a mother questioned by the state, her husband violent, Rutherford had few options. She took refuge where she could find it. When Junius Booker turned violent, the media framed the assault in terms of race and gender. The court apparently did not. Rutherford did not merit protection as a white woman. Her violations of segregation mitigated her claim to protection by the state.

While the article reporting Booker's assault in the *Times-Dispatch* was more than two pages long and provided a detailed description of the attack, his trial was less newsworthy. He was indicted in July for malicious wounding with intent to "maim, disfigure, disable, and kill," found guilty, and sentenced to five years on the road force.[33] The newspaper never reported his conviction. Booker avoided charges of attempted rape because, in the court's eyes, Rutherford had crossed into space where she did not belong. In the process, she had placed herself beyond the reach of white male protection. Neither Rutherford's whiteness, nor her womanhood, nor both together carried sufficient power to transform Booker's violence into a serious racial transgression.

Whether an alleged assault occurred in a rural or an urban area had some effect on the charges black men faced, but that factor alone cannot account for the variety of charges against black men or the widely disparate sentences they received. White authorities paid close attention not only to where an assault occurred but also to the exact nature of a black man's actions toward a white woman. For the legal system, determining whether an accused black man should be convicted of rape, attempted rape, or a nonsexual charge was fraught with complications.[34] Its decisions reflected local contexts and how whites in general, and legal authorities in particular, interpreted ambiguous actions. Juries given a choice of crimes also may have considered the effect of the assailant's actions on the victim. According to Virginia law in the twentieth century, unlike in the nineteenth, evidence of the emission of semen was not required for a jury to convict a man of rape. Virginia law said that penetration, however slight, with force and against a woman's will, was sufficient for a crime to be called rape. To juries, then, whether or not a rape had been committed should have been quite clear. Newspapers reporting a "criminal assault" often informed the public that the assailant had "accomplished his purpose," indicating penetration. Among the few existing legal records that contain the victim's testimony surrounding the issue of penetration are those of the Mickens and Legions cases. Clarice Pye, who accused Joseph Mickens of rape in 1941, answered affirmatively when she was asked by the prosecutor whether Mickens "actually entered her." Viola Miller, who accused Samuel Legions of rape in 1943, also affirmed that Legions had penetrated her "with his male organ."[35] One can assume that white women in other cases answered similar questions. Though it is possible that juries did convict black men for rape when no penetration had occurred, there would have been little motivation for doing so. The punishments for rape and attempted rape were virtually identical. Virginia law limited imprisonment for attempted rape to between three and eighteen years and imprisonment for rape to between five and twenty years, but it allowed capital punishment for both crimes.[36] Convicting a man of rape instead of attempted rape did not necessarily allow the jury to impose a significantly more severe punishment.

While on the one hand, juries may have convicted men of rape without evidence of penetration, on the other, they may have opted to convict men of attempted rape instead of rape, since both attempted rape and rape were capital crimes, to protect the reputation of the victim. No white person stated this openly, but the evidence suggests that in cases involving young white girls, convicting their assailants of attempted rape rather than rape reassured the white public that the victims had not been "ruined" by sexual intercourse with black men. Will Finney was charged with rape in 1908 when he attacked his employer's eleven-year-old daughter as she was gathering berries. The jury found him guilty of attempted rape, not rape, and he was sentenced to death.[37] In 1918, Stanfield Sherman was indicted for rape but found guilty of attempted rape and sentenced to death for an assault on a six-year-old girl.[38] And Paul Hairston was tried for rape and found guilty of attempted rape for an assault on a fourteen-year-old girl in 1919.[39] There are no existing records of the testimony regarding penetration in these cases, but it is possible that the young girls' lack of knowledge of sexual intercourse made their testimony regarding penetration unclear.[40] White southerners viewed the rape of a white woman by a black man as the ultimate despoliation—a fate "worse than death." Returning a verdict that implied a white victim had not actually been raped allowed the jury to repair the tattered remains of a white woman's or girl's reputation shredded by the sexual attention of a black man.

In some cases where men were charged with assaulting white women, Virginia juries focused on determining if black men intended to commit a sexual crime, and then convicted them accordingly. When white women testified that black men achieved penetration, the intent of the criminal act was presumably clear. But when there was no penetration, juries faced the more difficult task of deciding the intent of actions that may not have been explicitly sexual. Some cases were clear-cut. Records of the trial of Charles Gillespie in 1909, for example, state that he seized his victim, beat her, threw her upon the ground, raised her clothes, and tore her underclothes, all while he threatened to kill her with a knife. Her torn underclothes presumably made his intent clear, and the jury convicted him of attempted rape after deliberating a scant two and a half minutes.[41] In Jasper Morrison's case, he was charged in 1920 with the attempted rape of a five-year-old girl. After hearing testimony of his actions, the jurors determined that there was sufficient proof that Morrison tried to force sexual relations and they convicted him of attempted rape and sentenced him to eighteen years in prison. In his petition for pardon several years later, Morrison tried to make a distinction between sexual contact and rape. He claimed that although he had exposed his genitals and rubbed himself against the girl in an effort to masturbate, he had no intention of raping her. The governor rejected his petition for early release because he either was unconvinced that such a distinction could be made or believed that Morrison's argument was a self-serving spin on otherwise incriminating evidence.[42]

The actions that juries considered adequate evidence of black men's intent to rape white women, however, were not always clear-cut, nor were they interpreted consistently from case to case. As the trial records indicate, juries used their own judgment, or their own prejudices, to decipher black men's intentions. Most cases in which white women accused black men of some form of assault resulted in charges for a sexual crime. Of the 288 cases under study, 221 included a charge either of rape, of attempted rape, or of assault with the intent to commit rape. Many of these cases included charges for other crimes, such as robbery or murder. The numbers imply that prosecuting attorneys and juries suspected black men's actions would culminate in sexual assault regardless of whether those actions included clear steps necessary to accomplish penetration, such as pulling up a woman's clothing. White juries' determinations likely arose from the emotion provoked by charges of black-on-white assault. For example, in 1927, Robert Sims was convicted of attempted rape and sentenced to ten years in prison. Five years later, the judge who tried his case petitioned for his release, noting that at the time, there was "a good deal of hysteria" about Sims's alleged crime. Community furor, in the judge's view, overshadowed a more balanced view of Sims's actions. "The evidence showing a criminal [sexual] intent was weak," he wrote, "and would hardly have sustained anything but a misdemeanor if the accused had not made such a strong effort to escape."[43] In 1937, in another case, although court officials acknowledged that Louis Riddick's actions showed no sexual intent he received a life sentence for attempted rape. In recommending that Riddick be given a conditional pardon after he had served twenty years, the parole board noted that Riddick's intentions were unclear. The white woman he assaulted had testified that Riddick "entered the second floor of her home and engaged in a struggle with her, though nothing was actually said or done to indicate it was a sex attack."[44] That admission played a significant role in his winning his freedom.

Juries did not always impose the most severe sentences allowed by law, even in cases in which they might reasonably infer black men intended to commit rape. Harrison Waller, for example, in 1906 received a sentence of eighteen years in prison after he broke into a woman's home, threw her upon the bed, and pulled up her clothing.[45] In 1909, Frank Baylor also received an eighteen-year sentence for grabbing a woman, dragging her into some bushes, and throwing her to the ground.[46] At the time, eighteen years or death were the maximum penalties that juries could impose for a conviction of attempted rape. In 1922, Ralph Green was convicted of attempted rape; he received a twelve-year sentence for leading a young girl into the woods by the hand.[47] On the other hand, men were convicted of attempted rape when their actions clearly indicated no sexual intent, and they received vastly disparate sentences for similar actions. Jim Acree, for example, received a death sentence in 1923 for chasing a young white girl, even though she and several of her friends testified that he never laid a hand on her. The sentence was later commuted.[48] Raymond Alsberry received a twelve-year sentence in 1930 for attempted rape after he dragged a woman into an alley and choked her.[49] Theodore Roosevelt Wilson was convicted in 1922 and sentenced to eighteen years in prison for attempted rape; the indictment charged him with laying hands on his victim and choking her.[50] These sentences attest to the latitude Virginia law granted to juries to determine sentences, but they also suggest that a white women's accusations alone were insufficient to merit ultimate punishment.

Juries' decisions to convict black men of attempted rape do not appear to have been a function of the degree of violence black men used. Attacks labeled as attempted rapes did not necessarily involve greater violence than did simple assaults. Raymond Alsberry's crime seems hardly more violent than Charles Harris throwing a newspaper over his victim's head and choking her. Harris, however, was only convicted of assault and battery and sentenced to one year on the road force.[51] Alsberry spent twelve years in prison. One might interpret the disparities in sentences in numerous ways. Harris's crime occurred in Richmond, a considerably larger city than Winchester, where Alsberry faced trial. Alsberry faced trial in 1930, sixteen years after Harris's crime, and Alsberry had recently been indicted for forging a check prior to being indicted for attempted rape. Dragging his victim into an alley might have been interpreted as his attempt to find the seclusion necessary to commit rape. The widely varying sentences that black men received for similar actions should dispel the belief that a crude calculus of inflicted harm alone determined the sentences black men served. Indeed, any conclusive assertions about why jurors chose particular sentences are difficult to make. What is clear, however, is that white Virginians did not see all violations of white women as equally harmful or threatening to white supremacy. Jurors determined that black men who committed violent acts against white women did not always have rape as their ultimate goal.

Similarly, jurors also determined that not all black men were willing to use force to achieve sexual gratification. Rather than invariably spurring mob violence or a death sentence, black men's nonviolent actions that suggested affection or desire toward white women elicited various responses in the legal system. Black men who made these kinds of advances were usually convicted, but they received lesser punishment. The case of Tom Williams illustrates the various ways interactions between white women and black men could be interpreted. In 1909, the *Richmond Times-Dispatch* reported that police arrested Williams after he entered the home of his white neighbor and put his arms about her. Apparently, she screamed and Williams fled.[52] Williams was later indicted for attempted rape. His indictment stated that "he did grab hold of and attempt to pull off the clothing of the said Rosa Ann Perdue, and did attempt to rape," a considerably different version of the assault than that described in the paper.[53] The jury appeared to endorse the newspaper's version, finding Williams guilty of assault and battery rather than attempted rape and sentencing him to six months in jail and fining him $50. Coleman Crews's case in 1924 was similar. The *Richmond Times-Dispatch* reported that he attempted to assault a white woman but in a subsequent article stated that the evidence did not warrant a felony charge. The warrant for Crews, however, stated that he entered the woman's home and assaulted her by laying his hands upon her.[54] Both Williams's and Crews's actions could easily have been interpreted as preludes to rape. Yet in both cases, whites judged the men's actions as simple assault. Their sentences suggest that whites at least occasionally hewed to the rules of evidence. Neither Williams nor Crews displayed any intention to use force to gratify desire, evidence of which was necessary for a conviction of attempted rape. The judge in a case from 1910 made this point explicit in his instructions to the jury. He stated there must be "force or attempted force, coupled with an attempt to gratify the lustful desire, against the consent of the female, notwithstanding resistance on her part; and the mere fact that the accused may have had a desire to have sexual intercourse with the female is not sufficient to justify a conviction for the crime of attempted rape."[55] A jury could not convict a black man of attempted rape merely because he made what appeared to be sexual advances. After all, all black men supposedly harbored sexual desire for white women and found them irresistible.

Courts recognized that black men's physical expressions of sexual desire for white women could exist separately from a willingness to use force to satisfy that desire, but Virginia's courts were not always consistent in how they determined the relationship between desire and force. In cases where an assailant used force and there was physical evidence of sexual desire, juries voted to convict him of attempted rape even if it was unclear that his goal was intercourse. In 1920, Henry Hart was accused of an attempted assault on Virginia Garber, a seventeen-year-old "simple, good, unsophisticated, country girl."[56] At Hart's trial, Garber testified that as she was walking early in the morning, Hart threw an old skirt over her head and put his hand over her mouth. As they wrestled in the middle of the road, two white men passed by but did not intervene. Their presence, however, spooked Hart and he released Garber. Garber also testified that she was not bruised or thrown down, nor were her clothes torn. "Hart did not put his hands under her clothes nor use any vulgar language or make to her any improper proposal," though he did kiss her when he released her. When police arrested Hart and searched him, however, they found "stains of seminal fluid that seemed to be fresh" on his underclothes. The jury considered the stains as evidence of an intent to rape, and Hart was convicted and sentenced to death. The Virginia Supreme Court of Appeals upheld the verdict, writing that "the discharge of seminal fluid had rendered the accused impotent to accomplish his purpose for the time being. And the parting kiss and the blandishments [not to tell] . . . were sufficient evidence to warrant the jury in believing that the aforesaid purpose [rape] of the accused still remained fixed." His crime warranted death because of the possibility that he might try to rape again.[57]

The legal system considered Hart's apparent premature ejaculation sufficient evidence that he was willing to gratify his sexual desire by force. Similarly, in Charles Gillespie's case, the fact that he removed his victim's underclothes clearly indicated to the jury his intent to commit rape. In many other cases, however, physical contact between white women and black men was ambiguous. A black man could be convicted of attempted rape for a variety of actions, ranging from grabbing or dragging a woman to being on the verge of penetration. According to Virginia's legal system, any of the actions that fell within this range were indicative of an intent to rape. But sexual arousal or desire alone did not imply that black men were willing to use force.

The issues of desire, force, and intent became murkier when black men claimed that they did not know that the women they attacked were white. Insisting that they were ignorant of the woman's race suggests their understanding that much of the perceived severity of their crime stemmed from the woman's whiteness. Shifting a jury's attention away from the race of the victim could change its interpretation of black men's actions. Whites viewed black men's assaults of white women as particularly egregious, and often, though not always, as prima facie evidence of a desire to commit rape. At the same time, however, whites occasionally lent credibility to the testimony that black men offered in their own defense, particularly that they did not intend to commit that most heinous of crimes, an assault of a white woman, as a case from Norfolk in 1910 shows.

Lucy Upshur, a young white woman, was attacked on a Sunday night, as she was walking to the home of a friend. She reported that she noticed a young black man following her, became nervous, and began to run. The black man, later identified as Percy Forby, caught up with her, grabbed her by the throat, threw her to the ground, and climbed on top of her. She fought and screamed before losing consciousness; her screams attracted the attention of several white men, who captured Forby as he tried to flee. Newspapers both in Richmond and in Norfolk reported the attack, describing how Upshur fought "wildly" until her screams brought help and praising her rescuers for their bravery. The *Richmond Times-Dispatch* reported that "there was evidence to show that the negro's attempt was more than robbery," implying that Forby intended to rape Upshur had he had the opportunity. The *Portsmouth Star* linked Upshur's assault to a series of attacks by black men against white women reported to have occurred in the same area, suggesting that Forby was responsible for those as well.[58]

Despite the "excitement" aroused by reports of the assault, the suspicions that Forby was responsible for other assaults against white women, and his indictment for attempted rape, he was only convicted of assault. According to Forby, the attack was a case of mistaken identity. He meant to attack another woman who was black and, indeed, thought he was doing so. The specifics of the defense's argument are in the judge's final instruction:

> If the jury believes from the evidence that the defendant seized with his hands the neck of the prosecutrix under the bona fied

but mistaken belief that she was Bessie Harris [a black woman], then the nature and quality of the offense is the same as if it had actually been committed against Bessie Harris, and if they further believe from the evidence that in committing said act as aforesaid, the defendant was not actuated by anger or improper motive, and did not intend to inflict injury or to commit any other act than that which he actually did commit, then they are instructed that he, the defendant, was at most guilty of technical assault and if the jury find him guilty of this offense, they shall consider these mitigating circumstances in fixing his punishment.[59]

By instructing the jury as he did, the judge literally erased Upshur's whiteness, making it irrelevant to the case. The conviction of the defendant became dependent on his motive as *he* defined it, rather than on whites' interpretation of his actions. The struggle could have been interpreted as an affront to both racial and gender hierarchies, but because Forby believed he was attacking a woman of his own race, there was no racial or sexual violation. He had merely attacked a "black" woman. Judging the assault as if Forby were attacking a black woman significantly mitigated his crime. His defense, moreover, reassured the white community that Forby did not have sexual interest in white women. Forby, though a suspect in other local attacks and even identified by two other women as their assailant, was never brought to trial again.

Forby was not the only black man who in his defense claimed that he did not know his victim was white. In 1918, Andrew Johnson, whose alleged crime was not as serious as Forby's, also argued that he didn't know his victim was white. Official records of Johnson's case are unavailable, since he was tried in police court rather than in the circuit court, but, according to news reports, Johnson had written notes to a woman who was employed at the same place he worked. He was charged with the vague crime of "annoying a white woman." He claimed that he thought "the woman was a mulatto." He was fined $250 and placed on a twelve-month, $250 bond for his good behavior. His fine was substantial, but he spent no time in jail and faced no charges of sexual assault.[60]

Clarence Brown, in his request for conditional pardon, also tried to claim mistaken identity as a mitigating factor. In 1939, he and his friend Jim Holland were convicted and sentenced to life in prison for an attempted attack on two white women returning home from a fair in Rocky Mount, Virginia. In his statement to police, Brown said that he had seen the women leaving the fair, but he insisted that he had not realized they were white. He also claimed that he "didn't do anything but grab the girl, that is all I did—I turned her loose."[61] Carter Lee, the commonwealth's attorney who prosecuted the case, believed that both Brown and Holland should have been sentenced to death, not because their actions were so heinous but because of the intentions behind them. Lee argued that the two men "agreed between themselves that they would wait until two white girls came along and rape them." Lee contended that the two black men had specifically targeted white women, although he had no evidence to support this claim. He recommended against a pardon.[62] The governor apparently agreed and refused to grant either man pardon. Brown and Lee each asserted that the race of the alleged victims played a role in the attack. Brown, knowing that his crime would be judged less severely had his victims been black, claimed that the fact that the women were white was accidental, and thus irrelevant. The prosecuting attorney, however, made the victim's whiteness the central motivating force in the crime. Specifically targeting white women represented a distinct threat to racial boundaries, and Brown's life sentence likely reflected the mercy of the court. To both men, the race of the victim was a deciding factor in the disposition of the case.

Race undoubtedly mattered. The race of black men's female victims fundamentally shaped white perceptions of their crimes. Black assailants, white legal officials, and white jurors nevertheless debated the role a victim's race played in a crime. In Forby's case, his perception of his victim's race, rather than the reality, determined the jury's verdict. In Johnson's case, the judge only grudgingly accepted Johnson's claim that he thought the woman to whom he sent letters was not white. Like Forby, Johnson was convicted of a crime, but it was not a sexual one. In Brown's case, both the prosecution and the defendant agreed that the victim's race was preeminent, but they disagreed about whether the victim's race motivated Brown to commit the crime. He claimed ignorance while the prosecuting attorney claimed conspiracy. In all three cases, the role of the victim's race was contested, and the judge's or jury's interpretation of that role ultimately determined the severity of the assault. A woman's own sense of racial identity and her interpretation of events, once she made the charge, played no role whatsoever.

When an accused black man claimed that he did not intend to attack a white woman but had assaulted one whom he mistakenly believed to be black, he attempted to set white men's minds at ease. The claim reassured them that black men's violence was not directed at white women specifically and was not the outgrowth of supposedly irresistible lustful desires or a vengeful rage against white supremacy. Nevertheless, it is unclear which aspect of black-on-white rape most disturbed whites. Was it blacks' willingness to use force to satisfy lustful desires, or was it the presence of those very desires themselves? That southerners in the twentieth century so readily responded with extralegal violence to the most incidental of contact between white women and black men and continually harped on how the end of slavery had released the intrinsic savagery of African Americans has often led historians to conclude that it was the desire for white women alone that put black men in danger. Yet, most lynchings were not in response to sexual crimes against white women. Most involved charges of murder.[63] Murder, especially of black men's landlords or employers, represented violent rebellion against white authority in ways that sexual desire for white women alone did not. The ways in which whites responded to black men's verbal expressions of their desire for white women supports this conclusion. Several cases in this study revolve around black men's explicit solicitations for sexual relations with white women. Whites' debates about these cases reveal that it was not necessarily the desire itself that troubled whites. After all, such desire mirrored white men's own desires and their beliefs about black men's sexual nature. Evidence of black men's sexual desire for white women confirmed the racial hierarchy. Black men's sexual desire for white women only became problematic when they showed a willingness to satisfy that desire with force.

Because Virginia law required evidence of both force and sexual intent to convict a man for attempted rape, juries were not entirely free to force their own prejudices onto a given case, nor could they use the law as a tool to enforce the racial hierarchy completely and predictably. Yet the courts allowed white juries considerable latitude in interpreting the nature of black men's crimes, offering them the option of several crimes, including attempted rape, in their deliberations about guilt or innocence. Although the law stipulated what evidence was required to convict for these crimes, it was up to the jury to determine the facts of a case and whether the evidentiary requirements had been met. Jury verdicts, then, certainly were not perfectly clear cultural windows onto white attitudes about behavior, but they do represent more than merely the unbiased process of law. How white jurors decided to apply the rules of evidence does provide insight into white social and cultural beliefs about the intentions behind black men's actions and the degree to which they threatened the racial hierarchy. Even though the judge in Percy Forby's case instructed the jury to acquit him of attempted rape if they believed Forby's claim that he

thought he was attacking a black woman, the jury was still free to conclude that it was merely a self-serving lie. Similarly, although Virginia law
required evidence both of sexual desire and of the intention to use force to
gratify that desire to prove attempted rape, many juries voted to convict
black men of attempted rape without any clear evidence of sexual intent
or of willingness to use force. Within broad limits, juries ultimately chose
how they applied the law.

Examining the many cases of black men's attempted rape and assault
of white women uncovers an almost bewildering array of actions and
punishments. What is clear is that a black man's verbal expression of
sexual desire for white women was far less serious than his vague or
undefined actions that could be interpreted as an attempt to gratify sexual
desire by force. White southerners could countenance black men's expressed desire for white women, believing that such "natural" expressions did not threaten the racial and gender hierarchy. Only the "unnatural" attempt to satisfy their innate desires required a response.

The distinction the law made between desire and force, or intent and
action, becomes most clear in cases where the defendant made little or no
overt attempt physically to touch or assault the victim but merely requested sexual relations verbally. In pardon deliberations, legal officials
conceded that mere expressions of desire represented less serious offenses
than acting based on that desire. Although black men accused of propositioning white women did not always escape with merely a conviction for
assault, they usually received short sentences.

Sexual desire alone, then, was not enough to upset social norms, as
Frank Lynch's case in 1920 shows. Frank Lynch's actions betrayed curiosity about white women's sexual allure. He was accused of knocking at
the door of Mary Martin, a white woman, while her husband was away,
and saying, "Say, Mrs. Martin, I want to kiss a white woman; I want to see
what it is like to kiss a white woman." She replied, "No sir." Lynch then
placed his hand on her shoulder and said, "I didn't mean to insult you."
When she told him to leave, he did. Lynch was convicted of assault and
battery and sentenced to a prison term and fined.[64] Lynch appealed his
conviction on the grounds that the evidence was insufficient to prove
assault and battery. In their judgment affirming his conviction, the justices
agreed that the law defining which actions constituted the crime of assault
and battery was vague, but they pointed out that the conviction was
meant to protect "the sacredness of the person" or "prevent breaches
of the peace," suggesting that even such seemingly innocuous requests
could stir up white outrage. The court justified its opinion through its

interpretation of Lynch's actions following his solicitation. Though one might read Lynch's placing his hand on Martin's shoulder as part of an apology, the justices read it, as did the jury, as unwarranted physical contact, which constituted assault. Significantly, Lynch's curiosity about sexual relations with a white woman was not factored into this determination. His words were impertinent, rude, "grossly insulting," and forward, but not to the extent that they constituted a sexual assault.[65]

Similarly, in 1918, Rufus Jackson received a six-year sentence for three separate counts of assault with intent to commit rape against three different white women. His crimes, however, centered on intent rather than force. He was convicted based on the jury's determination that he intended to rape the women by force, though his actions consisted solely of approaching the women on a Richmond bridge at night, placing his hand on their arms or sleeves, and propositioning them. His sentence indicates the jury's belief that the assaults were not especially serious.[66] In Martin Wiley's case in 1921, his supposed intent took precedence over his actions. He was indicted for attempted rape after demanding "to have carnal knowledge" of his white victim and then rushing at her. Although the jury found him guilty as charged, they sentenced him to only one year in jail and fined him $1,000. This punishment was below the minimum term of three years for attempted rape and was more in line with a conviction for assault. Moreover, the jury's comparatively mild sentence stands in stark contrast to the apparent furor the crime initially ignited. The media reported that after Wiley's arrest, the victim and her husband personally urged an angry crowd gathered at the courthouse to refrain from violence and allow the law to take its course.[67]

Black men's expressions of sexual desire for white women accorded with the ideology of segregation. White women who were propositioned by black men retained the power of refusal and, through their indignation, reasserted their racial superiority. White women could usually do this without the interference of a white male protector. Solicitations for sexual relations could remain confined between the two parties and thus did not necessarily challenge white male prerogatives. Black men's expressions of desire affirmed the southern racial, sexual, and social order in another way as well. It proved that white women were extremely desirable. Frank Lynch was so curious about kissing a white woman that he was willing to risk a jail sentence. Solicitation affirmed white women's desirability while it maintained their untouchability. That black men asked these women for sexual relations suggests that they knew they could not act on their desires without permission. Viewing cases of solicitation in this manner confirmed what white men told themselves all along—that white women were both desirable and untouchable. Black men's desire for white women reaffirmed the racial hierarchy without breaching the boundaries between the races.

The problem with solicitation, of course, and what made it a crime, was that, in white southerners' view there was always the potential that a black man, frustrated after being rebuffed, might resort to force, thus violating both racial and gender boundaries. In crossing those boundaries, however, black men also reinforced them. In their desire for and willingness to take by force what they could not have—the bodies of white women—black men confirmed the value of white women's bodies, and the values of the culture that put them on the pedestal. Black-on-white sexual assaults thus served important cultural functions. They simultaneously threatened and affirmed the social order by confirming the appropriateness of white women's exalted position, the rectitude of white supremacy, and the logic—even if it represented an impossibility—of black men's attempts to join white men in their sexual access to white women. Each assault provided an opportunity for whites to reassert the color line, not merely by punishing black men for their alleged transgressions but by continually reinforcing the values embedded in segregation and defining where the boundary between appropriate and inappropriate interaction lay. In the process, these cases allowed both whites and blacks to negotiate the meanings of gendered whiteness and gendered blackness.

Ultimately, in cases of black-on-white rape, courts determined that some contact between white women and black men was clearly accidental and thus should not be severely punished. At other times, they determined that contact was not accidental. At the same time, nonaccidental contact was not always interpreted as sexual. Virginia courts occasionally recognized black men's apparent insolence toward white women for what it was—the result of accidental contact or a contest over the use of public space, and thus a violation of social, not sexual, boundaries. Officials also made distinctions between the level of threat to the social order inherent in black men's violent actions against white women and inherent in their nonviolent expressions of sexual desire. The decisions of legal officials, and the juries who determined the outcomes of criminal cases, suggest that whites attributed different social meanings to different allegations of assault, contingent upon a specific array of conditions. Not every case invoked the familiar racial script of the black beast rapist.

In cases in which whites did invoke the racial script, however, its power could decrease over time. Convicted black men frequently petitioned the governor for pardon, and the arguments of legal officials indicate that long after the fact, whites reevaluated the actions for which black men were convicted of rape or attempted rape. Opinions of legal authorities not only justified pardon; they manifested a fundamental reshaping of acceptable interactions between black men and white women. Significantly, white opinions about which actions were appropriate and which were not changed from the time a man was convicted to when he requested pardon. Evidence that had overwhelmingly swayed white jurors to vote for conviction took on new meaning in the eyes of white legal officials years later.

Specific actions were reinterpreted only when they met certain preconditions. Prison sentences made it possible for legal officials to reevaluate cases, as convicted assailants serving prison terms remained alive, and thus could request executive clemency. Men who had been executed obviously could not ask that legal officials take another look at their case. Prison sentences, which, in legal officials' views, were often indicative of doubt in the minds of the jurors, also justified reevaluating the severity of the assaults themselves. Exploring both legal officials' and the public's evaluation of a crime reveals that perceptions of its severity changed over time. A crime that might have caused community outrage at the time it was committed might be judged to be relatively minor several years later.

George Griffin was convicted in 1906 of attempted rape and sentenced to fifteen years in prison. At the time, the *Culpeper Exponent* called Griffin's actions "brutal" and "fiendish."[68] Local feeling against him was high, and Griffin was quickly moved to another county for safekeeping. By 1916, when the governor received Griffin's petition for pardon, the tempers of local community members, including the victim's relatives, had cooled, and they agreed that "the ends of justice have been fully met."[69] Griffin's actions also seemed less brutal and fiendish to the commonwealth's attorney: "My recollection is that the circumstances were not very aggravated and that the only evidence against him was that of the young white girl and that her evidence was only to the fact that he put his hand on her and made indecent proposals." The governor granted Griffin a pardon.[70]

Time altered the perceptions of the legal officials who prosecuted James Acree in a different way. Acree, at age eighteen, was convicted of attempted rape on a "schoolgirl" in 1923. He was sentenced to death, but the governor commuted his sentence to life in prison because Acree was judged to be feebleminded.[71] First in 1930 and again in 1939, Acree petitioned for release. His lawyer argued that the case was not "aggravated": "There was, apparently, no plot or design, there was no actual physical violence done, neither was the attempt long continued, nor pressed with any degree of determination." The testimony of the alleged victim herself supported the lawyer's claim that Acree's actions really were not so serious: "Though the indictment contained allegations of physical contact, yet the young lady testified at the trial that her assailant never had his hands on her."[72] In his letter to Governor Pollard in 1930 Acree insisted that he did not "get justice." He wrote, "The plaintiff testified in court that I chased her, but did not catch her, or place my hands on her. . . . It therefore appears to me that being accused of a crime of that nature, owing to my color made me guilty."[73] Acree and his attorney argued that his actions did not represent a grave violation of the color line. The prosecuting attorney, James S. Easley, endorsed Acree's petition in 1939 but in an indirect way. He stated: "The fact that I am unable to clearly recall this case indicates to my mind that there was nothing particularly aggrevating [sic] about the circumstances and that the facts related in the application are probably correct." He agreed to recommend a pardon, despite the fact that Acree's actions had originally been judged serious enough to merit the death penalty. Acree was released in 1939.[74]

Acree and Griffin owed their releases to the ability of time to alter perceptions about the seriousness of their actions toward white women. Actions that merited severe punishment at the time they were committed seemed less threatening years later. In pardon proceedings, white officials could allow considerations of a prisoner's youth or more balanced interpretations of his supposed actions to override the fact that the offense was committed by a black man against a white woman. Whether larger social trends influenced white officials' reevaluations of the severity of cases is unclear. Evidence indicates that pardon officials made such judgments on a case-by-case basis, with little formal procedure other than that they requested the opinions of the presiding judge and the prosecuting attorney.

White court officials' treatment of cases of assault by black men on white women shows that they considered the bodies of white women to be protected territory. Though whites did not always agree on what punishment served justice, they were largely unanimous in their belief that by encroaching on the bodies of white women, black men committed a crime against what indictment forms referred to as "the peace and dignity" of Virginia. By punishing black men, white men reasserted the boundaries of the social order and promoted public safety. That white juries composed entirely of men voted to convict the vast majority of accused black men underscores this point. Although whites may have disagreed on what constituted appropriate punishment, they did not question the need for punishment.

Rather than being evaluated in a predictable fashion by like-minded white officials who viewed every encounter between a white woman and a black man as an implicit threat to white supremacy, black men's alleged crimes appear to have been judged with the specific circumstances, relationships, and events surrounding them in mind. This is not to say that black men were always guilty, nor that they received just punishment for their alleged actions. On the contrary, racial prejudice marred all of these cases, and black men lived perpetually in the shadow of the electric chair, and, to a lesser extent, the lynch mob. That so many black men received any punishment at all for such minor violations of white women's persons underscores that criminal courts in Virginia could punish black men for *any* interaction with a white woman. Nevertheless, though Virginians clearly believed that black men represented sexual danger to white women, they did not interpret all of black men's actions according to this model. Whites' attitudes about these cases indicate that they believed that black men interacted with white women in other than sexual ways.

The judgments white legal officials and jurors made in cases of black-on-white assault did not occur in a vacuum, nor did they involve disinterested parties. White legal officials, and the system of segregation and white supremacy that they represented, privileged white interests over black and male interests over female. Cases of black-on-white assault represented violations of the racial and sexual order, but they also represented unique opportunities for whites to reestablish and affirm appropriate relations in a racially divided society. Upholding the social order, however, did not invariably mean that white elites always gave precedence to the accounts and actions of whites over those of blacks. Instead, legal officials buttressed the social order through complicated and dynamic deliberations about community relationships. This process is revealed in the disagreements among whites about what constituted "justice" for black men accused by white women. The cases over which officials deliberated also illuminate contested power relationships between white women and white men.

CHAPTER 3

Serving the Ends of Justice

Punishment, Protection, and the Power of Whiteness

Black-on-white rape, and white responses to it, exposed the unequal distribution of power in southern society. At their most basic level, legal and extralegal responses to rape demonstrated the power of whites to control black men's fates. Black men accused of assault had the least ability to direct their lives once they were accused and were literally at the mercy of whites. The disposition of cases, from arrest to deliberations of pardon, however, reflected larger conflicts among whites over access to the privileges of whiteness. The power over individual black men, and over the black population as a whole, stood at the heart of whiteness in the South. After all, the racial hierarchy was the primary social hierarchy that whites openly acknowledged and publicly committed themselves to defending. The focus on white supremacy and black inferiority served to obscure potent class and gender hierarchies that were equally fundamental in shaping southern social relations. The racial solidarity implied in the rhetoric of protecting white women rendered invisible women's subordination under patriarchy and poor whites' lack of social, economic, and political power. Black-on-white rape cases in many ways represented white solidarity at its height, and the overwhelming conviction rate of accused black men attests to the fact that, to a considerable degree, all whites acted out of shared racial interests when white women accused black men of rape. Ironically, however, these cases also provide a revealing window on the limits of white unity as rape cases simultaneously exposed fractures in whiteness created by class and gender divisions.

Whites' ability to accuse black men of assault and to control the dominant narrative of the crime enabled them to define violations and threats to the racial hierarchy. It allowed whites to claim themselves victims of harm and to assign blame. Rather than merely recounting tales of violence, narratives of assault verbally mapped the contours around appropriate and inappropriate relations and delineated the boundaries of blackness and whiteness, with their attendant access to social power. For white women, invoking white men's promise of protection publicly proclaimed their whiteness. For white men, providing protection, either through lynching, through participating in the resulting trial, or through influencing the sentences black men served demonstrated their own racial identity. Cases of black-on-white assault thus became a vehicle through which whites claimed their place under the mantle of white power. At the same time, through the legal system, whites harnessed the authority of the state to promote the interests of individual whites, as well as white supremacy.

Trials, decisions about appropriate sentences, and debates over pardon became the battlegrounds on which whites sought to control access to white privilege, which was symbolically and literally manifested in the bodies of accused men. Once juries returned their verdicts, considerations of appropriate sentences became the arena through which different groups of whites sought to balance the prerogatives of whiteness. White officials sought to endow the legal process with a degree of legitimacy by limiting the ability of whites to punish black men arbitrarily. The legal system provided the vehicle by which legal officials prevented marginalized whites from using accusations to further their own goals. Finally, the entire legal process, from trial through pardon, became the means by which white men sought to contain the power that segregation, and its attendant rhetoric about protection, gave white women. After all, it was white women's accusations that placed individual black men's fates in the hands of often-angry whites, and it was white women's words that set the entire process in motion. In short, women briefly were able to dictate the actions of men.

The competing agendas among whites and their beliefs about the relationship between black-on-white assault and the social order often appear in debates about appropriate punishment. Whites used their arguments about what punishment black men deserved as a way to promote their understanding of the harm a given assault did to the social order. Severe violations of the color line merited the most severe penalties. At the same time, the punishments black men received, many whites argued, sent definite messages to the black community about the limits of white toleration when blacks violated the rules of racial interaction. By insisting that their opinions about black men's fates be heard, whites claimed their right to participate in creating and refining the racial order. In whites' ability to influence decisions about punishment was the power to define the standards of social behavior for both blacks and whites, and, by extension, to shape the social order itself. Paradoxically, the exercise of patriarchal protection that was at the heart of white supremacy simultaneously challenged and supported racial, class, and gender hierarchies, creating situations in which white solidarity was sacrificed to protect class and patriarchal privilege.

Idealized segregation suggested that all whites exercised equal power over all blacks. In reality, however, some whites possessed more power than others. Cases of black-on-white rape brought these inequalities to light. They created opportunities for some whites to exercise the power to punish black men (and white women), while they simultaneously limited the ability of other whites to trade on the privileges of their race. Crimes against white women set the seemingly rigid boundaries controlling interracial interaction in sharp relief. The power to determine whether a black man had harmed a white woman forced whites to rank explicitly both the assailant and the victim in the community. Whoever had control over defining what actions represented a racial trespass and who could be violated by those actions could order social relations, and thus control the social hierarchy and the larger social order. The white men who defined black men's actions as criminal and who made the decisions about black men's guilt and punishments ultimately determined the distribution of power among all whites.

In some cases, debates about punishment were confined to disagreements over the effect of punishment on public order. Some whites argued that severe punishment prevented future mob violence, and others insisted that it merely demonstrated racial discrimination in the legal system. John Wood's case provides a good example of the contours of this debate. Wood had been convicted in 1925 of attempting to assault two

University of Virginia summer school students in their dorm room. Wood was sentenced to death, but it was clear that he had not committed the crime alone—the two women testified that they fought more than one assailant in their room that night. Authorities, moreover, agreed that John Wood did not have the mental capacity to plan and execute the crime on his own. He had a long history of mental instability and had been diagnosed as feebleminded. Despite Wood's testimony against his alleged accomplices, however, the two other black men accused of participating in the crime were acquitted. Shortly after their trials, Wood's attorney petitioned the governor to have his death sentence commuted to life in prison. As part of his deliberations, Governor Byrd sent Frank Bane, the commissioner of public welfare, to Charlottesville, the community in which the crime had been committed, to ascertain public attitudes about the crime and Wood's sentence.[1]

Bane found a divided white community. Business leaders expressed some concern for the integrity of the criminal justice system. Though Bane could find "no great interest in the case," among the business and professional men, he found that the majority were in favor of commuting Wood's sentence. Many of them, Bane said, including Mr. Waddell, vice president of the People's National Bank of Charlottesville, "state that they have very serious doubts as to whether the negro in question is guilty at all." Though this was not a universal opinion—R. C. Minor, vice president of the First National Bank favored Wood's execution—Bane believed that it represented the majority view: not only did legal officials responsible for Wood's trial believe the majority of white citizens desired commuting his sentence, they also stated that many whites believed that Wood's conviction and sentence were connected to his race. "They [legal officials]," wrote Bane, "state further that they believe the best interests of the community will be served by the suggested action [commutation], and they are further of the opinion that if John Wood is electrocuted a great many citizens of the county and city will be of the opinion that he was electrocuted primarily because he happened to be a negro."[2]

Members of the university community disagreed and expressed their opinions more forcefully. Several of them framed their concerns within the rubric of white womanhood: they were more interested in the message commutation would send to the community than in whether or not Wood was guilty. University officials responsible for the few female students on the university grounds noted the burden they carried for white women's safety. To them, severe punishment would deter other black men from committing similar assaults. Dr. Charles Maphis was most emphatic that Wood's sentence not be commuted: "[A]s Dean of the Summer Quarter, the public looks to me for protection for the girls who come here." Wood should be executed, he argued, both as a deterrent to other black men and as a message to whites that the legal system effectively protected white women, making extralegal protection unnecessary. "[I]f the law does not protect these women, the Klu Klux Klan [sic] and others will take it into their own hands to do it. . . . The failure to carry out the verdict of the jury in his case would . . . lead to mob rule." Maphis reiterated his position several months later, writing, "I am of the opinion that it would be against public policy to commute Wood's sentence, and that if any attack of a white woman should occur in this community within a reasonable period, and the man should be apprehended, he would likely be lynched."[3]

The superintendent of the university hospital in Charlottesville, John Hornsby, also worried that any mercy granted John Wood would have dire implications for future public order. As the supervisor of the female nurses and nursing students at the hospital, he understood his duty to protect white women. "I am keenly interested because I have 120 young women here under my guardianship and I have 50 negroes working for me in the Hospital, and I feel my responsibility." He believed that commuting Wood's sentence would be interpreted by the black employees at the hospital as a license to attack white women, and specifically white female nursing students. Leniency toward Wood might provoke more assaults, creating a temptation for his black employees and increased danger for the nursing students under his care.[4]

Numerous white men in Charlottesville claimed a say in Wood's fate, and all believed they spoke for the good of the larger community. Those in favor of commutation believed that hasty judgments based on racial discrimination undermined the ability of the law to punish violators of the social order. Others argued that the deterrent value of swift and severe punishment kept both blacks and whites in line. Whether they privileged concerns about white women's protection or the integrity of the legal system, each claimed the power to define the danger an assault represented to the social order and the right to calibrate the appropriate response. The governor dodged both sets of questions, commuting Wood's sentence to life in prison and citing as justifications his mental condition, his youth at the time of the crime, his poor background, and his lack of education.[5]

John Hornsby was not alone in expressing concern that lenient punishments affected interactions between all white women and all black men. Other cases exposed debates about the effect of tangled interracial relationships on the behavior of both whites and blacks. Many cases illuminate issues far beyond the protection of white womanhood. In May 1920, for example, a Pulaski County jury convicted Jasper Morrison, a seventeen-year-old "mulatto," of attempting to rape the five-year-old daughter of his white employer, John Buford. Morrison took the stand in his own defense, denying that he had any intention of forcibly raping the girl. He admitted that "he did rub himself against the limbs of the child, it being a form of masturbation, but that no force was used, nor did [Morrison] intend to use any force."[6] Five years after Morrison's conviction, Governor E. Lee Trinkle began to receive petitions requesting Morrison's release. For the next five years, various whites in Pulaski County argued the merits of Morrison's petitions, and, in the end, it appears that he served his full sentence. The petitions reveal that Morrison's case embodied the contested boundaries around acceptable interactions across racial lines. Few disputed that Morrison's actions, even if only intended as masturbation, constituted a breech of appropriate behavior between blacks and whites. Nevertheless, there was some debate over whether his sentence, eighteen years in prison, was too severe for his actions. His lawyer, R. L. Lindsay, argued that it was, insisting that Morrison "deserve[d] a chance in life." John Buford, the father of the victim, disagreed, stating his steadfast opposition to pardon and assuring the governor that a decision in favor of Morrison's release "would be criticized by most of all the best people."[7]

The white man most strenuously pushing for Morrison's release, Jim McGavock, however, was not one of the "best people." Curiously, he was both Morrison's white father and the foreman of the grand jury who indicted him. Although McGavock did not refer to his relationship with the convicted boy, both Morrison's lawyer and John Buford noted it and suggested that it was common knowledge in the community. In the eyes of other whites, however, by working on Morrison's behalf and implicitly acknowledging his relationship with Morrison's mother, McGavock forfeited his claim as a white man to influence Morrison's punishment. John Buford took specific steps to derail McGavock's efforts, writing the governor on several occasions and noting McGavock's complicated relationship to the case. At one point he warned, "I do not know what kind of steps Jim McGavock will take. He tried to get me to give my consent [to Morrison's release], but I will never do it as long as I live." Buford apparently had the position and prestige to influence the governor. He affected a personal tone in his pleas, addressing the governor as "My dear Lee" and inquiring about the status of the governor's agricultural interests. Buford's efforts were successful. He claimed the right to determine Morrison's fate, challenging McGavock's status as a white man and his related ability to interfere in the case.[8]

Morrison's lawyer also questioned McGavock's fitness to participate in the deliberations over Morrison's sentence. He implied that McGavock's interracial relationship and acknowledgment of his son tarnished McGavock's whiteness and thus reduced his social power. He lamented that "a man like Jim McGavock ma[d]e such a mess of his life" but nonetheless saw a way to use Morrison's white paternity as a justification for pardon. Lindsay blamed Morrison's mixed parentage, and the inherent contradictions in segregation, for the assault itself: "[I]t is a pity that there must always be so long as black and white live together this intermingling of blood. The white in [Morrison] always calling for its own blood and the negro in him holding him back to lower levels."[9] Because the crime stemmed from McGavock's inability to act within racial boundaries, the state could not punish the son for his actions. Because Morrison was biologically driven to unnatural acts, any sanction the state imposed would essentially punish Morrison for the sins of his father.

Debates about Jasper Morrison's fate concerned not merely the crime itself but also the behavior of both blacks and whites, and their access to public power. McGavock's relationship with Morrison's mother was certainly not the only one of its kind. White men's sexual exploitation of black women has a long and sordid history in the South. Nevertheless, whites believed it was inappropriate for McGavock to use his power as a white man to promote the interests of a son who was the product of an illicit relationship. Such a man, whites argued, should not be able to use his race to shape the fate of a white girl's assailant, even if, and perhaps especially if, that black man was his son. Jim McGavock had no automatic right to social power merely because he was white, and he certainly had no right to confer the benefits of his race on his nonwhite son.

Ultimately, however, it was Virginia's governors who decided black men's fates when petitions for clemency came across their desks. Consequently, these debates offer contradictory conclusions. Many white men articulated their belief that, as white men, they deserved a say in defining black men's crimes and their assaults on white supremacy and in how convicted men should be punished. By offering their opinion, whites were claiming access to one privilege of whiteness, control over black men. They argued that while some whites possessed this right, others forfeited it through their inappropriate behavior. Yet most participants in these discussions could not force state and legal authorities to act on their advice. The state controlled the fate of black men, and the state ultimately held the power to define and preserve the social order.

Representatives of white institutional power, moreover, frequently used their authority to balance the community's need for retribution against black men with official conceptions of what constituted justice. Whiteness granted the power to influence decisions about black men but not always the wisdom to balance outrage with mercy. White anger created a blunt and inefficient instrument of racial control. Legal authorities, sworn to replace outrage with the commitment to rational order through law, ideally possessed the clarity of vision to weigh the competing desires for retribution and white ideas of civilized justice. Black men faced white public ire in the form of the jury, and white officials conceded that white anger shaped jury verdicts and sentences. In these cases, legal authorities and the governor used their power to refine justice and thus limited the power of juries as representatives of white popular opinion. Punishment of black men was necessary, but it nonetheless might require adjustment using the power that both whiteness and Virginia law conferred upon legal officials.

Judges, prosecuting attorneys, court clerks, and law enforcement officials used clemency petitions to bring black men's sentences in line with their ideas of appropriate punishment. Lee Williams stood accused of attempted rape in 1917; he was convicted and sentenced to five years. The judge in his case believed Williams was deprived of a fair trial because of the nature of the crime. He pointed out that the evidence against Williams was not sufficient to sustain a guilty verdict. Williams, however, had no legal counsel, so, terrified and fearing the white community's wrath, he had pleaded guilty. The judge, conscious of William's predicament, "gave him the shortest term under the law which is five years in the Penitentiary"[10] and acted further on his behalf. "I gave him to understand at the time that after he had served one or two years, I would help him to receive a pardon and I am now writing to say that I think he has been sufficiently punished." The judge was almost as good as his word; Williams was released after he had served two and a half years.[11]

Robert Sims, accused of an assault on Mary L. Shapard in 1927, faced a similar situation. When he was arrested, Sims allegedly confessed that he had "touched the woman" but denied that he intended to rape her.[12] Sims pleaded guilty to attempted rape and was sentenced to ten years.[13] In 1932, the judge who tried the case wrote to the governor on Sims's behalf. "From the evidence as related to me by the officers," he wrote, "I had serious doubt whether a conviction for attempted rape could be sustained. . . . The evidence showing criminal intent was weak and would hardly have sustained anything but a misdemeanor if the accused had not made such a strong effort to escape." The judge asserted that Sims was "not a bad man, though he is not very bright," and emphasized that his family "are respectable colored citizens of the county." In light of these facts, the judge believed that Sims had been sufficiently punished.[14] Reordering the relevant facts, the judge privileged Sims's age and family reputation over the white woman's claim to protection. The judge's actions refined the relationship between Sims's actions and his place in segregated society, a measure public opinion was too clouded by outrage to make.

Legal officials acknowledged the power of white outrage, and they used their authority to counteract it by altering the dominant narrative of the crime. John Roberson was accused of attempted rape in 1907. His victim, a white woman named Mrs. Gallier, testified that she had been sleeping in bed with her husband and child when Roberson allegedly entered the room, pulled off the covers, and attempted to assault her. A jury convicted Roberson and sentenced him to fifteen years in prison. Judge Frank P. Christian, who presided over the case, was dissatisfied by the verdict of the jury, and three years later he wrote to the governor on Roberson's behalf. Christian emphasized Roberson's claim that he had been drunk and mistakenly entered the Gallier's house, thinking it was his own. The atmosphere of outrage caused whites to ignore a more reasonable explanation for Roberson's otherwise baffling actions. Surely no black man, the judge suggested, would attempt to assault a white woman whose husband was next to her on the bed. Christian argued that if Roberson truly intended to commit rape, "no Virginia jury would have permitted a negro to escape under such circumstances with fifteen years in the penitentiary. . . . It looks to me as though there has been somewhat a miscarriage of justice in this case and the horrible crime charged more considered by the jury than the evidence, and I do not think you would make an error in some commutation of his term." The commonwealth's attorney agreed. They had been unable at trial, however, to outweigh white emotion with reason. The jury sentenced Roberson to fifteen years despite the arguments of the prosecuting attorney "that five years in penitentiary was all the negro should receive according to law, and I practically argued this to the jury." Once the jury returned its verdict, legal officials used the power entrusted to them by the state to correct a "miscarriage" of justice and give Roberson a more appropriate sentence. He was pardoned after serving four years.[15] These cases show that white authorities could not always control the jury's decisions about guilt and appropriate sentences at the time of trial. Juries applied the law as they so fit, not always adhering to the expert judgments of legal officials. By waiting several years and then petitioning for conditional pardon, however, legal officials were able to impose their definitions of the crime and their ideas of justice on the cases tried in their courtrooms.[16]

The white community, however, also utilized forms of leverage other than mob violence to influence the actions of legal officials. Whites asserted their collective power when they believed that white law enforcement officials had failed in their duty to protect white women. They occasionally used their legitimate power as citizens and voters to influence how officers handled accusations of assault. William Green and Walter Williams, both black men, were convicted in Salem, Virginia, in 1925 of "peeping" and were each fined $50. Neighbors had seen Green and Williams several times peeking into the windows of a white widow's home as her two daughters dressed. The neighbors reported the men's actions to the police, but police failed to catch the men in the act. Four white neighbors established a watch, and the two men were eventually arrested. Filling the void created by the failure of law enforcement to arrest the offenders, the white community forced the legal system to act, thereby delineating what sorts of behavior by blacks the white community would tolerate. Dissatisfied with authorities' inaction, the white community, in the *Richmond Times-Dispatch*'s words, "put an end to the terrorizing of the family."[17]

Whites did not always agree about the danger black men's actions represented. In their efforts to shape official responses to crimes, they sought to harness the power of the state to enact their standards of justice according to their conceptions of the crime. In a society based on racial hierarchy, the ability to draw the line between appropriate and inappropriate interactions between whites and blacks represented considerable public power in local communities. Contests between authorities and the white community over control of black men's fates not only attest to a fractured white community; they also illuminate white efforts to protect white supremacy without leveling class distinctions among whites. In the eyes of white officials, black men guilty of crimes against white women deserved severe punishment, but only within the bounds of an accepted white power structure controlled by legal authorities themselves. The rest of the white community, however, might disagree and express its disagreement in public and political ways.

In October 1927, in the farming community of Smithville, Virginia, fifteen-year-old Hilda Barlow was raped and murdered. After witnesses reported that they had seen Shirley Winnegan leaving the scene, police quickly arrested him and charged him with the crime.[18] Word of the murder soon spread, and a mob of more than 200 men amassed to lynch Winnegan. By evening, Winnegan had been transferred to two different jails before finally being placed in Richmond for safekeeping. The mob was determined to exact its brand of justice. They traveled to several local jails, interrogated the sheriff as to Winnegan's whereabouts, and agreed to disperse only when they learned that Winnegan was being held in Richmond.[19] Thwarted in its attempt to seize Winnegan, the white community criticized law enforcement officials for protecting him, arguing that the mob that chased Winnegan across three jurisdictions had a right to enforce lynch justice. County officials, however, insisted they had only "done their duty to uphold the law."[20]

The white community believed, however, that the failure of the sheriff and the commonwealth's attorney to relinquish their prisoner in the face of popular opinion constituted a breach of the authority of their offices and a subversion of the will of the people. It was a violation of office sufficient to mandate their removal. Ten days after Hilda Barlow's murder and approximately two weeks before a local election, 1,200 citizens of Isle of Wight County met to repudiate the nominations for sheriff and commonwealth's attorney and initiate a write-in campaign for alternate candidates.[21] Talk soon moved to larger issues, which formed the core of the community's complaint: law enforcement officials, according to one participant, failed "to make our grand old county safe for women and children." Another declared he wanted people in office who represented his interests: "We want men who will serve the masses and not the classes." To the meeting's participants, officials' declarations that they were sworn to uphold the law demonstrated a misplaced loyalty to elite institutions and a failure to protect the patriarchal interests of common (white and male) citizens. Claims that state institutions did not "make this grand old county safe for women and children" implied that legal authorities ignored the popular will, compromised popular concerns—even the lives of their wives and children—and trampled the rights of citizens. There was no racial solidarity in the aftermath of Winnegan's crime. There was a contest among whites over who had the power not only to decide Winnegan's fate but to determine the relationship among law, order, and patriarchal authority, defined as the ability to protect homes, women, and children. Shortly before the election, circulars appeared around the community urging voters to "Remember, protection of the home comes before party."[22] Both the sheriff and the commonwealth's attorney lost their bids for reelection, becoming political casualties in the battle over who would shape the meaning of white supremacy. Which whites, ultimately, had the power to punish crimes against the social order?

Winnegan's case appears to be the only instance in Virginia in which the white community punished legal officials at the polls for their handling of a black man's crime. Community members' actions underscored their belief that interference in legal procedures was justified when elite-controlled structures proved unsatisfactory. Both sides claimed to have the best interests of the community at heart. But each side defined those interests differently. Officials placed their oaths of office above their revulsion over Winnegan's crime and argued that the legal system had sole power to judge and punish black men; their responsibility to legal precedent rose above white men's honor and the need for "protection." In contrast, the public promoted its interest in swift, severe, and popular punishment and utilized legitimate channels of political protest to assert its view. Both sides argued that their primary duty was to control the fate of blacks who challenged the racial order.

No one attempted to argue that Winnegan did not present a danger to white society. He was quickly tried, sentenced to death, and executed. Any other reputation he may have had in the community was overshadowed by his new identity as rapist and murderer. Black men's reputations were important considerations in defining a black man's threat to the racial order, but they did not usually affect decisions about guilt or innocence or even sentencing at trial. Often black men's reputations came into play in decisions about pardon. Court and state officials evaluated black men's acquiescence to segregation in the community prior to the crime to determine their fitness for release. Black men who had "known their place" before the crime, even though they had been convicted, still might receive conditional pardon. The assailant's reputation, age, mental ability, or whether he was drunk or not could become mitigating factors. The white community weighed these factors to determine not only whether a black man intended to harm a white woman but also whether he intended to attack racial boundaries and flout the system of segregation as well. Men who, due to any of these factors, could not comprehend the rules of racial interaction were less likely to be seen by whites as attempting to usurp the racial and gender privileges of white men. Significantly, however, it was the testimony of whites that supplied evidence of a convicted man's understanding and acceptance of his place in segregated society, as well as his respect for white authority. Whites alone determined whether a black man "knew his place."

Whites most strenuously condemned black men who appeared to purposefully violate racial taboos. They insisted that black men's crimes against white women represented both their natural tendencies and their attempts to seize or exert power. Deliberate, planned assaults were calculated attempts to seize the privileges allowed white men rather than impulsive acts of lust. Owen Goggin's assault on Elizabeth Nance in 1914 illustrates how evidence of premeditation alarmed whites. After the governor received a petition to commute his death sentence to life in prison, Henry Humphreys, who prosecuted the case, wrote to the governor urging him to put Goggin to death. Goggin's crime, he argued, was not serious merely because he had violently assaulted a white woman. It was the intelligence with which Goggin planned the crime that made him a dire threat. According to Humphreys, Goggin "showed considerable cunning. . . . The evidence of premeditation is overwhelming, as a few minutes before he struck Mrs. Nance on the head with the ax, he walked into the room where she was sitting at the table with her three small children, and remarked to her 'I see by this newspaper that they have put the Allens in the chair.' He then went and closed both the front and rear hall doors, and returned to the dining room, where he made the attack."[23] The community, shocked by the brutality of the assault, was also horrified to realize that Goggin had the intelligence to plan an attack. His "cunning" in making sure Nance was without male protection by casually searching the house while she breakfasted made plain that he had not merely acted on a lustful impulse. As a petition against commutation stated, Goggin "knew exactly what he was doing."[24] The facts of the crime demonstrated to whites the danger of Goggin's assault. His desire for his white employer's wife, and the lengths he went to satisfy it, translated into a desire for his employer's racial and gender status. Goggin was not satisfied with his "place." By these considerations, he deserved to die, and the governor declined to interfere in his case.

Authorities made a similar argument in Henry Jones's case in 1929. He was convicted of raping his white employer's wife, who after the assault promised not to report him if he would spare her life. Believing her, Jones made no attempt to escape. She nonetheless reported the assault to authorities, and Jones was convicted and sentenced to death. His lawyer attempted to have his sentence commuted, concluding that Jones must have been either insane or feebleminded not to attempt to flee after committing what was commonly understood to be the most egregious of crimes. Arthur W. James, who investigated Jones's petition, challenged the claim that Jones was mentally deficient and did not understand what he was doing: "He was perfectly conscious of the seriousness of his offense and he employed considerable intelligence in planning" it. Cognizant of the social meaning of his actions, Jones had no grounds to argue his life should be spared, and he was executed two weeks after James penned his report.[25]

Black men who "knew their place" and displayed appropriate respect for the racial hierarchy were more likely to be spared the full force of the law. The episodic lapses of black men who were generally willing to act according to segregation's rules were interpreted as less dangerous to the racial order. For example, John Spencer, who was convicted of rape in 1919 and sentenced to five years in prison, was released after one year. A group of white men petitioned the governor to grant him conditional pardon, arguing that Spencer "has always been regarded as an honest well behaved colored man, knowing his place and attending to his own business."[26] Similarly, Coleman Crews's one-year sentence for assault was suspended after nine months. Officials noted in his pardon that he had "always previously borne a good reputation."[27] These black men understood and accepted their subordination to white authority, so their release posed no threat to white supremacy.

Other black men were intellectually incapable of comprehending the South's taboo on sexual relations between white women and black men. Although they might represent a physical danger to white women, their attacks did not always represent a conscious assault on segregation or the social order. Their impulsive attempts to force white women into sexual intercourse, though terrifying to the particular white woman involved, did not pose significant danger to the rest of white society, and thus merited less severe punishment. The decision to commute John Wood's death sentence grew out of this sort of consideration. Whites apparently supported commutation because Wood, who was mentally incompetent, was "led" into the crime by two other black men of "superior intelligence" who were acquitted. By this logic, Wood himself posed no threat to white women as long as he was not coerced by others.[28] These same whites believed that the men who allegedly engineered the assault—most thought Wood mentally incapable of doing so himself—would have deserved execution had they been convicted. It was not the actions themselves, then, that determined the severity of the assault but the intent behind them. John Wood's accomplices apparently knew full well what they were doing in ways that Wood himself could not.

G. Johnson, the clerk of the court at James Smith's trial in 1917, also connected Smith's mental ability with the severity of the crime in his statement recommending pardon in 1926. He argued that "Smith was not of sufficient mentality, while not a lunatic, to understand the enormity of the crime, and while he was guilty in law, not knowing what he had done, its purport, and connection with society, I doubted if a criminal court such as ours fitted in his case."[29] Smith was released after serving nine years of an eighteen-year sentence.[30] For many whites, they could only conclude that any black man who attempted to assault a white woman must be insane. When Jacob Gatling was shot while trying to force his way into a white woman's home, whites could express only bafflement. As the newspaper reported, "He was considered trustworthy. Some think he became suddenly insane."[31]

Legal officials made similar arguments that young offenders, usually under seventeen years of age, should be spared the extreme penalty. Like black men with mental disabilities, young black boys could not be expected to understand the full implications of their actions. Supporters of Gabriele Battaile, who was convicted of rape in 1906, petitioned the governor to commute his death sentence, arguing that at only about fourteen or fifteen years of age, Battaile was "intensely ignorant." Three clergymen wrote that Battaile "does not realize whatever the gravity of the crime or his own conditions, in fact, judging from his actions and attitudes, he seems to think that his act was mere child's play. . . . That he has committed the crime there is no doubt in our minds, but because of his youthfulness and his dense ignorance," the men requested his sentence be commuted.[32] In this instance, the governor was not sympathetic. Jasper Morrison's father made a similar argument, saying his son did not realize "that even the appearance, the first gesture towards the commission of this crime upon a white female in this state would lead to his quick extinction or at least heavy punishment."[33] Neither of these young boys understood the importance of white woman's purity to the exercise of white authority, and, consequently, their crimes were not interpreted as open challenges to white power. Youthful misunderstanding was not always accepted as a mitigating factor, but the fact that numerous petitions requested it to be considered as such suggests that petitioners believed it might sway a governor to extend pardon.

Most young black men convicted of crimes against white girls in Virginia were not put to death, a fact that reflected white beliefs that they could still be taught to respect their place in the racial order. Several were sentenced to reform school, where whites hoped they would be rehabilitated. Allen Ball, for example, was accused in 1909 of attempting to assault an eight-year-old white girl. Though he was indicted for a felony and he pleaded guilty, he was committed to the Negro Reformatory Association of Virginia for an indeterminate length of time. Interestingly, the judge imposed this sentence with the consent not of the victim's father but with that of Ball's father.[34] Jacob Jefferson's case in 1916 was similar. Accused of assaulting a five-year-old white girl, Jefferson pleaded guilty to simple assault rather than attempted rape and was sentenced to time in the same institution.[35] These young men may have been spared the death penalty because they were accused of assaulting very young girls who themselves could not yet understand the extreme nature of the violation. Black boys' lack of understanding of racial taboos and society's perceptions of young children's sexual innocence together made the harm to young victim's seem less severe, and thus the crime a less serious threat to racial norms.

The length of time black youths could expect to remain at a reform school often depended on the population at the schools themselves, which were frequently overcrowded.[36] But black boys incarcerated for assaults on young white females could be released in as little time as six months if their family situation proved adequate. Powell H. Smith was sent to the reformatory association in June 1918 after being convicted in Loudoun County for assaulting a white girl. The judge ruled that he had been allowed to "run wild" and had "no parental control." When Smith's father, however, returned from the army at the end of World War I, officials agreed to release Smith on the condition that his "father is around to exercise control." Smith was released in December 1918, after only six months.[37]

Concerns about parental authority played a significant role in determining whether black youths accused of assaulting white girls presented a threat to the social order. To legal officials, and probably to most other Virginians at the time, the home provided the best place to learn the rules of a segregated society. White legal officials expected black parents to inculcate into their children the appropriate norms and behaviors expected of a subservient population. Assaulting a white girl certainly subverted those expectations, but legal authorities only rarely determined that black youths accused of such crimes deserved the ultimate penalty. More frequently, they viewed the actions of black boys as a problem of socialization. They were too young to realize their appropriate role in a segregated society and the importance of the South's most sacred taboo against sexual interaction between black men and white women. They could not be held accountable for their actions in the same way that grown men could be. Once these youthful offenders adequately internalized white prescriptions about black subordination, they would no longer represent a threat to white women or to white supremacy. Although whites believed black men harbored an inherent desire for white women, the behavioral norms of segregation, learned and internalized by most black males in their youth, should contain those desires. The failure to follow segregation's rules, then, was an anomaly, not an inevitability. Segregation and socialization together could supersede nature to control black men's behavior.

Court officials were less forgiving of repeat offenders. Authorities might attempt to reform young black boys with an alternate form of punishment, but if those efforts failed, they faced severe sentences. In 1931, Loo Rooster Jarvis, a fifteen-year-old, was accused of a sexual crime against a white woman. The nature of the charges against him was unclear, and legal officials later conceded the possibility that the relationship was consensual. Nevertheless, in lieu of a trial, Jarvis was sent to the Central State Hospital, Virginia's mental institution for African Americans, where he was sterilized. Authorities apparently hoped to reduce his criminal tendencies, as well as to prevent him from passing them on to the next generation.[38] Jarvis escaped from Central State Hospital after three years, and six months later he was charged with raping another white girl. He received a life sentence. Legal authorities wasted no more time with efforts at reform.[39]

As eugenicists argued that controlled reproduction would eliminate social problems, including crime, they clamored for the sterilization and segregation of youthful black offenders.[40] Arthur W. James, a commissioner of the public welfare in Virginia, cited the case of a fifteen-year-old boy, probably Willie Lewis Younger, who was diagnosed as feebleminded but for whom there was no institutional care. After being returned to the community following a year's detention for an unspecified offense, Younger allegedly raped a four-year-old white girl and was sentenced to life in prison. James lamented the lack of institutional care for this boy pointing out that his crime would have been prevented had he been incarcerated at the appropriate mental institution.[41] Younger was pardoned after serving nine years of his life sentence, at which time legal authorities determined his sentence was too severe.[42]

In considering pardons, white officials carefully weighed the effect an

assault had on white supremacy and retained the ultimate power to identify and address the harm it caused. Officials often relied on the opinions
of local whites who knew the reputations of assailants, but the judges and
prosecutors who conducted the trials had the most influence over the
governor's decision to grant a conditional pardon. Like the power to determine punishment for black men, the power to determine the exact
nature and degree of harm their assault caused also shaped the boundaries around appropriate interactions. A calibration of the harm caused to
a specific female victim also influenced pardon decisions. Although white
men during the trials of black men accused of assaulting white women
reacted harshly to the damage inflicted on female victims, once the convicted black men were in jail, whites debated black men's fates in a way
that suggests that the harm white women experienced was not so griev-
ous after all. Local white men might occasionally express concern over
their responsibility to protect white women, but their discussions over
punishment and pardon rarely included concern that these men continued to represent a threat to white women. Most deliberations never
mentioned the interests of white women or the duty of white men to
protect white women by keeping convicted men in prison.

Occasionally governors considered the opinions of white husbands or
fathers in their pardon deliberations, but they rarely considered those of
the victims themselves. The opposition of the victim's family to the convicted man's pardon was no sure impediment to pardon, and indeed, in
considerations over John Wood's sentence, officials clearly stated that public order superseded the interests of victims in their deliberations.[43] In the
few pardon cases in which officials mentioned the victim, it was often to
reassure themselves that concern for the victim was irrelevant. If the victim had died, for example, concerns about her sense of security were obviously moot. Sarah Patterson's death cleared the way for Walter Moore's
release in 1924. The judge scrawled at the bottom of a letter from the
governor's office, "In light of . . . the death of the old woman . . . I would not
oppose pardon."[44] The death of Albert Cogbill's victim also opened the
way for his pardon.[45] Other officials reasoned that the release of an alleged
assailant could cause the victim no harm if she had left the area. Albert
Clark was convicted in 1932 for an attempted rape of a thirteen-year-old
girl, and he received a sentence of twenty years in prison. After eight years,
the governor received a petition requesting his release. The prosecuting
attorney, in giving his approval, noted that the victim was working in West
Virginia, "so I doubt that it makes really so much difference to the girl
herself as to whether or not this man is pardoned."[46] An official involved in

the pardon proceedings of William Hundley, who was convicted of house-breaking with intent to commit rape in 1904, pointed out to the governor that the victim's husband had moved the family from the area, "so that his family would no longer feel any insecurity from the man's release."[47] Similar considerations fueled requests by legal officials that black men be pardoned provided that they not return to the community in which the victim lived. Significantly, officials expressed no concern for the safety of the white women living in proximity to released assailants' new places of residence. So much for protecting white women. These kinds of attitudes suggest the view that assaults harmed particular women but did not threaten the safety and integrity of white womanhood in general.

Officials' statements in pardon deliberations also seemingly contradict general attitudes about the effect of black men's assaults on white women. Southern rhetoric termed a black man's rape of a white woman a fate "many times more brutal than death itself"[48] and insisted that lynching spared the victim from having to recount her ordeal at trial. The rhetoric of white womanhood presumed that any assault by a black man on a white woman caused tremendous social, psychological, and physical damage. Yet the definition of harm was more nebulous. In some cases, whites assumed that rape by a black man tainted white victims physically. Some women, for example, received venereal disease from their assailants, which became important evidence against them.[49] But the damage sexual assaults did to white female victims went beyond the physical. In 1940, after accusing four black men of abducting and raping her, a twenty-six-year-old widow was fired from her job and evicted from her boarding-house because of her "notoriety" and the announcement that one of her alleged rapists had syphilis.[50] Rape contaminated victims physically and morally and undoubtedly affected women's relationships with the white men in their lives. White men could not articulate the idea that white women victims of black rapists were untouchable, but the view that rape was a fate worse than death conveyed the sentiment. One newspaper editor justified lynching by citing the effects of rape: it crushed the "peace and joy" out of women's lives.[51]

Only in the last twenty-five years have doctors and psychologists recognized rape to cause severe physical and psychological trauma for its victims. Recent studies show that up to one-third of rape victims suffer from post-traumatic stress disorder, a severe psychiatric problem most commonly associated with combat veterans. As many as half of rape victims never fully recover from their ordeals and suffer lifelong chronic depression.[52] Few people in the early twentieth century would have con-

sidered rape to cause such lasting damage. Evidence suggests that, despite calling black-on-white rape a fate worse than death, some white
southerners seemed strangely ambivalent about its effects. Many news
reports of black-on-white rape intimated that the harm to victims was not
so severe. News reports described one attack victim, who was later determined to have been robbed rather than raped, as being "none the worse
for wear."[53] The eight-year-old girl who Russell Ellett allegedly raped and
choked into unconsciousness was described in news reports as being "not
seriously hurt."[54] The attorney for John Henry McCann in 1939 even argued that a sexual assault on a young girl was less serious than that on a
woman because a girl's innocence and ignorance about sexual matters
protected her from fully understanding her violation. "This kind of attempt to rape," he asserted, "where the victim's size and age make full
consummation impossible; where the victim is not injured, and where her
very innocence protects her from long after effects of shock; and where
there is no temptation to other men to attempt such violence; is much less
dangerous to society than attempts on mature girls."[55] McCann's lawyer
may have been grasping at straws in an attempt to save his client, but he
may also have believed his argument would persuade a judge to spare
McCann's life. He was unsuccessful; McCann died in the electric chair.

Psychologists who study sexual trauma now insist that sexual innocence in no way protects child victims, but white southerners in this time
period evidently believed otherwise. Young girls' ignorance about sexual
relations may have inadvertently worked in black men's favor in another
way, as they frequently did not possess the vocabulary to articulate what
had happened to them. The "little schoolgirl" who James Smith allegedly
raped, for example, may have spared him the death penalty in 1917 because, according to court documents, "it is questionable as to whether or
not she really knew or had reason to observe" what rape was. "Had the
little girl been keenly alive to what such a thing was . . . there is hardly a
question that the sentence would have been death."[56] These young girls, if
not entirely innocent of sexual matters, were surely unable to understand
whites' beliefs about the devastating nature of black men's crimes on
white females.

The rhetoric suggested that the magnitude of the damage an assault
inflicted on a woman was directly related to her place in the social order
and to her position as the repository of white civilization and racial purity.
According to popular view, an assault by a black man defiled a woman's
virtue and tarnished her whiteness. In reality, evidence suggests that
white men considered that the degree of harm done to the victim was

related to how the assault affected a white woman's ability to perform her accepted social role in the community. Evidence that an assault victim was able to fulfill her social role after the incident could prompt officials to conclude either that the assault was less severe than originally thought or that the harm done to her had dissipated. Either argument could be used in favor of black men's release.

Few legal records provide information about a victim's later actions, especially after the jury reached its verdict. Clemency papers occasionally hint about white women's lives and reputations in the community. Court-house records, such as wills and marriage records, also give faint clues about white women's experiences after the conclusion of a trial. County marriage records might indicate the victim married. In cases in which there is no record of a subsequent marriage, however, it is impossible to determine a woman's later marital status. Moreover, for married women, it is difficult to determine whether or how being the victim of an assault affected her and her husband's marriage relationship. One detective in-vestigating sex crimes in the 1950s noted in a popular article that it was not unusual for the husband of a rape victim to look "at his wife with a distaste he could not stifle." He went on to speculate "that some women might have been so fearful of their husbands reactions that they felt it wiser to keep their woes to themselves."[57] For single white women com-ing of age in the first half of the twentieth century, however, eventual marriage was the expected life trajectory, and, in the popular imagination, being wives and mothers were women's most exalted roles. Many people believed that a woman who had been the victim of a rape by a black man was tainted or "ruined," making her an undesirable marriage partner. This view may account for the tendency of juries to convict men accused of assaulting young girls of attempted rape rather than rape.

Some records, however, contain statements officials made in favor of the release of convicted black men that suggest that the harm white women experienced as victims was not "worse than death" but in fact transitory. Their statements stemmed not from any conversations with the women themselves but rather from information about their lives after the assault. In several cases, officials cited the victim's eventual marriage, and even childbearing, as evidence that the crime was not as severe as orig-inally thought. Officials did not say so directly, but in the decision to release Bernard Fleming, who was convicted of rape and sentenced to life in prison, they pointed out that even though the victim lived in the area, she had since married. Indeed, this information overrode her father's opposition to Fleming's release.[58] Similarly, officials noted that the white victim of Loo Rooster Jarvis had since married and had two children, though they decided to delay his release because of his mental instability.[59] In the eyes of white men around them or of those they married, women who were raped and were able to live respectable lives and fulfill their expected social roles afterward demonstrated that the damage of rape had faded. If a victim's family, a microcosm of society, could carry on, then severe punishment was not necessary to exorcise a black man's misdeeds. If an assault had not disrupted the accepted social order because the victim remained integrated in white society, then the convicted assailant's release would not threaten the social order either.

White women's claims of assault themselves, however, threatened the social order in an entirely different way. White women's accusations forced white men to fulfill their rhetorical promises of protection by exacting retribution against accused black men. At the same time, an accusation represented an implicit rebuke of white men, who had failed in their duty to keep white women safe from black men. In the face of white men's failure, according to the code of chivalry, white women could demand and compel action in defense of their honor and virtue, placing them, albeit temporarily, in control of white men's actions. This temporary power inverted the traditional social order. In most cases, white men accepted this temporary reversal, belatedly upholding their duty as white men by convicting the black men white women accused. Nevertheless, throughout the legal process, white men sought to contain the implications of white women's accusations. White fathers, husbands, and law enforcement officials manipulated women's testimony and pressured women to identify particular black men as their assailants. The ability of white men to shape white women's accounts of assault and, as will become more clear in subsequent chapters, their ability to act as final arbiters over white women's behavior, restored a gender hierarchy disrupted by white women's accusations. Indeed, by provoking chivalry, white women learned that the key to the sheltered arena of white womanhood remained in white men's hands.[60]

White women may have been viewed as in need of protection, but their actions in the face of assault contradicted their image of weakness and dependency. Women often fought back when they believed black men threatened violence. Some leveled weapons at intruders; some struggled in hand-to-hand combat. A thirteen-year-old girl in North Carolina successfully fought off her assailant after he snatched her up from her bed and carried her to the woods.[61] Other women grabbed the handiest defensive weapons they could find, battering their assailants with axes, sticks, handbags, guns, and even their own brute strength. At her home, Mrs. Vick Fuller tussled with a black man who, armed with a pistol, demanded money; she eventually "threw" him out of her front door. She quickly locked the door and called for help to her neighbors from her window.[62] Still other women used ingenuity to resist their attackers. While Judith Alexander struggled against her rapist in 1956, she managed to lift her phone off the receiver in the vain hope that someone on the party line might hear the assault and come to her rescue. After the rape, when her assailant searched her house for money, she told him she would cash a check for $100 and have it for him the next day. Her ploy failed to work, as Junius Henderson Dandridge did not return and was not apprehended for several days, but news reports celebrated Alexander's "shrewdness" nonetheless.[63]

Reports of these kinds of incidents celebrated the "plucky" women who managed to foil attackers and were familiar fare in Virginia's newspapers throughout the period.[64] Rather than merely lamenting episodes of black men assaulting white women, newspapers applauded women who shed supposed female passivity and used violence or quick wits in their own defense. Such stories both entertained readers and instructed women on how to defend themselves. Their actions celebrated or not, when faced with an assailant and fearing a sexual attack, many women had little choice but to muster their physical resources against the attack. Women were most vulnerable to all kinds of crime when their fathers, sons, and husbands were absent. Many women recounted efforts by their assailants to ascertain whether protection was nearby and described the various strategies would-be assailants used to determine that a husband was away. Mrs. W. F. Adams of Richmond, Virginia, whose husband was at work, was in her kitchen when a black man came to her door, ostensibly begging for food. Seeing no one else with her, he knocked her down and robbed her.[65] A white woman in Asheville, North Carolina, was attacked after her husband left to go to the store.[66] Mrs. Frank Railey was forced to defend herself for a different reason: newspapers described her husband as "feeble." Hearing a noise at night, she got up to investigate because he could not. She encountered a black man at the door who dragged her into the yard and shot her three times.[67] These instances revealed not only women's vulnerability but also some black men's ingenuity. They confirmed whites' fear that blacks' shrewdness emerged most clearly in criminal behavior. Perhaps more disconcerting for whites, these incidents suggested that black men possessed a degree of intelligence, an "evil genius" committed to immoral rather than noble purposes.

Regardless of the success with which white women thwarted attacks, their experiences proved that white men's protection could be unreliable. Indeed, legal officials assumed that the mere presence of a white man was sufficient to frighten away most black men willing to attempt an assault. In authorities' view, when faced with black assailants, white men would, by definition, defend a white woman, even at the risk of their own lives. Consequently, white officials interpreted the presence of an able-bodied white man during a reported assault as strong evidence that no crime had in fact occurred. A case from 1943 provides an apt example. Viola Miller and her husband, Ralph, accused Samuel Legions, a black man, of break-ing into their bedroom while they slept. They both testified that Legions ordered Ralph Miller to remain in the bedroom and to quiet the couple's crying infant while Legions took Viola Miller into the kitchen and raped her. Legions was convicted and sentenced to death. He appealed his con-viction to the Virginia Supreme Court. In its decision, the court wrote that the fact that there was "no resistance from either the prosecutrix or her husband, except the ineffectual and feeble efforts of the latter . . . does such shocking violence to any righteous conception of human conduct as to be unbelievable even to the most credulous and naïve."[68] Basing their deci-sion on the assumption that all white men would fight to the death to prevent their wives from being assaulted by black men, the court con-cluded that the husband's presence at the scene of the crime sufficiently undermined the Millers' account of rape to justify Samuel Legions's ac-quittal. Throwing out his conviction, the court affirmed the equation of white men's presence with protection.[69]

For most women, however, white male defenders were nowhere to be found. The absence of male protection in most of these cases reveals a larger conflict in the rhetoric surrounding chivalry and white woman-hood. When white women accused black men of assault, they implicitly accused white men of failing to provide adequate protection, a fundamen-tal breach of white men's patriarchal duty. More troubling, however, was the view that in assaulting white women, black men were, in effect, point-ing out, and even capitalizing on, the inadequacies of white men. Had white men been present, these cases suggested, no assault would have occurred. Yet, in practice, the code of chivalry did not insist that white men consciously work to prevent black men's assaults on white women, other than through the supposed deterrent of severe punishment or lynching. The code of chivalry merely promised retaliation when black men's ac-tions brought white men's failures to light. Little wonder white men re-acted so violently.

White men's draconian responses to many alleged assaults may have stemmed in part from guilt created by the inherent paradoxes of segregation. White men's economic interests and their sense of honor often came into conflict. White men frequently scaled rhetorical heights expounding their sacred duty to protect their women, occasionally even placing it above their citizenship in importance. The *Richmond Times-Dispatch*, in condoning the lynching of William Page (described in Chapter 1), applauded the victim's father, who led the lynch mob, as "a staunch old Virginian who places the safety of his womenfolk first and the majesty of the commonwealth second." His economic concerns, however, seemed paramount; he employed Page on his farm, creating the opportunity for Page to encounter his daughter.[70] Despite the importance that protecting white women played in forming white men's racial identity, and despite the danger that all black men supposedly presented to all white women, white husbands and fathers continued to act in ways that theoretically put their wives and daughters at risk. They employed black men as laborers, left their wives and daughters alone—or worse, with only black farmhands—on isolated farms, and allowed day-to-day interactions on country roads, on city streets, and in local stores.

The case of Will Finney, in 1908, is another example of the consequences of white men's economic decisions. Local whites considered Finney to be "a dangerous man to be running around loose" and "a mean negro," yet the father of the eight-year-old girl he was convicted of assaulting still chose to employ him on his farm, allowing direct contact between Finney and his wife and daughter.[71] Many white men would not sacrifice their economic well-being in order to prevent their wives and daughters from coming into contact with black men, contact that many white southerners believed could easily turn into violent sexual assault. Nor did they seem particularly willing to allow able-bodied laborers to languish in prison for their full sentences—it was frequently convicted men's employers who initiated petitions for pardon. Both Robert Price's petition for conditional pardon in 1918 and Alexander Garrison's in 1919 were submitted by former employers who hoped to rehire the men upon their release.[72]

These contradictions, and the strains they created, conditioned white men's responses to interracial incidents. White men's sense of guilt and responsibility becomes clear in their efforts to hide assaults from the white community. In 1909, the *Richmond Times-Dispatch* reported a white woman's attack and included her husband's response: "Fearing that the details of a vicious attack on his wife might be brought to public notice, a citizen of N. First Street, near whose home a brutal attack was committed some weeks ago, refused to tell police of the occurrence." The assault only came to light when police went to the victim's home during an unrelated investigation.[73] The husband's reluctance to report the attack on his wife betrayed his shame and sense of failure, and perhaps his wife's as well. Although one might argue that this man's efforts to hide the crime stemmed from his belief that public disclosure of the assault would leave an indelible stain on his wife's psyche or character, it is also likely that he believed the stain of the assault would spread to him, establishing his own inadequacy as a husband and a white man.[74] The Virginia Supreme Court stated as much in its decision in the Legions case, in which it determined that the husband's failure to provide protection justified the acquittal of his wife's assailant: "In the presence of a tragedy that could mean nothing but disgrace and humiliation to the wife of his bosom, to himself, and to his children, he was servile as a slave."[75] The supreme court gave no quarter in this regard. By comparing the husband's cowardice to slavish servility, the court effectively stripped him of his whiteness. Chivalrous valor, after all, represented the essence of white masculinity and white supremacy.

While an accusation of assault tacitly acknowledged white men's impotence in the face of hypersexual black men (a double blow to their white masculinity), it simultaneously demonstrated the power of women's whiteness at its height. Under the right conditions, virtually any action by a black man toward a white woman, however innocent, could land black men in serious jeopardy. Through their identification of black assailants, violated white women demanded that white men restore their honor through a conviction and a stiff sentence.[76] White men generally acceded to white women's demands. Although any assault represented white men's inadequate protection, retribution enabled white men to fulfill their promise of protection retroactively, either through lynching or through the legal system. Each assault justified Jim Crow and the vigilantly maintained color line. Nevertheless, white women's power, even after an assault by a black man, was not absolute. Once a woman made an accusation, she lost control over the description of events that she alone experienced. White men reclaimed their position atop both the racial and gender social order by controlling the meaning, and even the content, of white women's narratives of assault and limiting the degree of protection that compromised white women could expect. They did so at the same time they appeared to be defending white women's honor through the courts, further buttressing segregation as a rational and progressive, if patriarchal, solution to the "Negro problem."

To see their accused assailants brought to justice, white women relied on a criminal justice system controlled by white men. White women's own words and experiences could be the catalyst for punishment, but in the process of investigation and criminal trial, women's voices were drowned out by the legal system. Well before trial, white men as husbands or as legal authorities manipulated and at times even disregarded white women's statements about their assaults. The process of finding and identifying the assailant was the most likely context for conflict between victims and white men. Fannie Chenault, who was assaulted in Richmond in 1914, for example, discovered that police increasingly doubted her story the longer she was unable to identify a suspect. When newspapers reported as much, she named the next suspect brought before her as her assailant, even though she had previously rejected him as the right man. The man was eventually acquitted by a jury because of doubts about the accuracy of her identification.[77] That same year, Lizzie Skiles expressed uncertainty about whether Clarence Nixon was the man who had raped her while her husband was away, as did her mother who witnessed the assault. As her husband later told the defense attorney, faced with their indecision, he "got behind them and made them come up" and identify Nixon as the assailant. As a result of that uncertain identification, Nixon was convicted, sentenced to death, and eventually executed.[78]

Once forced to identify Nixon, Skiles played her part and testified against him. Indeed, once the trial concluded with Nixon's death sentence, she countered efforts by local whites to have the sentence commuted. She insisted that "the nature of the crime is such that executive clemency could not be considered if you are convinced as to his guilt. The jury having passed sentence, it remains with you to sustain the jury who heard the case." White men, she implied, had a duty to vindicate her by seeing Nixon punished: "Even though he be a negro, I would not want him punished if I were not sure that he was the man."[79] Once Skiles conformed her testimony to white men's expectations, they made a great show of deferring to her wishes. The governor noted the importance of her request. He wrote that he "had carefully examined the application of Clarence Nixon and all the evidence you have produced in connection with a letter I have just received from Mrs. Skiles, and under the circumstances will have to decline to interfere."[80] If she played her part at trial, she argued, then white men's responsibilities were clear.

Lizzie Skiles's testimony was shaped by her husband's insistence that she identify Nixon as her attacker, making it difficult for her to resist. Other white women refused to go along. When Annie Ross reported that she had been assaulted in 1920 and Robert Williams was brought before her, she refused to identify him as her assailant. Police coerced Williams into confessing and then used that confession to obtain his conviction and death sentence. Ross, his supposed victim, had refused to testify against him. In fact, she had not even appeared at his trial.[81] Doc Bacon in 1903 was also convicted without the testimony of the women he allegedly attacked. She happened to be his former employer and insisted he was innocent.[82] In both these instances, white men assumed white women's prerogatives, reshaping women's narratives of assault at will to serve their own ends.

Annie Ross and Lizzie Skiles conformed to the image of respectable women, and when they claimed they were raped, their reputations demanded the deference from the legal system. Skiles's husband's insistence that she identify Nixon as her assailant also provided a necessary salve to his wounded pride. While the assault itself highlighted his failure to protect his wife, the conviction and execution of the man she named as her assailant were crucial means of restoring her family's honor, an imperative for her husband, even if it meant executing an innocent man. This perhaps explains her plea to the governor that Nixon's death sentence be carried out. The officers responding to Annie Ross's accusation, too, seemed intent on exacting retribution for their lapses in protection. White men reasserted their patriarchal authority by constraining women's voices once an accusation was made. White men amplified women's claims when they served white men's interests, and they silenced or ignored women's claims when they did not. Although white women had the power to accuse black men, white men alone claimed the power to punish them. In the same vein, white men determined the severity of the punishment black men received, thus controlling the degree of protection certain white women could expect.

When a white woman accused a black man of assault, she claimed social power by demanding redress through a legal system controlled by white men. But white women's social power came through their whiteness, whiteness that both made them vulnerable to attack and subordinated them to white men. White husbands and fathers exercised their social power by pressing charges, demanding that the legal system respond to the harm inflicted on their families. For poor white men with little economic or political power, the violation of their wives and daughters became a primary means of claiming the powers of whiteness, of allying themselves with their white betters. Counting on the power of white solidarity in cases of black-on-white rape, poor whites deliberately used women's ability to cry rape as leverage in unrelated disputes and as a means of claiming the privileges of whiteness. While charges of black-on-white rape presented white unity at its height, white authorities nevertheless balanced the need for racial hierarchy with the need to support class hierarchy. Even poor white men claimed their right and duty to defend white women by pressing their wives' or daughters' cases through the legal system, but white authorities circumscribed the power of their whiteness. They helped to convict the men poor white women accused, but they asserted their authority to determine the punishment black men received. No case presents this more clearly than that of Luther Tyler.

In February 1914, in Goochland County, a rural county east of Richmond, Luther Tyler was indicted for the rape of Pearl Johnson.[83] B. D. Johnson and his wife, Pearl, had lived in the county with their three small children for about two years on a rented property two miles from the nearest white neighbors. At trial, Luther Tyler was convicted and sentenced to death. In its petition to have Tyler's death sentence commuted, the defense pointed to significant inconsistencies in Pearl Johnson's account of the rape.[84] Aspects of her testimony apparently defied credibility. The defense asserted that the victim's husband was cutting wood 250 yards from the house in which the rape allegedly took place and that the sound of the ax could be heard clearly in the house itself. B. D. Johnson could have returned to the house at any time, and the sound of the ax "was a distinct warning to anyone that protection was near." The victim herself was surrounded by her children, who could have gone for help. There also was no physical evidence of rape, and Mrs. Johnson never received medical attention. There were no torn garments, no disheveled hair, no bloodstains, and no incriminating evidence on any of Luther Tyler's clothes. More significantly, she and her husband waited a full day before reporting the assault to authorities and only did so after consulting with a white neighbor, George Bowles. Instead, the defense went on, they "calmly retired that night without having aroused anyone to arrest or hunt out the *known* criminal. This has always been considered a suspicious circumstance." In addition, Luther Tyler had made no attempt to escape during the thirty-six hours between the alleged assault and his arrest, as whites assumed any guilty black man would do.[85]

The character of the Johnson family, the defense argued, reflected their general lack of credibility. By 1914, when Pearl Johnson accused Luther Tyler of rape, her family had become unpopular in the area. An affidavit signed by several citizens called B. D. Johnson's reputation for truth and honesty "bad" and pointed out that his father had been caught in a steel trap trying to steal corn from his neighbor. Pearl Johnson was illegitimate and "had no lawful father," and both the Johnsons were "people of a low order."[86] Their reputation made their testimony suspect. "It is manifest that a man of the poor character that Johnson bears would be more likely to swear falsely than a man of good character," the defense noted. "The whole conduct of this man is inconsistent with the claim that his wife was raped and her evidence would have been stronger without it."[87]

Luther Tyler's lawyer argued that the charge of rape actually stemmed from an unrelated dispute. Luther Tyler's mother testified that on the night of the alleged assault, George Bowles had come to her house demanding sex. He became angry when she refused: "He wanted to stay with me but I refused to let him do so, and he got mad and when he left he said 'You watch and see of something don't happen.' " Laura Tyler further testified that B. D. Johnson had come to her house shortly before Christmas looking for Luther. He told her "that he had heard that Luther had seen his sister [Eliza Johnson] and a man in improper connection, and he wanted to know who the man was, and asked me to find out from Luther and to let him know when I went to the mill." Laura Tyler also said that Eliza Johnson was "a common woman and so generally considered." Luther Tyler later denied in his testimony that he had ever seen "Johnson's sister with a man and never said anything to anyone about it," but Johnson confirmed under oath that he had gone to the Tyler home to find out from Luther the name of his sister's lover.[88] The charge of rape was a means of exacting revenge on the Tyler family. By refusing sexual relations with a white man and withholding information about the sexual indiscretions of Johnson's sister, the Tyler family had implicitly challenged Bowles and Johnson's white power. The charge of rape was the two men's attempt to harness the power of the state to assert their superiority.

In claiming Pearl Johnson was raped, Bowles and Johnson tried to use the legal system, through its commitment to protect white women, to assert their white masculinity. They demanded that their whiteness be treated with the same respect as that of elite men. Luther's lawyer argued that Pearl Johnson did not deserve the protection provided by the legal system and asked the governor to prevent Johnson and Bowles from using the courts to gain access to social power usually denied them as poor men of bad character. Punishing a well-regarded black family at the whim of insulted, "no-count" whites harmed the integrity of the courts and ultimately harmed the racial order as well. Legal officials had a duty to restrict white women's power to accuse black men because it could be manipulated by unscrupulous white men. As Tyler's lawyer wrote, "[A] woman tells a tale and men believe it. They believe because their passions and prejudices want them to believe and arouse them to act." Smith turned the trope of protection of white womanhood on its head, insisting that "while women must be protected, men, even negroes, must have some protection [too]." Requesting a stay of execution to allow time to prove Tyler's innocence, he concluded, "[S]ome day in the near future truth will triumph and the dumb mouth of facts now silent will show the innocence of the accused."[89]

Alexander Forward, the governor's secretary, was skeptical. The defense attorney attributed Pearl Johnson's charge to "an hallucination or perhaps, to a plot." Forward pointed out to the governor that "there was nothing against her character, but that she is illegitimate," and he found it "difficult to conceive why the woman should have said she had been assaulted when she had not, or of why she should have bruised herself."[90] As an illegitimate daughter with a poor reputation in the community and three children to support, her ability to choose freely her role in the charade would have been limited. Her bruises could have been the evidence of the means her husband used to convince her to claim rape to exact revenge on Tyler's family.

Though Forward was confused about the case, the governor was less so. He commuted Luther Tyler's death sentence to life imprisonment. In weighing the words of two disreputable white men and a woman who was illegitimate against those of a respectable black family, he chose the latter. In so doing, he conceded the need to prevent low-class whites from claiming the full measure of their whiteness and forcing the hands of their betters. Although the legal system acknowledged their power as whites by convicting Luther Tyler, it simultaneously limited that power by asserting that the violation of Pearl Johnson, if it even occurred at all, did not merit the extreme penalty prescribed by the jury. The state would step in to protect black men who found themselves at the mercy of whites seeking to manipulate white power for their own ends.

Luther Tyler was not electrocuted, but it was probably little comfort for him to anticipate life in prison for a crime that many thought never took place. The *Richmond Times-Dispatch* reported that he escaped from jail in 1920, but he was eventually captured and returned to prison. In 1928, Governor Byrd's office received a petition for pardon from Luther Tyler. His file includes reference to an affidavit signed by George Bowles in which he recanted his trial testimony, bolstering Tyler's claims of innocence and his allegations that the charges against him grew out of unrelated disputes. It is unclear whether state officials released him from prison.[91]

Tyler's case demonstrates the efforts elite whites made to protect white supremacy and to uphold class hierarchies. White officials may have made decisions based on their desire to protect their own authority. The rhetoric of white womanhood demanded that the state protect all white women, regardless of class or character, but this mandate created uncomfortable problems for elite whites. Their power, and the entire social order in which that power operated, was predicated not only on white supremacy but also on white elites' authority over poor whites and women. Considerations of class hierarchy required elites to limit the social power marginalized groups could demand because of their race. By convicting Luther Tyler, the court and the state bowed to white supremacy, but by commuting Tyler's death sentence, white elites checked the power of women and poor whites and presumably reassured themselves that the sentences black men received represented justice. Poor whites could not arbitrarily demand that black men be put to death and abscond with the power that rightfully belonged in the hands of legal authorities. By retaining control over black men's fates, legal authorities maintained their power at the expense of poor whites. Decisions that favored blacks over whites of "low order" might appear to have undermined segregation. Rather than threaten the racial hierarchy, however, these actions actually buttressed a social order whose structure united the privileges of race and the prerogatives of class position.

White authorities would act even more forcefully on African American men's behalf when they determined that white women had used the social power granted to them because of their race to illegitimate ends. When white men challenged the prerogatives of race they supported white women's subordination in the southern social order. Assaults on women occurred in a world in which, despite the best efforts of whites, the races could not be perfectly segregated. Many of these incidents involved people who did not conform to stereotypes: the accused black man was not always a lust-crazed, savage beast; the victim was not always a pristine example of southern womanhood. These realities created a gap between the heated rhetoric that surrounded any discussion of interracial rape and the disposition of cases in the real world. White men might talk of their duty to protect white women, and they might convict most men accused of assaults against them, but some women deserved more protection than others, and some women's bodies could hardly be violated. Ultimately, white men believed, some white women deserved almost no protection at all. On the other hand, white male prerogatives deserved protection at all times.

CHAPTER 4

Not Considered Worthy of the Respect of Decent People

The Color of Character in Black-on-White Rape Cases

Rape has historically been a crime in which the actions of the victim have mattered as much or more than the actions of the accused assailant. Scrutiny into the victim's sexual history, her activities on the night of the assault, her style of dress, her reputation in the community, her relationship, if any, with her assailant, were and are common experiences for rape victims, making many women reluctant to report the crime at all. Unlike in virtually any other crime, the victim's own claim of violation was rarely accepted on its face. Most states routinely required corroboration of the victim's testimony, and the chastity of the victim was always relevant at trial. Courts assumed, as did most jurors, that if a woman had consented to sexual relations once, she was more likely to consent to sexual relations in the future. Rape trials, in short, became public examinations of the woman's suitability as a victim. The law defined rape as carnal knowledge by force and without consent. In practice, the law made it clear that there were many women who could not be raped at all. Most women, especially those who violated accepted standards of morality, rarely found redress through the legal system.[1] Despite frequent avowals to the contrary, the treatment of rape victims in the courtroom and the seeming unwillingness of juries to convict men accused of rape suggest that society historically has considered rape a minor or, perhaps more accurately, a rare crime and continues to do so today.

One noted exception to this formulation of rape in the American legal system throughout the twentieth century, and even before, involved cases in which the assailant was a person of color and the victim was white. In those cases, according to the dominant paradigm, the legal system almost automatically accepted women's claims of violation and prosecuted their accused assailants severely.[2] The overwhelming willingness of whites to believe African American men had a propensity to rape white women stems from the relationship between sexuality, public power, and racial inequality after emancipation. After white southerners turned to the law and to extralegal violence as tools of racial control, the rhetoric of black-on-white rape grew to mythic proportions. The rhetoric contributed to the willingness of whites to accept claims of rape made by white women against men of other races. By the twentieth century, the cloak of chivalry supposedly spread its protection around all white women regardless of their class or character.[3] Cultural beliefs shaped legal practice. Presumably, the character of the victim no longer played a role in rape cases involving black assailants and white victims. Legal officials, law enforcement, and the public automatically and predictably replaced their usual skepticism and suspicions of women who cried rape with the assumption that all white women's accusations of rape were entirely credible as long as the men they accused were black.

White southern men, however, despite their rhetoric to the contrary, were not so willing to endow all white women with the unfettered power to accuse black men of rape. At trial, white men upheld their duty to protect white women and usually convicted the black men white women named as their assailants. After conviction, however, questions about a white woman's suitability as victim appeared in considerations for conditional pardon.[4] Concerns about the character of the victim indicate that white women who accused black men of rape faced the same skepticism that all victims of rape faced, though usually at a different point in the legal process and tending toward a different result. Their accused assailants still received punishment, though not to the full extent of the law. More important, however, questions of character illuminate conflicts over the degree to which whiteness entitled white women to protection. The construct of white womanhood was not the unquestioned possession of all women who bore white skin. Instead, a white woman's status always depended upon her abiding by the rules of racial interaction and the norms of appropriate class and gender behavior. Honor and reputation were continuously evolving entities, shaped by the perceptions of others.[5] In their discussions of black men's petitions for pardon, white legal officials decided that women who failed to abide by the rules of appropriate behavior could not claim whiteness and expect white men's full protection. Withholding or limiting protection from white victims ultimately was a means by which white men constrained white women's power to accuse black men, and retained control of white men's actions. The willingness of white men to shift the judgment to white women's actions rather than those of black men, as they did in most other rape cases, helped set right a social order knocked out of kilter by the assault itself.

Considerations for pardon, in essence, represented the efforts of some elite whites to "correct" the justice imposed by the trial jury, adjusting the punishment to reflect more accurately their perceptions of the seriousness of the crime. Assaulting disreputable white women did not represent a direct challenge to the system of racial hierarchy since these women were not representatives of white womanhood. Their behavior moved them outside of chivalry's protective shield. They were not the embodiments of white womanhood that the rhetoric imagined. More important, cases involving "disreputable" women suggest the malleability of white women's racial identity. A woman's whiteness was composed not only of her race and her gender but also of her class and reputation. It was not a fixed entity, but rather it shifted according to a woman's behavior and her apparent willingness to uphold normative ideas of women's appropriate behavior and morality and white ideas of proper racial etiquette. Rather than contradicting the racial ideology expounded in instances like the Scottsboro case in 1931, considerations about the character of white victims refined and reinforced white supremacy. Some women were more white than others, and some women's behavior blurred their racial status. To merit the full protection promised to white women, women had to perfectly perform their whiteness, behaving at all times as white women should. White women who failed to uphold expected standards of behavior watched the privileges they received as white women erode before their eyes. White men's unwillingness to inflict the extreme penalty in every case checked white women's seemingly unlimited power to accuse and compel white men's response. Denying some women full protection under the code of chivalry ultimately reflected white men's understanding that these women were less white.[6]

This chapter explores how white men examined and understood the role white women's characters played in cases of black-on-white rape. The experience of Fannie Chenault, a white woman who claimed she was attacked in 1914, provides one useful vehicle for examining white judgments about women's behavior before, during, and even long after an assault. Fannie Chenault's case is unusual in that debates about her worthiness as a victim occurred publicly in the media during the trial, and whites openly acknowledged that innuendoes about her compromised reputation contributed to the acquittal of the man she accused. Nevertheless, the case illuminates how white southerners determined which women were deserving of white men's protection. Chenault did not behave as a white woman raped by a black man should, and thus she forfeited her claim to white men's protection.

Fannie Chenault was a twenty-six-year-old, unmarried stenographer and Sunday school teacher who lived with her widowed father outside Richmond.[7] One night, on her way home from the trolley stop, a black man dragged her into some bushes and held her captive for more than three hours, repeatedly trying to rape her. He was apparently too drunk to succeed. When the black man released her that night, she immediately went home and told her father, who notified police. Initially, Richmond newspapers reported local outrage over the assault. The *Richmond Virginian's* headlines announced, "Negro Brute Assaults Miss Fannie Chenault"; the *Richmond Times-Dispatch* reported, "Girl Attacked by Negro Fiend." These accounts described Chenault as being in a "frightful condition, her clothes torn and disheveled" and "half-dead from her frightful experience."[8] Papers warned of possible extralegal violence, speculating, "Should the negro be taken in the county, there is little hope of his ever reaching jail, as the citizens are aroused to a high pitch, and declare that should he be caught, his body will grace the limb of a tree."[9] Local emotions apparently calmed, and within a day, eleven black men were being held as suspects, waiting to be identified by Chenault. Eventually, Chenault identified John Clements as her assailant. Curiously, he had been brought before her twice previously and both times she had failed to identify him as her attacker.

Three of Richmond's four daily newspapers followed the case closely, and their reports track Chenault's descent from being the paragon of white womanly virtue to a woman with questionable credibility. In the first reports of the assault, newspapers presented her as an exemplar of the attributes of true womanhood. One paper described her as pretty and later reported that "Miss Chenault is one of the most prominent young women of Henrico County, and is held in high esteem by all with whom she is acquainted."[10] As she exasperated police by rejecting the suspects they brought before her, friends insisted that it was precisely her moral and conscientious character and her fear of punishing the wrong man that caused her indecision in identifying her assailant.[11]

Revelations about her actions both during and after the assault, however, soon threatened her status as innocent victim. Police questioned her level of resistance during the attack, wondering why she did not call for help, attempt to escape, or attempt to grab her assailant's weapon at any time during the three-hour assault.[12] As she described her actions, she acknowledged how carefully she weighed her options: "I knew the cost of screaming, and I knew the cost of silence. I thought it through quickly, as I was forced to do, and I determined to keep quiet."[13] She was unwilling to die to protect her honor, as truly virtuous women were expected to do. That admission was the first of many strikes against her that ultimately rendered her unworthy of protection.

Once Chenault identified Clements as her assailant, much of the case's coverage focused on the defense strategy. The defense's case revolved around three axes: that Chenault's identification of Clements as her assailant was unreliable; that over the course of the assault, she had made an insufficient attempt either to resist or to escape; and, finally, that she had made conflicting statements regarding the nature of the assault. The question of her identification was the least controversial means of securing acquittal. Using this tactic, the defense could agree that Chenault had indeed been the victim of a brutal attack but that she had made a mistake in identifying the culprit. This approach cast no aspersions on her credibility, only on her powers of observation. The other two prongs of the defense were more problematic. First, by asserting that her resistance was inadequate, the defense implied that Chenault's failure to escape, or to draw attention to the attack, signaled consent. Miss Chenault, however, had already stated to the newspapers that she made a conscious choice not to resist. In making her choice between "the cost of screaming and the cost of silence," she opted for a strategy that inadvertently helped the defense's cause. The second problematic tactic of the defense focused on Chenault's conflicting statements about whether she was raped. She initially told police that she had been raped but later changed her statement. In Chenault's attempt to protect her reputation by publicly declaring that she was not "ruined," she, along with her family and her doctors, had inadvertently given ammunition to the defense.

At trial, the defense's most effective assault on Fannie Chenault's claims, however, concerned whether or not a respectable woman could or should use words commonly understood to be "vulgar."[14] The morning after the assault, Chenault had described her experience to Officer McMahon in detail. Because the statement was intended to be informal, no stenographer was present to record it word for word. In committing it to paper, McMahon testified at the preliminary hearing, he had substituted a few words for those Chenault used to make the meaning more clear and concise. He then gave Miss Chenault the statement to read, which she did, and she signed it.[15]

During the trial, most testimony surrounding the statement involved whether Chenault herself had used specific "vulgar" words or whether they had been substituted by the police. Although McMahon conceded that he might have substituted the words, he asserted that Chenault had consented to the words, as shown by her signature, which was tantamount to actually saying them. She testified that the police had promised not to use the statement against her, indicating her own concern about the document's content.[16] The prosecution countered the defense's contention that Chenault used the words on her own. One attorney for the prosecution agreed that "yes, there were some words and phrases used in the statement which I think an innocent young woman should not have known about and should not have used." But he argued that if Chenault had used vulgar words herself, it was only after they had been used by McMahon or they were the exact words spoken to her by her assailant during the attack.[17] According to the newspaper, the fact that the statement appeared in the first person, as Chenault's own words, left a lingering impression.[18]

At the end of the trial, before the jury was to begin deliberations, an attorney for the defense requested that Chenault read the statement aloud in court. The prosecution protested, but the judge ruled that the statement "was evidence and could be considered by the jurors any way they saw fit." Chenault took the stand and testified without "embarrassment" that the statement was substantially correct. She pointed out the words that she had not used and stated that she did not know the meaning of some of the words attributed to her. Nevertheless, the statement impressed the jury: "The jurors paid close attention to the reading of the statement, several of them leaning over and putting their hands behind their ears to catch every word. Others appeared to be surprised and shocked at some of the foul language used. The general impression was that the statement would seriously hurt the chances of the prosecution in securing a verdict of guilty carrying with it the death penalty."[19] Apparently, Fannie Chenault's knowledge of foul language, not whether Clements had actually attacked her, would determine his guilt or innocence.

The jury voted to acquit Clements. Jurors justified their decision to the local papers, remarking, "We found Clements not guilty because in our judgment, Miss Chenault, the one person on earth who should have known, did not appear to be sufficiently positive in her identification."[20] Prosecutors issued a statement asserting their belief that the evidence was sufficient for conviction, and one added, "Mr. Chenault [the victim's father] is heart-broken at the verdict and I feel very sorry for him. I think however, that the jury acquitted Clements on the grounds of lack of identification and not because it doubted the truth or sincerity of Miss Chenault."[21] Despite these assertions, the statement attributed to Chenault had a critical effect on her reputation. By placing her on the stand and asking her to speak the "foul language," the court literally put the words in her mouth. Her use of the words in the statement raised suspicions about her innocence, making the jury unwilling to convict Clements, even though he was black. The problem of identification added to this unwillingness but also provided a convenient mask for the jury, which apparently considered Chenault's supposed lack of good character in its verdict.

The speculation that Chenault used language that no truly innocent woman should have known represented the culmination of a swirl of allegations about her character, mirroring the character assassination experienced by many victims of rape. Fannie Chenault's experience indicates that regardless of their race, white women's character remained a contested issue among male officials. The attorneys involved in Chenault's case specifically stated that even though the man she accused was black, examinations of her character were legitimate avenues of inquiry. Attorneys on both sides of the case told the media on several occasions that though questioning the character of the victim was distasteful, it was nonetheless legitimate when a man's life was at stake.[22] Indeed, a prosecuting attorney petitioning for the release of a black man convicted of an attempted rape in another case justified examining the victim's character by insisting that immorality affected the credibility of the complaining witness.[23] Questioning the victim's character remained a legitimate aspect of black-on-white rape trials in the twentieth century.

In Fannie Chenault's case, the prosecution's assertion that the jury's verdict reflected doubts about the legal issue of identification rather than Chenault's "truth or sincerity" also followed an accepted pattern among Virginia jurists. White Virginians were usually loath to question openly the character of the victim in cases of black-on-white rape. Moreover, few defendants attacked their victim's character directly at trial because they were unwilling to risk the anger such accusations might provoke in a white, male jury. Most allegations about the victim's poor reputation appeared in petitions for executive clemency submitted by black men after they had served a portion of their sentence and were generally confined to the safely private considerations of state officials and court officers. Legal officials frequently gathered the opinions of community members when making their decisions, and white male officials and community members were more willing to strip the cloak of chivalry from suspect white women after conviction than at trial. Indeed, even unsubstantiated statements about the victim's character could be deciding factors in petitions for clemency. For "compromised" women in the twentieth century, the cloak of chivalry offered only temporary protection at best.

No Virginia governor stated on paper that his decision to pardon a black man convicted of a sexual crime against a white woman derived solely from allegations about the victim's character. In cases in which legal officials cited information about the victim's character, they usually followed the example of John Clements's jury, noting other issues as well, such as the defendant's mental state or the victim's inability to positively identify the assailant. These other issues often took precedence over character in the formal statement of a governor's decision. John Will Bond, for example, was convicted of attempted rape in 1906 and sentenced to eighteen years in prison. His former employer, E. A. Edwards, argued that Bond should be released because his crime was not aggravated and because he was not likely to repeat the offense on more prominent women: "The woman was a white one (but was of doubtful character) and I'm sure the boy was aware of the fact [and this] was one reason why he insulted her."[24] O. B. Wright forwarded Edwards's arguments in a letter of his own: "I fully realize the charge against this man is a serious one, if it was rape or just a scare by unbecoming language I am not prepared to say and what was the character of the woman is a question too. There are a great many white people here that seem to put themselves on a level with niggers."[25] The governor refused to release Bond until 1920, when the attorney who prosecuted the case wrote the governor that Bond's "mental state was *congenitally* very inferior."[26] Information about Bond's mental state was part of trial testimony, but in 1920 it reappeared to bolster a petition for pardon previously based solely on the victim's reputation. The governor pardoned Bond soon after receiving the prosecutor's recommendation. Bond's mental incapacity provided a more convenient rationale for the governor's decision than did the victim's reputation.

Similarly, legal authorities justified James Yager's release by pointing to questions about the victim's identification of him as her assailant, but allegations about her character played a role as well. Yager was arrested in 1922 for an assault on Annie Beahm, an unmarried nurse. The case initially caused considerable excitement in the community. The *Richmond Times-Dispatch* reported that people were milling about the streets discussing the incident when news of the crime spread and that Beahm's three brothers traveled from Washington, D.C., to aid in the search for her assailant, prompting officials to worry that their presence might lead to violence. Yager was eventually arrested, tried in a neighboring county, and sentenced to twenty years in prison.[27] Four years after the trial, legal officials petitioned Governor Harry Byrd to release Yager. Several officials argued that Beahm was mistaken in her identification. One suggested that the sentence alone indicated reasonable doubt: "The very action of the jury shows that they were not satisfied of the guilt of the accused. Had they been, there is not a doubt about the fact in my humble judgment but that they would have fixed death as the penalty in their verdict." He cryptically concluded that "subsequent developments" had reinforced his and other officials' opinion.[28] The prosecuting attorney agreed that the mistaken identification of Yager justified a pardon, but he also made Yager's appeal for pardon more powerful when he said, "I have also heard rumors to the effect that the moral reputation of this witness [Annie Beahm] was not what it might have been. Of course I have no positive evidence to substantiate these facts."[29] Fact or rumor, allegations about the victim's character were important enough to bring to the governor's attention. They sufficiently bolstered claims of misidentification that were apparent at trial. Governor Byrd agreed to grant Yager a conditional pardon after he served just under five years, the minimum penalty under Virginia law for a convicted rapist.[30]

The white male officials who argued for Yager's release and Governor Byrd, who granted it, rested their arguments primarily on the safe legal ground of identification. This tactic allowed them to avoid openly challenging the victim's testimony that she had been raped. They could argue that, in her hysteria—which is usually interpreted as evidence of correct identification—the victim had identified the wrong man as her assailant. In Yager's case, although questions about the victim's identification may have been raised at trial, the volatile nature of the case outweighed those issues. Authorities raised them after Yager had served a minimum sentence. Allegations about her character further diminished the credibility of her identification. Character was an important factor in the governor's willingness to grant Yager a pardon, but it was not a factor that he needed to acknowledge.

Issues of character appeared most frequently in applications for pardon, but Fannie Chenault's case remains instructive. It demonstrates that concerns about rape victims' credibility could surface at trial and that they revolved around a woman's willingness to conform to behavior whites expected both of respectable women and of women who had been assaulted. Fannie Chenault's behavior and reputation dominated the case shortly after she identified Clements as her assailant. Despite news reports that Miss Chenault was a Sunday school teacher and that she was kind, popular and pretty, well liked at work, and respectable, public gossip nonetheless sprouted. Though it is unclear exactly what the nature of the gossip was, it was enough to cause her family to issue a statement promising an aggressive investigation to find the origins of such reports. A family friend chastised the public for such doubts, chiding, "It is shameful that this case should have aroused any other sentiment than cases of this kind usually awaken—that of resentment of the atrocious treatment Miss Chenault received when attacked by her brutal assailant."[31] Eventually, the Chenault family hired attorney Isaac A. Diggs both to aid the prosecution and to protect Fannie's reputation. Diggs issued another statement to the paper, averring that "it is a fact that vile, slanderous and outrageously false rumors have been circulated about the young woman and there is evidence to show that they are absolutely false."[32] Rumors about her were so widespread that one newspaper took an unprecedented step. It published a picture of her under the headline, "Miss Fannie Chenault, the Victim of Assault and Unkind Opinion" in the hopes that "a faithful likeness of the young lady might make its appeal to the thoughtful. It is a remarkable thing that despite the fact that the defense attorneys dare not attack her character, and despite the testimony of her family physician and another doctor to her chaste life, a large number of otherwise fair-minded people have permitted themselves to be misled by gossip and suspicion." Fannie Chenault's picture showed her to be an attractive young woman, with her head held high, wearing a white dress.[33]

What cast doubt upon Chenault's moral character went beyond her use of foul language or vague, unspecified rumors that ultimately forced her family to take action. Considerations about her suitability as a victim deserving white men's protection implicated virtually every area of her life. Her behavior as a dutiful daughter came under attack. The defense suggested that Fannie Chenault kept late hours, which became a source of familial strife. The defense's cross-examination of her father focused on their intergenerational conflict:

> "Don't you know that you slapped your daughter's jaw that night and beat her for staying out so late?"
> "I did not."
> "Did you strike your daughter at all that night?"
> "No."
> "Did you ever slap her for staying out late?"
> "No."[34]

The *Richmond Evening Journal* reported that when "asked if she had ever been out all night she stated that she had several times been out all night." The media also speculated about her social life, suggesting at one point that she was involved in a relationship with another witness in the case who was considerably younger than she. Finally, there was concern about whether or not she was a virgin, despite two physicians' testimony to her "chaste life."[35]

In 1940, Lucille Hartless faced similar scrutiny of her relationships with men. Hartless agreed to go out with a married white man she had known several months at her work. In the course of their date, he took her to a secluded area and became "fresh." She resisted his advances, and he reportedly told her she could either give in or walk home. She decided to walk home. She later told police that as she walked, a car carrying four black men stopped alongside her and offered her a ride. Figuring there was safety in numbers, she accepted. She later told police that the men took turns beating and raping her.[36] All four men insisted they were innocent of rape and claimed that when they picked her up, she had already been beaten, presumably by her white date.[37] They were convicted at trial, and each received a sentence of ten years in prison, far below the maximum term of life in prison and far more lenient than the death penalty they might have received. Another issue apparently cast doubt on Hartless's claim that she was an innocent victim. She had left her job that night in the company of a married man, raising implications of adultery. Although she had claimed to repulse his advances, he had nonetheless taken liberties with her. She was a woman who found herself at the mercy of social attitudes regarding dating and sex, which tacitly blamed her for getting herself into such a predicament in the first place. If she had been truly virtuous, the theory went, she never would have accepted a date with a married man, and no honorable man would have tried to take advantage of her.[38]

Occasionally, the victim's poor reputation was sufficient to prevent the case from even entering the legal system. Luther Winston, for example, was arrested in October 1915 and charged with rape. The victim, Mrs. Nora Salmon, claimed that Winston had raped her in her home. Her husband promptly reported the assault to police. Several days later, the magistrate dismissed the case. Though the report on the incident in the *Richmond Times-Dispatch* gave no reason for the dismissal, it did say that "both Salmon and his wife . . . are well known in police circles and Magistrate Smith suggested that they better leave the county in ten days." Further discrediting the Salmons' character, the superintendent of the Children's Home Society of Virginia declared Nora Salmon was "not a suitable character to raise her child" and took custody of her four-year-old daughter.[39] The Salmons' previous record with local authorities destroyed the credibility they needed to make a rape charge stick, even against a black man. Nora Salmon's bad character outweighed her whiteness.

Lee Ernest Bell's case did not even merit the attention of the local media. He was arrested in 1925 and charged with rape. His sister, living in Ohio, wrote the NAACP requesting its help. J. H. Pollard, Bell's lawyer, assured the Richmond branch of the NAACP that their services were not necessary. He believed there "need be no alarm" since he did not "think it is a rape case as the character of the girl is doubtful." Pollard was accurate in his estimation; the case never came to trial.[40]

A white woman's suitability as a victim, however, concerned more than her previous reputation. How she behaved during the assault and shortly thereafter, in many eyes, constituted important evidence about what had occurred between victim and assailant, whether she had identified the appropriate suspect, and the degree of harm the assault inflicted on her. One aspect of Fannie Chenault's behavior that raised the eyebrows of authorities, and those of the public as well, was her seemingly feeble efforts to resist or escape. They wondered suspiciously why there had been no opportunity throughout her three-hour ordeal to escape or call for help. Her failing to even risk an escape attempt suggested that she remained with her assailant by choice, negating her claims of nonconsent to sexual relations. These concerns ultimately became less important than her behavior subsequent to the attack. The defense closely questioned her father about her demeanor in the hours immediately following the assault. According to the original report, Chenault made her way home after the assault and woke her father, who then saddled his horse and went to alert the authorities.[41] According to Mr. Chenault's testimony, he did exactly what would be expected of a man who had just found out his daughter had been raped. But on cross-examination his version of events did not seem so convincing. When he returned home from reporting his daughter's abduction and assault, he said, he found her sleeping peacefully. "She was not tossing or groaning was she?" he was asked. "No," he replied. That she was able to sleep peacefully after being horribly assaulted contradicted accepted assumptions about the very nature of black-on-white assault. Since most whites considered rape by a black man to be a fate worse than death, the idea of a rape victim being calm enough to sleep after her ordeal defied belief. Consequently, women who were not sufficiently hysterical or traumatized might find their claims of assault questioned. Officials supporting Vander Lee Gibson's petition for pardon challenged his alleged victim's story of assault for similar reasons. An officer responding to the assault stated that she did not "appear at the time to be outraged or particularly excited as, in my opinion, a white woman would be who had been raped by a negro." His statements were supported with evidence that the victim was a prostitute who was in jail on a drunk and disorderly charge when the assault allegedly occurred.[42]

Truly innocent victims of rape behaved as did Bertha Ferguson, who accused Alfred Wright of rape in 1912. Summarizing her behavior, the prosecuting attorney noted that Ferguson bore clear signs of assault: "[T]here was [sic] scratches on her face and neck where he choked her, she spat blood for several days afterwards from the choking, she made her screams immediately." She also behaved appropriately: she "soon afterwards went into hysterics, and was unconscious for several hours and had the Doctor's attendance."[43] Annie Beahm, who accused James Yager of rape in 1920, also displayed all the symptoms appropriate for a victim of rape. Four days after the assault, she remained under the care of a physician, who said that her condition was serious. When Yager was caught, he was brought before Beahm. She identified him by exclaiming, "He's the man who attacked me"; then she collapsed into a faint.[44] Her extreme reaction at her initial identification should have leant credibility to her testimony, making Yager's subsequent pardon four years after his conviction because of doubts about her identification all the more surprising.

In Fannie Chenault's case, more shocking than her ability to sleep was her behavior the following morning. Shortly after the assault, headlines in the *Evening Journal* announced that Chenault "Attended Church Day after Crime" and referred to the "unprecedented action" as "a shock to her family." In response, she said that "she considered it her Christian duty to be with her [Sunday school] class that morning." Two days later, it was reported, she clarified her position: "Miss Chenault told Officer Hardy that she was so nervous Sunday morning that she did not fully realize the situation; otherwise she would not have attended church."[45] The public's shock about her church attendance grew out of Virginians' expectations about the shame all victims of rape supposedly felt. The public's horrified surprise, however, also grew out of public understanding of what actually occurred between Chenault and her attacker. Though no newspaper reported it directly, all assumed, as their readers likely did, that having been held for three hours, Miss Chenault had undoubtedly been raped. Reports called the assault "brutal," "horrible," and an "atrocity" and noted that her clothing was torn, that he "mistreated" her, and that her assailant would be brought up on a "capital charge"—all implying rape.[46] Then the story changed. Richmond newspapers covering the assault reported that Chenault's doctor had issued a statement that Clements, by now arrested and identified as her assailant, had not raped her; he had "failed to accomplish his purpose."[47] Her doctor insisted that any statements she had made previously to the police were because of her ordeal. "Under the circumstances it would have been impossible for Miss Chenault to have given an accurate account of what occurred," he argued.[48] On the stand, Chenault attempted to clear up the confusion regarding her original statement that she had been raped. According to the *Richmond Evening Journal*, she testified that "[a]t the time she had not known actually what constituted an accomplished assault, but had since ascertained. Dr. Collins had informed her in several points in regard to which she had made different statements through ignorance."[49]

This statement on the stand revealed much about Chenault. When she attended church, the community wondered how she could have physically managed to get herself to church if she had been so mistreated? Her testimony on the stand indicated that she was able to attend church because she had not been so mistreated.[50] But the community also wondered how she could show her face in church after being the victim of a rape. A woman who was raped, who was *truly violated*, would have been too humiliated to appear in church, defiling a house of worship with her defiled body. Chenault's only defense to this charge was ultimate purity and innocence: she did not even know what constituted rape, and she could not know that she should not show her face. Her appearance in church thus proved her innocence, making her free from the taint that would have ruined her if she actually had been raped by an African American man. News reports conceded this possibility: "What appeared to have been a mistake in her going to church the next day, upon consideration by any reasonable person, shows too plainly it was the providence of God to let all who will see that she had not been the victim of his most vile designs. Had he accomplished his purpose, she could never have been physically able to have gone to her place of worship where she had always found her greatest pleasure."[51] That Chenault faced criticism for attending church after being assaulted suggests not only the degree of public humiliation rape victims experienced but also how their every move after the assault was scrutinized for compliance with popular expectations of the aftereffects of rape. Apparently, to achieve retribution against a rapist, the victim could risk no "mistakes" in her behavior.

Though the church controversy receded, Chenault failed to behave with the shame and humiliation demanded by the public. Reports described Chenault at the preliminary hearing as seeming "to take a lively interest in the proceedings," and as appearing not "to mind the stares of the crowd."[52] In their reports of her testimony on the second day of the hearings, newspaper articles continued to cast her simultaneously as victim and as seasoned celebrity. Alert, interested, and not much ashamed of what had happened to her, Fannie Chenault appeared to be enjoying her notoriety. And notoriety she had, for "[t]he courtroom and the corridors of the courthouse were packed with curiosity seekers."[53]

As the proceedings continued from June to October, public interest did not abate. Newspapers became more frank about the motive for the crowd's interest: "Many of those present came out of idle curiosity in anticipation of hearing Miss Chenault relate the details of the alleged crime."[54] According to the *Times-Dispatch*, many attended "merely to get a 'thrill' or to hear the sensational features of the case exploited in open court."[55] The *Evening Journal* identified who these "thrill" seekers were: "forty or fifty young men who were waiting to hear Miss Chenault testify."[56] Her story had become folk pornography, and she was the object of titillated male attention.[57] This was not the shrinking, frail, white woman whose assailant should be lynched to spare her the ordeal of a trial. To observers, it appeared as though the trial was no ordeal for her at all. In other words, she did not adequately perform her whiteness and thus lost the protection seemingly guaranteed to her by the color of her skin. Questions about Chenault's behavior became consuming enough to justify the acquittal of the man she named as her assailant. After Clement's acquittal, the case quickly disappeared from the newspapers. The remaining records are silent as to how Chenault's experience affected her subsequent status. For other white women, their behavior was scrutinized long after the trial.

Rape victims' later failure to abide by the norms of middle-class morality often justified the release of their convicted assailants, even years after the crime. Wilson Allen, for example, was convicted of an attempted rape of seventeen-year-old Maggie Storm in 1916 and sentenced to eighteen years in prison. Eleven years later, the current commonwealth's attorney, William B. Sanders, wrote the governor expressing his belief that Allen had been sufficiently punished. He came to this conclusion because subsequent revelations had caused him to have doubts about the truthfulness of the victim's testimony. The attorney learned that three years after Allen's conviction, Storm, whom he described as "a great big Buxom unmarried young white woman," had opened a "bawdy house," a development, he argued, that tarnished the reliability of her initial testimony: "Taking [this] into consideration, I had serious doubts whether during the trial she told the whole truth. Of course I realize that the law does not permit a man to assault a lewd woman, at the same time her lewdness if it exists can always be shown by the defense in cases of this nature in order to affect the credibility of the testimony of the prosecutrix." Storm's later actions called into question her claim to innocence and, by extension, to white men's protection. More important, despite the jury's verdict defining her as an innocent victim, she remained suspect to male legal officials. When her behavior failed to conform to that of a true victim, they were willing to use their authority to seek the release of her convicted assailant. As Sanders wrote, "I just felt . . . that this man had been sufficiently punished; and I arrived at this conclusion from what I heard at the trial of this case and what I learned about the woman afterwards."[58] The governor declined to release Allen because he had made several attempts to escape from prison, but he did agree to shorten his sentence.

John Boone fared a little better. He was convicted of attempted rape in 1900 and sentenced to sixteen years in prison. After Boone served six years of his sentence, the presiding judge and the prosecuting attorney wrote to Governor Swanson requesting Boone's pardon. At trial, the defense had argued that the interaction between the defendant and the prosecuting witness was a case of prostitution rather than attempted rape. By 1906, both the judge and the commonwealth's attorney at trial agreed: "Since this trial it has become well known that this Mrs. Fulford [the victim], who had not long lived in the county at that time, was a most disreputable character, who afterwards created much trouble in the neighborhood. Beleiving [sic] that on this account her word was unreliable, and that it was really a case of solicitation, and not attempt at rape, we think that the sentence of sixteen years found by the jury, was too great, and that the prisoner should now be pardoned."[59] Significantly, at trial, the jury, with little knowledge of Fulford's character or reputation, had judged her testimony to be credible. It was only after she had developed a reputation that her testimony became unreliable. Governor Swanson granted the request for pardon, and Boone was released. Years after the conviction of their assailants, both Maggie Storm and Mrs. Fulford lost the advantage their whiteness gave them.

Certainly women like Maggie Storm and Mrs. Fulford were not the paragons of white female virtue that the rhetoric of white womanhood invoked. That they resorted to prostitution across color lines demonstrates their position at the lowest end of the socioeconomic spectrum. Class position of the victim alone, however, did not always accurately reflect her character. Fannie Chenault was routinely reported to be the daughter of a prominent farmer and from a well-regarded family. Nevertheless, poor white women did not receive the same consideration that elite women received. Virginia courts and legal officials did not go so far as to say explicitly that lower-class women could not be raped, but they did concede that raping lower-class women was not as serious as assaulting more elite women related to "prominent" men. Most black men accused of assaulting poor women still were convicted, but the class of the victim was a factor in determining the length of sentence and whether the convicted assailant was an appropriate candidate for pardon.

John Bailey was convicted in 1903 for the attempted rape of "a young married lady." The media reported excitement over the case, and Bailey was moved to a remote location for his safekeeping after the victim identified him as her assailant. He was convicted and sentenced to eighteen years in prison.[60] In 1914, Bailey petitioned for a conditional pardon because he was suffering from tuberculosis. Both the presiding judge and the prosecuting attorney wrote to Governor Stuart recommending that Bailey's petition be granted. The commonwealth's attorney of Sussex County confined his recommendation to Bailey's health. The presiding judge, however, remarked that Bailey was charged with an attempted rape upon a white woman "who was of a very humble station in life." Further mitigating Bailey's crime, the judge continued, the evidence "showed that no damage was done to the woman." After eleven and a half years, the judge felt the victim's class had diminished the severity of Bailey's offense. Despite the recommendations of the legal officials who convicted

Bailey, the governor refused to grant Bailey a pardon, probably because his illness made him a public health hazard.[61]

The class status of white women also could influence the sentences that white juries would impose on convicted black men. Two black men convicted of "peeping" into the home of a white widow and her daughters, for example, were fined $50 each. The women worked at the nearby Viscose plant, and the *Roanoke Times* reported that they inhabited a house near the "colored settlement." Harassing poor women living at the racial margins without male protection did not represent a serious affront to the racial hierarchy, and the men received minor punishments.[62] The behavior of the neighbors who observed the men's activities and who eventually captured them for police is also instructive. The two men had been seen at the women's windows on several occasions before the neighbors took action on the women's behalf. But neighbors were not always so tolerant of violations of white women's privacy. In 1921, a black man seen peering into the windows of a prominent white woman's home was shot by her neighbor.[63] Apparently, violating elite white women's privacy was more serious than repeated violations of poor women already accustomed to living among African Americans.

Few cases made direct reference to the specific social or economic class of the victim as a mitigating factor. It is clear, however, that cases in which women's reputations were suspect, or where legal officials thought the women themselves had compromised racial boundaries, almost invariably involved women of lower status. Living at the margins of white society allowed for more interracial interaction that violated the mandates of Jim Crow. Women living in proximity to African Americans did not necessarily have the luxury of adhering to the dictates of white womanhood. For some women, poverty necessitated economic exchanges such as prostitution; for others it meant being unable to afford to live in all-white areas, which theoretically insulated women from contact with black men. For still other women, poverty necessitated wage labor, which could bring them into contact with black men that elite women could avoid. Poverty made women more vulnerable to assault. It perhaps also led potential assailants to believe that these women were not white enough or of high enough status to be included in white men's rhetorical promises of protection.

Virgie Thorpe's personal circumstances appeared to mitigate the offenses of the three black men convicted of raping her in 1914. Thorpe, described in newspapers as feebleminded, both lived at and worked as a cook in an almshouse. While there, she met Mort Hill, James Henry Bynum, and Lewis Hardy, who apparently gave her a drugged alcoholic beverage and raped her while she was unconscious. They were convicted of rape and sentenced to fifteen years in prison.[64] Six years later, after the men had received a conditional pardon, the attorney representing Lewis Hardy and Mort Hill wrote the governor thanking him for his decision. In that letter, he insisted that "whilst these negroes committed a grave indiscretion, they were innocent of the crime of which they were convicted." He then played down the issue of Virgie Thorpe's consent, writing that the men were convicted because of "the natural prejudice that the white race has against negroes cohabiting with white women, whether it with, or without, the consent of the woman."[65] Since Virgie Thorpe was apparently unconscious at the time of the assault, obtaining her consent was presumably impossible. Her status as a mentally disabled poor woman (and one who foolishly drank alcohol given to her by black men), however, downgraded the offense from a felony to a "grave indiscretion."

Albert Clark was arrested on a charge of attempting to rape thirteen-year-old Virginia Hotchkiss in 1932.[66] He was convicted of attempted rape and sentenced to twenty years in prison. Eight years later, the governor received a petition requesting that Clark be granted a conditional pardon.[67] Potter Sterne, the commonwealth's attorney, explained his views of the case to the governor and described the circumstances of the assault. Albert Clark had spoken to Virginia Hotchkiss on several occasions prior to the assault, asking if he could come home with her. She refused each time, not understanding "what Clark had in mind at the time." On the occasion of the assault, however, "it was very clear what he intended to do and was trying to do." Clark threw her on the ground, got on top of her, and tried to pull down her underclothing. To Sterne, there was no doubt whatsoever that if Virginia Hotchkiss had not resisted strenuously, Clark would have raped her. He was willing to consider, however, mitigating factors that might allow for Clark's release. He pointed out that Clark was feebleminded, which would make him less responsible for his actions because he would have little understanding of the severity of his crime or its possible consequences. But Sterne also conceded that the victim's class status, "in relation to the position in society, if that term may be used," made Clark's actions more reasonable. The victim's father was the janitor at the local high school, and he frequently had members of his family, including Virginia, help him clean the school in the late afternoons. Though Sterne would not cast aspersions on Virginia Hotchkiss's character, claiming that by all accounts she "behaved herself entirely proper[ly]," he nonetheless thought it possible that her social station contributed to Clark's conclusion that she might accept his advances. "I can see that it may be possible that Albert Clark felt differently toward this girl who assisted in cleaning up the school from the way he might have felt towards some other girl who was not doing that kind of work."[68] Sterne's speculations about Clark's motivations for attacking Hotchkiss were linked to elite white southern assumptions about class and racial interactions. He suggested that Clark's attempt at rape in part stemmed from his belief that Hotchkiss's low status made her exempt from southern prohibitions on sexual relations between white women and black men. The power of Hotchkiss's white skin should have placed her out of Clark's reach, but it was offset by her class status, which made her sexually available.

John Broaddus seems to have made a similar calculation, though he, too, was arrested and convicted for attempted rape in 1918. Broaddus, who, by all accounts, was an enterprising young man, went to the home of Nellie Richards to buy fruit trees and livestock from her father. Though Richards's father owned his farm, he also had to support eleven children. Broaddus admitted that he made sexual advances to Richards but insisted that he did not intend to use force. He apparently believed she might consent,[69] and her class status allegedly contributed to this belief. The jury's verdict suggests that, though they found Broaddus's behavior troubling, it represented a minor threat to the racial hierarchy. Though convicted of attempted rape, he received a sentence of only five years in prison. The class status of both Hotchkiss and Richards made their respective assailants' actions more understandable. These women were vulnerable in ways that elite women were not, suggesting to their assailants that a sexual relationship might be welcome, despite legal and cultural rules against it.[70]

These cases reveal the ambiguous position of poor white women who accused black men of assault. Juries accepted most of these women's claims of violation and convicted the men they accused, but evidence of juries' skepticism toward victims appeared in their sentences. Black men like John Broaddus received sentences well below the maximum allowed by law or were granted conditional pardon and released before they had served their full sentences. One judge revealed perhaps more than he realized about the confluence of class and character when he urged Governor Byrd to allow Henry Jones's death sentence to be carried out in 1929: "A good woman, the mother of several children, the wife of a substantial farmer, was horribly outraged in her own home. Under the circumstances . . . I felt it was my duty to impose the maximum sentence."[71]

Assaults committed against white women who were less "good" and connected to less prominent white men were considered less severe and believed to merit less severe penalty. Sexual assaults against poor women did not threaten the social order to the same extent that those against their elite counterparts did, perhaps because of lingering beliefs that poor women were inherently less moral.[72] That black men realized this also reassured elites that they knew elite white women were off limits.

Other evidence suggests that some white women themselves, aware of elite attitudes about poor women's character, believed that the legal system would not protect their interests. The case involving Lucy Powell is instructive in this regard. Powell accused Ad Armistead and Arthur Lewis, both black men, of trying to rape her on two separate occasions in 1915.[73] Both assaults occurred on her family's farm and were interrupted by approaching family members, and it is possible that both instances were interrupted consensual encounters.[74] Powell, however, was the illegitimate daughter of a woman who was herself illegitimate and therefore lived at the margins of respectability.[75] Regardless of what occurred between Powell and the two men, Powell's reputation made it unlikely that her case would elicit community outrage. Rather than go to the police, Powell took her mother's advice and accepted monetary restitution from both men. It was only when she believed that the two men had hired another black man, William Clark, to kill her that she took her case to authorities. Armistead and Lewis were subsequently arrested and charged with attempted rape. Both men were convicted and sentenced to three years in prison, the most lenient sentence allowed by law. The defense's instructions to the jury included a reference to Powell's reputation for being of "unchaste character," which offered further evidence of her marginalized status in the white community. The defense stated that if the jury believed that the state proved that the two men attempted to assault her, it must convict them, regardless of the evidence about her poor character.[76] That the defense even raised the issue of Powell's character in a case involving a white woman and two black men attests to the limited protection unchaste white women could expect from white men. The jury did its duty and provided legal retribution, but only to the minimum degree required by law. Perhaps fearing as much, Lucy Powell initially tried to negotiate recompense on her own, outside of the legal system. She turned to white authorities only when she believed her life was in danger. Significantly, later evidence supports the contention that a guilty verdict did not restore her credibility as a white woman in the community. Three years after Armistead and Lewis would have completed their sentences, census records reveal that Ad Armistead had returned to Fredericksburg, where the assault occurred, and was living with his wife and three children. He apparently did not fear for his safety, despite his conviction for attempting to rape a local white woman. Lucy Powell, however, was gone.[77]

Making insinuations about a woman's suitability as victim involved more than issues of her reputation for chastity. Legal officials' attention to where the attack occurred, as well as where the victim lived, located issues of a woman's character in the physical space she occupied. Common understandings of certain spaces translated into beliefs about a woman's respectability and her relationship to the full spectrum of appropriate norms and behaviors expected of white women. West Jones, for example, was convicted of attempted rape and robbery and received eighteen-year sentences for each charge, to be served consecutively. Eleven years later, Jones appealed to Governor John Pollard for conditional pardon. The deputy clerk at the Corporation Court of Newport News, where Jones was tried, wrote the governor to state his "impressions" regarding the case. He implicitly questioned the victim's character because of the location of the attack, which occurred on a *"poorly lighted street*, in the North West section of the city, one seldom used by people whose business was in the open."[78] Occupying suspect physical space, white women themselves became suspect as victims, even though in this case, there was no other indication that the victim's character was compromised. Pollard agreed to pardon Jones.

Legal officials also raised suspicions about the character of women who lived in questionable areas. In a world that was legally, ideologically, and socially divided by race, residing in a black neighborhood, or even a mixed neighborhood, moved some white women outside the legal system's full protection. Men accused of raping women who lived on the margins of white society were still convicted, but they were not given the extreme penalty, and the female victim's place of residence could be a consideration in requests for pardon. Walter Moore's request was one such case. He was convicted in 1914 for the rape of a sixty-four-year-old widow, Sarah E. Patterson. Patterson testified that she had known Moore since he was a child and thus had no difficulty identifying him as her attacker. Moore's lawyer, R. W. Kime, believed that the victim's lifestyle may have contributed to her rape: she "had for years been making her home amongst the colored people; I do not mean to say that she lived in the house with colored people, but she lived in their neighborhood." Refraining from directly stating that Patterson's residing outside the boundaries of white society mitigated Moore's crime, Kime nevertheless believed that where Patterson lived affected the case. The governor resisted

Kime's argument for another four years and did not release Moore until 1924, after his victim, Sarah Patterson, had died.[79]

Other cases also indicated that blacks and whites living in proximity troubled legal officials, echoing Kime's insinuations that inappropriate relationships across racial lines were inevitable in mixed neighborhoods. Sentences given to black men accused of violating racial boundaries with white women served as important warnings to communities to maintain a racially segregated social order. Solomon Douglas provides a perfect example. He was convicted of assaulting a white woman but given only a six-month sentence because he argued that the charge grew out of an unrelated dispute. Despite receiving little more than a slap on the wrist after being charged with a capital offense, Douglas appealed to the governor to suspend his sentence. In response to Douglas's appeal, the commonwealth's attorney wrote the governor urging him to deny Douglas's request, arguing, "She [the victim] is a white woman, and both live in a community made up of negroes and whites; and a pardon to this negro would have a bad effect on other negroes." In the prosecuting attorney's eyes, pardoning Douglas would encourage inappropriate racial relations, perhaps prompting other black men to seek relationships with white women. The governor apparently agreed with the commonwealth's attorney, and Douglas served his sentence. The argument was not that Douglas's sentence was just but rather that it was a means to affirm the cultural norms of the larger segregated community.[80]

Legal officials tiptoed around making claims about a woman's character based solely on where she lived. Failing to live in segregated communities was often a problem of poverty, not necessarily of insufficient racial pride. But some white victims, or even their families, also failed to maintain social segregation from blacks, which inherently tarnished their reputation as respectable whites. Raising suspicions about the moral character of a victim's family reflected then-current scientific beliefs that qualities like moral rectitude or "criminality" were hereditary. Harry Laughlin, one of America's foremost promoters of hereditary determinism and "racial integrity," noted the existence of a "shiftless, ignorant, and worthless class of anti-social whites" in the South.[81] In pointing out the moral character of victims' families, defense attorneys implied that the sexual violations of these women were not serious racial transgressions and indeed grew out of their families' inappropriate relationships across racial lines. These assaults, therefore, did not threaten the racial order. White women's suitability as victims, like their whiteness, was tied to their ability to live up to general prescriptions about white women's behavior. Standards about appropriate behavior naturally extended to their families' perceived willingness to abide by the rules both of segregation and of general lawful conduct.

Daniel Johnson was convicted in 1903 of attempted rape and sentenced to twelve years in prison. Johnson's lawyer, Micajah Woods, arguing for his release, claimed that Johnson's actions were really not very serious, "scarcely in the range of attempted rape—a mere fondling of her—*without force*," and thus his sentence was too severe.[82] In addition, Woods blamed the reputation of the victim's family and its violation of racial etiquette for encouraging Johnson's actions. According to Woods, "the prosecutrix is one of a notorious Shiflett class from Shiflett Hollow in the Blue Ridge and this colored boy was received and treated in the family as though he was their social equal and while perhaps he made some improper advances to this woman, I have never considered that his conduct warranted such a severe penalty." Contrasting the respectability of members of the Johnson's family, who were "among the most respectable colored people in the county," with that of the victim, Mrs. Lamb, who he claimed "does not bear a good reputation," he encouraged the governor to grant Johnson's request for pardon. Allegations that the victim had herself transgressed racial boundaries by "accepting" Johnson as a "social equal," a term that implied sexual access, as well as her family's general reputation, justified Johnson's early release. Johnson's lawyer subtly suggested that it was reasonable for Johnson to presume that, after being treated as a social equal, his advances would be welcome. Johnson was released after serving half of his twelve-year sentence.[83]

Social segregation, like spatial segregation, was crucial to maintaining white supremacy, but not all whites held themselves above blacks. John Will Bond's lawyer spoke to this fact when he insisted that "there are a great many white people here that seem to put themselves on a level with niggers."[84] Bond received a pardon after serving ten years of an eighteen-year sentence. Significantly, lawyers for Bond and Johnson admitted that both men had made unwanted sexual advances to white women. Nevertheless, these women placed themselves on the margins of white protection because assaults were the natural and inevitable outcome of such relationships. They, and perhaps their families as well, had stepped out from under the cloak of chivalry of their own volition. Such racial and sexual independence amounted to a rejection of their privileged status as whites and a repudiation of access to the full measure of patriarchal protection.

According to legal and scientific authorities, bad character was a family trait. Nevertheless, the victim herself did not need to demonstrate that she actually possessed a bad character for authorities to justify her convicted assailant's release. James Holmes owed his early release to the behavior of the victim's parents. Holmes was charged with the attempted rape of sixteen-year-old Swannie Lassiter in 1925. Newspapers gave considerable attention to the assault. The *Richmond Times-Dispatch* placed its report of the attack on the front page, with a headline, "Blackstone Girl Brutally Beaten."[85] Swannie Lassiter claimed that while she was walking home from work, Holmes leaped out at her, knocked her down, and tried to drag her into the woods, presumably to rape her. He was only stopped by her resistance and the appearance of a black woman, Laura Crawley, walking along the road. When James Holmes and his older brother George were brought before both Lassiter and Crawley, they stated that George looked like the assailant, but they were positive that it was not James. James was returned to the police station by his father when he confessed to him that he had been wearing his brother's clothing and had been at the scene of the alleged crime. Though Lassiter and Crawley could not identify Holmes as the assailant, Holmes confessed, pleaded guilty, and was sentenced to ten years in prison for attempted rape.[86]

Five years later, Holmes's father, George, a painter in Blackstone, petitioned the governor to release his son. The petition was submitted at the urging of the commonwealth's attorney of Nottoway County and the judge who tried the case, both of whom supported the elder George Holmes's petition and referred to him as "one of the best negroes in Nottoway County."[87] They based their support for Holmes's petition on the reputation of the Lassiter family. At the time of the crime, the family's reputation was less significant than its racial status. According to the petition, "the Lassiter family did not bear a good reputation at that time [of the crime], but they were white people, and their home standing was not considered in the case of the Commonwealth against James Holmes." Five years later, however, the court could no longer ignore that the family continually violated standards of appropriate conduct: "Her father and mother have both been convicted in Nottoway County within the past several years of selling liquor. Mrs. Lassiter has been arrested on several occasions on other charges. Her house has the reputation of being absolutely disreputable, and these people are not now considered worthy of the respect of decent people at Blackstone. Mrs. Lassiter is now in Nottoway county jail charged with murder."[88] The murder charge exhausted the community's patience, and legal authorities were now willing to release her daughter's assailant. The governor concurred, and Holmes was released in February 1931. Legal officials admitted that Holmes spent five years in prison largely because Swannie Lassiter was white, but her race was later outweighed by her family's disregard for the law. Significantly, Lassiter had left the area not long after Holmes's conviction, so Holmes's release ultimately hinged on the actions of her parents.

In considerations of executive clemency, the victim's character gained importance especially in relation to the characters of others. The reputation of Swannie Lassiter's family was poor in comparison to that of George Holmes, who forced his son to turn himself in to police. Similarly, Daniel Johnson's sentence was thought to be too extreme not simply because he only fondled a disreputable woman, but also because he came from a well-respected black family. A victim's and her assailant's characters were a compilation of class status, race, and reputation. They became especially salient when one party's character was judged relative to that of the other. Because reputation was a matter of association, and even heredity, local beliefs about the character of the victim's family could be an important indicator of the victim's character, and thus the convicted man's fitness for release.

Carrying on inappropriate relationships, sexual or not, across racial lines was often central to the poor reputation of a white family. Any white who was "on social terms" with African Americans possessed a bad character, and, in cases of black-on-white rape, a bad character became proof that the violation of the color line in the assault was minor. Once white women engaged in "inappropriate" relationships with black men, their right to refuse physical contact instigated by those men diminished. These women figuratively lost their whiteness. Engaging in social relations with African Americans placed white women on the margins of white protection because such relationships placed white women outside white space. It tacitly acknowledged that an assault or an attempted assault was the inevitable outcome of such relationships. Accusations of social intimacy were used by a defendant as evidence to mitigate his crime and thus make him a more attractive candidate for pardon. The fact that a charge of rape grew out of inappropriate relations across racial lines, however, would not guarantee a convicted black man's release. Conviction and prison terms represented warnings white officials sent to blacks about the consequences of interracial relations. Punishment also proved white officials' desire to control even nonviolent or consensual contact.

An incident involving John Johnson is a case in point. Not only were the facts of his case contested long after the jury handed down its verdict, but the decision concerning his pardon depended less on what actually occurred between the defendant and the victim than it did on how their relationship was interpreted. White understandings of that relationship, however, could not be separated from their reputations and the familial context in which the relationship developed.

John Johnson's case first came to the attention of the media when he and the fifteen-year-old daughter of his employer were reported missing. Authorities located them two days later, after they had been seen in a nearby town amicably purchasing supplies. The girl, who later claimed Johnson had raped her, appeared to be Johnson's willing companion. He was quickly arrested, convicted of rape, and sentenced to twenty years in prison.[89] Eight years later, however, Johnson began to write the governor requesting a conditional pardon, offering an alternative interpretation of their trip. He insisted that he had not assaulted the girl and indeed had only taken her out of town at her request. Johnson argued that the "sweetheart" of the young girl asked Johnson to facilitate the trip as a rendezvous, and Johnson speculated that the couple was planning to elope.

Johnson knew his audience, and he carefully tiptoed around the volatile issues of race and sex. In his first letter, he acknowledged his respect for "his superior, the white race," as well as for "what the white man's law does to negroes who even intend to abuse a white girl." Johnson insisted that his conviction resulted largely because of his race; the jury wrongly inferred that Johnson, as a black man, could not have innocent intentions toward a white girl. More relevant to his situation, he argued, was her reputation as a "bad girl" in the community. Two months later, Johnson wrote again to plead for the governor's intervention. He insisted that he was innocent of the charge, that he had been duped by the alleged victim. He was "under the impression at the time that she was absolutely decent and respectable . . . but it developed later that her character was none too good and she had probably been associated with colored men, and which I am convinced was her reason for later changing her story and saying I raped her." His white victim, he argued, had used a rape charge to cover her own, possibly interracial, sexual relations. Johnson also wrote that she was pregnant at the time and later married the white father of the child and that he believed this represented evidence of her unchaste character.[90]

After receiving a letter from Johnson's former employer, who insisted Johnson and the girl traveled to see Johnson's wife, who was a midwife, Governor Peery wrote to both the prosecuting attorney and the presiding judge requesting their opinions. Redmond I. Roop, the commonwealth's attorney, wrote that the facts given by both Johnson and his former employer contradicted the evidence at trial: "No evidence was introduced or hinted at tending to show that [the girl in question] had ever been intimate with anyone else, nor was she pregnant." Instead, he argued, Johnson had played on the victim's emotions, using the trip to see her sweetheart as a ploy to create the opportunity to rape her. Judge Gregory, by this point a justice on the Supreme Court of Appeals of Virginia, saw things differently. He professed himself unable to "reconcile" a "good many circumstances" of the case. For him, however, the purpose of the trip was largely irrelevant. The critical issue was the interaction between the victim's white family and Johnson, their black tenant: "The girl's parents permitted her to associate with this negro while he was a tenant on the farm of the parents. He was also permitted to be a guest and dine at the same table of the parents. In this way, he was almost a member of the family." The judge, referring to the testimony of the girl and the doctors who had examined her, said it was "proven beyond a doubt that on several occasions he had been guilty of immoral conduct with this girl, but there were certain indications which showed that it may have been by her consent." He argued that Johnson had been sufficiently punished and should be released.[91]

There was no consensus among Johnson and his employer and the court officers about what had occurred between Johnson and his alleged victim on their trip. The prosecuting attorney's statement denied assertions that the victim was sexually active or pregnant, though the judge claimed the medical evidence showed the opposite. These allegations may have been common knowledge in the community, and may have been sufficient to save Johnson from the death penalty. The statements of the judge, however, reiterate how important whites believed it was to guard the color line in white homes. The judge never intimated that Johnson was wrongly convicted, even though he suspected that the sexual relations resulting in the rape charge were consensual. The parents blurred the appropriate boundaries surrounding relations between white employer and black employee, and between a white family and a black man by treating Johnson as a guest. They thus created space for illicit interracial sexual relations to occur. Because the victim's parents were partially to blame for allowing a social relationship to develop, in the judge's opinion, Johnson had been sufficiently punished and should be released. The governor denied Johnson's petition without comment, so his final reasoning is unknown. His refusal to release Johnson suggests that, despite the actions of the victim's parents and the victim's possible consent, and despite the fact that no one could agree on exactly what had occurred between Johnson and his victim or how to interpret the evidence, his "crime"—be it rape, interracial sex, or inappropriate relations with a white family—was serious and he should serve his full sentence.

Character was not a simple issue. Accusers of black men benefited enormously from their status as whites, and a white woman's word was usually enough to convict the black man she accused. But often white elites judged how white women's actions accorded with their own idealized notions of behavior when white women accused black men of assaulting them. A guilty verdict did not guarantee a woman's place in the sheltered arena of white womanhood. Indeed, her credibility and innocence remained only as long as she conformed to social standards. For the victim, the trial was never over. A white woman's reputation and her behavior before, during, and even after the alleged assault could influence the sentence a black man received and the length of time he would ultimately serve. Issues of character, weighted by white women's conformity to accepted notions of who or what constituted an appropriate victim, informed juries' and legal officials' decisions. A black man's reputation and the general character of his family played a role as well. Through their decisions, white men contained white women's power to accuse men of rape. White women who violated white moral codes or whose families engaged in inappropriate relations across color lines merited only limited defense. Considerations about women's class and willingness to uphold gender norms determined the power of their whiteness. Only when paired with respectability did whiteness grant women true social power and earn them the full measure of white men's protection. Issues of gender could cancel or temper considerations concerning race. The cloak of chivalry was indeed thin at the edges.

CHAPTER 5

Telling Tales

White Women, False Accusations, and the Conundrum of Consent

Considerations of character in cases of black-on-white rape revolved around public perceptions of white women's behavior, but they did not always include insinuations that white women outright lied when they made their accusations against black men. Nevertheless, the ability to accuse black men of rape gave all white women an effective tool for getting themselves out of compromising situations. "Crying rape" against black men fed into white fears about black men as rapists and thus provided an ideal means for white women to divert attention away from their own social and sexual indiscretions. In most cases, allegations that a woman falsified a charge rarely entered into discussion. In some cases, a woman's injuries or the wounds she inflicted on her assailant in self-defense made it clear that she had indeed been assaulted. Of course, there was also little doubt that a woman was assaulted if she had been murdered. In many other cases, whites evidently accepted the victim's account with little skepticism, as long as she could identify the appropriate suspect. White Virginians, however, did believe that white women falsely accused black men of rape to serve their own ends.

Those cases in which whites acknowledged women's duplicity illuminate another aspect of the paradox of segregation. Despite being structured around patriarchal control of women, segregation gave women one particular form of social power: the ability to accuse black men of rape. But with that power came the ability to abuse it. When white women did abuse it, whites eventually abandoned racial solidarity. At the same time, because white women used charges of rape to mask their own sexual indiscretions, indiscretions that the white community very well may have known about, the cases themselves undermined white pretensions about white female virtue. Despite the rhetoric of protection that accompanied these cases initially, the subtext of illicit sexual activity eventually rose to the surface in considerations of pardon. These allegations challenged both the purity of all white women and the supremacy of white civilization itself, of which female virtue was the ideological cornerstone. In the cases in which white women cried rape to cover sexual relationships with black men, white women's consent itself became a paradox. Theoretically, no white woman would ever consent to sexual relations with a black man, but white men constantly confronted the possibility, as well as the reality, that some white women freely chose black men as sexual partners. In the face of white women's inability or unwillingness to protect racial purity, white men called on black men to subvert their innate natures and step in to protect the color line when white women failed.

In 1906, Mabel Risley told police that she and her fiancé, Forest Gooding, had been attacked by a black man while they were walking in a public park after dark. Risley later amended her story, saying that the assailant had raped her while Gooding went for help. One week after the assault, Joseph Thomas was arrested on an unrelated charge. Risley identified Thomas as her assailant in a lineup, as did Gooding. Thomas was tried, convicted of rape, and sentenced to death.[1] The Virginia Supreme Court of Appeals affirmed Thomas's conviction, but a dissenting opinion raised questions about Risley's claim of rape. There was very little corroborating evidence, and in her initial statement to police, Risley said nothing about being raped. Justice J. Cardwell insisted that "the natural horror of this particular crime diverted the attention of the jury from a proper consideration of the evidence."[2] These issues justified the commutation of Thomas's death sentence to life in prison.

Twelve years later, the prosecutor in Thomas's case, Crandall Mackey, who was now a judge, argued that Thomas should be released. Mackey argued that he was unconvinced that Risley had accurately identified her assailant and stated that his doubts were solidified by a statement made by Risley herself. "When I talked to her last and asked her if she was absolutely certain that Joe Thomas was the man," he recounted, "she said as near as I can recall, 'What is the difference if he is not the man[;] it is one less nigger in the world if they hang him.' . . . I think that she was ready to identify anyone who looked like the man."[3] Her response troubled Mackey enough to argue for Thomas's release, though the governor refused his petition.

Risley's frank admission that she did not care if she identified the correct man, as long as the man held responsible was black, convinced the prosecuting attorney that Thomas was innocent. Risley's willingness to sacrifice an innocent black man, however, also raised more fundamental questions about her credibility. Mackey petitioned a second time for Thomas's release, and this time he shifted his focus from Mabel Risley's racism to questions about her reputation for chastity. He insisted that "there were circumstances in the case which cast a great deal of doubt as to whether Miss Risley was ever raped." He did not raise new information concerning Thomas's case, but he drew a parallel with another case. Shortly after Thomas's conviction, a young white woman who lived next door to Mackey accused a black man of raping her and shooting her escort. After an investigation, she admitted that her brother had caught her and her escort engaging in sexual activity and had fired the shot. Shortly thereafter, this woman married the escort. Mackey pointed out that in the time between Risley's assault and the trial, she and Gooding married. He insinuated that Risley cried rape to hide her premarital sexual relations. In Mackey's eyes, Risley was no longer an innocent victim requiring white men's protection. Instead, she was a conniving woman willing to use her power as a white woman to manipulate a racist legal system to cover up her own indiscretions. She had never needed white men's protection and she certainly did not deserve it. With the focus of the petition squarely on the victim, the governor agreed that sufficient doubt had been raised regarding Thomas's guilt. He was released in 1922.[4] Thomas's possible innocence alone did not justify his release. Only when questions about his guilt were paired with allegations that Risley abused her power as a white woman—abused her very whiteness itself—by manipulating social fears of black rapists was Thomas's freedom justified.

Risley's statement that executing Thomas even if innocent would result in "one less nigger" stripped the veneer from white legal officials' pretensions that their judgments in cases of black-on-white rape represented justice and likely accounted for officials' disgust toward her. Their disgust, however, also reflected their awareness that white women could use beliefs about black men as rapists as a tool to achieve to their own ends. White women could manipulate white men's worst fears to their own advantage. Indeed, the alleged victim in Thomas's case seemed mystified that legal officials were at all concerned about Thomas's innocence. Regardless of whether he committed rape against her, according to white ideology, the potential was there. In her eyes, trials involving cases of black-on-white rape were never intended to achieve justice. Her statements suggest that she believed she was well within her rights as a white woman to sacrifice a black man to save her reputation.

In 1914, Luther Tyler's lawyer astutely noted that white men's racial ideology granted all white women power: "A woman tells a tale, and men believe it. They believe because their passions and prejudices want them to believe and arouse them to act."[5] White women had the social power to manipulate white men through charges of rape because their accusations accorded with white men's beliefs about black men's innate natures and because an accusation allowed white men to exert control over the bodies of black men. Indeed, Joseph Thomas became a suspect in Risley's rape simply because he had been arrested on another unrelated charge, perhaps one for which there was less chance of conviction. For some women, crying rape was the path of least resistance when they violated moral standards, as some white men acknowledged. Crandall Mackey speculated, with no evidence whatsoever, that Mabel Risley accused Thomas of rape to hide her own sexual relations with her intended husband.

It was less likely that women would be accused of a false accusation at trial, though it was not impossible. When defendants or courts proved that women lied for their own illicit motives, the women faced public indignation. Dorothy Skaggs, whose case is discussed in the introduction to this book, claimed that she was hit over the head, dragged into an alley, and raped to hide her relationship with a married man. She eventually identified William Harper as her assailant; he was quickly convicted and sentenced to death. His lawyer immediately motioned for a new trial and produced numerous white witnesses who claimed that the victim was lying to hide an affair. In the face of considerable testimony suggesting that Skaggs manufactured a rape charge to hide her relationship with another man, public opinion turned against her. The defense easily raised allegations of previous drug use, as well as suggestions that she had cheated on her husband in the past, all of which appeared in the newspapers. At Harper's second trial, he was quickly acquitted. After the trial, she and a female friend who testified on her behalf were tried for perjury.[6] In the widespread publicity of the case, whites agreed that she was not a white woman worthy of protection. They not only denied her the power to accuse black men and condemned her publicly, but the legal system also sought to punish her for abusing a power reserved for respectable white women. One newspaper editor even questioned whether white women in general were sufficiently trustworthy to carry such power.[7]

Not only white women used charges of rape against black men. A white community could come together and use a charge of rape to exile an unpopular black man. Henry L. Taylor claimed as much when he protested the accusations against him in 1931. He was accused of attempting to rape a young white woman on a country road. The victim, Minnie Coombs, did not see her assailant because he threw a coat over her head, but she claimed to recognize his voice. Taylor was arrested when bloodhounds tracked him to his home.[8] Taylor insisted, however, that the charges were being "used as a means, or a cloak, of not only casting a shadow upon [him], causing him distress, embarrassment, and humiliation, but [also] upon his relatives, associates and friends." Moreover, he believed that the charges, and specifically the efforts by the prosecution to have him incarcerated in a mental institution, represented a vendetta "by some he is not liked in the community in which he lives, and that there is more or less a local clamor by some parties in that community that [he] be driven from the community without cause, reason, or right; and further that this prosecution is simply a device to accomplish such purpose."[9] Taylor's trial was beset by difficulties. The judge became ill after a day of testimony, forcing the dismissal of the jury. At a second trial, Taylor was convicted and sentenced to three years in prison, the minimum prison term allowed by law. The verdict was overturned because the prosecution failed to prove that the bloodhounds were purebred, and only the tracking ability of purebred bloodhounds was admissible in court. The court declined to try Taylor again.[10] Taylor reportedly died in his native Westmoreland County in 1956, so he was apparently able to resist attempts to run him out of the community.

Whites used accusations of rape to exact revenge on blacks who may not have been guilty of rape but who had offended whites in other ways. For whites who had little access to legitimate forms of social power other than the color of their skin, in particular, accusing black men of rape served as a trump card through which they could demand the help of more elite whites and the power of the legal system to pursue their claims. Making accusations against black men also carried considerable symbolic power. It represented an attempt by marginalized whites to assert their whiteness and thereby lay claim to the privileges theoretically endowed all whites because of their race. Accusing black men of the most horrific of interracial crimes—the rape of a white woman—became a means by which non-elite whites with little social power sought to invoke the power of their race to bolster their social status.

Elite whites, however, believed that using false accusations of rape as leverage in interracial disputes was an illegitimate use of white power and indeed also upset the social order. Leery of publicly undermining white racial solidarity, white elites usually validated poor whites' allegations by convicting the black men they accused. But powerful whites also acknowledged when poor whites called on white solidarity to further their own individual interests by giving convicted black men short sentences or granting them pardon. These decisions did not mean that black men received justice. After all, innocent black men like Luther Tyler and Joseph Thomas spent years in prison. Instead, the decisions on the part of elites represented efforts to balance competing social hierarchies—to contain the power of poor whites to play the race card and to discourage white women from using accusations of rape to hide their own moral failings. Elites let whites who used charges of rape or assault against black men to get themselves out of tight situations know that their efforts would not always be successful and would not necessarily provide an expedient route to white respectability or social status.

The actions of white women who made allegations of rape also concerned white men. According to them, white women of low status who cried rape used their charges to seize the privileges of whiteness that their class and sexual behavior denied them. Non-elite white women who violated the rules of segregation by engaging in sexual relationships with black men threatened white men's patriarchal authority by flouting white men's ability to control sexual access to women. White men contained these women by denying them full protection as white women. In response to women who cried rape, white men worked to blend racial control with class and gender control and to prevent suspect women from claiming the status promised to them by the color of their skin. In effect, white men barred some white women from using their whiteness to dictate the actions of their betters. They thus released black men accused by women who were seeking to hide consensual relationships and even ignored the claims of some white women they believed used charges of rape as means of revenge, as Calm Williams learned.

Calm Williams was charged with the rape of a fifteen-year-old white girl in December of 1945. C. Anderson Davis, the minister of a local church, in his request to the NAACP for legal aid, wrote that the rape charge stemmed from a dispute between Williams and the alleged victim. The girl, after borrowing money from Williams to obtain a hotel room, asked him to help her procure men interested in paying her for sex. When she asked Williams for an additional fifteen dollars and he refused, she accused him of rape. According to Davis, this was not the first time she had engaged in prostitution: "The girl has a very bad record. She has been all over the country with different soldiers and has been sentenced to the state school of correction twice." As it turned out, the NAACP's help was unnecessary since Williams was never tried for any crime.[11] Using a rape charge to punish Williams placed the girl entirely outside the bounds of white male protection, and officials ultimately disregarded her accusation.

Cases in which women used charges of rape as leverage in other disputes reveal another aspect of interracial relations. They occurred in the context of a hidden underside to segregated southern society. Though laws strictly enforced racial separation at the public and institutional level, poor whites and blacks often interacted in their daily lives. Williams's accuser apparently knew him well enough to enlist his aid for her work as a prostitute. Blacks and whites lived near each other, exchanged goods and commodities, socialized together, and formed intimate relationships, all in apparent contradiction to the dictates of segregation. Many of these interactions were not entirely dominated by racial hierarchy. Both parties maintained some control over their interactions. Nevertheless, when disputes arose between whites and blacks at the lower end of the social spectrum, whites sought advantage by calling for the support of elite whites. Using their racial status, poor whites could use charges of rape to enlist the help of elite whites, and the public institutions controlled by them, to maneuver for advantage or to exact revenge. Unlike in Calm Williams's case, when disputes between these groups exploded in charges of rape, they usually resulted in conviction. Black men could spend years in prison on dubious charges, but the legal system eventually justified release because of doubts about the motives of the accusers.

Court officials and even juries showed little sympathy for white women who accused black men to serve their own purposes. Women often received harsh censure while their male accomplices did not, as Sallie Sigman discovered when she accused Solomon Douglas of attempted rape in 1921. Sigman, a married woman living near Schoolfield, Virginia, in Pittsylvania County, charged that Douglas came to her door when her husband was not at home. "Not realizing that the caller was a negro," she opened the door. After being informed that Sigman's husband was away,

Douglas allegedly stated, "It's not your husband I want but you," and he proceeded to force his way into the house. Sigman ran and got her husband's revolver and shot Douglas twice. Douglas ran but was caught by police. Sigman identified Douglas as her assailant, noting that he "had dealings" with her husband.[12] In January 1922, Douglas was indicted for attempted rape but was convicted only of misdemeanor assault. He was sentenced to six months in jail and fined $100. He appealed his conviction to the Supreme Court of Appeals of Virginia, but his case was dismissed when he could not afford to have the transcript of his trial produced, and he was remanded to jail.[13] Douglas's acquittal for attempted rape and his minor sentence for an assault on a white woman, though not unprecedented, was surprising because Douglas was already a convicted criminal. He had previously been acquitted of murder but spent three years in prison on an unrelated conviction for attempted rape.[14] Douglas was also well entrenched in the criminal culture that flourished during Prohibition, as were Percy Sigman and his wife, Sallie. Douglas argued that their criminal interaction ultimately resulted in the accusation against him.

Prior to Sallie Sigman's charge of rape, Percy Sigman had been arrested and charged with violating the Prohibition laws. According to the law enforcement officials who signed Douglas's petition for pardon, "The prosecutrix and her husband had been suspected of being bootleggers by all the officers in and around Schoolfield for some time." Solomon Douglas was one of their regular customers, and he testified at trial that he had purchased whiskey from the Sigmans on many occasions and, on the night in question, had gone to the Sigman home and purchased a pint of whiskey for two dollars. He claimed he made no attempt to rape Sallie. At this point, Sigman had been indicted, and Sallie Sigman suspected that Douglas had turned in the couple to authorities. According to Douglas's attorney, she "saw her chance to get even with them and woman-like started this hue and cry." The Sigmans allegedly ambushed Douglas and shot him twice and then swore out a complaint against him for attempted rape. Though Percy Sigman was acquitted of the Prohibition charges against him, his sister-in-law was arrested several days after Douglas's trial with several gallons of whiskey in the car she was driving—a car that belonged to the Sigmans.[15] Douglas's attorney had very little sympathy for the Sigmans, and, ignoring Sallie Sigman's race, insisted her gender only exacerbated the depravity of her actions. "It is deplorable that people of this character and especially a woman," he said, "will resort to such low means in order to accomplish their heinous purposes."[16]

Few legal officials involved in clemency proceedings disputed the facts as they were set forth by the defense, but the facts had been presented at Douglas's trial and considered by the jury and were reflected in the jury's verdict and sentence. Douglas's conviction for misdemeanor assault and his minor sentence indicated the credence that the jury placed in his account of events. Judge Richard Ker wrote the governor that he saw no reason to recommend clemency as "all questions of the credibility of the prosecuting witness [were] disposed of by the verdict of the jury." The commonwealth's attorney also recommended against clemency, writing, "She [Sallie Sigman] is a white woman, and both live in a community made up of negroes and whites; and a pardon to this negro would have a bad effect on other negroes." Despite the belief of the deputy sheriff and the justice of the peace of Schoolfield that Douglas's conviction represented a miscarriage of justice, Governor Trinkle refused to pardon him. "The question of facts was presented to the jury," he asserted, "and I do not feel that I would be justified in overriding this verdict." Evidently, Solomon Douglas served his sentence for assault.[17]

The jury's verdict in Solomon Douglas's case was indeed ambiguous. Presented with evidence that Sallie Sigman's charge grew out of a desire for revenge and her participation in criminal activities, the jury nonetheless decided to convict Douglas. Such a conviction represented the jury's lack of comfort with the parties' casual, if illegal, commerce across racial and gender lines. Sallie Sigman's participation in that criminal culture and her willingness to accuse a black man of rape as a means of revenge encouraged the jury to limit the power endowed to her by her race. The decision on the part of the judge and the prosecuting attorney not to support Douglas's petition was equally ambiguous. Declining to comment on Douglas's allegations, the commonwealth's attorney placed broader issues of social order over questions of justice. Douglas should not be released because that action might encourage other African Americans who lived in mixed communities. What exactly it would encourage them to do was unclear. Attack white women or engage in illegal activities across racial and gender lines? Either activity was equally destabilizing to the carefully monitored racial, gender, and class hierarchies.

The events surrounding the Sigmans' and Solomon Douglas's relationship attest to the hidden culture of cross-racial and cross-gender interactions that occurred despite carefully constructed laws separating the races. The Sigmans and Douglas, and many other whites and blacks, engaged in casual commercial exchanges, dominated not by rules of white supremacy and racial domination but by the laws of supply and demand.[18] Douglas and Sallie Sigman acted as equals in their exchange of money for whiskey. Sallie Sigman only resorted to the power her white-ness gave her when she believed Douglas had violated the rules surround-ing their commercial exchange. She may have thought that because of her race, her accusations would not be questioned, that they represented a fool-proof means of revenge. The men composing the jury that convicted Douglas were not so cooperative. To them, her whiteness and even her gender did not carry great weight. Her gender was largely erased when Douglas was convicted of a nonsexual offense. Her class and her charac-ter, and those of her husband, overrode consideration of her race and sex.

The rhetoric surrounding black-on-white rape insisted that all white women could call on white men and the legal system to avenge their honor. This ideology created a means by which poor women could poten-tially improve their status. Charging rape was a way for a woman to obscure public knowledge of her social and sexual misdeeds and to re-claim the higher ground of respectability. White women, however, found that crying rape was not always an effective means of reclaiming white status. The jury determined that Douglas's attempted rape of Sallie Sig-man was only a misdemeanor, a resounding judgment of the minimal threat her violation was to the racial hierarchy. Moreover, a final event suggests that Sallie Sigman's charges did little to improve her status in the community. After serving his sentence, Douglas returned to Pittsylvania County. Eight years later he was charged with violating the Prohibition laws.[19] He apparently felt little concern about returning to the community in which he had been convicted of assaulting a white woman. The subse-quent charges lodged against him, however, suggest that he continued to live within the criminal subculture of the community.

Charges of rape could cover a variety of misdeeds by white women, but none was so potentially damning to white women's status as allegations of consensual sexual relations with black men. Making accusations of rape to hide interracial affairs was the most obvious way in which white women used accusations against black men to achieve their own ends. Ida B. Wells, as early as 1892, asserted that numerous lynchings grew out of white women's efforts to mask relations with black lovers. "Nobody in this sec-tion believes the old threadbare lie that Negro men assault white women," she asserted. "If southern white men are not careful, they will over-reach themselves and public sentiment will have a reaction; a conclusion will then be reached which will be very damaging to the moral reputation of their women."[20] Accusing black lovers of rape renarrated a white woman's sexual indiscretion in a way that protected her respectability. The legal definition of rape negated white women's complicity in interracial sexual relations as it simultaneously proclaimed their access to white male protection. Freed from responsibility for their actions, these women hoped to reclaim their status as the repository of white, racial purity.

Sexual purity and chastity lay at the heart of idealized notions of white womanhood. The essence of whiteness for women was their sexual segregation from black men. To acknowledge consensual relations with a black man meant voluntarily rejecting the core of white femininity and the ultimate forfeiture of white status and privilege. Sexual relationships across the color line were so devastating to white women's status that white men presumed women would never acknowledge them. The prosecution in Samuel Legions case in 1943 argued that the fact that the alleged victim admitted to authorities she had sexual relations with the defendant in itself proved she did not consent: "No person who was the author of her own shame would be so callous as to freely tell others about such an experience with a negro man."[21] In theory, the fear of social ostracism and humiliation would prevent white women from acknowledging they had consensual relationships with black men. One prosecutor, outraged that a convicted man had even suggested the victim consented to relations, averred that it gave "her [the victim] the worse humiliation." Claiming she consented, regardless of whether or not she did, he continued, "would disgrace her forever in the eyes of the public."[22]

Black men, however, were usually convicted despite any rumors that a consensual relationship led to a charge of rape, especially since white women did not admit such relationships in court. There is no evidence that any case between 1900 and 1960 resulted in an acquittal after the alleged victim openly took responsibility for a sexual relationship, and no white woman pleaded with a jury to spare her black lover. For their part, black men were also reluctant to base their defense on the claim that they were engaged in consensual relationships, knowing they risked antagonizing white male jury members. In 1908, for example, Lee Strother waited until after his conviction to tell his attorney he had been having an ongoing affair with the woman who charged him with rape. Strother admitted giving false testimony on the stand because he believed basing his defense on consent would ultimately hurt his case. He reportedly told his lawyer that "if they [sic] jury had not believed him they would have hung him and if they did believe him and turn him out [acquitted him], the white folks would have killed him."[23] In most cases, the course of legal action, at least on the surface, conformed to the familiar paradigm—no sexual relationship between a white woman and a black man could ever be voluntary, and black men faced punishment for any such accusation.

And, as with most actions contradictory to the rhetoric of black-on-white rape, questions about the victim's consent usually appeared in petitions for executive clemency.

Questions of consent remained central to all rape cases, regardless of the races of the parties involved. By defining rape as carnal relations by force and against the will of the victim, the law placed the burden of proving nonconsent on the victim. Courts required women charging rape to demonstrate they did not consent to sexual intercourse by providing evidence that they strenuously resisted the assault.[24] This requirement ostensibly served to protect men from false charges. In practice, it made rape difficult to prove, protecting guilty, as well as innocent, men. It ultimately worked to give most men unfettered sexual access to most women, as long as they left few physical marks of violence to be used against them in court. The resistance requirement, however, was not so stringently applied in cases of black-on-white rape. According to twentieth-century cultural norms, especially in the South, nonwhite men had no right to sexual access to white women; therefore the law in no way sought to protect that right by placing the burden of proving rape on white women who made the accusation. Because whites assumed that white women would never consent to sexual relations with black men, white women who accused black men theoretically did not need to prove their nonconsent through resistance in court.

Lurking fears that white women might consent to relations with black men, however, complicated these assumptions. In many cases, white women still needed to provide some evidence that they did indeed resist. Such evidence assured jurors that their assumptions about white women held true: white women viewed any sexual contact with black men as abhorrent. At the same time, it ensured that even black-on-white cases conformed to the letter of the law, preventing troublesome precedents that later might be called upon in cases when white men were accused of rape. Virginia judges thus instructed juries on the relationship between consent and resistance even in cases of black-on-white rape.

In 1929, the judge presiding over the trial of Joe Gibbs, a black man accused of assaulting two white girls, instructed the jury that to convict Gibbs of rape, the law required that "such force is essential to the crime as may be adequate to overcome the resistance of the woman."[25] Similarly, at Charlie Brown's trial in 1941, the jury received instructions that if the victim consented to sexual relations, "it will not be rape." But the judge specified what constituted consent: "A consent induced by fear of bodily harm or personal violence is not consent, and resistance on the part of the woman is not necessary when it is dangerous and absolutely useless to resist, or that there is dread or fear of death or bodily injury on the part of the woman."[26] The judge in John Anderson's case made the most explicit statement regarding the resistance requirement. Like the judge in Brown's case, this judge specified that consent induced by fear did not count. But he went on to state the level of resistance required by law: "Resistance by the woman must be more than mere verbal expressions, but there must be the exercise of every means of faculty within the woman's power to resist penetration, under the circumstances, and that the persistence in such resistance must continue until such offense is consummated." If the jurors did not find that the victim's resistance met this threshold, they could not find Anderson guilty of rape even though he was black. Indeed, the judge combined this instruction with the specific warning that the jury could not be influenced by the fact that Anderson was a black man accused of raping a white woman.[27]

Once the law was explained to them, however, jurors could choose to apply it how they wished, and they arrived at their verdicts through the matrix of their cultural assumptions. In the cases described above, all the defendants were originally sentenced to death, suggesting that however these women responded to their assaults, the jury believed that what they did met the threshold of adequate resistance. By informing the jury of the state's requirement of resistance, however, the court worked to uphold important precedents about patriarchal privilege that also informed intraracial cases. Determining whether the victim displayed adequate resistance was left to the jurors, who ultimately judged whether a woman had resisted by "every means of faculty within the [her] power," regardless of the race of the assailant.

For females under the age of consent, however, the law presumed that they did not have the maturity to give consent to sexual relations with any man, let alone African Americans, so whether or not they resisted was moot. In Paul Hairston's case, the instructions to the jury suggest that he claimed that his victim, a white fourteen-year-old girl, had consented to his advances. The judge instructed the jury twice that any consent on her part was irrelevant, since she was underage and therefore could not legally give her consent. Whether or not the defendant believed she was above the age of consent was also of no relevance.[28] Nevertheless, courts did not assume that all white women, especially those under the age of consent, were innocent victims of black men's designs. J. R. H. Alexander, the prosecutor in James Washington's rape case, wrote the governor that it was routine to investigate the reputation and credibility of rape victims even when they were below the age of consent. "I would naturally investigate her reputation," he asserted, "and I did not hear a breath against her." Only later did he point out that "[i]n any event, the girl is only fourteen years old so that his statement [suggesting consensual relations] does not in any way help his plight."[29] He penned this note on legal procedure after Washington's father suggested that the charge against Washington grew out of an ongoing consensual relationship.[30] Even in cases in which white girls accused black men of sexual violence, and even in cases in which the law stated that consent and character should have no relevance in questions of guilt or innocence, legal officials nonetheless considered the possibility of consent when they debated black men's fates. They also realized that even though the issue of consent might have no legal relevance, it nonetheless remained a factor jurors would likely consider. Consensual relations between black men and white women, in white men's minds, were real possibilities despite the rhetoric to the contrary. Consequently, legal officials approached *all* rape victims with a degree of distrust.

Questions about the victim's consent were not confined to the victim and her alleged assailant, however. Courts confronted whether husbands or fathers who controlled sexual access to their white wives and daughters could consent to sexual relations for them. Randolph Hockaday, a black man, was convicted of attempted rape in 1937 after his drinking partner, Clarence Branch, a white man, exchanged sexual access to his daughter for whiskey and then held her down to allow Hockaday to have sex with her. Branch, however, was convicted of attempted rape as well, and both men received sentences of life in prison.[31] Similarly, in 1952, a white husband tried to force his wife into sexual relations with their black gardener. Both men were indicted, but the judge later dismissed the charges when the wife recanted her statement to police. She was arrested for making a false statement.[32] Clarence Branch, and possibly others as well, apparently believed they were exercising their patriarchal privileges, one of which, under common law, was sexual property rights over female family members, an understanding the state recognized when it solicited the opinions of husbands and fathers rather than of victims themselves in pardon considerations. The courts, however, limited the extent to which white men controlled women's sexual lives. In a segregated society, white women's sexuality had important public implications. Upholding the color line by preventing sexual interaction between white women and black men outweighed white men's patriarchal right to control sexual access to their female kin.[33]

Despite white assumptions, white women did consent to sexual relations with black men. It is clear that in the late nineteenth and early twentieth centuries, white prostitutes in Richmond "secretly sold their favors to colored men."[34] The opinion of the Supreme Court of Alabama in overturning the verdict of a black man convicted of raping a white prostitute conceded that white prostitutes did service black men, though the court hoped only rarely. In Georgia, saloons for drinking, gambling, and prostitution were frequently interracial.[35] Wilson Allen and John Boone's petitions for clemency, discussed in Chapter 4, revolved around allegations that their alleged victims were prostitutes. In all of these instances, white women apparently consented to sex with black men for economic reasons, if not out of desire.

Other evidence suggests that consensual relationships did not always involve prostitution. Melton A. McLaurin, in his memoir of growing up in the segregated South, wrote that consensual relationships between white women and black men were common knowledge in southern communities.[36] In Virginia in the 1920s, activists concerned with promoting the purity of the white race convinced the Virginia General Assembly to pass laws strengthening prohibitions on interracial marriage. As part of activists' efforts to improve the law, they provided what they believed to be evidence documenting that sexual relationships between white women and black men continued without any interference from local authorities or the public.[37] White authorities clearly did not intervene in all instances of sexual relations between white women and black men. Many relationships continued without community interference, even if they were common knowledge among whites. Whites' willful blindness helped resolve the conundrum of consent: that white women supposedly would never consent to sex with black men yet frequently did. Ignoring these relationships denied their existence. Whites' insistence that the cases that were publicly exposed only involved low-status white women, in turn, confirmed that the definition of true white women indicated middle-class respectability. As their sexual relationships with blacks attested, white women at the lower end of the social and economic spectrum were less white, having reduced themselves to the level of blacks.

Although any sexual relationship between a white woman and a black man could be potentially explosive, evidence from cases that did spur legal intervention indicates that communities occasionally moderated their responses. Though no Virginia community openly advocated sexual relations across racial lines—indeed, all southern states had laws explicitly prohibiting interracial marriage—when cross-racial relationships came to light, they did not always result in rape charges. Loo Rooster Jarvis received a life sentence after he was twice accused of having sex with a white woman. Legal officials acknowledged that his first violation might have involved an ongoing sexual relationship with a white woman. When that first relationship came to the attention of authorities, they placed Jarvis in Central State Hospital and sterilized him rather than convicting him of a crime. In 1941, Leewood Ashby was not charged with rape for his relationship with a white woman, but he was convicted of the more ambiguous charge of "carnal knowledge of a white woman." He was sentenced to three years in prison and fined, but he was granted a conditional pardon a year early.[38] White communities policed these relationships, but they did not consider them rapes.

Evidence suggests that communities brought consensual interracial sexual relationships to the attention of authorities when the participants violated other community moral standards. Jacob Duncan, for example, was arrested in 1927 for an assault on a young girl. Danville officer Ira Harris initiated the proceedings after reporting that he had seen Duncan "lure the girl from her home to his dwelling."[39] The *Danville Register* reported that "[r]esidents of the neighborhood in which the girl lived had seen her with the Negro man and had grown suspicious." After his arrest, police removed Duncan to Lynchburg because they feared mob violence.[40] The role of the victim, who was under the age of consent, remained shadowy. The newspaper merely stated that "the girl was taken to police headquarters where she made a statement which, police say, support the charge," suggesting that she did not make her accusation entirely willingly.[41] In September, Duncan pleaded guilty to rape, insisting that his plea was not an admission of guilt but rather a means of avoiding the death penalty. He was sentenced to eighteen years in prison.[42]

Four years later, Duncan's wife began to petition the governor to release her husband. She vaguely referred to the details of Duncan's alleged crime ("It was concerning a white girl being at his home") and focused instead on her need for Duncan's financial support.[43] The governor, however, refused to grant Duncan a pardon. John W. Carter, the prosecutor in the case, saw "no reason in the world why parole should be granted at the present time." From the tone of Carter's letter, time had not diminished his feelings of outrage regarding the case.[44] The chief of police, J. H. Martin, concurred with Carter's assessment. According to Martin, Duncan was "a notorious character" and "was unable to hold a job because of his lazy and shiftless habits." The circumstances of Duncan's arrest most incensed Martin: "He had this girl come to his house several times each week *until* the entire neighborhood was scandalized. He was caught in the very act one night by Lieutenant I. H. Harris of this department, who had been watching his house."[45] Martin's letter suggests that Duncan's relationship with the unnamed white girl was common knowledge in the community, and indeed, Duncan and his lover did very little to hide it. Only over time did the sensibilities of the neighborhood become inflamed. Duncan's crime, then, was not merely having engaged in the relationship, but also the manner in which he and the girl conducted it: brazenly, frequently, and with little concern for discretion. In white male officials' view, Duncan had no regard for the color line, or a related gender line, and he flouted both repeatedly with a white minor.

White women's illicit relationships with black men negated their role as the repository of white virtue and honor, undermined white men's sexual control over white women, and potentially threatened the racial hierarchy by compromising white racial purity. Some white women apparently were unconcerned about their lost status. Others took great care to hide their relationships and called them rape when they feared exposure. For these women, public exposure came at an intolerable social cost, though not so intolerable as to forego the relationship in the first place.[46] These white women resorted to the only form of power they had when the long reach of southern social norms, steeped in racism, tradition, and patriarchy, appeared ready to call them to account. Their actions are understandable, though they are not forgivable, since they traded black men's lives for their own reputations. Crying rape, however, did not always shield white women from the full consequences of their actions. In an effort to constrain their efforts, white men could become the allies of accused black men, united as men against women's power to accuse them of rape.

As with issues of character, allegations that a relationship was consensual rarely were made at trial. Most appeared in petitions for clemency, away from open public debate and usually long after any furor caused by the assault had dissipated. As in the case of the victim's character, white juries usually voted to convict accused men as a tangible representation of their duty to protect all white women, even if the relationship was consensual and known throughout the white community. Only after whites could say the law had taken its course and they had defended white women's honor did whites balance the need to affirm the racial hierarchy with the need to address white women's own failings and shore up masculine privilege.

Charles Wilson, for example, was convicted of rape in 1904 and sentenced to twenty years in prison. Eleven years later, he appealed to the governor for executive clemency. The commonwealth's attorney recommended that the governor grant Wilson's request, stating that the white woman who made the charge "was not of the best reputation."[47] The presiding judge in Wilson's trial advocated his release more forcefully, placing responsibility for it on the female victim, whom he argued engaged in inappropriate relations with African American men. Wilson's conviction, he argued, "depended almost entirely on the statement of the prosecutrix, a white woman who was admittedly on intimate social terms with this man and other negroes in the neighborhood, and I am informed that since Charles Wilson's conviction of *an attempt to commit rape*, she has continued the association. A strong suspicion existed at the time that the charge was made to cloak the woman's own lewdness."[48] Wilson was released scarcely two weeks after Judge Tyler penned his recommendation.

The judge's statements suggest that the accusation represented a strategy by which the alleged victim hoped to reassert her white womanhood and claim its privileges despite her social and sexual misdeeds. As a woman whose skin was white, despite her tarnished reputation, she retained considerable power. Charles Wilson served eleven years for a rape that, in the opinion of legal authorities, may never have occurred. However, local knowledge of her reputation and her racial transgressions limited the protection such a woman could claim. Although Wilson would be punished, he would not pay with his life. Releasing him from prison, perhaps to return to the community, warned white women of the consequences of inappropriate relations across the color line, regardless of whether or not an assault occurred.[49]

White men acknowledged that even black men were at the mercy of women, because they, like white men, could be falsely accused of rape. Black men who engaged in affairs with disreputable, unscrupulous white women were most at peril; these women, whites believed, were most likely to engage in sexual relations with black men and most likely to stoop to making false accusations in an attempt to salvage their reputations. Nevertheless, at least initially, their accusations still commanded white men's response. Not all black men, however, were equally guilty in the eyes of white men. When black men engaged in affairs with a certain amount of discretion, or with some evidence of reluctance, white men might acknowledge their common gender interests with black men, and extend their support to black men as *men*. Indeed, white men could sympathize with black men who were victimized by desperate white women.

The *Richmond Times-Dispatch* reported that Paul Washington was arrested for rape on August 16, 1925. The victim was Della Payne, a married woman who, at the time of the assault, was separated from her husband and working as a housekeeper for a bedridden elderly man. She claimed that Washington broke into the house of her employer during the night and assaulted her. She reported the assault the next morning and named Washington as her assailant. When questioned by police at his home, Washington denied committing the assault and insisted that he had been in bed sleeping the entire night with his wife, who corroborated his statement. Circumstantial evidence at Washington's home, however, contradicted both of their stories. At the time of the alleged assault, it had been raining heavily, and police found a set of Washington's clothes soaking wet and hanging to dry at his home. His wet clothes led police to believe that Washington had been out in the rain the previous night, and they arrested him for Payne's rape.[50]

A jury found Washington guilty and sentenced him to life in prison. Efforts to have the judge set aside the verdict failed, and Washington was incarcerated.[51] Several years later, Washington petitioned the governor for conditional pardon with the support of the sheriff and the commonwealth's attorney who originally arrested, prosecuted, and convicted him. When Washington wrote the sheriff to ask for his help in getting the sentence reduced, the sheriff replied that he believed Washington was innocent and should not be in prison at all. His own investigation, he believed, cleared Washington of all charges.[52]

The sheriff wrote to Governor Pollard's secretary regarding Washington's petition for clemency in October 1932. His letter addressed his concerns about Washington's conviction at length. One of the most damning pieces of evidence against Washington was that his shoes matched prints found at the scene of the crime. Washington's shoes were very distinctive: three nails in the heel left a unique imprint. Payne had testified that Washington entered through the window in the back room of the house where she was sleeping, committed the assault, and left without walking through other areas of the house. According to the sheriff, however, the marks made by his shoes suggested he was familiar with the house:

> In tracing these nail prints one could easily see that Washington had been a frequent visitor to the Payne home and that he had worn these shoes on many visits there, as these prints were in all the rooms in the house and on the two porches, front and back. One other thing was very plain: that Washington had made many trips from the room which was claimed he entered and

which was the kitchen of the house through the room in which
Mrs. Payne claimed she slept and used as a bed room to the
third room and bed side of the invalid man showing conclu-
sively in my judgment, that he had frequently taken the invalid
food and water.

Washington had been in the house many times and "was invited there and
encouraged to be there by Mrs. Della Payne."[53] His footprints were also
found "even under the table in the kitchen . . . the imprints under the
kitchen table indicated that the wearer of that shoe had eaten meals at that
table."[54] Payne not only had sex with Washington but had violated other
cardinal rules of segregation as well.

At the time, the footprints concerned Sheriff Dyche enough to question
Washington about them after the jury returned with its verdict. Washington admitted that he had been a frequent visitor to Payne's house. By the
time the sheriff discovered this, Payne had left Virginia. She was gone for
several years, and the sheriff was apparently (or perhaps conveniently)
unable to locate her to question her about her relationship with Washington until immediately prior to Washington's petition. During his interview with Payne, the sheriff "accused her of carrying on an illicit affair
with Paul Washington. She broke down and cried, but would not at any
time deny the accusation nor did she affirm the accusation. All that she
would say was, 'I would be afraid for Washington to be released for fear
he might attack me,' which is a very slim excuse."[55]

When faced with the sheriff's accusations, Della Payne found herself in
an untenable situation. If she had carried on an affair with Washington,
her testimony in court would constitute perjury. Indeed, the year before in
Norfolk, as discussed earlier in this chapter, Dorothy Skaggs had been
convicted of perjury for falsely accusing a black man named William
Harper of rape. That case had received significant press coverage throughout the state, and it is possible that Payne worried she would face similar
charges. Washington's release would likely worry her—either her rapist
was free, or the man she falsely accused might seek revenge. The sheriff
had his own theories. He was sure "she would like to admit the truth," he
asserted, "but I am afraid she will never do so for the reason that she
would not want to admit having such conduct with a colored man and
would rather see him spend his days in the penitentiary, although innocent, than to suffer that disgrace."[56]

Payne had another more pressing reason for accusing Washington. According to the sheriff, she separated from her husband "something like a

year just before the trial . . . ; he refused to attend the trial or to take any interest in the case, though [the prosecutor] made efforts to get him to do so, urging him, for the sake of appearances at least, to attend the trial." Sheriff Dyche wrote that Washington was held in the Allegheny County jail for over six months before he was brought to trial because Payne was pregnant. This delay suggests that authorities at least considered the possibility that the charge of rape grew out of a preexisting consensual relationship. The baby would expose Payne's affair and reveal that her lover was black. "Of course," the sheriff continued, "being a married woman and having a white husband, the fear came over her that the unborn child might be black and she connived the scheme of rape accusing Paul Washington because he was about to break with her, thereby preparing to 'kill two birds with one stone.' " After the birth of the child, the sheriff visited Payne's home. He "found that the child was white."[57] Sheriff Dyche believed that Paul Washington was the victim of a scheming woman who used a charge of rape to explain the birth of what she feared would be a mixed-race child. "Mrs. Payne claimed that Paul Washington made only one trip to her house. That statement is untrue and, if that is untrue, any statement she made concerning this case is liable to be just as untrue."[58] The prosecuting attorney, when asked by the governor, also recommended that Washington receive a conditional pardon.[59]

With hindsight, of course, one can understand Washington's reluctance to reveal the nature of his relationship with Della Payne. Though nowhere does any news report mention that the communities of Covington and Clifton Forge were outraged by the assault, Washington felt himself in a precarious position. Washington's confession to the sheriff also revealed why, beyond her pregnancy, Payne made her accusation when she did. According to Washington, their affair had been going on for over a year, perhaps even before she separated from her husband. Washington admitted that he did indeed travel to Payne's home on the night in question and did have consensual sexual relations with her. But on that night he told her he was breaking off their affair, that "he had become afraid that their relations were going to be found out, that he would be punished, and that he was not going to have any further relations with her." She went the next morning to her father and accused Washington of rape.[60]

Paul Washington was released from prison in April 1933, after spending seven years in prison for engaging in a consensual sexual relationship with a white woman. Ultimately, court officials and the governor believed Washington's version of events over Payne's, despite the fact that she never changed her story. Her cry of rape lends credence to arguments that any white woman could successfully accuse a black man of rape regardless of the quality of the physical evidence. When she found herself scorned, pregnant, and alone, she was able to call upon the formal authority of the state to press her claim for innocence and respectability. But her actions, when revealed by the sheriff, placed her in a more untenable category. She was scorned, rejected by a black man, and desperate, and she had lied. The role of the woman scorned was one that all men, white or black, recognized and feared. Her motives for naming Washington for rape created an alliance between a black man and the white authorities who were supposed to protect white women. Paul Washington was a man wronged by a desperate woman; he was no longer solely identified by his blackness. She lost the cloak of chivalry she had claimed because of her whiteness.

Sympathy for Washington grew out of a common fear of false accusations of rape by vindictive women who illegitimately manipulated their sexual power to exert control over men, the community, and their own situations. Washington's advocates acknowledged that Della Payne's position, being pregnant and separated from her husband, caused her to "cry rape" in order to save her reputation. White women's accusations demanded that white men take action, and white men usually complied. But when women used their power to shield themselves from the consequences of their moral failings, white men abandoned racial solidarity. Indeed, once Washington served what whites believed to be an appropriate sentence, they rallied to his support.

The plight of John Spencer, another black man accused of rape, also created an alliance between him and white male supporters in his community. In his case, however, that alliance did not pivot around a common fear of women. Rather, it revolved around men's common sexual desire for women. In Spencer's case, the desire on the part of a black man for a white woman did not elicit white hysteria, violence, or the rhetoric of protecting white women. Instead, it operated as a catalyst for his release.

Spencer was tried and convicted of rape in Page County in October 1919. The woman who accused him was Cora Sours, an eighteen-year-old, unmarried, white woman. Spencer's conviction occurred without much fanfare. The court records are sparse, and evidently, his trial was quick and without incident. The assault itself never received news coverage, and there is no evidence that reports of an assault on a white woman by a black man caused any expressions of outrage in the community. Spencer, a fifty-one-year-old married laborer, was sentenced to the minimum term of five years in prison.[61]

In November 1920, Spencer's attorney, R. S. Parks, wrote to the governor requesting Spencer's release. He enclosed a petition signed by eight other white men, including a lawyer, a doctor, an insurance salesman, a newspaper editor, and a local merchant, from the community. In their petition, the men contended that Spencer was only guilty of adultery. Spencer, according to the petition, had "always been regarded as an honest well behaved colored man, knowing his place and attending to his own business." For several years, he had worked as a driver, hauling supplies in a horse and wagon from the town of Luray to Skyland, a summer resort nearby. Cora Sours lived along his route, and "she would come out to the road and get on the wagon and ride back and forth with him. . . . [S]he was seen with her arm around him and in other ways showed her intimacy or fondness for the man."[62] At no point in the trial did Spencer deny that sexual intercourse had occurred between Sours and himself. At issue was whether that intercourse constituted rape.

The existing clemency files do not indicate whether Spencer attempted to use his relationship with Sours as his defense. Nor does the file reveal why the case came to the attention of the authorities, though there are several possible reasons. Cora Sours, knowing that her relationship with Spencer was causing community comment, may have made the charge to save her reputation. Her family may have made the accusation for her to save their reputation. Neither the letter from Spencer's attorney nor the petition on his behalf discussed the reputation of the victim or her family. Cora Sours never married in Page County. Census records, however, show that Sours's family worked as farm laborers, and several women named Sours worked as domestic servants in white households, so she likely came from the lower end of the socioeconomic spectrum. Sours's presence in Spencer's wagon on a public road, however, suggests that she was not concerned about being seen showing affection for a black man. The charge could have arisen, as it did in the Jacob Duncan case, from community intolerance. After turning a blind eye to Spencer and Sours's relationship, the community may have reached the end of its toleration. The couple may have been too brazen or may have met too frequently, or the community may have been interested in sending a message to the African American community to deter any other black men from similar actions. This last explanation seems to have the most supporting evidence. Both the letter from Spencer's attorney and the petition insisted that any deterrent effect had been accomplished.

Regardless of who charged him, Spencer received a sentence of five years and soon found himself with a cohort of white men pleading his cause. The signers of the petition did not believe that Spencer's actions threatened existing racial hierarchies. The focus of their argument was that Spencer had done no more than any man would have done, and they did not believe that Spencer should suffer additional punishment because he had succumbed to temptation. They, as men, sympathized with Spencer's desire. The fact that his desire was for a white woman did not materially change the case, other than causing a guilty verdict where none otherwise would have occurred. According to Parks, Spencer's temptation was certainly increased by the fact that Cora Sours was white, but that only made his eventual capitulation to that desire the more understandable: "That the man was guilty of violation of law, in that he had time and again had sexual intercourse with the woman was not denied by him but admitted, and the [ev]idence clearly showed that she visited the negro, rode up and down the road with him with her arms around him and threw herself in his way and he took what was thrown at him, as many mwn [sic] would have done, especially a negro man would feel himself complimented and ivited [invited?] by a woman of a different and superior race."[63] The petition signed by the community echoed Park's assertions: "We did not believe then and we do not believe now that rape was committed and the man only did what others might have done, take what was offered and thrown at him."[64] Spencer, after all, was a man. He could hardly be blamed for accepting the attentions of a young woman.

At the time of the trial, Parks had asked the court to set aside the verdict as contrary to the evidence, but the court declined to do so. The judge refused to set aside a verdict just because he did not agree with it, telling Parks that he thought "it better to let the verdict stand, as there was admission of adultery, and it would serve as a deterrent to other negroes not to interfere with white women."[65] Through the actions of the jury, the Luray community had completed its duty to protect segregation, for which white women were merely the proxy. But their verdict was not an unqualified endorsement of the victim's testimony. The short sentence, the minimum allowed for a conviction, underscored the jury's misgivings. Moreover, it allowed the court officials to step in after the message had been sent to the black community. Luray whites would convict black men for engaging in affairs with white women. White men, however, in consideration of the temptations of sex, would adjust the verdict according to their understanding of Spencer's offense. Conviction gave a nod to conventional ideology and rhetoric. Spencer's pardon gave a nudge and a wink to black men as men. All men felt the temptations of the flesh in the presence of a willing and insistent woman. All men might stand together to let a man, even a black one, off the hook for succumbing to their natural desires.

Both Washington's and Spencer's actions in the case mitigated their offenses. Washington, realizing he was violating racial rules, sought to end his affair. He showed proper respect for the consequences of his actions. Spencer was an older African American man who had always known his place. More important, both were in situations with which white men could sympathize and indeed in which they could envision themselves. Few men could resist a woman who threw herself at him— certainly one whose reputation in the community may already have been tarnished. All men knew the fear that a woman might accuse them of rape to serve her own purposes. In both cases, they acknowledged the need to protect white women from black men, but as soon as they could, they adjusted the sentences to reflect more accurately their "crimes."

These two cases also attest to official efforts men made to police personal relationships that did not conform to the public mandates of segregation. Black men who visibly flouted the dictates of racial separation opened themselves to charges. Their punishments served as warnings to all African Americans that white women were off limits, even when the women themselves were willing participants or perhaps even aggressors. Black men's convictions confirm the belief that interracial sexual relationships represented a violation of southern social norms and compromised the racial hierarchy. Juries did their duty by at least appearing to protect white womanhood and to punish black men's offenses. But their protection was qualified, and light sentences and community support for early release speaks to their ambivalence. Short sentences reflected white men's understanding of black men's vulnerability, white men's distrust of white women's truthfulness, and white women's ability to manipulate white men's actions through accusations of rape. White men felt compelled to convict black men, but they also acted to limit the havoc accusations of unscrupulous women could wreak on the lives of African American men.

This, in essence, was the conundrum of consent: the ideological impossibility of white women's consent to sexual relations with black men amidst numerous instances of that very thing. White women were the highest symbol of white civilization and the guardians of racial purity, yet they were simultaneously untrustworthy, irrational, and at times, even willing partners in illegal sex with black men. In acting on white women's invitations, black men violated their duty to the racial hierarchy and thus ensured their convictions in court. White authorities through the courts demonstrated their expectation that black men must at all times sublimate their innate desire for white women and resist temptation, especially in the face of a willing and insistent white woman. In the face of some white women's inadequate racial pride, it thus became the responsibility of black men to protect and uphold white women's purity and virtue, as well as the color line itself. Although whites frequently compromised their racial status, it was up to blacks to defend it, thereby preventing "no-count" whites from challenging the supposedly self-evident validity of white superiority."[66] It was black men, then, who were required to restore the racial hierarchy, and protect white men's prerogative to have sole sexual access to white women.

Some white women accused black men of assault to get themselves out of compromising situations and prevent public discovery of their moral transgressions. This fear of discovery was uniquely female, and, because of a racialized double standard, similar moral indiscretions would not have threatened the reputation of white men. White women's reputations comprised the currency of their social status, and the loss of that reputation could very well mean the loss of their livelihoods, their marriages, and the sources of their material support. Indeed, in response to a friend who asked Dorothy Skaggs why she was willing to risk the life of an innocent man, she apparently replied, "I couldn't afford to lose my husband over this."[67] Her concerns did not center on her fear of divorce but rather upon losing the money her husband sent her every month, which was her primary means of support. Faced with such a loss, it is perhaps not surprising that some white women called on one of the few socially accepted forms of power they possessed in a patriarchal and segregated society: the power to shift responsibility for their own misdeeds to the shoulders of black men, either men they knew intimately or anonymous strangers. Their actions carried grave consequences for black men, some of whom, like Lee Strother, lost their lives.

Yet women's efforts to save their reputations often resulted in unforeseen consequences. Some accusing white women apparently suffered pangs of guilt for false accusations. Governor Tuck received an anonymous letter in 1946 claiming to be from the white woman who had accused Fred Butler of rape in 1945. Telling the governor that she accused Butler "to save my name," she begged that he be released. "I cannot sleep or be at rest for the great wrong and injustice I did to a colored man who is serving a life sentence on account of the lies I told which [are] all untrue."[68] When Della Payne was confronted by the sheriff about her relationship with her former lover, Paul Washington, she refused to say a word but cried bitterly and profusely. Her actions forced her to leave the state but perhaps also left her consumed by guilt. They surely spelled the end of an affair she had wanted to continue when she made her accusation. Dorothy Skaggs and her husband also vowed to leave Virginia once their legal troubles concluded, so overwhelming was the negative publicity surrounding her actions.[69] In the midst of Skaggs's perjury trial, one newspaper editor went so far as to suggest that the law should be amended to insist that women provide corroborative evidence for claims of rape.[70] The dishonesty of a few accusing women threatened the perceived integrity of all accusing women. Accusing a black man of rape may have seemed a logical strategy to solve white women's immediate problems, but it simultaneously created others.

White tolerance for some interracial relationships refines historical understanding of sexuality and white womanhood in the segregated South. The only sexual relationships that represented an open threat to white supremacy were those perpetrated against women who were the paragons of white womanhood. In trials involving black-on-white rape accusations, white men punished black men who attempted to seize white patriarchal privilege. Whites presumed that trials, like lynchings, served as a deterrent to other black men who might consider similar actions. They showed black men the possible consequences of any relationship with a white woman and reiterated black men's duty to protect white supremacy, even if white women would not.

The cases described in this chapter also suggest, however, that legal authorities were concerned about more than black men who transgressed racial boundaries. Many white women's conduct was also troubling. These women were different from the white women extolled in racist rhetoric about black beast rapists; they were less worthy of protection. Indeed, they were less white. Lowering themselves socially and sexually to what whites insisted was the level of blacks effectively erased the racial hierarchy and exposed the lie at the heart of white supremacy. African American men had to be controlled as a means of containing errant white women whose own actions upended the social order. Black men risked incarceration for failing to help marginal whites act their part, for, in essence, enabling whites to erode claims to white superiority. At the same time, short sentences and conditional pardons reminded poor whites, and especially white women, of the consequences of their own transgressions and reinforced elite white men's power to police both white women's and black men's conduct.

The willingness of white men to grant black men the benefit of the doubt worked to balance the prerogatives of race, gender, and class in the Jim Crow South. Questioning the claims of tarnished white women who cried rape lent a degree of credibility to the legal system, assuring the community—both white and black—that, for the most part, only truly egregious violations of racial norms received the most severe sanctions. It also allowed white men to check the power given to white women because of their race. A woman's whiteness did not entitle her to undisputed power over black men; nor did it grant her the unconditional power to command white men to fulfill their promise of protection. More important, in limiting the degree of protection some women received, white men preserved their power to act as the final arbiters of not only white women's behavior but also the ideal of white womanhood, an ideal that permeated every aspect of white women's lives. The occasional willingness on the part of white, male juries to acquit black men accused of raping white women, and the decisions by legal authorities to release convicted black men long before they completed their sentences, might seem to undermine white supremacy. In reality, decisions that appeared to favor black men reinforced a social order structured on more than racial hierarchy. They affirmed a system of power in which hierarchies of race, gender, and class worked together. Southern social structure relied not only on white domination but also on the subservience of women at all levels of society. Granting some black men reprieve ultimately reinforced all white women's obligation to obey.[71]

CHAPTER 6

An Altogether New and Different Spirit

African American Strategies of Resistance and Leverage

Chapters 1–5 discuss cases of black-on-white rape primarily in terms of the power struggles they created
among whites, both women and men. They also demonstrate how whites
sought to balance the competing hierarchies of race, gender, and class that
together structured southern society. The focus on white responses to
claims of rape, along with the high conviction rate of accused black men,
might suggest that whites could exert exclusive or absolute power and
influence over these cases. One might conclude that the African American
community was held hostage to white interpretations of the crime and
merely watched while the legal system exacted its retribution on black
men. Focusing only on white power, however, denies any possibility for
black agency. Yet, even in a racially segregated and white-dominated society, African Americans created and utilized forms of resistance and
manipulated subtle modes of power.[1] Although their power was never
equivalent to that of whites, African Americans nonetheless found ways

to exert pressure on the white community and the legal system, even in cases of black-on-white rape.

The sheer variety of sentences black men received after having been convicted of assaulting white women suggests the presence of such pressure. Though 87 percent of accused black men were convicted of some crime, the vast majority were not punished to the limit of the law. While 48 (21 percent of the 230 convicted men) of those not sentenced to death received the maximum prison sentences allowed under Virginia law, the majority received lesser sentences. Fifty-two convicted men (23 percent of the 230 convicted men) received sentences of five years or less. The variety of sentences indicates a more complex interaction between race and gender in these cases, and the black community played a role in shaping that interaction. Despite being removed from the direct control of the criminal justice system, African Americans developed ways to influence it at a distance. They shaped how whites viewed different cases, and even encouraged whites to alter their perceptions of the role of race in crimes involving white women and black men. Ultimately, African Americans and their allies were able to convince whites that certain cases did not threaten the social order. Their ability to affect these cases underscores African Americans' access to some degree of power.

Any discussion of rape and resistance must address the possibility that black men's assaults on white women themselves were a means of opposing white supremacy. Historians seem loathe to acknowledge this possibility not only because rape is a "dishonorable" form of opposition but also because acknowledging its possibility seems to confirm the racist assumptions of white demagogues who have equated African American desires for political and economic power with their supposed desire for sexual access to white women.[2] Moreover, it assumes that some black men did indeed deliberately attack and rape white women, that not all accused men were framed by unscrupulous white women; this, too, among some scholars and partisans, is an explosive contention. Nevertheless, black men's motivations for assault are worthy of scrutiny, as are others' perceptions of those motivations.

Southern white apologists such as William Alexander Percy and W. J. Cash grudgingly conceded that African Americans' supposed tendency toward criminality might spring from their racial oppression. Cash acknowledged that violence could be a form of redress against powerful whites, and Percy suggested that black violence against other blacks represented a displacement of their hatred for whites. Neither author specifically targeted rape in his analysis, but their writings suggest that some whites believed crime was a logical and expected response to a system that condemned blacks to poverty and exploitation.[3] Other white southern commentators saw assaults by black men on white women specifically as a form of revenge. Philip Alexander Bruce, an avowed racist, commenting on what he perceived to be a rise in crime among blacks after emancipation, is but one example. He wrote that the black rapist of a white woman took "that fiendish delight in the degradation of his victim which he always shows when he can reek [sic] his vengeance upon one whom he has hitherto been compelled to fear; and here, the white woman in his power is, for the time being, the representative of that race which as always overawed him."[4] Bruce was not alone in his analysis of black crime. In 1900, at a conference on race conditions and problems, Alexander C. King, a prominent attorney from Atlanta, made similar claims. "To criminal tendency is added race animosity," he asserted, "and this in the brute with passions of the lowest order, incites to the assault on women of the other race. He will triumph over the other race in the person of a woman of that race."[5] Criminality, these white men argued, stemmed from blacks' unfitness for freedom, and became, through attacks on white women, a means of revenge against white men. White women victims were pawns in a dispute among men, the tools of battle if not yet the trophies of victory.

Critics of southern segregation also saw black men's assaults on white women as forms of revenge. Lillian Smith attributed assaults on white women to a "few angry bitter ignorant negroes" who fought back "the only way they knew how: by assaulting white women. It didn't happen often but it happened, and it was a powerful and suicidal revenge."[6] Like other scholars writing at approximately the same time, she insisted that black men did not randomly choose to target white women because of white women's vulnerability but rather in retaliation for the years of abuse white men had inflicted upon African American women. W. E. B. Du Bois placed white men's rape of black women at the heart of black anger toward whites. Arguing there was much he could forgive in whites' treatment of blacks, he drew the line at rape: "But one thing I shall never forgive, neither in this world nor the world to come: its [the white South's] wanton and continued and persistent insulting of the black womanhood which it sought and seeks to prostitute to its lust."[7] Du Bois, however, stopped short of calling black male rage a motive for raping white women. Other writers made the connection explicitly. John Dollard, in his sociological study of a town in Mississippi, called assaults on white women reprisals for the treatment of black women, pointing out that as a means of revenge they were a "way to hurt the white man most."[8] Gunnar Myrdal suggested that whites' fears of black men raping white women grew out of their own troubled consciences for their treatment of black women.[9] However they articulated black men's motives, these scholars saw white men's mistreatment of black women at the heart of black men's rage.

By the 1940s, raping white women as a form of revenge had become a familiar trope in black literature.[10] In the 1960s, radical black activists continued this inflammatory stance. Radical groups like the Black Panthers made masculine sexuality a pivotal part of their ideology, placing sexual stereotypes at the heart of racialized political power.[11] For some radicals, rape was a revolutionary act. Activists such as Calvin C. Hernton, Eldridge Cleaver, Frantz Fanon, and LeRoi Jones (Amiri Baraka) endowed the rape of white women with political meaning. Hernton believed black men's rape of white women grew out of the frustrations caused by living in a segregated society and suggested that under Jim Crow, "in every black man who grows up in the South, there is a rapist no matter how hidden."[12] Cleaver was most direct in his assertions that sexual violence was a means of resisting racial oppression. "Rape was an insurrectionary act," he wrote. "It delighted me that I was defying and trampling upon the white man's law, upon his system of values, and that I was defiling his women—and this point, I believe, was the most satisfying to me because I was very resentful over the historical fact of how the white man has used the black woman. I felt I was getting revenge."[13] These depictions of rape confirmed white southerners worst fears, that sex with white women was an expression of black power, a means of opposing white supremacy, and a tool of political struggle. Black men's rape of white women struck at the heart of white southerners' racial ideology and struck at the core of white men's masculine pretensions. After all, white men had placed white women on the pedestal, thereby making them both a target and a trophy of racial strife.

Outlining what motives social commentators believed were behind black-on-white rape does little, however, to illuminate the motives of men actually convicted of rape. In the mid-twentieth century, experts constructed rape as a symptom of psychological and biological pathology. Until the later part of the twentieth century, experts in criminology, the legal system, and medical science argued that rape was the act of sick and aberrant individual men. Regardless of how they classified individual rapists, scholars studying rape in the 1950s and 1960s defined the urge to rape, while not a specific psychiatric abnormality, as part of a "character disorder."[14] Usually citing the influence of domineering females, such theorists believed rapists were abnormal men unable to meet their sexual needs through normal means. Judges and prosecutors trying men accused of rape in the early twentieth century, however, would not have used psychological terminology to describe rapists' crimes, nor would newspaper reporters in their coverage of cases. Rapists, in these men's view, simply could not control their lustful impulses, though they might concede that the inability to control the sex impulse was itself a character disorder. Descriptions of black men as "lust-crazed fiends" or "lustful brutes" in accounts of assaults reflect this understanding of sexual violence as biological imperative. The prosecutor in Buford Morton's 1947 trial, for example, described Morton as a "beast" who was intent on satisfying his "hellish lust for sex."[15]

Recent feminist analyses have shifted our understanding of rape away from a focus on desire for sex to a crime of violence and power. Feminists argue that rape is a form of social control, the fear of which serves to "keep women in their place."[16] Rather than rape growing out of pathology, feminist scholars have argued that because social definitions of sexuality eroticize male aggression and dominance, as well as female passivity, rape is merely a "crude exaggeration of prevailing norms."[17] Scholars have increasingly separated rape from sexual expression, seeing rape as a crime in which the perpetrator uses forced sexual interaction to control and humiliate his victim as he aggrandizes himself. At the same time that feminist scholars enlarged our understanding of rape as a crime of power, they simultaneously reinforced the popular image of a rapist as a black man. Focusing their attention on rape as an aspect of male domination, they overlooked the interdependence of racial and gender hierarchies. For women of color especially, rape has also historically been a crime of racial terror, and a means of enforcing and reinforcing white supremacy.[18]

The only direct expression of convicted black men's motives can be found in a study done by Diana Scully in the 1970s and 1980s. Scully interviewed 114 convicted rapists in Virginia penitentiaries, 41 of whom were black men convicted of raping white women.[19] According to her interviews, rape was a means of revenge or punishment, with the victim either representing the collective liability of all women or being a substitute for a particular woman against whom the rapist bore a grievance. In some cases, the victim represented all women, and the assault was meant to "put her in her place." Other men used rape to gain sexual access to unavailable or unwilling women, viewing rape as a rewarding challenge and as a means of enhancing their self-image, never believing they would be caught. Most saw rape as "a rewarding, low-risk act."[20]

The motives of black men convicted of raping white women echoed the motives Scully found among rapists in general. Most did not view their actions as political acts but rather as a means of sexual access, a view that, according to Scully, confirmed the power of the racial hierarchy:

> Sexual access to white women, not racial hostility, was the most common theme. Sexual curiosity about white women was evident in these interviews—a curiosity no doubt stimulated by the excessive images of white women as sex objects projected by the dominant white male culture. Blocked by racial barriers from normal access, these men used rape to gain access to unavailable white women. . . . Raping white women was variously described as "the ultimate experience" and "a feeling of status, power, macho." For another man, raping a white woman had a special appeal because it violated a "known taboo," making it more dangerous and, thus more exciting to him than raping a black woman.[21]

Although we cannot determine the precise motivations of convicted black men from the existing records of the cases of black-on-white rape that comprise this study, we can draw some tentative conclusions by applying more recent understandings of sexual violence to the past (an admittedly dangerous prospect). Using a modern framework, we might speculate that most men probably did not see their crimes as part of a direct assault on white supremacy. But as rape is now understood as a crime of power, anger, or control, and because convicted rapists described their acts in terms of retaliation or punishment, it is possible that some black men used the assault of white women as an act of revenge.

In existing case files, black men's statements of motive, which are primarily located in confessions, did not articulate rape as a crime of power. They identified their motives according to contemporary understandings of the crime as one of lustful impulse. Black men stated that they "wanted a piece of tail" or "took some pussy," not that they violated white women to make a political statement or in retaliation for a perceived wrong. But, then again, it is unlikely they would express these latter motivations. During a potentially coercive interrogation, many black men probably eventually told white men what they thought they wanted to hear. More important, already in a potentially life-threatening situation, no black man would further inflame white male authorities by speaking the language of political power and struggle. For a black man to baldly state that his actions were intended as an attack on white supremacy would only have increased the likelihood that he would receive the death penalty.

But why not attack white men themselves? There are two ways to answer this question. First, as recent analyses of lynching have shown, black men did, in fact, turn their anger against white men. Although white southerners justified lynching by invoking the myth of the black beast rapist, less than a quarter of lynchings resulted from allegations that the lynched man assaulted a white women. Most black men were lynched for having assaulted or murdered white men.[22] Evidently, assaulting white women was a less "suicidal" way to express anger at white men, because, at least in Virginia, most black men convicted of assaulting white women did not pay with their lives. Second, one can argue that black men's assaults of white women were inherently political acts aimed at white men because of the way white southerners defined the role of white women. As rhetoric about both southern racial ideology and gender hierarchy shows, the southern social order was based on white male hegemony.[23] White southerners elevated white women as idealized embodiments of racial purity and white civilization at the same time that women remained subordinate to white men. White men's mastery over their dependents was an important aspect of their identity as men. White women's vulnerability thus represented the core of the social order. Southern whites conflated public power with manhood and interpreted any attempts by African American men to achieve political and civil rights as attempts to seize white men's sexual control over white women, a charge that most African Americans vigorously denied.[24] Regardless of any individual black man's motivations, any assault on a white woman struck at the heart of white men's patriarchal and racial power. Black-on-white rape was indelibly intertwined with a system of racial and sexual subordination; ideologies about both race and gender made white women likely targets for black men's rage, their sexual curiosity, and in white eyes, their desire for political and civil rights.

Despite the power of white southerners' rhetoric and their fears of black men as rapists, however, African Americans were not entirely prevented from influencing the legal system once they were accused of assault. They utilized numerous forms of both resistance and leverage to shape the legal process. African Americans engaged in acts of resistance in which they directly and openly opposed the white legal structure, and they protested its treatment of black men accused of crimes against white women. Black men might escape or try in other ways to delay legal procedures to allow outrage to dissipate. They also might enlist the help of civil rights organizations in their cases. In addition, the black community might contribute to accused men's defense funds, articulate less incendiary explanations for black men's actions, or attempt collective retribution for extralegal action using their power as laborers and consumers. The opportunities for blacks to protest whites' abuses of power and their ability to oppose the legal structure directly were limited, and they were not always successful, but acts of resistance did occur and they attest to the ability of African Americans, both collectively and individually, to challenge white authority and public power.

Leverage, in contrast to resistance, involved often indirect acts of opposition to white hegemonic power that occurred within the framework of white-controlled institutions, such as the legal system.[25] Leverage reflected the black community's ability to carve out and utilize both direct and indirect mechanisms of power and influence. Like a lever, these mechanisms magnified the small amounts of power blacks could exert, often through intermediaries—such as leaders in the black community, or, more often, white patrons or white lawyers—and usually at a distance. Forms of leverage might be as simple as supplying a black man with an alibi or the private intercession by respected black leaders (or, occasionally, in the case of young offenders, their parents) outside the formal legal process. Some black men might invoke their good character to mitigate their alleged offense; some might have others invoke the poor character of the alleged victim. In the latter case, this assistance often came from white patrons who could supply especially powerful leverage to reduce the charges, or lighten the sentences of black men without the risk of inflaming the white community.

Exploring these indirect channels of power reveals that segregation was not a fixed entity based on white domination and black subordination but rather a continually contested one. Segregation, moreover, did not always divide communities into racial coalitions. When confronted with cases of black-on-white rape, many whites had conflicted loyalties because of their relationships with African Americans. Especially when they involved work relationships, these cases reveal the dynamic aspect of patronage, and the push and pull of deference and obligation. Through the mechanisms of power, blacks challenged the community norms and standards of white supremacy, and struggled—even in a structure that systematically deprived them of power—to influence the process of drawing the color line. Because these mechanisms often operated through intermediaries, blacks could influence the legal process without seeming to threaten white power. The leverage African Americans brought to bear could not entirely counteract white power. Nevertheless, conceding inequality does not also concede that blacks had *no* power or no ability to act as conscious moral agents.

Exerting leverage on black-on-white rape cases in the first half of the twentieth century rarely involved a direct assault on racial inequality. The black community often actively opposed whites' definition of the events that resulted in accusations against black men, but they also worked within the legal and social structure to bend local understanding of events to their own advantage. African Americans were strategic in their actions, seeking advantage in individual cases and pressing arguments that they felt would be most effective in achieving their ends. They could not seek directly to overturn the aspects of southern culture that made black men vulnerable to white women's accusations without increasing the risk of extralegal violence. But within the existing legal structure, they sought to mitigate the effect of that culture on individual black men. Only after the development of an organized civil rights movement did the African American community, mostly through the black press, directly attack racism in the legal system and white assumptions about black men, white women, and rape.

Within the criminal justice system blacks sought to gain advantage in a given case without awakening white wrath that would doom their cause; consequently, they often sought sources of power that were hidden from most white eyes. Glenda Gilmore underscores the elusiveness of black action in her analysis of progressive reform, arguing that black women reformers "used their invisibility to construct a web of social service and civic institutions that remained hidden from and therefore invisible to whites." Black women took the "straw" allocated to them by disenfranchisement and "made bricks."[26] The work of African Americans on behalf of black men accused of assaulting white women was, in some ways, similar to what Gilmore describes. Many activities, by both women and men, usually remained invisible to whites and thus to the historical record as well.

The invisibility of black leverage presents the historian with very real problems. The existing sources articulate debates about how to punish black men primarily through the mouths of white men. Who put the terms of the debates in those mouths is more difficult to determine. White defense lawyers rarely acknowledged the sources of their arguments or even the rumors they presented to legal officials. The sentences handed down to convicted black assailants, by their very variety, prove that judges and juries acknowledged mitigating circumstances, but the sources of those circumstances are unknown. It is impossible to know how many black ministers, community leaders, prominent reform-minded African American women, or even desperate family members spoke with the judges and sheriffs presiding over a given case or knew members of the jury personally. Such relationships could be exploited in the hopes of winning leniency. Leverage appears most clearly in the petitions for pardon filed by black men already convicted of assaults. In these petitions, white lawyers, influenced by black interests, argued that more lenient sentences served the ends of justice.

Acts of resistance—direct opposition to the treatment of black men accused of rape in the legal system—because of their straightforward nature, are somewhat easier to pinpoint than acts of leverage. But, because whites rarely conceded that blacks would have any desire to oppose the system of white supremacy, sources usually did not define black actions as political protest. Locating acts of resistance to whites' treatment of black men accused of rape requires reading between the lines. African Americans did engage in a variety of activities that demonstrated a refusal to acquiesce to the familiar progression of legal events. Through escape, through mobilization of friends, family, or African American organizations, or through organized and public protest, blacks opposed the power whites wielded through, or sometimes outside, the legal system. Through such actions, blacks acted as agents on their own behalf.

One subtle form of protest implicitly challenged whites' understandings of black-on-white rapes and called into question the assumptions that whites routinely made regarding the actions of black men toward white women. Black newspapers did this by providing alternative narratives of the crime that shifted the focus from white fears that all black men desired white women to other cultural and social issues. For example, William Thomas, discussed in Chapter 2, was convicted and sentenced to death in 1927 after he allegedly lunged at a white woman who was alone in a schoolhouse. The black press argued that he was not attempting to rape her. Instead, it asserted, Thomas, who was new to the area and poor and hungry, had merely asked her for a piece of bread and she became frightened when he went to take it.[27] This revised explanation of Thomas's actions shifted the focus from black men's alleged propensity to rape white women to the reality of poverty and hunger among blacks in Virginia. Revised narratives also highlighted what the African American community believed to be white women's irrational fear of black men. Which account of Thomas's actions was more accurate is impossible to say. For whites, unsurprisingly, a narrative of assault that centered on a black man's sexual desires made more sense than did one that centered on his hunger. Because whites controlled the mechanisms of the legal system, their interpretation carried authority

An alternative explanation of events that may have proved more effective involved the four black men accused of raping Lucille Hartless in Richmond in 1940, discussed in Chapter 4. Hartless claimed that her white date abandoned her after she spurned his sexual advances. Far from home, she accepted a ride from four black youths who took her to a secluded spot, where they beat and raped her. The four men argued that when she appeared at the side of the road and begged for a ride, she had already been beaten. This alternative scenario shifted attention away from the volatile issue of interracial rape and focused on another reality: that white men denied sexual access to seemingly available and vulnerable women could become violent. At the same time, the counternarrative of the four Good Samaritans created a more complicated picture of interactions across race and gender lines. Black men could have nonsexual, benevolent intentions toward white women. Even more pointed, black men, in some instances, could treat white women better than did white men. These notions could have triggered white rage, as they undercut white men's patriarchal and chivalrous pretensions. In the case of the four black youths, it is more than likely that the alternative narrative helped to shift sympathy away from the victim, especially because her white date was married. Although the four men were convicted of rape, their sentences of ten years in prison were surprisingly lenient.[28]

One popular, if perhaps spontaneous, form of resistance was simply to absent oneself from the legal process itself. Many black men, when they feared arrest was imminent, fled the area. News reports of black-on-white assault often focused not on assaults themselves but on the efforts by whites to catch suspected assailants, and they attest to the frequency that suspected black men used escape as a method of opposing the criminal justice system. In 1916, after allegedly assaulting two white schoolgirls, John Henry Williams fled on foot from Nottoway County. He was captured on a cattle farm in a neighboring county by a posse whose triumphant picture was published in the *Richmond Times-Dispatch*. He confessed, was sentenced to death, and was executed six weeks after the crime.[29] Williams did not escape the legal process but managed to avoid its grasp for four days. In white eyes, fleeing represented a tacit admission of guilt, and Williams's effort to escape fanned white outrage over the assault.[30] Short-term escape, then, was not always a successful means of avoiding the imposition of white ideas of justice. Nevertheless, if a black

man could successfully escape—and many assailants were never caught—
whites were unable to exact retribution.

Often the delay between the time a man was accused and eventually
brought to trial allowed whites' outrage to dissipate enough that jurors
would hear evidence with an open mind. Richard Jackson provides a case
in point. He was accused of raping a middle-aged white woman in her
barn. Despite the fact that his shovel was at the scene of the crime, Jackson
claimed he was in Baltimore on the night of the rape. He remained at his
home in Washington, D.C., forcing Fairfax County authorities to obtain his
extradition, which he fought vigorously. He was not brought to trial until
two years after the crime, at which point he was acquitted.[31] His legal
battle to prevent extradition worked in his favor. Though the *Fairfax Herald*
covered the attack and the search for suspects extensively in 1922, it made
no mention of Jackson's extradition to Fairfax, his trial, or the jury's verdict in 1924.[32] Without the tinder of racial hysteria, Jackson's trial, like
most rape trials of white men, resulted in the defendant's acquittal. Richard Jackson may not have consciously described his actions as resistance
when he fought his extradition, but his efforts successfully prevented
white outrage from dictating his fate in the legal system.

Convicted men also protested their sentences with their feet—they escaped from prison. Preston Waters was convicted of attempting to rape a
white woman who claimed a black man had accosted her on a city street in
1923. She identified Waters as her assailant, the jury convicted him, and he
was sentenced to fifteen years in prison. Four years after his conviction,
Waters escaped from prison and remained at large for more than a year. In
1932, several years after his recapture, he wrote Governor Pollard requesting a conditional pardon. In his request, he insisted that he escaped because he was wrongly convicted. "Knowing that I was serving an unjust
sentence," he wrote, "I was bitter, and escaped from the prison." The
attorney who prosecuted his case acknowledged that there was no evidence indicating Waters's intent to commit rape. The governor agreed to
grant a pardon but refused to release Waters until he had made up the
time he was free. All told, Waters spent more than eight years behind
bars.[33]

Fleeing arrest or escaping from prison were dangerous forms of resistance, ones that could justify the use of lethal force by law enforcement.
It is unclear whether the men who sought to avoid their trials or their
sentences were acting out of a sense of racial injustice or self-preservation.
Preston Waters was something of an exception in this regard. He explicitly
made the connection between what he believed to be the "little justice" in

his sentence and his decision to escape. He also attributed his continuing plight to his status as a prisoner. "As to my case, from long experience, I know that I will not [be] believed in the [recitation] of my case. I know that the word of no prisoner is ever believed." Waters's letter made clear his belief that his status as a black man convicted of assaulting a white woman guaranteed that no white official would give credence to his claims of innocence.[34]

Accused black men also challenged racial discrimination in the legal process. In 1921, Charles Green, who was indicted for attempted rape and robbery, protested his experience in a racist legal system, and, in an unusual move, insisted his protest be included in the trial record. Lillie Priddy, his alleged victim, testified that as they passed along a road, Green tipped his hat to her and then struck her with a stick and tried to assault her. When her cries attracted help, he allegedly fled with her pocketbook. Priddy's pocketbook, however, was found, with all its contents, lying in the road about six feet from the scene of the crime.[35] Green was eventually tried and acquitted of attempted rape, but he was convicted of robbery. The jury's sentence of eighteen years, however, was the maximum prison term for attempted rape. As part of his anticipated appeal, Green requested that a notation be made in the court order that Green had protested the exclusion of "all persons of African descent and of all other races, except the caucasian race," from serving on both the grand jury and petit jury and that he had moved to have his indictment quashed on those grounds. The court had heard his arguments and had rejected the pleas and in the record, insisted that "no person or persons of color or of African descent were excluded."[36] In specifically targeting the discriminatory practices routinely used by southern courts, Green's protest anticipated later, more successful challenges of court procedures. Racial discrimination in jury selection, however, would not be declared unconstitutional until 1934.[37]

Green's protest, even without the help of any civil rights organizations, was an early iteration of the later civil rights strategy of Charles Houston, Thurgood Marshall, and the NAACP Legal Defense and Education Fund, which used strategic appeals to have specific discriminatory practices declared unconstitutional. Green appealed his case on the grounds that there was no evidence he had taken Priddy's pocketbook. The only testimony of theft came from Priddy herself, who acknowledged she was unconscious and never saw Green take the bag or have it in his possession. The Virginia Supreme Court of Appeals reversed his conviction, and Chesterfield County declined to retry his case. The Virginia Supreme Court's judgment, however, did not address discrimination in jury selection, and it is not clear whether Green raised it in his petition. The text of the court's judgment called his petition for a writ of error "so inartificially drawn that it is difficult to say where errors are assigned,"[38] an assertion that may have been little more than an attempt to avoid the issue.

Green's case may not have attracted the help of the NAACP because it did not accord with their long-term strategy. Rather than taking on any case of discrimination, the organization chose to take action only when it felt the time was ripe for successful appeal and in cases that were appropriate vehicles for targeting specific laws. As it often informed people seeking its aid, the NAACP handled only cases in which an "injustice has been done or is about to be done because of race or color prejudice and where entry by the Association will result in a favorable decision affecting the rights of colored people in general."[39] The NAACP did not see itself as, and continually reminded blacks that it was not, a "legal aid society." It also avoided cases in which the inflammatory nature of a crime, in white eyes, would overshadow any constitutional claims it might make. Its approach to civil rights law had the unfortunate effect of sacrificing individuals who were the targets of specific discrimination. The NAACP waited for cases that fit its strategy rather than developing a strategy in response to the cases that came to its attention.[40] Despite this stated approach, African Americans continued to bring cases of black men accused of assaulting white women to the attention of the NAACP. Although Virginians notified the NAACP of the plights of numerous accused black men, the organization became involved in relatively few cases. Consequently, most Virginia cases receive little more than scant mention in the NAACP's manuscript collection. The New York office referred some cases to local branches and refused some cases outright.

Calling on the NAACP for help was risky because southern whites resented the organization's stated goals and their interference. Though there is no evidence that whites threatened blacks in Virginia who tried to enlist the help of the NAACP, histories of the organization and memoirs of African Americans attest to the anger such actions could inspire among whites.[41]

The requests for help that were directed to the NAACP in Virginia reveal a vibrant network of activists working on behalf of accused men. The New York office of the NAACP often referred cases to local activists, inspiring a wide network of official and unofficial allies to rally to the cause. For example, Lee Ernest Bell's attorney advised that the group's help was unnecessary because the alleged victim had a poor reputation.

However, Bell's sister, who lived in Toledo, Ohio, brought the case to the attention of the New York office of the NAACP, and the secretary of the Richmond branch looked into it. Protest against accused black men's treatment in the legal system, then, was not confined to the locale of an assault, and protest voiced by family and supporters hundreds of miles away could garner support for black men. Moreover, if blacks were leery of calling on the NAACP for fear of white response, this network could more safely enlist its help from a distance.[42]

Like members of the NAACP, other politically active African Americans advocated using strategic appeals to oppose racism in the criminal justice system. Philip Jones, for example, was convicted of raping and murdering two sisters in 1934, and he eventually was executed.[43] At first, the NAACP took considerable interest in the case. J. Byron Hopkins Jr. of the Richmond branch interviewed Jones, but when the NAACP was convinced of the integrity of Jones's confession, they bowed out of the case.[44] Although the NAACP believed that little could be gained from the Jones case, Joseph Simpson, a writer for the *Richmond Planet*, argued that the black community could benefit from raising issues on Philip Jones's behalf. Acknowledging Jones's probable guilt, Simpson urged the NAACP, "or some other interested body," to appeal Jones's conviction on procedural issues that affected all black men charged with crimes. According to Simpson, Jones's case provided a prime opportunity to protest elements of the legal process, like jury selection, precisely because there was nothing to lose: "Jones had already been sentenced to death and an appeal in his case on the jury issue, resulting in a new trial, would have a profound and lasting effect on Virginia jurisprudence," even if it could not save Jones's life.[45]

Neither the NAACP nor any other interested group took up Simpson's call, but his urging is nonetheless significant. Simpson was clearly aware of the efforts of the attorneys involved in the Scottsboro case, and he was looking for cases in Virginia that would press the same points. He urged Virginia's African Americans to begin protesting their denials of due process, which may not have occurred in Philip Jones's case but did so in general. In his mind, it mattered little that blacks in Virginia were much less likely to be lynched than in other southern states. There was plenty of room to protest how blacks were treated within the legal system. Simpson made his call in a newspaper with an unabashedly political agenda, so his claims about the lack of due process for black defendants would have had resonance for his reading audience. Rather than taking on the entire case against Philip Jones, which was futile anyway, Simpson argued, the black community could make enormous long-term gains in the legal system through a narrow, tactical appeal.

Unlike Simpson, however, other black newspaper reporters wrote public appeals designed solely to win convicted men mercy. Rather than attacking racism in the legal system, as Joseph Simpson advocated, they usually sought to present an argument that avoided accusing whites of racial discrimination. Before the late 1940s, rather than addressing the larger issue of racial disparity in punishment, or attacking white Virginians' irrational fear of black men's propensity to attack white women, the black press concentrated on attacking specific issues in a given case. Shirley Winnegan, for example, was convicted of raping and murdering Hilda Barlow in 1927 and was sentenced to death (see Chapter 3). Rather than arguing that Winnegan was innocent of the crime or convicted by a jury fraught with racial prejudice the *Richmond Planet* attacked the jury's decision to execute a man previously determined to be insane. Winnegan's supporters, in their editorials and letters to the governor, confined their protest to these grounds, hoping not to gain Winnegan's release but to save his life.[46] They were unsuccessful, and Winnegan was executed.

Like the NAACP, the black press was strategic in the cases they chose to cover. Although their appeals for mercy did not always directly attack discrimination in the legal process, they did focus on the extreme punishment that many black men received from white juries. Consequently, black newspapers made little mention of black men who fared well before the legal system, either by being acquitted or by receiving a light sentence, a commutation, or a conditional pardon. Concerned with exposing the endemic racism of both the legal system and southern society in general, the black press would understandably be reluctant to publicize instances when the system upheld black men's interests over those of white women. Similarly, the black press was usually reluctant to publicize instances in which blacks threatened or attempted violent retribution as a form of protest, because it did not want to appear to support violent insurrection. The strategies of the black press, however, often provided the means by which the black community as a whole could act collectively to protect black men from the worst ravages of the legal system.

Even if African Americans were not involved directly in cases of black-on-white rape, they still found ways to demonstrate their opposition to the legal system. Virginia's black press in the 1930s printed numerous articles following the cases of accused black men throughout Virginia and the South, including that of the nine men accused in Scottsboro, Alabama. In that instance, articles instructed people where to send donations to support the men's legal defense. These kinds of activities sent a message to Virginia's whites about how local African Americans' felt about racial discrimination in the legal system, and underscore the importance of the black press to an incipient civil rights movement.

Similarly, the black press protested the 1949 convictions of seven black men in Martinsville, Virginia, who had been accused of raping a white minister's wife. All seven men were executed in 1951 despite vigorous protest. With the help of the black press, African Americans showed their collective sense of injustice by creating a fund to support the families of the men.[47] Rather than viewing them as brutal rapists, the black community remembered the men as human beings with families, and placed their conviction and sentence within a context of systemic racial discrimination. After the Martinsville Seven case, protest against the treatment of black men accused of rape in the legal system no longer functioned on a case-by-case basis. As Chapter 7 shows, the widespread racial disparities in punishment for rape in Virginia demonstrated by the seven men's lawyers changed the nature of the debate about interracial rape in Virginia, placing all such cases in the larger context of the fight for civil rights and equal treatment under the law.[48]

Other accused black men benefited from more organized efforts on their behalf. Any accused man who hoped for justice or at least mercy needed competent legal counsel, and often the help of the black community to pay for it. John Clements, who was acquitted of assaulting Fannie Chenault in 1914, owed his release in part to the vigorous efforts of his defense attorneys. Clements worked as a laborer at a dairy and probably could not have afforded his legal fees on his own. Though his lawyers expressed a willingness to handle Clements's defense for no fee, they received compensation from the Civic Improvement League, a "local negro organization," as well as from a "citizen of Henrico who has serious doubts as to the guilt of Clements."[49]

In the case of Clarence Howard, who was convicted of raping and beating a white woman in a store in Farmville, Virginia, in 1938 and received a sentence of death, the black community played a role in his eventual release. After his arrest in West Virginia, he claimed that he had never been to Farmville, Virginia, until he had been brought there by officials as a suspect in the case. He insisted he was working as a day laborer in Kentucky at the time of the crime. Howard nevertheless pleaded guilty because, he reportedly told the court, "he couldn't beat the case. You all say I did it and I have no witnesses."[50] The witnesses in Kentucky who could testify to his whereabouts at the time of the crime were not able to get to Farmville. Though "prominent negroes in the vicinity of Farm-ville" attempted to raise money to bring the witnesses to testify, they were unsuccessful, and attempts to win Howard a new trial based on their testimony were also unsuccessful. Howard's conviction stood until he received a conditional pardon in 1949 because of "strong doubt as to his guilt."[51]

When whites exacted punishment through extralegal beatings, shoot-ings, or lynchings, Virginia's African American community also engaged in collective protest, providing clear evidence that blacks did not remain silent when they believed the standards of accepted relations between whites and blacks had been violated, especially in a state where lynching was not the norm. Though newspapers reported only a few instances of collective protest, there were certainly others. Roosevelt Woodson's insin-uations about a white woman provoked one such collective protest in 1929. A white man overhead him making an "insulting" remark about a white woman while he was working. The white man allegedly knocked Woodson down and reported the remark to the woman's husband. Later that night, the woman's husband and his brothers "administered" a beat-ing on Woodson. After the beating, according to newspaper reports, a group of black men began to gather in cars at the filling station operated by the woman's brother. The men paraded down the streets of Carrsville, where the incident took place. Police arrested them for "unlawful assem-bly" before violence occurred, but authorities reported that the men were armed and waiting for an additional twenty-five men and were planning to retaliate for Woodson's beating. The *Richmond Times-Dispatch* reported that the parade "intimidated citizens and terrorized the neighborhood."[52] News reports, moreover, said that the parade was in response to the treat-ment Woodson had received at the hands of whites who had circum-vented the law. The eight men who were arrested were each sentenced to three months in jail and fined a hefty $300. Despite the black men's quick arrest, their activities nonetheless concerned whites, who feared that a gathering of armed blacks might represent a more general uprising against white power.

No white response to black-on-white rape was a more egregious viola-tion of due process than lynching. Whites used lynching to force blacks into their "place," and it demonstrated to all blacks the potential conse-quences of their failing to abide by southern social and legal codes.[53] Generally powerless to prevent them, though there are instances where the black community successfully hid a mob's intended victim, African

Americans recognized lynchings as an abuse of the power of white supremacy in a "civilized" society that claimed to be bound by the rule of law. It is no surprise that some of the earliest efforts of collective action by African Americans, both men and women, on their own behalf was to end extralegal executions.[54] Less well-known, however, are local community actions to protest specific lynchings. One such event occurred in Virginia in 1917.

William Page was lynched in Northumberland County, Virginia. The sequence of events leading up to his lynching were not unusual. He was accused of attempting to assault two white girls, the daughter and the niece of the prominent white farmer who employed him. The *Richmond Times-Dispatch*'s account of Page's subsequent lynching reads like a melodrama; it described an inevitable punishment exacted by "earnest" and "hardworking" men seeking speedy justice, who came together and dispersed in near-supernatural anonymity, like "a bolt from a clear sky." Page was taken from the sheriff by a crowd of masked men who "seemed to have risen as if by magic." "His appeals for clemency [were] born back on the wind to the sheriff" without reply, and after being allowed to spend a few minutes with his wife and mother, he was taken to the "negro settlement" and hanged from a giant oak "beneath which the pickaninnies play daily" in the yard of the schoolhouse. Less than four hours elapsed between the alleged assault and Page's death.[55] The account of William Page's violent death at the hands of a mob is different from subsequent reports of lynching, carrying none of the vilification of lynch mobs that the Virginia media would soon develop. Accounts of Page's lynching fit easily within most southern justifications of lynching—that it was understandable and unavoidable retaliation, undertaken by a crowd solemn and purposeful in its unpleasant duty, when black men committed the "unspeakable" offense of assaulting white women.[56]

Several days after Page's death, the *Times-Dispatch* reported that any excitement caused by the lynching had "died out almost as quickly as it was fanned into flame." The commonwealth's attorney of Northumberland County was beginning an investigation of the lynching, but white reporters claimed that the local community, even the African Americans, supported the mob's actions: "As far as could be ascertained today, negroes generally seemed satisfied with the verdict of the armed band that executed the negro and that he had received only proper punishment." As proof, the newspaper pointed out that Page's family refused to accept the body for burial or "to have anything to do with it."[57] The black community may have appeared conciliatory to prevent reprisals. Or, as Fitzhugh Brundage points out, refusal to accept lynched men's bodies for burial, and the costs that such burial incurred, could be a form of protest to lynching itself. As the aunt of a man lynched in Alexandria, Virginia, in 1897 argued, "As the [white] people killed him, they will have to bury him."[58]

There was other evidence that the blacks living in Northumberland were decidedly outraged about Page's illegal execution. An editorial in the *Richmond Planet* insisted that "[c]olored folks know that the rapist is as dangerous to the colored folks as to white ones and they will serve on a jury to land him in an electric chair as quickly as the white man." Despite articulating a common abhorrence for the crime of rape, however, the *Planet* argued that the full facts of the case were unknown and, as presented by whites, defied belief. "We cannot understand how William Page could have been guilty of attempted criminal assault unless he was demented," it asserted. "To outrage a woman with another yelling female in the vicinity is well-nigh an impossibility and yet this is what is alleged to have been done." The *Planet* modulated its condemnation, insisting that it was not in favor of racial amalgamation but that it nonetheless found the account of the assault questionable. Lynch law must go, it argued, but primarily because it did not allow unlikely accounts of assault to go unchallenged.[59] Maintaining a reasoned tone that focused on legal issues and avoiding any mention of white barbarity were part of the paper's strategy. In this way it could circumvent any charges by whites that the black press encouraged interracial sexual congress or criminal activity.

Though, according to the white press, events in Northumberland occurred with a relentless inevitability, and though the black press carefully stated its grounds for opposition, the black community in Northumberland did not remain quiet for long. Despite previously reporting that the black community seemed satisfied with Page's execution, the *Times-Dispatch* hinted at doubts among whites that this was indeed so. It expressed whites' relief that a black religious revival that took place not long after Page's death ended without becoming a catalyst for protest and that "leaders among the colored people, when they found there was no question of the guilt of Page, lent their full influence toward quieting their people."[60] Six weeks after Page's death, however, the paper reported, with some surprise, that there were "indications of trouble" in the Heathsville black community, where Page had lived. Immediately after the lynching, "the colored people were thought to have taken it quietly and entirely without resentment." It was even thought that some blacks agreed that

Page's death was a just punishment. This view, it later developed, was "erroneous." According to the *Richmond Times-Dispatch*,

> It has been discovered that many secret meetings have been held, and that a prominent citizen and land owner who farms extensively, has been boycotted by the race, every negro refusing to work for him at any price or under any conditions, believing they had found he was one of the lynchers. It was learned also that those who might have been prevailed upon to work for him had been intimidated. They were threatened with a beating to the finish if they gave him any assistance. An altogether new and different spirit is being manifested among the colored people now. Wages have doubled and negro help can scarcely be gotten at any price.

Occurring almost immediately after the East St. Louis riot and the NAACP's protest march in response, this "new and different spirit" marked the birth of the modern civil rights movement. Such effective collective action, however, the paper insisted, could not have been solely the result of black initiative, and it blamed the uprising on outside agitators. "Many accuse German spies as being at the bottom of the trouble."[61]

Blacks in Heathsville were able to harness their power as laborers to demonstrate their anger at the white men who killed William Page. Their activities—discovering the identity of the lynchers themselves, organizing the boycott, and policing the black community to ensure that the boycott was successful—required a good deal of coordination. Though the *Richmond Times-Dispatch* did concede that blacks were protesting Page's lynching, it nonetheless could not believe the black community was sophisticated or organized enough on its own to accomplish such a successful protest. The black press called the protest a harbinger of things to come. The *Norfolk Journal and Guide* warned that any more lynchings would deprive whites of their labor force, since other blacks would surely adopt the tactics of those in Heathsville.[62]

There is no evidence in the historical record that other communities in Virginia used similar tactics, though this lack of evidence does not mean that similar protests did not occur. White newspapers may have been loath to publish accounts of black collective action precisely because they might encourage other blacks to protest any unfair treatment. But even if these events were singular in their approach and effectiveness, that does not minimize their importance. At the very least, the actions of African Americans in William Page's community and of the friends of Roosevelt

Woodson suggest that blacks did not meekly accept white subordination and did not quietly accept whites' decisions to circumvent the legal process. Voices actively raised against such injustices informed whites where blacks located the boundaries between appropriate and inappropriate action across racial lines. And though blacks were not always able to enforce those boundaries, their protests pushed against white ideas of interracial interaction and carved out room to maneuver. Few white farmers in Northumberland County would be quite so willing to take the law into their own hands in the future after seeing their crops—their very livelihoods—jeopardized.

Through escaping the law, pointing out discriminatory legal practices, enlisting the aid of civil rights organizations, and organizing collective actions against specific whites, African Americans directly opposed whites' control over the legal process that tried black men accused of raping white women. Whether fleeing, escaping, or refusing to work for members of a lynch mob, such actions underscored black outrage over white ideas of justice when white women were attacked. Some acts of resistance were noteworthy in their very daring. Though blacks did not openly oppose the white judicial system often, and instances of outright opposition appear rarely in the historical record, they did exert some power over the courts. Blacks used leverage to shape the legal process, operating within the legal system, rather than in opposition to it.

That in some instances black men accused of assaulting white women were not prosecuted suggests that something overpowered the force of the evidence or the white woman's charges. In some cases, the decision to decline to prosecute was made in exchange for some other form of punishment, such as an accused man's agreement to leave the state or to be confined in a juvenile reform school or even a mental hospital.[63]

One case in particular, however, sheds light on one way blacks were able to negotiate with legal officials and to convince them to drop plans to prosecute black men suspected of assaulting white women. Some African American parents could exert leverage on behalf of their children, as Ralph Green was bitterly aware. He, along with several other black youths, was charged with attempted rape for attacking a ten-year-old girl in 1922. Despite being only fifteen, he was found guilty and sentenced to twelve years in prison.[64] Eight years later, Ralph Green wrote the governor requesting a conditional pardon. The superintendent of the prison was reluctant to recommend clemency because Green had attempted to escape from prison, but he expressed some sympathy for Green's situation. "I feel all of this boy's trouble is not his own fault. It is simply because no one looked after him when he was younger and he was just allowed to roam the streets without any home supervision." On the other hand, Green's sister, Carrie L. Hill, who also wrote on his behalf, wrote that his conviction was fundamentally unfair. He had been arrested with other black boys who had participated in the assault but who had escaped charges. "The rest of the boys' fathers and mothers got them out," she wrote, "but Ralph did not have anyone to see after him." Though the governor refused to release him, he did remove the additional sentence Green received for attempting to escape from prison.[65] In the case of the boys who were not incarcerated, their young ages may have made it easier for legal officials to agree to drop charges, but age alone, as Ralph Green's experience attests, was not enough to change the authorities' minds.

That the vast majority of men who were accused of assaulting white women were not punished to the limit of the law suggests that during the trial, blacks were able to exert some degree of influence over the trial process and the opinions of the jury. The presence of the convicted man's family, friends, or other supporters in the courtroom may have influenced the jury by placing the defendant within the community. Whites also may have been more reluctant to execute a familiar black man, one whose reputation was known in the community, who was a husband and a father, a tenant, or a hand. Historians have documented that whites often criticized the black population as a whole but made exceptions for "their" blacks. Men who were part of the community web of relationships were less threatening than itinerant black men, as long as they were not accused of assaulting the wives and daughters of their employers.[66]

When black men were accused of assaulting white women, the black community might rally behind an accused man by hiding him or helping him to leave the area. They might testify to his character in court. They also might provide the accused man with an alibi. Testimony about alibis provided an important form of leverage. It allowed blacks to contradict the word of a white woman or other white witnesses without directly accusing whites of false testimony. It also provided the jury or legal officials with justifications for lenience when there were questions about the accused man's guilt or the victim's character. An alibi also allowed whites in the criminal justice system to acquit an accused assailant or grant him pardon without dismissing the woman's account of her assault. In accepting an alibi the court could still express sympathy for the woman as victim of violence while attributing the accused man's release to her unfortunate but understandable mistake in identifying her assailant.

Black men and white women did not, of course, testify on an equal footing before white juries. White men usually were more likely to believe the word of a white woman, even when it was directly contradicted by a black man. L. W. Lane stated that he and other white men automatically accepted white women's testimony over that of black men when he testified against Lee Archer's defense motion for a change of venue in 1913: "[I]f the girl were positive in her identification of the man, he [Lane] would believe her statement against that of a dozen Negro witnesses who might testify that the accused was at another place and he believed everybody else would do the same."[67] Whites believed blacks were inherently dishonest, an assumption only exacerbated when blacks faced criminal charges. Whites' perception that the testimony of whites was more credible than that of African Americans' shaped the clemency process as well, as Alex Hatton's experience shows. Hatton had been convicted in 1918 for committing at least one of a series of thirteen assaults on white women between October 1917 and March 1918 in Norfolk. The evidence must have been scanty because he was sentenced to only eight years in prison. Two years later, his parents began to appeal for his pardon, claiming that he could not have committed most of the crimes because he was working in Connecticut at the time. Their appeals were refused in 1920 and 1921. He was finally granted pardon in 1922, when the governor received a letter from Hatton's Connecticut employer confirming his presence in the North at the time of the crimes.[68]

As a form of leverage, providing an alibi for a black man was not always successful; Lee Archer was convicted and executed despite such testimony. In other cases, it raised sufficient doubt to free an accused black man. A Richmond court, for example, dismissed charges of attempted rape against Sandy Brown when he produced six witnesses who testified that he had not left the railroad shanty where they were sleeping on the night of the alleged offense. Their testimony outweighed that of the victim, a white woman, who said she was "positive" he was the man.[69] Louise Dreves identified Bud Debero as her assailant by his voice and the light suit of clothing he was wearing when he allegedly assaulted her. He was acquitted when he produced witnesses who testified he had never owned such a suit. This testimony was strengthened by evidence that Dreves had initially identified another man as her assailant.[70]

Accused black men also called upon patronage relationships with whites to help their cause. Creating alliances with the white community was one of the most effective forms of leverage available to black men, as whites' testimony was less easily disregarded by other whites. These alliances attest to the complex relationships between blacks and whites in twentieth-century Virginia. Many whites and blacks enjoyed relationships not necessarily egalitarian but characterized by varying degrees of caring and benevolence that could continue for generations. The willingness of some whites to support black men accused of assaulting white women provides some of the best evidence that whites did not respond uniformly and predictably to white women's charges of interracial rape. It reveals the internal tension inherent in white paternalism, characterized both by deference and by mutual obligation.[71] At times paternalism protected white women, and at other times it protected black men. No case better illustrates the complexity of interracial relations than that of Leon Fry, accused, tried, and acquitted of an assault on a ten-year-old white girl in 1932.

Ethel Moyer, a young schoolgirl in Page County, told police that while she was walking home from the bus stop, a black man attacked her. Because his head was covered, and because he put something over her head as well, she was unable to give a detailed description of her attacker. Suspicion soon rested on Leon Fry, a black youth described as anywhere from seventeen to twenty-two years old. Fry lived and worked at a white home near where Moyer was attacked, and when police attempted to question him, he fled, dodging bullets shot at his back. He spent one night hidden in the woods before he turned himself in.[72]

After Fry's capture, coverage of the case shifted from the crime itself to efforts to preserve Fry's safety until trial. Rumors of community unrest prompted the Page County sheriff to move Fry to a more secure location. The Harrisonburg jail, reputed to be "mob-proof," became Fry's refuge for the next month. Not content to secure Fry behind three steel doors, Charles R. Fawley, the Harrisonburg sheriff, called in the Virginia militia, armed with fire hoses, pistols, "tear bombs," and "riot guns." Though Fry was reported to be "frightened almost white," Fawley announced that "no man would get the keys to the Harrisonburg jail except from my dead body." Militia guards continued to surround the jail for nearly a week, though no mobs ever appeared.[73] Throughout his confinement, Leon Fry professed his innocence. Evidence against him was largely circumstantial, as the victim could not precisely identify him, stating that "he looked like the man" after initially saying "he was too black." Police, however, found footprints that matched Fry's shoes near the scene of the attack, as well as several safety pins that officers claimed he routinely wore on his clothing.

Fortunately, Fry had friends in high places. Born to a black couple with numerous children, he had been living with and working for Nathan Sedgwick, the former sheriff of Page County, since the age of seven. News reports emphasized that Sedgwick had raised Fry since that point and was convinced of his innocence. Indeed, it was Sedgwick who accompanied Fry to the jail when he surrendered to authorities.[74] The unqualified endorsement of one of the most "prominent" members of the community improved Fry's legal position immeasurably. Sedgwick buttressed Fry's insistence that he was innocent by providing him with an alibi for all but fifteen minutes of the afternoon of the crime. Because of Sedgwick's support, the community became more willing to lend credence to reports of unfamiliar black men in the area and became skeptical of the victim's shaky identification, especially after Fry pointed out that he had known the victim for three years, and if he had indeed been her assailant, she would have been able to identify him with more certainty. The support of the former sheriff helped shift public opinion, and it also provided Fry with resources. Sedgwick hired Lynn Lucas, the son of the current sheriff of Page County, as Fry's defense counsel. He was joined by state senator Aubrey Weaver, who became interested in the case when he read reports that Fry might be innocent.[75]

Backed by a formidable defense team determined to establish his innocence, Fry's fortunes brightened. Although a preliminary hearing in Harrisonburg and the Page County grand jury decided he should face trial, the defense attorneys remained confident they could prove Fry's alibi and establish that other black men passed through the area at the time of the crime. They were not entirely successful. Fry's first trial resulted in a hung jury. But Fry's support from powerful whites took their toll on the victim and her family. While the media emphasized the "prominence of the family for whom the negro worked," they also noted that "[t]he little girl and her aunt, who is her guardian, have been in a highly nervous state since the former trial."[76] When they were called to testify in Fry's second trial, "both were very nervous and gave their testimony in a voice scarcely above a whisper."[77] The jury deliberated for less than forty-five minutes and voted to acquit.[78]

Leon Fry's patron, Nathan Sedgwick, was able to establish reasonable doubt about Fry's guilt in several ways. Not only did he provide for his legal defense and arrange for bail after the first trial, he lent Fry credibility. He provided the sanction of whiteness that prompted other whites to shift their focus from Fry's race to the specific details of the crime. With Fry protected by the whiteness and power of the former sheriff, the white community could justify their doubts about the victim's identification of Fry as her assailant and concede the possibility that another black man could have been in the area. They could believe Fry without directly disbelieving his victim. Ethel Moyer and her aunt, though white and female, could not compete with the status and social power of Fry's white patrons. Moyer's power as a white female victim of a black man diminished in the face of the public support offered Fry by white male figures of authority. The cost of the white community's support, in terms of the victim's suffering, was clear in the demeanor of Ethel Moyer and her aunt on the witness stand. After Fry's acquittal, no efforts were made to search for other possible suspects.

Whites could be powerful allies to black men accused of the rape or attempted rape of white women. Many black men sought to harness the power of their white employers on their behalf, and whites sought to influence the legal process in different ways and at different times.[79] Such support shielded the black man in the armor of white protection from white women who accused them, a curious inversion of southern exhortations to protect white women from black men. But the effect of that protective shield went beyond legal counsel or an alibi. Whites, and especially prominent white employers, could testify that a black man "knew his place" and was unlikely to commit what whites considered the most egregious violation of segregation. This kind of testimony assured whites that the black men in question accepted the racial hierarchy and were thus no real threat to whites or white supremacy. Consequently, white patronage did not come without cost to the African Americans that called upon it. Accused black men who used the support of white patrons were prevented from challenging either racial discrimination or the assumptions that surrounded interactions between white women and black men. Moreover, relying on patronage relations affirmed the very system—legally enforced racial inequality—that made black men vulnerable in the first place.

White patronage did not always lead to acquittal. Leon Fry's case is but one particularly well documented example. But with white support, many did received shorter sentences or win pardon. William Rose was charged with attempted rape in 1914. At his trial, his white employer and his employer's son and daughter all testified that he was working for them at the time of the assault. Rose was convicted and received a sentence of eighteen years in prison, but nine years later, the alibi and his employers' support contributed to his release.[80] As clemency files show, white legal officials were willing to change their understanding of an assault and shift attention away from race and toward other factors. As Richard "Reds" Jackson learned, by forcing Fairfax authorities to spend two years fighting for his extradition, the passage of time created more room to maneuver. After community outrage died down, a jury was more willing to listen to the defense's arguments. Similarly, in many cases, when juries sentenced black men to prison, the time a black man spent incarcerated cooled local tempers, and made legal officials more willing to examine other aspects of the case for mitigating circumstances.

In twentieth-century Virginia, whites often assumed black men's guilt regardless of the evidence, and more than one-quarter of accused black men paid with their lives, either through lynching or execution. Consequently, winning a prison term rather than a death sentence represented a victory of sorts. A jail term provided time for tempers inflamed by racial tension to cool. When that happened, the defense or the convicted man's supporters could begin to encourage officials to turn away from the inflammatory racial aspects of the case. White patrons could play an important role in this process. Once a black man had been convicted, it was not uncommon for whites to begin to work on his behalf. White patrons, moreover, could more easily raise issues about the character of the victim, shifting the focus in the case from race to gender. As the case of John Mays Jr. shows, it was not necessary for the victim herself to be tarnished by allegations of promiscuity. Character included not only the sexual and moral reputation of the victim but also her family's position and reputation, a combination made more potent when placed in contrast to the assailant's and his family's character and reputation. John Mays ultimately owed his release to the intervention of a white patron, who argued that poor character was not race specific.

John Mays Jr. was convicted in Nelson County in May 1923 of attempted rape and was sentenced to eighteen years. He was released from prison in December 1930 because of the recommendation of the trial judge and the commonwealth's attorney, his good record while in prison, and doubt as to whether he committed the crime. At the time that he was accused of rape, Mays was seventeen years old and working as a gardener for a local white doctor. His alleged victim was a seven-year-old white girl who testified that while she was on her way home from school she was accosted by a black man who carried her into the woods and attempted to rape her. Mays was arrested several hours later while he was working at the home of Dr. A. A. Sizer. The evidence against Mays was not strong, and S. B. Whitehead, the commonwealth's attorney, conceded that Mays's conviction sprang from the racial aspects of the case: "A mistake may have been made by the jury in determining this case and as the girl was white and he was a negro, that fact may have induces [sic] the jury to give him a long[er] term than they would otherwise have done."[81]

Most of the information regarding the case comes from Dr. Sizer's letters on Mays's behalf. He insisted that both Mays's character and his behavior indicated that he was not guilty of the crime. The Sizers had known Mays's family for more than three generations, and, according to Sizer, they all exhibited "integrity and humble faithfulness." Indeed, Sizer asserted, Mays "comes of our best negro stock" and was above reproach. He was devoutly religious and had been a preacher in the local African American church since he was fourteen. He was extremely intelligent, as Dr. Sizer had taught him alongside his own son. These were hardly the characteristics of a brutal black beast rapist.[82]

Sizer's language was not accidental. Framing his appeal in terms of heredity and intelligence demonstrated his understanding of the theories of eugenics—that the human race could be improved through selective breeding. Eugenical ideas became popular in Virginia as a more "enlightened" approach to managing the problems posed by "unfit" populations. *Buck v. Bell*, a case decided by the U.S. Supreme Court in 1924, won constitutional approval for compulsory eugenic sterilization. The case, in which the plaintiff, Carrie Buck, was described as a "moral imbecile," was the most famous legal case in Virginia in the 1920s and 1930s and was first heard in the county circuit court just south of where Mays faced trial. Neither the governor, nor any legal official involved in Mays's case, would have been unaware of the *Buck* decision's implications.[83] It is likely that Irving Whitehead, Carrie Buck's counsel, was the father of S. B. Whitehead, the man who prosecuted John Mays's case. Mays's patron could claim some eugenic expertise as well. Dr. Sizer's medical degree made him competent to pass judgment on the mental and moral "fitness" of both Mays and his victim, and the ideas of eugenics provided the framework for his petition on Mays's behalf.[84]

May's behavior at the time of his arrest reinforced his image as an unlikely rapist. He had not been absent from his work all day, to Sizer's knowledge, and he had made no attempt to escape after the assault, as whites believed a guilty man undoubtedly would have done. "When the child's father came up and told me what had happened," Sizer testified, "the boy was near the house cleaning up my yard, and while the man was talking he did not seem to be the least interested or concerned in what the man had to say, but kept on at work in spite of the fact that several hours elapsed before he was arrested." At the time of the arrest, after Mays had been accused by the young girl, he "seemed sincerely and utterly surprised." His actions, like his character, were hardly those of a guilty man.[85]

Sizer argued that the alleged victim also did not fit her role. Indeed, Sizer emphasized that the character of the victim's family could not compare to Mays's family reputation. "This little girl comes from our lowest breed of poor whites," he wrote. Though Sizer did not impugn the character of the victim herself, in the age of eugenics, character and heredity were indelibly intertwined. "Her mother is utterly immoral and without principle," he asserted; "and this child has been accustomed from her very babyhood to behold scenes of the grossest immorality. None of our welfare work affects her, she is brazenly immoral." The daughter was not only tainted by her mother's heredity, she was tainted by her mother's behavior as well. Poor genetic heritage, after all, reached its fullest expression in substandard behavior. These considerations, in his professional, scientific opinion, raised suspicions about her credibility as a complaining witness. He concluded, "It is therefore hard to say what effect such experiences may have had upon the child's imagination even at that tender age." Unwilling to base Mays's release solely on the issue of the girl's character, Sizer conceded that she might have been attacked but that she identified the wrong assailant. At the time of the assault, "there were many negroes at work in the quarries near her home and they were often seen in the woods."[86] Releasing Mays based on the girl's identification was far less controversial for the governor than publicly agreeing that the character of a victim, who was also a minor, alone changed the nature of the case.

Closing his final letter, Dr. Sizer appealed to the governor's and all Virginians' knowledge of Virginia's African American population, perhaps also alluding to Mays's accuser as an outsider. "The real Virginians know our Blacks," he wrote. "We know the heart can be pure and white under the blackest skin; and it is with this conviction that we appeal to our good governor." Sizer asked the governor to separate Mays's skin color from the cultural stigma associated with blackness. Mays, in his eyes, was "a defenseless negro, even though far more respectable than the family of the white girl who accused him." Sizer assured the governor that "nothing could induce me to sanction his release if I thought him guilty. I believe in justice for all regardless of color or creed and do sincerely hope that he may be given his freedom by Thanksgiving." Thanksgiving came and went, but the governor released Mays in time for Christmas in 1930.[87]

Dr. Sizer's intervention on Mays's behalf illustrates the tangled web of relationships in small communities. Respectability was not always a function of race, yet it was another criterion determining social position and worth. Mays came from a respectable, religious family that had been in the area for years, long enough to develop patronage relationships with powerful whites. Once inflamed racial feeling had died down, these relationships worked in Mays's favor. How Dr. Sizer framed his pleas for Mays's pardon is instructive as well. First, he based the victim's respectability on science, calling on Virginia's supposedly enlightened approach to race relations. Then he provided the governor with a noncontroversial justification for release. He alluded to questions of identification, a legitimate rationale dismissing the testimony of a white female victim, which appeared no where else in discussions of the case. Although the alleged victim was but seven years old, and well under the age of consent, she nonetheless had been tainted and corrupted. In Sizer's eyes, her family life and her environment cast doubt upon her credibility as a witness. Sizer carefully crafted a rationale for Mays's release, indicating to whites not only that Mays knew his place but also that his race diverted attention from more relevant issues. The case could not be understood according to the paradigm of black-on-white rape. Sizer shifted the focus from race to gender, class, and genetics, arguing that no matter what her race, the victim could not be trusted. He turned racial stereotypes on their heads: Mays's family was upstanding and the white victim was not. The governor and the legal officials who tried Mays concurred and granted Mays a pardon.

The black men who owed their release to allegations about the victim's character usually did not raise that issue themselves. It came at the hands of whites working on their behalf—lawyers, white patrons, or former employers. It would be far too inflammatory for a black person to argue publicly that a white woman was of compromised character. The origin of rumors about white women's characters, however, remained obscure. In some cases, rumors may have been brought to the ears of a white legal official or attorney by a member of the black community. Local blacks living in a community in which an assault occurred probably knew the position and reputation of both victim and assailant. This was even more likely if the alleged victim was poor, since poor whites and blacks often lived near each other and engaged in social and economic, if not sexual, relationships. Once outrage among whites over the assault had dissipated, the black community likely realized that allegations of a white woman's "lewdness" could be a powerful tool in the hands of whites working on behalf of a defendant. The passage of time, then, allowed gender to supersede race.

African Americans also exerted leverage by pointing to convicted assailants' youth or mental disability as mitigating factors in a case. Virginia governors commuted the death sentences of several black men convicted of assaults against white women when local authorities and the community raised the issue of youth or feeblemindedness. Will Finney, for example, was convicted in 1908 and sentenced to death. Governor Swanson commuted his sentence to life in prison after receiving a petition from the legal officials responsible for his trial and members of the community who insisted that Finney "is a negro of absolutely no intelligence and is known in the community in which he lives as a neighborhood idiot." They argued that because the "sentiment" against him was "so high" at the time of trial, court officials could not ascertain his mental status. After an investigation, the petitioners had determined that Finney "was not and is not at this time responsible for his acts." Finney's life was spared.[88] Similarly, in 1922, Preston Byrd, a fourteen-year-old who was arrested for attempted rape of an eight-year-old white girl, convicted of rape, and sentenced to five years in prison, was transferred to the Virginia Industrial School for Colored Boys five months after sentencing. Authorities had declared him feeble-minded, with an IQ of a nine-year-old.[89]

Youth and feeblemindedness were not guaranteed roads to clemency. Newspapers reported that John Henry Williams, convicted of rape and sentenced to death in 1916, attempted to "feign violent insanity" to avoid execution. After his removal to the state penitentiary, he reportedly "gave up the pretense and became resigned to his fate"; he was eventually executed.[90] Gabriel Battaile's case was more controversial. His supporters appealed for his life, arguing that Battaile was too young to realize the import of his actions. "It would be a disgrace to the fair name of Virginia (the mother of presidents) to allow a boy to be hung," one of them asserted.[91] Three African American ministers tied Battaile's unfamiliarity with racial norms to his youth. They argued that Battaile was "intensely ignorant and does not realize whatever the gravity of the crime or his own condition, in fact[,] judging from his actions and attitude he seems to think that his act was mere child's play."[92] To them, whether or not Battaile was guilty was secondary to his youth and ignorance; he was too young to have internalized the rules of segregation. Unfortunately for Battaile, the governor refused to commute his sentence and he was executed.

Petitions for clemency based on claims of youth or mental incapacity relied on the testimony of family members, doctors, and teachers who knew the defendant and who could bring such issues to the attention of the court or the governor. Parents, teachers, and religious authorities found arguments about age or intelligence to be safe and uncontroversial bases on which to fight for a convicted man's life. These appeals made no allegations about the character of the victim or her honesty, yet they shifted focus away from race. They argued that the crime committed by a black defendant was not a racial transgression but instead the result of youthful impulsiveness or mental illness or incompetence. By shaping appeals around these grounds, the black community reassured whites that it accepted and understood racial boundaries.

Family members of convicted men or convicted men themselves often based their appeals on more quotidian concerns: that parents, wife, or children needed financial support. Russell Ellett's mother requested her son be pardoned after he had served six years of an eighteen-year sentence for attempted rape. She noted that "he would be so much help to me if he were out, as I am a widow woman." She then added in a postscript, "I see where so many have been pardoned" that she saw no reason why her son's case should be any different. Her request was refused in 1920 and again in 1924, after the victim's father expressed his strenuous opposition.[93] In 1929, Beverly Carr received fifteen years in prison for attempted rape. In 1935, he submitted a petition for a conditional pardon signed by thirty-five members of the community. It argued that Carr was only fifteen at the time of the crime, that he had received an excessive sentence, and that his parents were old and needed someone to look after them—all factors justifying early release. His petition was refused.[94] Henry Smith's mother requested even less. She merely asked the governor to delay her son's execution. "If my boy must die," Susie Smith wrote, "will you give him thirty days more to live so that I can possibly be up and out and thereby be better prepared to stand up under the calamity wich [sic] I has always prayed to my God to never let me suffer?" Lest the governor miss her meaning, R. H. Bagby, Smith's attorney, enclosed his own note along with hers, writing, "The boy's mother has never been able to see him since his arrest, and it would be an act of charity to respite him so that she may do so before he dies." The governor refused, and Smith was executed on the day set in court, presumably without having said good-bye to his mother.[95]

These are but a few examples of a common phenomenon. Many families of black men begged Virginia governors to release their husbands, sons, or brothers because of economic need. Many convicted men asked for pardon on the same grounds. Overwhelmingly, such appeals alone were unsuccessful. Only when they were combined with an additional justification were governors willing to set a black man free. Family relationships, and the material obligations those relationships created, were not usually an effective form of leverage. People requesting clemency on the grounds of severe hardship did not always attempt a solely strategic approach. Susie Smith, for example, was illiterate and professed herself to be overcome with grief at her son's fate. In her letter, she spoke from her heart without consideration about whether she provided the governor legitimate grounds for her request. Governors were more concerned with exacting retribution for crimes, setting examples for the rest of society, and perhaps safeguarding their political positions than with the emotional and material needs of black families.[96]

African Americans who worked on behalf of convicted black men were acutely aware of the racial context in which they presented their appeals. They walked a fine line, consciously avoiding any hint that they were challenging the social order. Even if the racial furor over a specific assault had dissipated, unrelated controversies over the nature of race relations in the South influenced appeals for executive clemency, but not always as one would expect. The case of Fred Q. Butler, who was convicted in 1945 of attempted rape and sentenced to life in prison, is an example of how strategically invoking racial tension in one area could deflect tension from the issue of black-on-white assault.

Virginia Abbott, a relative of Butler, began writing Governor Stanley, requesting a pardon for Butler in 1955. Stanley responded that Butler needed to serve more time, since twelve years imprisonment on a life sentence was the minimum term required before the governor could consider pardon. She wrote again in 1957, stating that she desired "to see him free or partially free" and with his family for the holidays. She also alluded to the desegregation crisis facing Virginia after the Supreme Court's *Brown v. Board of Education* ruling. Noting the controversy over the state's response to desegregation and responding to Virginia's constitutional provision that governors could not serve consecutive terms in office, she wrote Stanley, "We wish it were possible for you to stay on until the state is at peace again over many troubles that has [sic] been confusing."[97] Governor Stanley refused Butler's petition without comment.

In 1958, Abbott began again to work for Fred Butler's release. The new governor, Lindsay Almond, was opposed to integration, going so far as to close Virginia's public schools rather than integrate them. Abbott was active in the African American schools in Amherst County, and in her appeals she continually praised Almond for his actions. She assured him that she prayed often for him and expressed her confidence:

> I hold a position in the civic work of our county (Amherst) and have always felt that the races are best served as they are, seperate [sic] schools. I work right along with our loyal superintendent . . . although I have to keep quiet at times, but they fully understand my attitude and the citizens here in our county are quite peaceable and the majority will hear me when I speak, I have gone out on my own at my personal expense when there has been any question as to whether a parent should ask that

their child or children should be admitted to white schools.
There has not been one so far who has asked for admittance.
There are a few of my race who are at odds with me on this
account but I keep quiet and move on and thank God there has
been no upheaval in our county.

She closed by asking the governor to keep her sentiments to himself,
unless he was discussing her work with her superintendent.[98]

Abbott received two letters in reply from Governor Almond, and both
thanked her profusely for the support she gave to his positions. Almond
wrote her for the last time the day after he granted Butler a conditional
pardon. In that last letter, he wrote, "You were very kind to mention in
such a nice way the grave problem that confronts us in this hour of crisis."[99] By the time he penned his second letter to Abbott, Almond had
suddenly reversed his position. Though he still felt that Virginia's schools
should remain segregated, he had called for the end to massive resistance,
believing that there were no more legal avenues that would allow the state
to circumvent the Supreme Court's ruling.

By assuring the governor he would have no trouble in Amherst County,
Abbott signaled her acceptance of a racial status quo in Virginia, despite
the decision of the Supreme Court. By placing the focus of her appeal on
her support for segregated schools, she could imply that releasing Butler
to her family would not result in more racial violence or agitation for civil
rights. She may have done so merely as a tactic to pacify Almond. By
signaling her support for white racial politics on one issue, she drew
attention away from the racial politics embedded in black-on-white rape.
In her letters, she hardly mentioned Fred Butler, or his fitness for release.
She avoided any discussion of whether or not Butler was denied due
process or had suffered from racial discrimination in sentencing, two
kinds of injustice that by 1958 were widely acknowledged by the black
press. Abbott's letters may attest to the conflict within the black community over the issue of segregation. But her work on Butler's behalf suggests how members of the black community could use racial issues as
leverage on convicted men's behalf.

The interracial environment provided the backdrop for any decision
regarding a black man's fate. Butler indeed may have owed his freedom to
Virginia Abbott's ability to assert common ground with the governor over
massive resistance. After all, the racial environment was complex, and
understandings across racial lines did not always conform to our ideals of
community loyalty or civil rights. Blacks and whites were not always

antagonistic toward one another. This complicated relationship between blacks and whites, though not readily apparent in existing sources, influenced cases where black men were accused of assaulting white women. When black men were sentenced to prison, the black community and the black defendant's supporters—not always one and the same—were sometimes able to shift the focus of the case away from interracial sexual assault to issues involving the victim's character or the defendant's age or mental status. Whites and blacks worked together in many cases and together sought to assure legal officials that racial norms had not been violated in an assault. They did this by rearticulating the narrative of a particular instance of cross-racial, cross-gender interaction and removing race as the sole motivating force.

Whites' occasional willingness to look beyond the defendant's race sheds light on the paradoxical nature of segregation. African Americans could challenge egregious abuses of white power even in a society where white power and racial hierarchy were accepted, and they often did so with the help of whites. Blacks were reluctant, for obvious reasons, to claim that the leverage they could exert represented political and public power, and whites were certainly unwilling to acknowledge that blacks had any access to such influence. Though southern society, dominated by racial hierarchy, sought to deprive blacks of control over interracial issues, blacks nonetheless made the most of the power they did have, and indeed wrung influence out of the most unlikely of sources. Loathe to have their actions lend credence to white fears that blacks were seeking to overthrow the social order, African Americans worked behind the scenes, drawing on personal relationships across racial and gender lines to advance their interests. Every instance of the use of leverage, and all the uses of leverage that remain hidden, reveal that the color line and the race-dominated legal system did not go uncontested.

These acts of resistance and leverage that African Americans utilized when black men were accused of assaults by white women were precursors to the organized civil rights movement. They attest to the ability of African Americans to fight for advantage on a case-by-case basis. Only rarely did the people involved in those cases articulate an understanding of black men's plight as part of the larger system of racial domination, though they may have recognized it as such. It was not until the late 1940s that the legal treatment of cases of black-on-white rape appeared in a new racial context. The role of the burgeoning civil rights movement in this process is the topic of the final chapter.

CHAPTER 7

Another Negro-Did-It Crime

Interracial Rape after World War II

In 1959, a young white married woman, the mother of four children, accused Sam Townes of rape. Louise Stephens claimed, and her scratches and bruises seemed to support her allegations, that Townes had come to her house, dragged her outside, and raped her twice. After his arrest, authorities sent him to Central State Hospital to determine if he was sane. The resulting report implied that Townes's relationship with Stephens was more involved than the violent encounter she described suggested. The report noted that the victim and her husband frequently drank together and that Louise Stephens was known for drinking heavily and "going out with a variety of men." Sam Townes, according to his aunt and uncle, also had a reputation for being a "woman chaser."[1]

Townes faced trial in 1960, and his counsel was Oliver Hill, a well-known civil rights lawyer. At Hill's advice, Townes pleaded guilty to rape, despite maintaining his innocence, and begged the court for mercy. He received a sentence of life in prison.[2] After his sentencing, Hill continued to work on Townes's behalf, eventually submitting a petition to the U.S. Supreme Court of Appeals for the Fourth Circuit. In his appeal, included in a petition for Townes's pardon nine years later, Hill explained why he had encouraged Townes's guilty plea. He argued that Virginia's discriminatory legal structure forced his client to plead guilty because in cases of black-on-white rape, a trial by jury ensured "an almost certain death penalty." A letter from the attorney who represented Townes in his 1969 pardon petition reiterated Hill's strategy. "Mr. Townes' trial counsel, S. W. Tucker and Oliver W. Hill," he wrote, "both testified that, had it not been for the racial factors involved (i.e., a Negro accused of raping a white woman in Mecklenburg County), they would not have been concerned about the possibility of a death sentence and would have acquiesced in his trial by jury on a plea of not guilty."[3]

Hill based his trial strategy on several sociological studies of rape prosecutions in the South that demonstrated that southern courts reserved the death penalty in rape cases for black men. Virginia was no different. Between 1908 and 1965, Virginia executed fifty-four men convicted of rape or attempted rape, all of them black.[4] These studies did not note that most black men convicted of assaulting white women—at least in Virginia—escaped with their lives. Hill, however, emphasized a common theme in rape defenses in the postwar period. Civil rights activists called attention to the enormous racial disparities in sentencing for rape in Virginia and throughout the South. By the 1950s, attorneys brandished statistics that supported their claims that black men received far harsher penalties for rape convictions than did white men. These statistics alone altered how many attorneys approached individual rape cases. Oliver Hill tended to urge accused black men to plead guilty so they would circumvent a jury's ability to sentence black men to death. Black men still could receive the death penalty in Virginia for rape, and between 1946 and 1960, five men, in addition to the seven in the Martinsville case, were executed. Thirteen others, including Sam Townes, received life sentences. Black-on-white rape remained an important symbol of white supremacy and black men's supposed danger. In 1949, the family of Cupid Diggs, for example, awoke to find a burning cross on their lawn after he was accused of assaulting a white woman.[5] But of the fifty-nine men who faced a Virginia court on some charge of sexual misbehavior with a white woman, including rape and attempted rape, sixteen saw the charges dismissed or were acquitted, three were committed to Central State Hospital, and an additional eight received sentences of less than one year. Together, twenty-seven, or over half, received little or no punishment. By the postwar period, death sentences for black men accused of crimes against white women were increasingly rare.[6]

The changing racial climate and evolving attitudes about women and sexuality altered how communities, both white and black, approached women's charges of rape. After World War II, African Americans became increasingly sensitized to racial injustices, and they frequently united in their efforts to combat racial oppression. In the area of rape, their efforts were often successful for a variety of reasons. Statistical proof of the racial disparities in sentencing provided a rallying point around which all African Americans could gather, and it placed the criminal prosecution of rape in Virginia within the discourse of agitation for racial equality. The black community vigorously supported accused black men, and the black press increasingly publicized the plight of black men accused of rape and ridiculed Virginia's whites for their intolerance of interracial interaction. And, as a result of other civil rights agitation in other arenas, African Americans began to sit on the grand juries that indicted accused rapists and the petit juries that tried cases of black-on-white rape.

Other changes that also worked to the benefit of accused black men had little direct connection to black activism. By the 1950s, juries in general appeared more suspicious of white women who claimed to have been raped by black men. Bolstered by popular Freudian theories, and troubled by women's more open sexual behavior, juries were less sympathetic toward accusing women when evidence revealed their other moral failings. The idea of neurotic women falsely crying rape to hide their sexual shenanigans became more widely accepted, while the myth of the black beast rapist began to fade. The African American press was not reticent about celebrating these changes. "Another Negro-Did-It Crime Flops," the *Norfolk Journal and Guide* announced in 1946; the article reported a case in which the white accuser admitted she fabricated her claim of rape.[7]

All these changes did not solely benefit black men. Comparing the punishments black men received for rape to those of white men naturally led to discussions of the legal system's apparent disinterest in prosecuting white men accused of assaulting black women. The black press and the black community began to protest vocally the sexual exploitation of black women. By the 1950s, increasing numbers of white men faced trial for, and a few were even convicted of, raping black women. While white women who accused black men of rape faced increasing scrutiny, black women, whose cries of rape had never before merited the attention of the courts, found white legal officials occasionally willing to prosecute their cases.

In many ways, the Second World War marked a new era in race relations. Fighting fascism made the promises of American democracy ring hollow at home. Bolstered by the "Double-V" campaign, for victory against fascism abroad and against racism at home, African Americans railed against the indignities that suffused their daily lives. Black men who served their country experienced segregation in the armed forces; they also traveled to areas in which segregation was less prominent or nonexistent; the contrast between the two experiences could be eye-opening. They returned to their homes less willing to tolerate the abuses of the past.[8] African American activism worked in lockstep with other developments. Decisions by the Supreme Court beginning in the 1930s and extending through 1954 chipped away at the legal structures of Jim Crow, outlawing the white primary, forbidding segregation on interstate transportation, ending restrictive covenants, allowing blacks into institutions of higher education, and, finally, ending segregation in public education.[9] With the withdrawal of constitutional approval for segregation in education, legal activists challenged segregation in all areas of southern life. Legal changes were accompanied by other expressions of support for civil rights. President Truman integrated the armed forces in 1948, which removed the federal government's stamp of legitimacy from institutional segregation. Truman also convened a committee of respected whites and blacks to make recommendations for improving African Americans' access to civil rights. In the 1940s and 1950s, Washington, D.C., began to desegregate public facilities, including hotels, restaurants, theaters, and parks. By the mid-1950s, a handful of African American men served in the U.S. Congress, while others served in state legislatures, and increasing numbers of African Americans received appointments in the federal government.[10]

None of these developments alone made African Americans less tolerant of whites' fear of black men as rapists. But an increasing willingness to protest injustice permeated all of these changes, and African Americans no longer remained silent in the face of inequality. In the years immediately after the end of the war, the black press pointedly jeered at whites' advocacy of the rape myth, as well as their initial willingness to believe any white woman's account of rape. Black newspapers also pointed out when white women's accusations did not conform to easily discernible facts and evidence. In the late 1940s, the *Norfolk Journal and Guide* even coined the phrase "Negro-Did-It" crimes. Its use implicitly criticized whites' assumptions that, unless proven otherwise, blacks were responsible for most crimes, and once accused were almost certainly guilty, regardless of the facts in the case. According to the black press, such charges often turned out to involve no criminal wrongdoing whatsoever by black men. A year after one headline announced, "Another Negro-Did-It Crime Flops," another insisted, "Negro-Did-It Crime Is Implausible."[11]

Both these headlines referred to cases just over state lines in North Carolina, where the *Norfolk Journal and Guide* had a large readership. But Virginia cases received similar scrutiny. In 1946, two black men, William Daniels and William Hayes, were arrested on charges of attempted rape. Two white women, one of whom was the wife of a Portsmouth city official, told police that as they were walking at night, a car carrying the two men passed them. It stopped some distance ahead, and the two men got out of the car and walked toward the women. They fled and called police from a nearby home, and police arrested the two men. When the case came before a trial justice, the two women conceded that the men had neither spoken to them nor been close enough to touch them. The judge immediately dismissed the charges, saying, "It is the duty of the court not to let prejudice interfere with the administration of justice." When the *Guide* first reported the case, it noted that it "had all the earmarks of being another one of those notorious Negro-did-it affairs."[12]

The black press's willingness to publish accounts of white women's unfounded accusations of rape explicitly challenged black men's treatment in the legal system. In labeling these cases as "Negro-Did-It" crimes, the black press pointedly insisted that whites rarely challenged white women's accounts of rape even in the face of contradictory evidence. Newspapers decried the fact that black men accused of crimes had to prove their innocence. That newspapers began to approach rape cases in this fashion reflected other developments. It drew attention to white men's lurking suspicions that women who charged rape were not always trustworthy. In the 1950s, changing ideas about women's sexuality made men more willing to believe that women claimed rape to save their reputations or to hide their own indiscretions. These suspicions even extended to white women who claimed to have been raped by black men. Any hint of misbehavior on a woman's part could diminish her credibility. With increasing acceptance of women's sexual desires whites were able to acknowledge openly that some white women sought out social and sexual relationships with black men. All of these postwar changes altered many black men's experiences in the legal system.

African Americans' insistence that whites railroaded black suspects also reflected a growing body of legal opinions and precedents. Despite the complexities involved in cases of black-on-white rape, black men paid with their lives at an astonishing rate. But southern justice was neither static nor monolithic. Black men were put to death for rape at a decreasing rate and, after 1938, the state of Virginia no longer executed black men for attempted rape, though the law permitted them to do so. Around the

South, various civil rights groups won legal victories in criminal cases at the appellate level, establishing the expectation of due process, fair legal procedure, and access to counsel for black defendants. For black men accused of rape after these decisions, however, the right to due process had an ironic outcome. It became increasingly difficult to overturn death sentences, as lawyers could find fewer and fewer procedural biases to target in appeals.[13] The focus on persistent racial disparity in punishment by the civil rights activists and the lawyers who defended accused men, however, would have a profound effect on the way in which the black community responded to charges of black-on-white rape. New forms of protests, along with other changing cultural factors, would result in fewer black men receiving severe sentences after being convicted of crimes against white women.

Drawing attention to racial disparities in sentencing first became a legal strategy in the case of seven black men accused of rape in Martinsville, Virginia, in 1949. The Martinsville Seven case is often compared to the Scottsboro case, but other than consisting of multiple black defendants and a white victim, there is little similarity between them. Few racial activists, other than the staunchest ones, proclaimed the innocence of the Martinsville men. The evidence that they had raped a white woman went uncontested in court. The woman told authorities that while walking after dark in the black section of town, four black men attacked and raped her. An additional three men joined them and raped her as well. The men were quickly identified and arrested. Facing overwhelming evidence of their guilt, the men claimed they were too drunk to be responsible for their actions, that the victim consented by failing to resist vigorously enough, and that the intercourse had not taken place.[14] The injuries sustained by the victim, which required many months of recovery, contradicted their claims. The men's trials took place over the course of eleven days, with six different juries, which all returned penalties of death.

Civil rights groups' previous gains in due-process guarantees severely limited the Martinsville attorneys' options to appeal the men's convictions. There was no evidence of mob action and no inflammatory racial rhetoric in press coverage of the case, and the judge made a considerable effort to mute the racial overtones of the trial. All the men were represented by competent legal counsel, and none claimed mistreatment by police. Their lawyers, with the backing of the NAACP, decided to try a new approach in their appeal. Rather than focus on discrimination in legal procedure, they decided to argue that discrimination in the punishment of blacks in capital cases represented a violation of the equal protection clause. They crafted their arguments with the help of recent social science research that indicated systemic racial disparities in sentencing. Citing Guy Johnson's ethnographic studies of homicide, they pointed out that blacks convicted of murdering whites were more likely to be sentenced to death and executed than blacks who killed blacks or whites who killed members of either race. They bolstered Johnson's findings with references to data from the Southern Conference Education Fund, which showed that 93 percent of southern men executed for rape between 1938 and 1948 were black.[15] Little of this evidence, however, related directly to rape in Virginia, so lawyers studied executions for rape in Virginia since 1908 and discovered that forty-five black men had been executed for rape or attempted rape in Virginia, while no white man had shared a similar fate.[16] These statistics demonstrated persistent racial discrimination in sentencing in Virginia, statistics that would be cited in many studies of race and the death penalty in subsequent years.[17] As a result of these findings, the U.S. Supreme Court ruled in 1972 in *Furman v. Georgia* that the death penalty was unconstitutional in its application. In a 1973 case, *Coker v. Georgia*, the U.S. Supreme Court ruled that the death penalty constituted cruel and unusual punishment for rape, not because of the racial disparity in its application, but because it was excessive punishment for a crime that involved no loss of life.[18] The NAACP's appeal in the Martinsville Seven case ultimately failed. In 1951, Virginia executed all seven men within days of each other, an unprecedented number of executions for any one crime in any state. Nevertheless, the arguments of their lawyers had a profound impact on how African Americans responded to charges of black-on-white rape in subsequent years. Arguing that racial discrimination in sentencing violated African Americans' right to equal protection placed rape cases squarely within the realm of civil rights activism in a way that individual criminal cases previously had not.[19] Rape cases became part of the struggle for civil rights.

While blacks paid more attention to white women's accusations against black men, whites seemed to pay less. Coverage of black-on-white rape cases was declining in the white press. Eric Rise, author of *The Martinsville Seven*, attributes this change to whites' desire to avoid racial hysteria and promote law and order. Editors of white dailies may have decided to minimize the impact of allegations of rape, both to avert mob violence and to preserve the appearance of a law-abiding society. White newspapers' desire to avoid inciting racial animosity and mob actions after rapes was not new. As early as the 1930s, in some locales, newspapers did not report white women's accounts of interracial assault, other than perhaps in a brief notice. At that time the black press, leery of reporting actions that seemed to confirm white stereotypes of black criminality, was reluctant to publish accounts of rape or the trials that followed. Black newspapers occasionally published protests of black men's treatment in the legal system, but almost without exception, they did not publish cases in which the legal system worked in black men's favor. After the Second World War both the black and the white press shifted their agendas. White newspapers noted assaults and trials of black men for rape but often without drawing attention to the racial aspects of any given case. Black newspapers used their coverage of rape trials to agitate for equal justice.

The defense tactic of pointing out racial disparities in punishment rarely seemed to sway a judge or jury alone, but it did apparently affect the advice that defense lawyers gave their clients. Oliver Hill encouraged Sam Townes to plead guilty to charges of rape specifically to avoid the death penalty. Other black men received similar counsel. Kenneth Weatherspoon, a naval man accused of raping a fifteen-year-old girl, pleaded guilty and refused to take the stand in his defense on the advice of his attorney, saying, "If I took the stand, I would have a chance of going to the electric chair." Weatherspoon received a life sentence.[20] Lloyd Junius Dobie received similar advice in 1956, and he waived his right to a jury trial and pleaded guilty before a judge. The judge sentenced him to death, however, and he was eventually executed.[21]

Other accused black men decided to take their chances with a jury, but the allegations of racial disparity in sentencing provided a subtext for the black press's coverage of each case. Albert Jackson Jr., for example, faced a jury when he was charged with raping a white woman in Charlottesville in 1951. He claimed that she was a prostitute who had sold him sexual favors. Police confirmed that when they came upon the couple, she stated, "Give me my five dollars." Jurors were unconvinced not only because witnesses testified to the victim's screams but also because she was covered with blood from injuries caused by the assault and police testified that she was incoherent afterward, unable even to tell them her name. This testimony, coupled with Jackson's inconsistent statements to police, convinced the jury of his guilt, and he was sentenced to death.[22]

When the Virginia Supreme Court upheld the jury's verdict, Jackson's attorneys began a concerted effort to convince the governor to commute his sentence to life in prison. Jackson received legal counsel from Spotswood Robinson, a lawyer who frequently worked for the NAACP, and Gregory Swanson, the first African American admitted to the University of Virginia School of Law in 1950. The lawyers argued that Jackson was mentally ill and thus should not be put to death. Jackson's attorneys also gathered a delegation to appear before Governor Battle to convince him to commute Jackson's sentence. They based part of their arguments for commutation on racial disparities in punishment, pointing out that no white man had ever been executed for rape in Virginia. This final appeal failed, however, and Jackson was executed in 1952.[23]

Willie A Dixon, an ex-serviceman, had better luck with his jury, but the black press also asserted that his sentence was largely a function of his race. Dixon's alleged crime hardly qualified as rape. He purportedly called a white woman repeatedly and asked her for a date. She called police, who set up a trap to catch her pursuer. Dixon was tried for attempted rape. At trial, his lawyer moved to have the charge of attempted rape dismissed because any evidence supporting it was purely speculative, but the judge refused. After deliberating one hour, the jury returned a verdict of guilty and sentenced Dixon to fifteen years in prison. Local African Americans were outraged over the severity of Dixon's punishment. The press pointed out that a black man recently convicted of murdering another black had received only a four-year sentence. Other community members compared Dixon's case to a recent case from North Carolina dubbed the "Looking Case" in the press. In that case, a black man named Mack Ingram had been charged with attempted rape for merely looking at a white woman, despite sworn testimony that he was never close enough to touch her. Ingram received a six-month sentence for assault, but his conviction was overturned by the North Carolina Supreme Court.[24]

Cases like those of Willie Dixon and Mack Ingram confirmed African Americans' perceptions that black men could be tried and convicted of rape after the most incidental of contact with white women. By the 1950s, however, Willie Dixon's case was becoming the exception rather than the rule. More cases proceeded like those of Mack Ingram, William Daniels, and William Hayes. In those cases, though they were charged with attempted rape for actions that did little more than scare white women, courts declined to punish them. Authorities continued to respond to white women's fears of strange black men with arrests, but the legal system would not support every charge made by white women or legitimate all white women's fears. This does not mean that white authorities no longer policed interracial interactions. Black men were still indicted for their interactions with white women. By the 1950s, however, black men who flouted taboos against interracial interaction in public generally were charged with only morals violations, and the white women involved with them often faced identical charges.

Charging black men (and white women) with morals violations was not entirely new. In 1939, three black men who allegedly had sex with a white minor and were charged with rape received fines for being of "not good fame." Likewise, most cases between 1900 and 1945 began with rape charges, and prosecutors chose to try the black men in question on lesser charges, or the juries chose to convict on a lesser charge, such as assault. By the 1950s, authorities seemed more willing to see cases of alleged rape or attempted rape as morals violations from the outset. Most of the cases described below appeared in black newspapers in major Virginia cities, and most of these charges involved urban couples, making it difficult to determine if police in rural areas were making similar kinds of arrests. The evidence suggests, however, that by the 1950s, though white authorities still punished public displays of interracial sexuality, they did so in less severe ways.

In 1952, James Menefield publicly violated the rules prohibiting sexual interaction between white women and black men. He and his companion were arrested as they were seated in a parked vehicle in the early hours of the morning. Both Menefield and Juanita Parsons, a white woman, worked together at McGuire Hospital in Richmond. Each was convicted in police court of being "a person not of good fame" and the court required each of them to post a $300 bond for good behavior. The court required them both to submit to a physical exam to determine if they had venereal disease, reflecting lingering beliefs among whites that blacks were a "syphilis-soaked race" that could contaminate whites.[25] The hospital also forced them to resign from their positions.[26] Charley Wallace faced similar charges, but in somewhat different circumstances. He was discovered "with Blonde in car" in a white neighborhood, and the woman had her arms about Wallace's neck. Like Menefield and Parsons, both Wallace and the "blonde," Elsie May Williams, posted $300 bonds for good behavior and submitted to medical tests. Wallace claimed that he was the "victim of circumstances." He had never seen the woman before she had opened the door of his car and asked for a ride. He could not explain why she had her arms about his neck, but he denied that they had been caught in a "love tryst."[27] In 1958, police arrested a black man and a white woman after observing them making love in a car parked on a well-known "lover's lane." The woman claimed to be so drunk that she did not know what she was doing. She received a sentence of two days in jail. Her black companion was found guilty of being a "person of ill fame" and was required to post a $500 bond for sixty days. Unable to come up with the money, he spent six months in jail.[28]

Black men and white women caught in apparently consensual sexual interactions faced relatively minor penalties, as long as they had the money to post bond and were free from venereal disease. But even in cases in which the interaction appeared coercive, black men no longer automatically faced charges of rape or attempted rape. Ernest Harris Jr., for example, was arrested in 1957 in New Kent County for, according to his indictment, detaining a white woman against her will with the intent to defile her. The incident began as both were driving on a dark road. After forcing the woman to pull over, Harris forced her at gunpoint to accompany him in his vehicle. At one point, according his alleged victim, he made "some kind of statement about wanting a woman, and apparently placed his hand on the victim's leg."[29] He eventually released her unharmed. After his arrest, Harris claimed to have been on a three-day drinking binge at the time of the crime.[30] With Oliver Hill as his legal counsel, Harris was charged with abduction, and his case was heard before a judge. The judge ruled him guilty, fined him, sentenced him to a year in jail, and then reduced the sentence to three months' probation at Hill's urging.[31] Harris's indictment for abduction placed him in serious legal jeopardy, but not to the same extent as a charge of attempted rape.

In 1950, Fletcher Jones also escaped serious legal difficulties for actions that could have led to charges of attempted rape. He was accused of exposing himself to a white boy and girl, asking the young girl to approach him, and then grabbing the girl. The white boy pulled her away, and they fled. Jones faced charges of assault and battery. The jury, however, acquitted him of all charges.[32] James Watkins also escaped serious charges for having allegedly harassed a white married woman for almost six months. When her husband was away, he would come into her house as she slept, scratch on her screens, or peer into her windows. The woman's husband, who finally caught Watkins in the act, quickly called police. Watkins received a twelve-month sentence for trespassing, not attempted rape.[33]

The variety of charges black men faced for actions against or indiscretions with white women reflects the changing social values and attitudes in law enforcement and adjudication. Blacks also benefited from changes in legal procedure that gave them increasing access to and influence over the legal process. The black press identified jury integration as having a significant impact on African Americans' experiences in the criminal justice system. In 1934, the U.S. Supreme Court ruled unconstitutional the systematic exclusion of minorities from grand and petit juries with *Norris v. Alabama*, but the decree did little to seat African Americans on criminal court juries. Blacks might have been chosen as token members of an initial jury pool, but then lawyers would exclude them in jury selection. In the 1947 case *Patton v. Mississippi*, the U.S. Supreme Court ruled that excluding members of the defendant's race impaired his or her right to a fair or impartial trial.[34] But high courts continued to affirm verdicts in southern criminal cases despite the allegations that courts purposely excluded racial minorities from jury service.[35]

In Virginia, however, blacks began to appear on criminal juries, even in cases of crimes against whites. In 1946, the *Norfolk Virginian-Pilot* reported the first black majority on a criminal jury when William Daniels was acquitted of stealing a radio.[36] The same year, the *Norfolk Journal and Guide* noted that for the first time, five African Americans had been seated on a criminal jury in Norfolk's Corporation Court. On trial was John Henry Mayo, a black man accused of attempted larceny. The judge in the case told the reporter that he found nothing particularly unusual about the case. He asserted that "he personally had found [blacks'] action to being summoned to serving no different from that of a white man" and insisted that his only "objective was to see that justice was impartially administered." The jury found Mayo guilty and fined him $50.[37] At the end of that year, the same paper published an article pointing out that in Portsmouth, a city adjoining Norfolk, blacks frequently outnumbered whites on juries. The reporter asserted that blacks had served to their credit for over ten years, and not merely as tokens meant to meet the requirements of Supreme Court decisions. The *Journal and Guide* assured its readers, perhaps too eagerly, that there "were no segregated brands [of justice] for white or black."[38]

The presence of blacks on juries in the Norfolk metropolitan area does not mean that blacks appeared on criminal juries throughout the state of Virginia. Few counties had a vibrant African American newspaper to inform readers of such developments. White newspapers, in their coverage of criminal cases, did occasionally mention the racial composition of juries, but it is impossible to determine in any systematic way whether rural Virginia counties also admitted blacks to jury duty. In cases of black-on-white rape covered in the black press, and occasionally the white press, it is apparent that African Americans did serve as jurors.

Virginia jurors made decisions not only about guilt but also about sentencing. The presence of black jurors could prevent white jurors from imposing severe sanctions if they voted to convict. Frasker Young, for example, faced charges of rape in 1949.[39] According to the *Richmond Afro-American*, a jury of ten whites and two blacks convicted him and sentenced him to twenty-five years in prison, a substantial term but considerably less substantial than the life term or the death sentence they could have imposed.[40] Raymond Palmer's experience was more unusual. He was arrested and charged with raping a white housewife and robbing her in her home in 1957. At his first trial, Palmer was convicted and sentenced to death. The judge overturned his conviction, ruling that the prosecution's assertion that the victim was pregnant at the time of the attack prejudiced the jury against the defendant. At Palmer's second trial, he faced a jury of eleven whites and one black man. That jury was unable to reach a verdict, and the judge declared a mistrial. Palmer's case was tried a third time, this time before just a judge, who found him guilty and sentenced him to life plus an additional forty years.[41]

In only one case did the black press credit African Americans serving on a jury with altering the outcome of a trial, and that case involved a white man tried for the rape of a black woman. In 1951, Clifford Wulk, a white marine officer, was accused of raping a sixteen-year-old black babysitter as he was taking her home. The girl made an immediate report of the assault to her parents, who took her to the police and to the hospital, where doctors confirmed the attack. Wulk was indicted in December, but his trial was repeatedly delayed until the NAACP dispatched lawyers to act as special prosecutors in the case. Wulk finally appeared in court to face trial in June 1952. After two days of testimony, the jury of six whites and six blacks could not reach a verdict, splitting along racial lines. The *Richmond Afro-American* announced that the hung jury "[m]ark[ed] the first time in Virginia's History that a Jury Has Split Down the Middle along Racial Lines." Six months later, however, shortly before the beginning of the second trial, the judge decided to drop the charges against Wulk, citing doubts about the state's ability to win a conviction, and released him. Though the NAACP protested the decision and mass meetings occurred in Spotsylvania County, Wulk was never retried.[42]

Despite blacks' greater participation in the legal process, there was little they could do when criminal prosecutions targeted men who challenged the racial hierarchy directly. Even in the 1950s, whites used charges of rape as a means of controlling African Americans who violated the norms of segregation. When this occurred, the African American community, depending on the circumstances of the case and its racial context, often had little recourse.

One such case occurred in Wythe County in 1953. In February, a white woman accused the black taxi driver she hired of rape. The driver, Willard Austin, denied the charge, but when he arrived for his preliminary hearing, a mob estimated at 300 people surrounded the courthouse. The fury of the mob, however, appeared to be short-lived. According to the cryptic comments of a white man overheard by a reporter for the black press, the charge at first inflamed the outrage of members of the white Wytheville community, who were "getting ready to lynch that boy all right. But now they know the facts, nobody cares anymore." The African American press did not report what those alleged "facts" were, but it speculated that "the charge against Austin was the result of competition in the taxicab business of Wytheville." Austin had owned a cab company in Wytheville since 1935. He employed white drivers and even white women to work in the company's office, and his cabs never carried black passengers.[43] Despite the fact that the case incited a mob, it never merited attention in the white press. Austin denied his guilt and a jury convicted him of rape and sentenced him to five years in prison, the minimum term possible (and, under Virginia's parole guidelines, Austin could be released from prison on parole in little more than a year). The black press made no mention of the trial or the jury's verdict.

In light of the comment that "nobody cares anymore," determining the reasons for the Wytheville jury's guilty verdict is difficult. The sentence imposed, however, suggests a certain degree of compromise. Austin's sentence may have been the jury's way of punishing him for being too successful and of giving white cab owners time to establish their businesses without his competition. The case thus served to reassert white control over taxi service in Wytheville. The minimum sentence, however, simultaneously sent a message that the victim's story was not entirely credible.

Bernard Skipper was not so lucky. A jury convicted him twice of rape and sentenced him to a lengthy prison term. The Virginia Supreme Court of Appeals overturned the initial verdict, ruling that the prosecution did not sufficiently prove Skipper's identity as the woman's rapist. Not only had she originally described a light-colored black man as her assailant (Skipper was very dark) and initially refused to identify him, the FBI had also determined that a black man's pubic hairs found at the scene did not match Skipper's. Skipper also produced three witnesses testifying that he was elsewhere at the time of the crime. The victim's unwillingness to identify Skipper as her assailant in a police lineup justified setting aside his first conviction. She refused to identify him verbally but later claimed that she knew "within myself instantly" that Skipper was the man who had broken into her apartment and raped her. She kept silent because, she said, "I did not want all of the publicity that goes with a trial, and I figured that all had been done to me that could be done."[44] It was not until several days later, after hearing from police that he had gotten into "some misconduct," that she identified him. "If this person is going to offend other people in society, we can't live in the world," she stated.[45] Deciding the judge's conduct encouraged the jury to accept her explanation for not identifying Skipper, the Virginia Supreme Court overturned the verdict and ordered a new trial. At his second trial, Skipper was again convicted and received a sentence of thirty-five years. Skipper appealed his second conviction, but it was affirmed by Virginia's higher court with little comment.[46]

Skipper's arrest for rape was not his first encounter with local law enforcement. Three months before the alleged rape, Skipper filed suit against the city of Lynchburg, alleging police brutality and requesting damages in the amount of $100,000. He charged that on two separate occasions police had detained him without cause and had beaten him. After a local investigation cleared the four men named in Skipper's suit, his charges prompted an investigation by the Justice Department.[47]

The white press took no notice of his police brutality suit, picking up Skipper's story only when he was charged in early October, first with burglary and then with rape. The black press, once Skipper was charged with rape, gave his trial only minimal coverage. As the trials for the criminal charges proceeded, his suit against the police department ground to a halt. The Justice Department abandoned its probe after receiving no cooperation from the Lynchburg police, who believed the investigation amounted to federal interference into state and local matters.[48] Skipper's suit against the police department was soon dismissed on a technicality.[49] Unencumbered by the civil suit, the Lynchburg court proceeded to try Skipper on one count of trespassing, two counts of burglary, one of which included allegations of attempted rape of a young black girl, and the rape charge levied by the white woman. Skipper was convicted on all counts and received a thirty-day sentence for trespass, seventeen years for the burglary charges, and, eventually, thirty-five years for rape.[50]

Given the chronology of events—Skipper's false arrests in June, his suit filed in August, an alleged rape in September, the felony charges in October, and the dismissal of his civil suit—one wonders if the Lynchburg courts targeted Skipper for unsolved or manufactured crimes in retaliation for his civil suit. His complaint against the police officers was sufficiently credible to merit the intervention of federal officials. Only after their withdrawal did Skipper face charges for other crimes. The white press, once Skipper had been charged with felonies, covered the proceedings of his civil suit in the same articles in which it followed the criminal proceedings, clearly associating the two. Its coverage may have served as a warning to other

African Americans about the limited redress they could expect from white courts when they charged racially motivated brutality, and emphasizing that federal intervention would provide no protection.

The black press became strangely silent after Lynchburg authorities filed criminal charges against Skipper. Its silence may have derived from a sense that racial agitation would only worsen his situation and perhaps from the fear that its initial support of his suit and the wide publicity it gave it had a hand in Skipper's additional legal troubles. Although African American activists placed their faith in the federal government and federal courts to redress long-standing racial grievances, it would serve no purpose to agitate for federal intervention in a case in which federal authorities had determined there was little they could do. Finally, the black press may have considered Skipper to be guilty of the crimes charged against him and determined not to contaminate its larger causes by associating with a criminal. Despite the silence of the black press, the fact that the criminal charges against Skipper were made so soon after he filed suit suggests that white officials used the power of the legal system to contain challenges to their racial prerogative, and there was little the black community, defense lawyers, or even federal authorities could do. The black community uttered little protest over Skipper's case. They may have been fearful of reprisals, or the protest they did muster may not have seemed important enough to include in white accounts of Skipper's legal battles.

Other black men, however, owed their successful defenses in court to the willingness of the African American community to support them vocally and financially. The case of Ruffin Junior Selby, in Princess Anne County in 1953, illustrates the forms of protest that the African American community could muster. Selby's case also underscores the community strength African American men could call upon in the 1950s, even when accused of rape and murder.

Ruffin Selby's case began on a spring evening when Carmelia Cravedi, a divorced white woman, went on a date with Dean L. Kirkendorfer, a white navy quartermaster. Late in the evening, they parked on a deserted and secluded road. Kirkendorfer apparently left the car to relieve himself, and was attacked by a person whom Cravedi described as "a big negro." Hit three times in the head with what authorities suspected was a crowbar, Kirkendorfer died, and the assailant dumped his body in the back seat of the car. The assailant then allegedly drove Cravedi deeper into the woods, where he raped her, beat her, and left her for dead. Three navy men out for a horseback ride discovered Kirkendorfer's car the following morning, with Cravedi slumped over the steering wheel.[51]

Police interviewed numerous suspects without success. Two weeks after the crime, police arrested Selby and, after grilling him for almost two days, charged him with rape, murder, and robbery. Selby denied any knowledge of the crime, but police noted that he lived near the crime scene, was large and "powerfully built," and had no alibi.[52] Though initially too traumatized by her ordeal to face suspects, Cravedi eventually identified Selby as the man who assaulted her and her companion in the woods. Cravedi's identification provided the only evidence of Selby's involvement in the crime. Fingerprints the FBI took from the scene belonged to neither the alleged victims nor the alleged assailant. Police found neither the murder weapon nor the two watches that the assailant took when he left the scene. Selby also was eventually able to provide an alibi for the time of the assault.

Despite the paucity of evidence against him, without competent legal help, Selby still faced possible conviction. Though the white press's coverage of the case avoided inflammatory racial rhetoric, the brutality of the crime alone could have turned the jury against any black man the police chose to arrest and charge. The black press, however, took up Selby's cause immediately. Convinced by Selby's claims of innocence, and concerned that he had been held without access to counsel for several days, the *Norfolk Journal and Guide* reported that a defense committee had formed to raise money and had hired a well-known Norfolk attorney, J. Hugo Madison, to represent Selby. When Madison, accompanied by a delegation from the NAACP, met his new client, Selby assured them that though he had been held for many hours by police, he had not been questioned for exceptionally long periods of time, nor had he experienced any mistreatment.[53]

Though Selby received a preliminary hearing in July, he did not stand trial until October. In the intervening months, the local chapter of the NAACP spearheaded a fund-raising effort to support his defense. By the time of his preliminary hearing, the fund had amassed over $1,000. Local support for Selby had exploded after what the *Journal and Guide* described as a "citizens' mass meeting" to publicize his case.[54] Much of the coverage of his case between arrest and trial focused on the fund-raising efforts on his behalf.[55] By the close of Selby's trial, the fund had amassed a total of more than $3,300, all but $250 of which went to pay legal fees, costs associated with trial, clerical help, a private detective, copies of Kirkendorfer's autopsy report, Cravedi's medical records, and fees for the court reporter.[56] The publicity of his plight also provided for his bail. Several neighbors, including one white man and two black men, mortgaged their homes and businesses to raise money for Selby's release until trial. The press reported that he spent the majority of his time thanking those who had contributed to his defense.[57]

In addition to publicizing efforts to raise money for Selby's defense and publishing the names of those who contributed as a means of thanks, the *Norfolk Journal and Guide* also connected Selby's case to another case of apparent racial injustice. Shortly before Selby's preliminary hearing, the paper published an article about the experience of William Harper, who was accused of raping a white woman in 1931 (discussed in the introduction). Harper was convicted and sentenced to death, but the intervention of concerned whites ultimately saved his life. At a second trial, he was acquitted when the defense produced several witnesses who testified that the victim, who was married, had been with her lover across state lines at the time of the assault. In 1953, Harper still lived in the Norfolk area and bore scars from the beating police gave him to coerce his confession. According to the article, Harper "still felt uncomfortable when he thought how he narrowly escaped death for a crime he did not commit."[58] The paper connected the two cases to underscore their similarities. Both men faced charges made by white women, both men vehemently claimed their innocence, and both cases pointed to a legal system that put black men exclusively in the shadow of the electric chair.

Justice eventually prevailed for Ruffin Selby, as it had for William Harper. At Selby's trial on the rape charge, which the state believed was its strongest case, the prosecution could produce little evidence, other than Carmelia Cravedi's shaky identification, that he was responsible for the crime. No physical evidence ever placed him at the scene, and the defense produced two witnesses accounting for his whereabouts at the time of the crime. The jury, composed of eleven whites and one black, voted to acquit Selby after deliberating less than fifteen minutes.[59] The courtroom burst into applause as the jury announced its verdict. Several weeks later, the commonwealth's attorney decided to dismiss the remaining charges of murder and robbery.

Selby certainly benefited from the lack of evidence against him. But he needed competent legal help to make certain the jury noted the prosecution's weak case. The funds raised by his supporters through the NAACP provided him with the counsel of some of the best attorneys in the area who would appear many times defending other African American clients. For the NAACP, the publicity surrounding Selby's case boosted their membership as well.[60]

Activities by African Americans and white supporters in cases like Ruffin Selby's illustrate well how organized activity could force the legal system to render a mode of justice to black men accused of assaulting white women. Mass meetings, defense funds, competent attorneys, and a jury that included African Americans helped to offset the disadvantages black men faced because of the racial configuration of the case. By the 1950s, black men were more likely to be acquitted of charges of raping white women, or to have the charges against them downgraded to lesser offenses. Certainly not every black man accused of a crime against a white woman benefited from these developments. But the chances of a black man being sentenced to death for the rape of a white woman decreased dramatically by 1950.[61]

The efforts of the African American community and of civil rights organizations played a large role in changing some black men's experiences in the legal system, but they did not work alone. New attitudes about white women's sexual nature prompted whites to look with suspicion on some white women's charges of rape. By the 1950s, common views of female sexuality posited that women were not always in conscious control of their sexual desires. These beliefs, which stemmed from Freudian theories of criminology popularized and developed more by Freud's disciples than Freud himself, took on pernicious form in the courtroom.

Freud's contribution to the theory that women desired to be raped is spotty at best. He is better known for advocating a theory of seduction, in which young girls, harboring an aggressive sexuality, cloaked their own sexual desires in fantasies of seduction. According to Freud, this projection might cause women to "fantasize" or "remember" sexual episodes as a means of "fulfilling dreams while denying their desire." Freud thus provided psychological justification for the "false accuser," whose stories of sexual violation really represented fantasies masking her own desire.[62] Freud said very little about women's fantasies of rape, though his ideas of the subconscious were taken up by his disciples and superimposed on women's sexual nature. The most famous of these disciples, and the most frequently quoted, was Helene Deutsch, who argued in the 1940s that women possessed an inherently masochistic sexual impulse. In her theories, because sexual intercourse for women was initially painful, women learned to find sexual pleasure in the pain of intercourse, and indeed required painful penetration in order to achieve sexual gratification. Thus, fantasies of rape were merely exaggerations of normal sexual desires for women. Deutsch extended her theories to assert that women could not be rape victims, arguing instead that the desire to be raped was a fundamental part of female sexuality.[63]

Helene Deutsch made the defense lawyers' job immeasurably easier because she argued that women subconsciously consented to rape, and indeed desired it. In her suggestion that women's subconscious masochistic tendencies should take precedence over their verbal expressions of conscious will Deutsch was a giant step away from her mentor. Sigmund Freud argued a woman's conscious desire to repel a rapist could become compromised by her subconscious desire to encourage the man's advances. He did not advocate that the woman's subconscious feelings could be used to excuse the man's actions in the face of her conscious, expressed lack of consent. For Freud, subconscious desires remained subordinate to the conscious will.[64]

Ideas about women's alleged fantasies of rape became a common addition to legal treatises on rape prosecutions in the postwar period. Legal theorists argued that despite a woman's resistance to assault and her willingness to go through the ordeal of a rape trial, she may have subconsciously desired to be violated, therefore relieving her attacker of criminal responsibility for his actions. In the 1940s, Henry Wigmore, one of the most famous authors on legal theory and evidence, even advocated that all rape victims be subjected to psychological analysis. He claimed that several psychiatrists had warned him that "fantasies of being raped are exceedingly common in women, indeed . . . they are probably universal." Wigmore asserted that women who charged rape often suffered from psychological disorders, which prompted them to bring false charges of rape against otherwise innocent men. "The unchaste (let us call it) mentality finds incidental but direct expression in the narration of imaginary sex incidents of which the narrator is the heroine or the victim."[65] Glanville Williams reiterated such beliefs in 1962, writing about the need for corroborative evidence in cases of rape. Unlike most other crimes, such as assault or robbery, in which the victim's statements of violation alone constituted sufficient proof that a crime occurred, rape required additional evidence because of women's alleged psychological makeup. According to Williams, "Sexual cases are particularly subject to the danger of deliberately false charges, resulting from sexual neurosis, phantasy, jealousy, spite, or simply a girl's refusal to admit that she consented to an act of which she is now ashamed."[66] A *Columbia Law Review* article made similar assertions, insisting that "stories of rape are frequently lies or fantasies."[67]

The legal system also treated women's rape claims with suspicion because many psychologists believed that women themselves did not know their own minds when it came to sexual activity. In essence, women often told men "no" when they meant "yes." Women, several articles insisted, enjoyed being overpowered sexually and often were attracted to, rather than repulsed by, aggressive men. As a *Stanford Law Review* article noted, "It is always difficult in rape cases to determine whether the female really meant no."[68] Ultimately, according to another influential article appearing in the *Yale Law Journal* in 1952, which relied on Freud for its conclusions, "[A] woman's need for sexual satisfaction may lead to the unconscious desire for forceful penetration, the coercion serving neatly to avoid the guilt feeling which might arise after willing participation." Charges of rape, then, frequently arose out of women's desire to avoid responsibility for their sexual activity and their supposed need for violence to satisfy sexual desire. "Fairness to the male suggests a conclusion of not guilty, despite signs of aggression, if his act was not contrary to the woman's formulated wishes," the article concluded.[69] Consequently, in the eyes of the law, verbal refusals of men's sexual advances, including screams or tears, were insufficient expression of women's will.

These beliefs about women's sexual psychology had significant effects on rape victims' experiences in the courtroom. Many juries and judges held women responsible for their rapes, despite women's protestations that sexual relations were truly against their will. Virginia was no different from other states in this regard, as various cases involving white men and women attest. In *Barker v. Commonwealth* in 1956, the Virginia Supreme Court of Appeals reversed the rape convictions of two men. The victim told police that she had met the men while she was waiting at a bus station and accepted their offer for a ride in their car. When she got into the car, the men beat her and raped her. The court reversed the men's convictions arguing that the victim's testimony was inherently unbelievable. Calling her actions "contrary to human experience," the court suggested that either she should have known not to accept a ride from two strangers or she secretly desired sexual relations with them. The court reiterated a similar ruling from an earlier case in which a woman accepted a ride with four men. Arguing that the woman presumably "knew something of the facts of life," having been married and divorced, she should have known better than to get in a car with strange men.[70] It was every woman's responsibility, these cases suggested, to avoid any situation in which a man might possibly claim that in coercing her into intercourse, he was acting upon her subconscious desire for sex.

Despite the court of appeal's scornful view of the women's actions, these appellate cases initially convinced juries of the assailant's guilt. Most cases did not, suggesting that these attitudes pervaded the public and not just appellate branches. Richard Chakejian's experience as a defendant in

1957 was more common. Chakejian, a white student at the University of Virginia, was accused of raping a white seventeen-year-old girl who had come to Charlottesville for a weekend of parties. He arranged to meet her back at his apartment, even though she had come as the date of one of his friends. When the girl arrived there, Chakejian raped her twice. Neighbors, hearing her screams, called police. At trial, the defense accused the girl of making "a play for him" and suggested that her accompanying him to his apartment late at night signaled her consent to sexual intercourse. In his closing statement, Chakejian's attorney told the jury that if the police had not arrived, "we wouldn't be here in court today," suggesting the girl only "cried rape" when confronted by police officers at the door of Chakejian's apartment. The jury of ten men and two women apparently agreed, voting to acquit Chakejian. They paid no heed to the fact that police arrived at his door because the victim was screaming loudly enough to alarm the neighbors.[71]

Most scholars of sexual violence note the effect of Freudian theories on attitudes toward the victims of sexual violence, but they maintain that such attitudes prevailed primarily in cases of rape between people of the same race, or in cases in which the assailant and victim were acquainted.[72] Women, especially white women, who claimed to have been raped by black men unfamiliar to them who had broken into their homes or apartments, supposedly escaped such suspicions. Helene Deutsch, in her theories of female psychosis, on the other hand, argued that white women who accused black men should face the strictest scrutiny precisely because they were especially prone to fantasize about being raped by black men and white men were so willing to believe them. According to Deutsch,

> The fact that the white men believe so readily the hysterical and masochistic fantasies and lies of the white women, who claim they have been assaulted and raped by negroes, is related to the fact that they (the men) sense the unconscious wishes of the women, the psychic reality of these declarations, and react emotionally to them as if they were real. The social situation permits them to discharge this emotion upon the negroes. . . . My own experience of accounts by white women of rape by Negroes (who are often subjected to terrible penalties as a result of these accusations) has convinced me that many fantastic stories are produced by the masochistic yearnings of these women.[73]

In her eyes, white women's accusations against black men in particular were the most likely to stem from repressed fantasies. Although cases in

Virginia between 1900 and 1945 overwhelmingly resulted in convictions, they also show that legal officials considered women's character and sexual experiences even when the men they accused of rape were black. At least at the pardon level, white men heeded Deutsch's advice.

Ideas about women's repressed sexual desires were legitimized by other social and cultural changes taking place in the 1940s and 1950s. Many social trends among the young, and throughout society in general, during this period caused concern about women's sexuality. Young teenagers began to date earlier, and marriage ages declined. Pregnancy out of wedlock, though disastrous to reputation, no longer signaled permanent ruin. Single white women could be "cured" of their neuroses and set on the road to true womanhood by giving up their children for adoption. Rock and roll music changed styles of dancing, and the increasing popularity of the automobile changed styles of courtship.[74] These changes influenced the treatment of rape cases. Raising suspicions about white women's sexual activity prior to being assaulted by black men did not automatically mean black men could expect to be freed by a jury, but the following cases suggest that the appearance of any impropriety cast a taint over a woman's charge of assault and might reduce the sentence her accused assailant received after conviction. These cases also signaled changes in the rhetorical code of chivalry that previously required all white men to protect all white women with their lives.

New social attitudes influenced the outcome of cases of black-on-white rape, especially those involving the growing number of white women who claimed they were assaulted while parked on a "lover's lane" or out with their white dates.[75] Ruffin Junior Selby's experience represented one such case. Carmelia Cravedi initially stated that they had become lost looking for a place to buy a cup of coffee. When that account raised suspicions, as they were found on a known "lover's lane," she stated that they had stopped for a cigarette. Kenneth Weatherspoon, the navy sailor who pleaded guilty of rape in order to avoid the death penalty in 1949, allegedly interrupted a white dating couple. According to the white press, Weatherspoon's fifteen-year-old victim and her companion were huddled in an alcove, "making up" after a fight, when Weatherspoon approached them. Under questioning from police, the girl admitted that her "parents did not permit her to stay out late and that her father had spanked her on several occasions for doing so."[76] The alleged attack on the high school students merited several articles in Norfolk's white newspapers, but the circumstances under which Weatherspoon attacked the girl gave those newspapers license to sexualize her. She was frequently described as pretty, attractive, or auburn-haired. Descriptions of other cases rarely merited so much comment on victims' physical appearances.[77] And, in Richmond, being caught parked with a black man could result in morals charges for white women, as several discovered.

Being caught in a tryst with a white date did not automatically taint the reputation of the alleged victim. Weatherspoon, after all, received life in prison. Other black men who interrupted white couples on dates also felt the full power of the law. Matthew Mack Callahan, in 1957, interrupted Doris Smith, a divorced mother of two, while she was out on a date with a white man. Callahan allegedly ordered the couple out of their car, beat her companion, and beat and raped Smith. He then held her hostage as he led police on a high-speed car chase. Though he initially eluded arrest, he was apprehended several days after the assault. His violent actions overawed her morally suspect behavior; he also received life in prison after pleading not guilty at trial.[78] In 1952, Lester Sawyer received a prison sentence of twenty years after being accused of attempting to rape a white woman parked in a car with her white male companion. Sawyer had denied the charge, testifying that, after becoming lost, he had asked the occupants of the car for directions and merely had gotten into a fight with the man after he was rude.[79]

Lester Sawyer's pleas of a "frame-up" did not sway the jury who voted to convict him, but in other cases, either authorities suspected that white women claimed rape to explain otherwise compromising circumstances or juries believed that the woman's own actions made her assault questionable. In Fairfax, Virginia, in 1955, four black youths accused of assaulting a white woman parked with her companion on a secluded lane themselves alluded to the illicit circumstances in which they encountered the woman. The four told police that they came upon the couple as the man had his hand up the woman's skirt and that the white couple asked the four young men not to report them to the police. The four were convicted of rape and received twenty-year sentences but were released in only seven years.[80] In 1951, Richmond's black press closely followed the case of a white woman who claimed that she had been assaulted by five black men. The case began when the woman and her white companion were arrested and charged with being of "ill-fame" after being discovered drinking in a Richmond park. The woman claimed she was raped, but police quickly discounted her story since a medical examination revealed no traces that she had been brutally assaulted six times. Within the month, the five men, one of whom was fourteen years of age, were released by police, with no charges filed. The *Richmond Afro-American* attributed their release to the collective protests of the black community, as well as her suspect story. The white press took little notice of the assault but did report that police dropped the charges against the men.[81]

No element of these "crimes" suggests shifts in white attitudes toward black-on-white rape more than the behavior whites expected of white men who witnessed assaults on white women. In earlier years, social beliefs about the horror of black men as rapists demanded that white men risk their lives to prevent such assaults. The failure of a white man to resist adequately the rape of a white woman under his care could be so unthinkable as to make a woman's charges of rape seem incredible.[82] As the cases from Virginia in the 1950s suggest, white men no longer believed it their duty to lay down their lives to protect white women from black men. Indeed, John Smith, one of the four youths convicted in 1955 in Fairfax, claimed that the white man offered the four sexual access to his white companion in exchange for not notifying police that the couple had parked for illicit purposes. The court either found his claim incredible or believed it did not mitigate his crime, but that he raised it at all signaled an acknowledged shift in men's sense of their chivalrous obligations.[83] Most of these white companions, whether or not the black man was armed, apparently gave little resistance to their date's assailants, other than going to find the police. The legal system supported their seeming "cowardice," since no white man was condemned either in the press or the courts for leaving a white woman under his care to a black assailant.

White men who witnessed sexual relations between their companions and black men thus were exonerated for failing to provide protection. In some cases, a man's failure to intervene even represented a form of sexual deviance that extended to the woman as well, whether or not she was a willing partner. In Virginia, in 1952, for example, Floyd Jewett, a white man, and Raymond Matthews, a black man who worked for the Jewetts as a gardener, faced charges of attempted rape after Jewett's wife told police that her husband had tried to "force her to make love to their colored gardener." Charges against both men were dropped when the woman, described as an "attractive redhead," changed her story. Offering little explanation for either her original charge or the change in her account, she merely noted that her husband and Matthews had been drinking together when she returned from work. After the judge dismissed the charges, Mrs. Jewett received a sentence of ninety days in jail for filing a false police report.[84] In 1959, the *Richmond Afro-American* published accounts of a fourteen-year-old black boy in North Carolina who accused a white couple of abducting him and forcing him to have sexual relations with the white woman while her husband watched. His account gained credibility when two other black youths claimed that the couple had also approached them but they were able to escape. The white woman was arrested on charges of "carnally knowing" one youth and attempting to "know" three others, while her husband was arrested on charges of aiding and abetting.[85] In both cases, white women faced charges for their acting out their husband's fantasies, and perhaps their own as well. Courts were willing to hold white women criminally responsible for sexual relations with black males that violated other morality laws.

By the end of the 1950s, whites and white authorities were no longer shocked by evidence that white women might consent to sexual relations with black men. Any suggestion of familiarity between white women and black men might be enough to acquit black men of charges filed against them by creating the possibility of consensual relations. George Washington, who was charged with attempted rape in Richmond in 1959, was acquitted after the victim, who was separated from her husband, admitted that during the alleged assault Washington called her by her first name, even though she claimed he was a stranger to her.[86] This seeming inconsistency in her testimony raised suspicions that her charge masked a more scandalous relationship, despite the absence of any evidence in that regard. In another case, Leon Woodley stood trial for rape in Portsmouth, Virginia, in 1953. After two separate juries in two separate trials failed to reach a verdict in his case, the prosecution decided to dismiss all charges against him, and he was released. The juries apparently could not decide which account of the alleged assault to believe. The victim claimed that Woodley dragged her into a field and raped her. He claimed that she approached him, asking about bus schedules, and then told him he could have sexual relations with her for five dollars. Though police reported that they saw her emerging from the field "hysterical," Woodley's account had sufficient credibility to prevent his conviction.[87] Philip Holley and Drexel Williams's experience in court six years later was similar. A white woman accused both men of raping her at the Arabia Shrine Temple in 1959. The two men disputed her account, claiming that she had approached them looking for whiskey. After the three sang and danced together for five hours, both men had consensual sexual relations with the woman. Philip Holley's first trial ended in a hung jury. Charges were dismissed completely when a separate jury acquitted his companion, Drexel Williams. Both the white and the black press covered the case, and both reported Williams's and Holley's claims that they had sex with the woman only after a prolonged afternoon of drinking and dancing.[88]

Juries were no longer as sympathetic to women who violated norms of proper behavior, and there is some evidence that black men were aware of this. John Clabon Taylor, one of the seven men convicted and executed in the Martinsville Seven case, openly acknowledged the role the victim's character could play when he warned the other men at the scene that "that was a Christian woman and it would cause us some trouble. . . . That if she was a drunk we might get by with it but I could tell from the way that she talked that she was a good woman."[89]

White women's and black men's conflicting accounts of what had occurred between them, as well as white couples concocting cover stories to hide their own indiscretions, comprise only a few of the challenges facing juries determining the facts behind rape charges. It was the job of the jury to establish which account best fit the facts of a case or best corresponded to what they knew about social, sexual, and racial relationships in the 1950s. Juries who were aware of the distinction society made between "bad" girls and "good" girls and of society's concerns about the sexual temptations inevitable when couples "petted" in the secluded confines of parked cars, treated allegations of assault arising from such circumstances with a degree of suspicion. Black men's claims of consensual sexual relations between white women and black men, rather than inciting white wrath, comported with jurors' views of modern sexual relationships and carried enough credibility to juries to merit a vote of acquittal. For white women who accused men of rape, whiteness, once their armor against character assault at trial, no longer shielded them from insinuations about their reputations. In the 1950s, theories of rape and women's sexual nature "proved" that a woman might cry rape after consensual sexual relations, and juries, acting on that knowledge, acquitted some accused black men and imposed reduced sentences on others.[90]

While white women were facing increased skepticism about their charges against black men, in Virginia black women's charges against white men were simultaneously gaining credibility. New ideas about women's sexual nature brought white women's experiences in rape trials more in line with those of black women, whose claims of sexual exploitation had long been ignored because of white ideas about black women's innate hypersexuality. At the same time, as the black community became increasingly vocal about the injustices black men faced in the legal system, they more frequently compared black men's experiences to those of white men accused of assaulting black women. Armed with the statistics of racial disparity in punishment, and long accustomed to white authorities' lack of interest in prosecuting white men, African Americans raised their voices against the sexual exploitation of black women. They used a variety of strategies, from raising funds to hire attorneys for victims, to criticizing persistent stereotypes about black women's supposed sexual nature, to pressuring law enforcement officers to arrest accused white men. The black press even reported instances of black men striking back against the harassment of black women. Their protests resulted in more trials for white men accused of assaulting black women, and an increasing number of convictions as well. These activities did not guarantee that black women received justice in a court of law, but the increase in the number of white men tried for assaulting black women itself represented considerable progress in protecting the civil rights of all African Americans.

The substantial change in official attitudes toward black women who accused white men of rape is all the more remarkable in light of Virginia's historic indifference to such crimes. Of the seventy cases of rape or attempted rape appealed to the Virginia Supreme Court of Appeals between 1908 and 1959, only two involved white men convicted of assaulting black women, though the court upheld the verdicts in both cases.[91] The first of those cases, which involved a white man accused of assaulting a thirty-two-year-old black woman, reached Virginia's highest court in 1936. At trial, the defendant, James King, attempted to prove that the woman was of poor character and had consented to sexual intercourse. He then invoked white stereotypes of black criminality when he claimed her injuries occurred when he resisted her attempt to rob him. The jury, however, accepted her account of forcible rape, and the Virginia Supreme Court affirmed King's conviction and sentence of ten years in prison.[92]

Despite the apparent legal victory for James King's victim, his conviction did not signal a change in attitude about white men accused of rape. If anything, the King conviction was an aberration. The racial composition of the cases appearing before the Virginia Supreme Court of Appeals alone, however, does not provide sufficient evidence of this point, as it heard so few rape cases, and their outcomes did not always reflect the attitudes of the local courts who tried the state's rape cases or of the white men who composed Virginia's juries. Analyzing every case of rape or attempted rape appearing before the local court of the city of Charlottesville is more revealing. Between 1920 and 1960, the court did not try a single case of rape or attempted rape involving a white man and a black woman.[93]

The evidence available underscores the contentions by scholars that white legal authorities throughout the United States, and in the South in particular, ignored sexual violence by white men against black women.[94]

White authorities arrested and tried white men for rape, but only infrequently. In 1944, Allen Gammon was convicted of raping a seventy-four-year-old black woman, and he received a sentence of six years in prison. Gammon's criminal tendencies probably appeared more serious to whites after he escaped from the jail where he was being held for trial.[95] After World War II, the black press became more vocal in publicizing black women's accounts of sexual assault. Black newspapers also reported cases in which black community members succeeded in pressuring white authorities to respond to black women's charges. In Amherst, Virginia, in 1948, respected African American community members convinced the commonwealth's attorney to arrest a white man for assault. The man, identified only as Dudley in the newspaper, had raped a black woman described as "feebleminded." Hearing of the assault, Virginia Abbott, who ten years later was instrumental in gaining a conditional pardon for Fred Butler, a black man convicted of rape, investigated the case with another couple. As a result of their efforts, police arrested Dudley for rape, but the judge reduced the charges to assault and fined Dudley $20 plus costs.[96] The case of Corbett A. Witt, a white man, appeared in the same paper. Witt was fined $350 for raping a pregnant black married woman, though, again, the judge reduced the charge to assault.[97] The black newspaper headline, "Rape of Expectant Mother by White Farmer Draws $350 Fine," announced that the courts were at least trying accused white rapists but simultaneously criticized the minimal penalties white men received when convicted.

The case against Carl Burleson and Leonard Davis, both white police officers in the Richmond police department, galvanized protest against the treatment of black women by white men and underscored the legal system's casual attitude toward such cases. In October 1946, Nannie Strayhorn, a thirty-two-year-old mother of two, accepted a ride to her home from the two officers after an argument on the street with her black male companion. Instead of taking her home, the two officers took her to the outskirts of town and took turns raping her. When they had finished, they dropped her off a few blocks from her home. At her house, Strayhorn told her brother what had happened. The next morning, accompanied by an attorney, Strayhorn and her brother filed a complaint at the police station. After she identified the two men, the officers were arrested. Both claimed their innocence, eventually asserting that they had picked up Strayhorn intending to charge her with being a person of ill fame. They had decided not to charge her when she begged them not to and had dropped her at home.[98]

The two men stood trial in Richmond the following January in separate trials. Both men pleaded not guilty. Both supplemented their testimony with numerous character witnesses who testified to their reputations for good behavior.[99] Juries found both men guilty of rape and sentenced them each to seven years in prison. Burleson skipped bail after his conviction but gave himself up a year later in Hawaii. Davis appealed his conviction to the Virginia Supreme Court of Appeals, arguing that the evidence did not sufficiently show that he had used force in raping Strayhorn. His lawyer argued to the jury, "As Shakespeare said, 'Protesting, she consented.' "[100] The court upheld the jury's verdict, ruling that because both men were armed, had carried Strayhorn to a remote and isolated location, and verbally abused her during the assault, she was sufficiently frightened for her life to justify her lack of overt resistance.[101]

The case against the two police officers received considerable attention in the black press, who condemned the two officers' gross abuse of their public authority. Though the black press expressed elation that the two men were convicted and applauded the Virginia Supreme Court's decision to uphold the verdict against Leonard Davis, the African American community was not entirely satisfied by the ultimate disposition of the case. The punishment the two men received, a mere seven-year prison sentence, rang hollow, given the treatment black men received for being accused of assaults against white women. "The verdict might be applauded," wrote the Norfolk Journal and Guide, "were not the penalty so farcical."[102] Indeed, the paper continued, to many African Americans, cases like that involving Nannie Strayhorn were representative of the inadequate protection accorded black women: "It is distressingly true that in no phase of the unequal dispensation of justice to which the American Negro is subjected in the courts of his country, does he fare worse than in cases in which his women have been criminally violated by sensuous white men. The studied refusal of white juries to accord the honor and virtue of Negro women the protection of the law is even reflected in the comparatively light punishment usually meted out to colored men convicted of attacking the women of their own race."[103] The Guide also noted that had the races of those in the case been reversed, the men would have received a far more severe sentence, perhaps even the death penalty.

The African American community's anger became even more heated when it heard rumors that the two men were petitioning the governor for conditional pardons less than two years after incarceration. In early 1949, Governor Battle received petitions signed by more than 550 whites asking for Burleson and Davis's release. The petition argued that their families needed the men and that they had previously been "good and upstanding" citizens. It included the names of the twelve members of the jury, who stated they had no objection to the men's pardon.[104] In September 1949, Governor Tuck received a petition and resolution from the Association for Justice in Virginia and America, presumably an African American organization, protesting the "impending" release of the two men. The resolution demanded "that Burleson and Davis serve their full sentences, or that every Negro man now in prison charged with raping a white woman be paroled at once."[105] After both the parole board and the judge who tried the case recommended against it, Governor Tuck apparently declined to grant the convicted men executive clemency. It is possible that both men were released on parole sometime in 1949, when they became eligible.[106]

Even as the number of cases in court involving white men and black women increased, the challenges blacks faced in obtaining legal redress remained substantial. The black press's regular recitation of crimes against black women reinforced how vulnerable black women could be to the violent attentions of white men. Black women reported being assaulted as they walked on the streets, returned from work, or waited for the bus.[107] Virginia Robinson accused a white cab driver of rape when he assaulted her after she hired him to take her home. He eventually was acquitted of rape but was convicted of malicious wounding for stabbing her and sentenced to ten years in prison.[108] One black woman was abducted by three white men while she was walking along the road arguing with her husband. Threatening the couple with a shotgun, the white men forced Sarah Johnson into their car and took her to their trailer home, where one of the men "performed certain indecent acts upon" her. George E. Downing, the only African American attorney in the county, acted as special prosecutor in the case. He charged the all-male, all-white jury, "I hope you twelve men will write a verdict that will protect the chastity of all our women, white or black." Two of the men were convicted of abduction and sentenced to three years in prison.[109]

No occupation placed black women in more danger than working in white households. Many black women accused white men of assaulting them while they were doing domestic work in their homes, or, especially for young black girls, when white fathers were returning them home after a night of baby-sitting. Freddie Lancaster assaulted his housemaid while she was cleaning the bathroom and then paid her one dollar for her housework. Though she waited five days to report the assault to authorities, he was charged with rape.[110] On the other hand, Garland Brock, a Suffolk County white man, was acquitted of statutory rape charges filed by the family of a thirteen-year-old girl who had worked in the man's home. His acquittal was somewhat surprising given that he admitted paying the young girl's maternity bills, an act many believed indicated he took responsibility for her pregnancy. A paternalistic relationship did not protect the girl from sexual exploitation and may have protected her assailant from punishment.[111]

Black families were aware of the dangers their young daughters faced. One mother of two black girls, aged ten and twelve, took what precautions she could when a white man named Wayne Pace asked if her daughters could baby-sit for his children. Figuring there was a certain safety in numbers, when she was unable to job herself, she sent both daughters together. She also took down the license plate number of the man's car. Despite her efforts, the man did attempt to rape both daughters in a secluded patch of woods. One escaped and ran for help. Pace was arrested and charged with attempted rape. A racially mixed jury deliberated thirty minutes before convicting him; they sentenced him to eighteen years in prison.[112]

In 1950, a twenty-three-year-old black mother accused Thomas Elkins of assaulting her when he took her home from baby-sitting his children. He apparently took a detour on the grounds of the University of Virginia and raped her. He then took her home and paid her three dollars for baby-sitting. Jefferson reported the assault to police, and Elkins was arrested and charged with rape. At his trial, Elkins testified that there was no time for him to rape Jefferson, as he had returned to his home within twenty minutes of leaving, a time frame confirmed by his wife and other white witnesses. A jury deliberated less than twenty minutes before voting to acquit Elkins.

Other testimony at Elkins's trial highlights additional difficulties black women faced in pressing their charges. When Jefferson went to University of Virginia hospital for medical treatment after the assault, the hospital refused to admit or examine her. She then went to a black physician, Dr. Ralph Brown, who examined her and prepared slides to use as possible evidence. When he sent those slides to the University of Virginia hospital for analysis, they refused to look at them. Despite the fact that the hospital provided medical care to both blacks and whites in separate wings, it refused to offer its services to a black woman who charged a white man with rape.[113]

Although Elkins was acquitted, newspaper coverage of testimony in the case did not indicate that Jefferson's character, or that of black women in general, became an explicit target for the defense. Direct attacks on the reputations of black women who claimed to be victims of sexual violence were often unnecessary because persistent stereotypes about the sexual

willingness of black women undergirded any defense strategy. Throughout the twentieth century, legal officials giving Virginia governors their
opinions on requests for clemency in cases involving black women often
stated that they viewed any charge of rape by a black woman with suspicion. In William Griffin's case in 1923, the prosecuting attorney stated that
common white beliefs about African American moral values guided his
actions. "I do not mean to infer that there should be one law for one class
of people and another law for another," he wrote; "but we all know that
there is one code of social ethics practiced by the negro race that is not
sanctioned by our own white race." He recommended that Griffin be
pardoned.[114] The commonwealth's attorney for Louisa County, in noting
an exception to white stereotypes of black morality, confirmed the rule.
Recommending against clemency for Tom Desper, a black man who received a sentence of eighteen years for rape, he wrote, "The rape in this
case was accomplished upon a colored woman, but one who was un-
usually respectable and against whom no evidence was or could be introduced to affect her reputation."[115] These sorts of stereotypes persisted into
the 1950s and influenced the defense strategies of white men accused of
assaulting black women. The two white men Barbara Scott accused of rape
argued that she consented to sexual intercourse with both men in front of
her black date. Their claims seemed far-fetched in light of her companion's resistance, his efforts to find the police once he was released, and
Scott's disheveled appearance and hysteria when police arrived.[116]

Because criminal records rarely contain detailed descriptions of trial
strategy, newspapers offer the best recapitulations of court testimony and
the arguments of the prosecution and the defense. The articles describing
the trials of white men accused of rape often contained some hint that the
defendants pointed to the race of the victim as a mitigating circumstance.
Joseph Rizzo, a white soldier, took the stand in his own defense when he
was accused of attempted rape. According to the Norfolk Journal and Guide,
Rizzo's attorney concentrated his defense arguments on Rizzo's service
record and the fact that "it was a colored woman who was testifying
against him." In this case, his tactics were successful; the jury acquitted Rizzo.[117] For white men accused of rape, the easiest defense was to
claim that sexual relations were consensual. This claim carried even more
weight with white authorities when the woman was black.

Well aware of Virginia's dismal record in convicting white men accused
of raping black women, the black community did not sit idly by. Buoyed
by an increasing number of successful cases protesting racial injustice, and
backed by a cohort of African American attorneys willing to defend the

rights not only of accused black men but also of victimized black women, African Americans sought to exert leverage over the legal process. Civil rights activists' intervention in interracial rape cases did not guarantee that black women received justice, however. Martin A. Martin, an attorney who frequently assisted the NAACP, observed the trial of Thomas Elkins, who was acquitted by a jury. In 1951, Oliver Hill represented the victim of Oscar Hopkins, a white man accused of attempted rape. Though Hopkins admitted to having sexual relations with the seventeen-year-old girl at trial, he was nonetheless acquitted.[118] The intervention of well-known black attorneys, many with ties to civil rights organizations, regardless of the jury's verdict, ultimately sent a message to the white community and legal authorities that the African American community considered legal redress for crimes against black women to be part of their quest for civil rights. The presence of such well-known men in the courtroom also exerted overt pressure on white officials to hold white men accountable for their actions.

When allegations of white-on-black rape became public, the black community also exerted leverage over the legal system in a variety of ways, many of them similar to the forms of resistance used when white women accused black men. Black citizens held mass meetings, raised funds for special prosecutors and lawyers to represent the interests of black victims, and criticized white authorities who treated the rape of black women by white men as minor crimes. African Americans around Goochland County, for example, vigorously protested in 1951 after they learned that a white youth identified as the assailant of a black girl was allowed to remain free for two days before he was arrested. According to the victim's family, Harold Parrish had attempted to assault the girl while he was bringing her to his mother's home to work. She escaped and reported the attack to her parents, who immediately notified police. When Oliver Hill called Goochland authorities two days later to inquire about the case, he was told Parrish had not yet been arrested. When the *Richmond Afro-American* called one hour later with the same inquiry, Parrish was in custody.

The delay in apprehending Parrish caused widespread anger in the black community. The *Afro-American* questioned whether the delay was "an election maneuver," noting that the commonwealth's attorney was up for reelection. Within days of Parrish's arrest, the black community took action. More than 225 county residents organized to raise funds for an attorney to help the girl's family prosecute the case. And civil rights organizations used the mobilized citizenry to address other concerns. James P.

Spencer of the Virginia Voters League and W. Lester Banks of the NAACP called for a mass meeting to instruct the community on the "value of voting and organization."[119] Parrish was indicted, but he was eventually acquitted.[120]

The 1950 case against William Whitley in Isle of Wight County provides another good example of the black community exerting leverage in the legal system. Whitley, a recently married white man, was charged with rape. He allegedly appeared at the home of a black girl and asked her parents if she could watch his elderly mother while he and his wife went to a movie. The parents agreed. Instead of taking the black girl to his home, Whitley drove around for two hours and then raped her at gunpoint. When he returned her to her home, she reported the attack to her parents, and her father confronted Whitley. Whitley admitted the rape, saying he had "been looking at her" for a long time. Her parents enlisted the help of Samuel Tucker, an NAACP attorney in Emporia, and other NAACP officials, including Roland D. Ealey and W. Lester Banks, and G. James Gilliam, executive secretary of the Negro Organization Society, to investigate the case. Whitley was arrested and indicted as a result of the investigation. According to the *Afro-American*, the case likely would have been hushed up had it not been for the NAACP's intervention.[121]

In spite of his confession and the black community's efforts, the jury on Whitley's case failed to hold him accountable for his actions. Local black citizens protested the all-white jury, given that African Americans represented a majority in the county. They also complained that white legal officials refused to use courtesy titles when addressing black witnesses, reflecting their lack of respect for them. Though civil rights attorneys worked with the prosecution, they could do little more than "flinch" and "grit their teeth" when the prosecutor asked a white defense witness, who was trying to portray the victim as a prostitute, to concede that "[i]t's nothing strange for a colored girl to have an illegitimate child." There was no indication that the victim had engaged in any previous sexual encounters, but the defense maintained that the sexual intercourse between the victim and defendant was consensual. Believing the defense's account, the jury voted to acquit Whitley.[122]

While the black press frequently covered the cases of black women who were raped, giving voice to the anger of their readers, the white press usually ignored them. The white press's lack of interest reflected the disinterest of southern whites as a whole. Though by the 1950s, white men accused of raping black women increasingly faced criminal trials, only rarely did those trials result in a conviction, and if conviction did result, the sentences were insignificant. Since the black press did not always report trial outcomes, exact figures regarding the disposition of cases are difficult to determine. Of the thirty-eight white men charged with assaults on black women between 1936 and 1960, trial dispositions are available for only twenty-four. Of those twenty-four men who were brought to trial, ten were acquitted outright and six were convicted, but the charges against them were reduced to some form of assault and they were only fined. Only six received sentences of longer than five years, and two received sentences of three years for abduction only. Civil rights activism could not guarantee that black women had their day in court, but these numbers represented improvement.

That civil rights activism could not ensure justice was not news to most African Americans in Virginia, and reports of assaults on black women frequently prompted black activists to protest the persistent racial disparities in sentences for men convicted of rape or attempted rape. Many cases encouraged the black press to compare the treatment of black men accused of raping white women to that of white men accused of raping black women. Vernon Frith, a white man, for example, was accused of rape by a mother of three in Martinsville in 1951. When the charges against Frith were dismissed because of the lack of evidence that the woman had been raped, the *Richmond Afro-American* printed the headline, "7 Colored to Die; 1 White Reprieve," making a direct comparison to the Martinsville Seven case. The dismissal of charges against Frith seemed doubly unjust since it occurred just as the Martinsville Seven were petitioning the governor to commute their sentences.[123] Whites brought up similar concerns. In 1957, for example, a white couple encountered two white men struggling to rape a black woman in a car in Richmond. They immediately blocked the car's escape, took its license plate number, and called police. Police arrested Charles Newcomb and Harlan Morrell for attempted rape. The men faced trial in police justice court and were convicted of being persons of ill fame and attempted assault and molesting. They were each fined $50 and placed on a $500 bond for good behavior. Protesting the verdict and the sentences the men received, which were light largely because they were white, Evelyn Ellerson, the white women who had interrupted the assault, declared, "If it had been the other way around, you know [what] would have happened. I don't think the verdict was fair at all."[124]

After the Martinsville Seven case, protesting racial disparities in punishment became a common aspect of African American news coverage of cases involving white-on-black rape. A 1951 editorial in the *Norfolk Journal and Guide* reminded its readers, "No Crime to Rape Negro Women in the Southland." Referring to a case involving six white servicemen accused of raping a young black mother, the *Guide* blasted a racist culture that tolerated crimes against black people: "The six young white men who committed this vile crime against a Negro woman probably got the foundation from their homes, churches, and schools. Here of all places they were taught that the proper place for their foot is on a Negro's neck. So what difference would it make to follow through with rape to satisfy their lust on a Negro woman. They probably have never in their lives been punished for anything they had done against a Negro."[125]

White men's callous treatment of black women and the legal system's refusal to hold them accountable eventually prompted open protest over white men's harassment of black women in general. As part of its coverage of a case in which a black man was arrested in Florida for saying "Hello, baby" to a white woman, the *Richmond Afro-American* published a prominent black women's thoughts on the subject. "I wish I had a nickel for every white man that said 'hello baby' to me," she said. "Just the other day, one of them said to me out of a clear blue sky—I don't know him at all—'You are certainly a beautiful brown-skinned woman.' I thought to myself what would happen if the situation were reversed—if I were a white woman and he was a colored man."[126] The obvious answer was that while black men might face serious legal charges, the white would not. And no legal recourse was available for black women insulted by such treatment. It was part of their everyday lives. In 1956, black men caused a "near-riot" when several white men were roaming the streets of Culpeper's black neighborhood looking for black women. After a black man began fighting with the two of the men, a crowd gathered. Culpeper authorities called out state troopers and arrested seven black men. The two white men were not arrested, while the black men received fifty-dollar fines for disorderly conduct.[127] That same year, another black man, Rudolph Valentino Henry, took the law into his own hands when a white man propositioned his wife in front of him. The two men scuffled, and Henry stabbed the white man to death. Dubbed the "wolf whistle slaying," Henry pleaded guilty to manslaughter. The judge, after hearing Henry's claims that he was only defending his wife, sentenced him to five years in prison and then suspended the sentence. Buoyed by the testimony of white police officers that they had received numerous complaints of white men molesting colored women in that neighborhood, Henry's suspended sentence was a victory for black men's right to defend black women against harassment.[128]

As part of its coverage of the case, the *Richmond Afro-American* printed an article describing how white men of all social strata came to African American neighborhoods at night: "Operating under what amounts to an immunity from arrest, the wolves, mashers, and sex perverts roam the poorly lighted streets" looking for illicit romance. Residents insisted the men's actions were getting worse, that they were no longer confining their harassment, as Rudolph Henry learned, to unescorted women. Violence often resulted.[129] As with the judge who suspended Rudolph Henry's sentence, some whites shared African Americans' outrage at black women's treatment and supported women who protected themselves from predatory white men. In 1959, a seventeen-year-old black girl was in a car with a married white man. When he began to assault her, she stabbed him to death with a knife she found in his car. A grand jury refused to indict her, but it also refused to indict the white man who had sexual relations with her thirteen-year-old sister that same night.[130]

These incidents do not necessarily imply that all whites were becoming less tolerant of white men's sexual harassment of black women. Most cases did not result in vindication of black women or indicate that black women would be free from the unwanted attentions of white men. But the increasing number of cases that came to trial, paired with the incidents in which violent protest of white men's harassment went unpunished, represented positive change. As it did for cases of black-on-white rape in the 1950s, the growing civil rights movement, with its development of legal strategies to protest segregation, benefited some black women who were the victims of rape. White women could no longer expect that their charges of rape would be accepted without question, and some white women were taken to task for their apparent sexual desire for black men. Counsel for black men convicted of rape could use the statistics produced by the Martinsville Seven case to protest racial disparities in punishment, and though this did not save all black men from the electric chair, it drastically decreased their chances of being put to death. White men, on the other hand, could no longer expect the same degree of impunity when they sought black women as sexual partners. White men were being convicted for interracial rape, and if the legal system was unwilling to protect black women, it might occasionally turn a blind eye to the black men and women who acted in its stead.

In 1927, Dr. John A. Hornsby, superintendent of the University of Virginia Hospital, wrote Governor Harry Byrd, urging him to allow a black man accused of assaulting two white university summer students to be put to death. He believed executing black men convicted of raping white women would act as a deterrent to other black men.[131] Twenty years later, when a black hospital employee was accused of attempting to assault several white female patients in their rooms, Hornsby's worst fears seemed to have come true. But by 1948, whites no longer viewed any move toward a white women as an imminent threat. Lewis Washington was arrested and indicted for attempted rape, but authorities allowed him to plead guilty to simple assault. He received a sentence of nine months in jail.[132] Lewis Washington, the accused worker, benefited from shifting race relations in the postwar era. His case was a harbinger of things to come, exemplifying the changes in how white legal authorities responded to many cases of black-on-white rape.

The postwar era brought changes to race relations in criminal justice, as in many areas of African American life. Federal courts were refusing to uphold segregation's legal underpinnings, and blacks were becoming increasingly vocal in their protests against racial injustice. These changes also affected the legal treatment of interracial rape in Virginia. As with all progress for civil rights, positive change took place amid continuing inequality, and such changes did not spell improvements for all African Americans who came before the legal system, either as accused defendants or as those seeking the legal system's protection. Nevertheless, the trajectory of change was important, both because it was part of the larger battle for racial justice and because it had real benefits for those unjustly affected. The legal system's treatment of interracial rape grew a small step more egalitarian. Black men received a modicum of due process and credibility, while white men faced increasing legal jeopardy for assaulting black women. White women who accused black men began to face the same suspicions that black women usually faced because of beliefs about their sexual nature. And black women, like white women, occasionally found courts and juries sympathetic to their accounts of violation. For black men unjustly accused, things improved. But for women of both races who experienced rape, the legal system continued to treat their charges with suspicion.

In 1912, Judge George J. Hundley declared that the crime of black-on-white rape "so excites, alarms, and arouses our people" that it represented "a deadly menace to the very framework of society itself."[1] Hundley largely spoke the truth: Virginians frequently rose up in anger when white women accused black men of rape. But as we have seen, an outraged community did not inevitably insist that black men pay for their alleged crimes with their lives. Local responses to these crimes were complicated and reveal a contested process of enforcing racial hierarchy and gender norms. Despite segregation's seemingly rigid rules, the boundaries around cross-racial and cross-gender interactions remained elastic. They could expand to accept or excuse some interactions between certain white women and certain black men, and they could contract to punish others. Despite white southerners' best efforts, blacks and whites did not exist in completely separate worlds, nor were they invariably antagonistic to one another when those worlds came into contact. When racial conflict erupted, whites did not always unite across class and gender lines, even in cases of black-on-white rape. Racial solidarity was contingent upon the simultaneous action of class and gender and far more elusive than the rhetoric of the white South would lead historians to believe.

The cases described in this book reveal the complexities and contradictions of a racially divided society. Whites and blacks inhabited the same streets in cities, worked in the same factories, stores, and hospitals, and lived close to one another in rural farming areas. They bought and consumed illegal alcohol together, and occasionally even ate together at the same table. In cities, where ambiguous racial interactions occurred frequently, white women became fearful around black men they did not know. The hustle and bustle of urban life pushed against the boundaries of racial separation. Interracial sexual relationships inevitably occurred without legal interference, despite the efforts of elite whites to prevent them. Indeed, more than any other factor, the local context controlled the disposition of cases of black-on-white rape. The participants in a case were members of a community, and their place and reputation in that community influenced events at trial and petitions for pardon. The reality of interracial relationships meant that not every interaction between a white woman and black man could be labeled a sexual threat, and allowed elite whites to give the benefit of the doubt to black men who either "knew their place" or were accused by potentially unscrupulous women.

Cases of black-on-white rape illuminate the struggles among whites and blacks and women and men that continued despite the seemingly absolute power of white men. Black men's convictions both asserted white power and theoretically proved the superiority of white civilization. They did not always represent white solidarity, however. White women had little formal public power, yet southern sexual ideology gave all white women, regardless of class or reputation, considerable ability to accuse black men of rape. Such power forced white men to act as white women's protectors and allowed white women to influence the fates of black men accused of rape. The cloak of chivalry that allegedly protected all white women, however, might only be a temporary cover for those whom white men deemed to be morally deficient. Black men's assaults of women who were judged to be less representative of white womanhood were perceived to be less of a threat to the social order.

Meanwhile, blacks also exerted power over the legal process, using leverage to temper the worst effects of white rage directed at black men. That African Americans were able to wield public power quietly attests to the continually contested nature of segregation, as blacks and whites negotiated the rules of racial interaction. Using their relationships with whites or their own communities, blacks opposed white interpretations of events and disputed the threat that whites argued black men's actions posed to the social order. Members of the African American community participated in these struggles from a disadvantaged position, but they nonetheless were able to influence decisions about black men's fates, especially as the century progressed.

These conclusions carry profound implications for understanding segregation as a system of racial control. The threat of violence and the strength of state and popular white power kept African Americans in a state of fear and buttressed a racial order that privileged white prerogatives. Yet the cases examined in this study suggest that segregation was neither rigid nor monolithic. Despite white efforts to construct a society in which whites and blacks occupied separate spaces, and in which white women remain subordinate to white men, relationships across racial lines, including sexual relationships between white women and black men, occurred, violating the mandates of both segregation and patriarchy. These relationships continued uninterrupted unless they publicly or excessively violated the mandates of segregation. The legal system punished black men who committed racial trespasses, but it could also chastise errant whites by releasing convicted black men. Accusations of black-on-white assault truly represented a world turned upside down, where black men sought to usurp white men's racial and sexual prerogatives, where white women controlled the actions of white men, and where poor and marginalized whites sought to capitalize on the power of their race. Public trials reclaimed public power for white men, acknowledging white women's power to accuse and punishing black men who committed racial trespasses. At the same time, white elites judged white women's complicity and limited the support disreputable women could expect from their betters. Over the course of the legal process, from arrest to pardon, elite whites were able to buttress the racial, gender, and class hierarchies on which their own preeminence depended.

The exclusive focus on Virginia raises the inevitable question of whether these conclusions apply to other southern states. Virginians prided themselves on their reliance on the legal system to patrol racial boundaries. Nevertheless, the rhetoric white Virginians used to condemn black-on-white rape matched that of other southerners, and the ideology undergirding racial relations and the social structure mirrored that of states throughout the South. The strength of Virginia's legal structure and the willingness of state authorities to use state power to quell mob violence partly explains the lack of mob murder. But as was the case in Virginia, the rhetoric of rape only spoke of what white southerners *thought* about black-on-white rape, not what they *did* in response to allegations of rape involving members of their communities. It is unlikely that once white southerners responded to allegations of black crime with extralegal violence, no other response was possible, even in the most violent states.

Scattered evidence indicates that white southerners responded to white women's accusations in a variety of ways. Virginia newspapers occasionally reported on the trial dispositions of cases of black-on-white assault from other southern states. In 1909, the *Richmond Times-Dispatch* reported that Charles Crumley, a black man, was saved from a mob in Florida after being accused of assaulting a white woman. He was acquitted at trial.[2] Preston Nelly was acquitted in Asheville, North Carolina, on a similar charge in 1925.[3] In South Carolina in 1931, a black man was convicted of attempting to rape a white woman and received a sentence of three years in prison.[4] The Richmond paper gave few details of the alleged crimes in these cases and provided little indication as to why these men were acquitted or received only minor punishments for crimes against white women. It does provide evidence, however, that Virginians were not alone in making distinctions among cases of black-on-white rape. In Florida, South Carolina, and North Carolina, at least, not every alleged assault by a black man against a white woman resulted in extralegal violence or punishment to the full extent of the law.

State appeals court records also provide considerable evidence that many cases of black-on-white rape made their way through the legal system. An examination of the records for Alabama, Georgia, Mississippi, North Carolina, and South Carolina reveals that approximately sixty cases of black-on-white rape or attempted rape were appealed after trial. Though these cases are useful, they probably represent only a handful of the cases that proceeded through the legal system, since most black defendants could not afford, or did not have grounds on which, to appeal their convictions. Appealed cases also give no indication of the number of black men who were acquitted or saw the charges against them dismissed. As in Virginia, cases appealed to higher courts in other southern states provide only a limited view of how local courts adjudicated the crimes brought to their attention.

At the very least, the sixty cases heard in the appellate courts of southern states provide considerable evidence that an accusation of rape did not inevitably lead to mob violence. Several cases noted that mobs of twenty to several hundred men gathered at news of the assault or the arrest of a suspect.[5] But those mobs did not derail the legal process. In other of these cases, justices expressed their responsibility to avoid a legal lynching. They stated that the nature of the crime, the assault by a black man against a white woman, alone convinced whites of black men's guilt, and therefore it was necessary to examine the evidence with additional caution.[6] Justices may have been unwilling to act entirely in opposition to public desires, as they upheld most convictions, but they apparently desired to maintain at least the appearance of integrity in the legal process.

Courts throughout the South also faced the same complexities in weighing the evidence in interracial crimes as did those in Virginia. Conformity to accepted patterns of behavior in violent crimes remained important in assessing black men's guilt. In some cases, the failure of black men accused of rape to act as whites expected black rapists to act injected doubt into white women's claims.[7] Court authorities in other states also struggled to determine when black men's actions carried a sexual threat and acknowledged that whites occasionally used charges of rape to gain leverage in unrelated disputes or to get themselves out of difficult situations. Blacks and whites in other southern states lived in proximity and carried on friendly relations. Not all white women avoided contact with black men. Some black men even argued openly in court that they maintained consensual sexual relationships with white women. The numerous cases of black-on-white rape appealed to higher courts throughout the South reveal a complicated web of community relationships that frequently crossed racial lines.[8] In short, the complicated efforts of Virginia legal officials to balance gender and class hierarchies as they sought to punish errant black men were mirrored in other southern states. The image of the black beast rapist and the innocent white female victim simply did not apply in every case.

Although few of black men's appeals were successful—of the sixty appellate cases examined, only sixteen convictions were reversed, and in every case, of course, local juries originally voted to convict—the arguments defendants crafted are nonetheless illuminating. Black men and their lawyers believed that evidence of the victim's inappropriate relationships or questionable character or of her consent might sway the court in their favor. More important, many of these arguments appeared in court testimony, indicating that even though such evidence might inflame white opinion against a defendant, defense counsels nonetheless decided to raise it. It is possible that in other cases where such evidence appeared, juries voted to acquit.

That southern whites did not always view interactions between white women and black men as criminal does not mean that the myth of the black beast rapist did not carry extraordinary power in the twentieth-century South. Black men fared worse than their white counterparts at every stage of the legal process and were far more likely to lose their lives after being accused of rape. Despite any protestations to the contrary, criminal trials did not necessarily uncover "the truth" about suspicious interactions. Juries were more likely to be swayed by a narrative of black criminality than by skepticism regarding the veracity of women's charges of rape or the possibility of mistaken identity. White men who controlled the legal process had the power to determine the punishment black men deserved for any racial trespass, and the jury's verdict usually aligned with white interpretations of events.

Fears of black men as criminals still color white perceptions of sexual crimes today. Scholars have demonstrated that black men accused of raping white women are more likely to be convicted and to receive more severe punishment than white men accused of raping women of any race.[9] Most white Americans still imagine a rapist as a black stranger leaping from the bushes. In Virginia, white women's accounts of rape against black men continue to carry tremendous power, even though they no longer spur angry mobs. As recently as 1995, a Virginia governor pardoned a black man who had been falsely accused of raping a white woman.[10] Cases like this one underscore the continuing dilemmas with which rape accusations are fraught. Rape is a crime that usually occurs without other witnesses, and the laws requiring corroborating evidence beyond the victim's testimony place a burden on the victims of rape that exists for victims of no other crime. The victim's identification of her assailant is crucial to conviction, and yet eyewitness identification in court is notoriously prone to error even among the most conscientious of witnesses. The probability of error only increases when witnesses attempt to identify suspects of another race. The release of convicted rapists who have been proved innocent by DNA evidence only underscores the difficulties accused men face.

Nevertheless, even today, despite the reforms in rape laws of the 1970s, the chances that a rape victim will see her rapist convicted in court remain abysmally small. Indeed, although efforts by groups like the Innocence Project reveal that innocent men are convicted, they also indicate that many guilty rapists never face a day in prison. They are never caught or someone else is punished for their crimes. Those innocent men who are convicted at trial are usually not the victims of unscrupulous or deceitful women exercising their only form of social power in a society that denies their concerns. They are the casualties of an imperfect criminal justice system. These cases demand that we put aside fears that acknowledging gender oppression will somehow lessen concern for racial oppression and instead work to understand how racism and sexism together support a social structure that works to the disadvantage of a great many. Only then can we create a society in which no one fears violence because of his or her race or sex.

NOTES

Abbreviations

EP   Secretary of the Commonwealth, Executive Papers, Accession
             35196, Library of Virginia Archives, Richmond, Va.
LOVA   Library of Virginia Archives, Richmond, Va.
PNAACP Papers of the NAACP on Microfilm, Alderman Library, University
             of Virginia, Charlottesville, Va.

Introduction

1. For an analysis of the Mann Act and its attempts to control illicit sexual relations, see Langum, *Crossing over the Line*.

2. Quoted in Carter, *Scottsboro*, 295.

3. "Scottsboro," in *Negro Songs of Protest*, collected by Lawrence Gellert, New York: American Music League.

4. Quoted in Goodman, *Stories of Scottsboro*, 227.

5. Quoted in Carter, *Scottsboro*, 269.

6. There was considerable editorial criticism of the guilty verdicts in white papers throughout the South. Other white southerners expressed their suspicion of women's charges in other ways. See Goodman, *Stories of Scottsboro*, 163–70.

7. Accounts of the Harper/Skaggs case are taken from the *Richmond Times-Dispatch*, the *Virginian Pilot and Norfolk Landmark*, and the *Portsmouth Star* between January and October 1931. The case papers are missing from the Norfolk Corporation Court in Norfolk, Virginia.

8. "Escape . . . ! From Shadow of the Electric Chair," *Norfolk Journal and Guide*, July 25, 1953. Twenty years later, in an article in the *Norfolk Journal and Guide* comparing his case to that of another black man accused of raping a white woman in 1953, Harper blamed his confession on a beating he received from police, from which he still bore scars on his head and legs.

9. "Harper again Placed on Trial for Life in Norfolk Court," *Portsmouth Star*, March 3, 1931; "New Trial Is Granted in Harper Case," *Portsmouth Star*, February 7, 1931.

10. "A Very Disquieting Case," *Richmond News-Leader*, March 7, 1931.

11. *Commonwealth v. Raymond Alsberry*, Common Law Order Book 11, p. 187, Winchester Corporation Court, Winchester, Va.; *Commonwealth v. Jacob Duncan*, Common Law Order Book 30, pp. 206, 233, 235, Danville Corporation Court, Danville, Va.; *Commonwealth v. Harold Taylor*, Common Law Order Book 19, pp. 91, 106, 119, 293, Richmond Hustings Court II, Richmond, Va.; "Negro Freed in Charge Involving Capital Crime," *Richmond Times-Dispatch*, November 16, 1931.

12. These cases represent those in which authorities arrested the man they believed to be responsible for the attack. There are numerous instances in which no suspect was ever apprehended. I located cases through reports in local newspapers, circuit court records, and the clemency papers of Virginia governors. Though I have surely missed a handful of cases, I am nonetheless confident that my sample is representative of all cases in Virginia. If anything, I have missed the low-profile cases that resulted in acquittal or very short sentences, making the assailant unlikely to bring his case to the governor's attention for pardon. This means that the percentage of "harsh" sentences may be exaggerated.

13. The number of men killed by extralegal violence includes two men who, after being chased by posses, were found hanged but whose deaths were ruled suicides. These incidents, in 1932 and 1935, occurred after Virginia had passed antilynching legislation. See "Denies Negro Was Tortured, Lynched," *Harrisonburg Daily News-Record*, September 23, 1932, and "Was It a Suicide?" *Richmond Planet*, May 25, 1935.

14. The dispositions of five cases are unknown.

15. Until 1924, the Virginia Code prescribed penalties of between three and eighteen years in prison or the death penalty for attempted rape and between five and twenty years in prison or death for rape. In 1924, the General Assembly extended the maximum prison sentence allowed by law to life in prison for both rape and attempted rape. This change resulted from juror complaints that the maximum prison terms were inadequate punishment in cases that they did not feel merited death. Several juries tried to lengthen the maximum prison term on their own, sentencing black men to death and simultaneously recommending the sentence be commuted to life imprisonment. In one case, that of Lee Strother in 1908, the governor refused to commute the sentence, saying that he was not bound by the jury's recommendation for mercy and saw no extenuating circumstances justifying commutation. In the case of Joe Gibbs in 1929, his sentence was commuted and he was granted a conditional pardon—similar to what is now parole, though without supervision—in 1947. He ultimately served eighteen years for his conviction of attempted rape. Rather than going through every application for conditional pardon, I examined a representative sample of cases for every year of the study and thus cannot accurately compare the number of men granted pardons and the number of those denied. This sample revealed that throughout the time period of this study, it was not uncommon for black men convicted of assaulting white women to be released before they completed their full sentences, and many returned to the communities in which they were convicted without further incident.

16. Each governor determined his own pardon policies, but most required those convicted of crimes to serve between one-third to two-thirds of their

sentences before they applied for conditional pardon. In life sentences, most governors required twelve years to pass before the convict applied for pardon.

17. There is a considerable body of literature that analyzes how case participants' preconceived notions of appropriate social relationships infiltrated the legal process and that uses legal trials as windows into culture. See, for example, Berry, *Pig Farmer's Daughter*, 4; Lazarus-Black and Hirsch, *Contested States*; Hariman, "Performing the Laws"; and Bennett, *Reconstructing Reality in the Courtroom*. In arguing that responses to black-on-white rape occurred on both a public front stage and a less-visible back stage, I am building on the work of several scholars in European history. See MacCannell, *Tourist*, 91–108; Greenhalgh, *Ephemeral Vistas*, 82–111; and Mitchell, *Colonizing Egypt*. These men develop the pathbreaking work of Goffman, *Presentation of the Self*.

18. The most comprehensive examination of executive clemency at the state level is Vivian M. L. Miller's study of the pardon process in Florida. Although I do not formally examine the governor's institutional power to grant clemency, concentrating instead on what those clemency decisions reveal about social relationships across race and gender lines, it is clear that, in many ways, Virginia's system operated similarly to Florida's. One important difference, however, is that the power to grant clemency in Virginia resided solely in the hands of the chief executive. See Miller, *Crime, Sexual Violence, and Clemency*. Several other works also touch on clemency and racial control. See, for example, Oshinsky, *Worse than Slavery*, and McMillen, *Dark Journey*.

19. See, for example, McGuire and Lydston, "Sexual Crimes among Southern Negroes."

20. Hodes, *White Women, Black Men*; Sommerville, "Rape Myth in the Old South"; Sommerville, "Rape, Race, and Castration"; Sommerville, "Rape Myth Reconsidered." Other scholars have also touched on interracial sexual relationships in the nineteenth-century South. See Edwards, "Disappearance of Susan Daniel"; Edwards, "Sexual Violence"; Bardaglio, "Rape and the Law"; and Bynum, *Unruly Women*, 117–18. Other scholarship reinforces Hodes's and Sommerville's contentions that antebellum southern communities could tolerate ongoing sexual relations between black men and white women. See Rothman, *Notorious in the Neighborhood*; Buckley, "Unfixing Race"; Lockley, "Crossing the Race Divide"; Rothman, "'To Be Freed from Thate Curs'"; and Mills, "Miscegenation and the Free Negro."

21. Hall, *Revolt against Chivalry*.

22. C. Vann Woodward's *Strange Career of Jim Crow* is the bellwether study of increasing racial antagonism at the turn of the twentieth century that sparked interest in the component parts of that antagonism, namely lynching and race riots. The scholarship on lynching in general and specific lynchings in particular is too numerous to list. Important and recent studies include Capeci, *Lynching of Cleo Wright*; Howard, *Lynchings*; Brundage, *Lynching in the New South*; Brundage, *Under Sentence of Death*; Smead, *Blood Justice*; and McGovern, *Anatomy of a Lynching*. One must also include Jacquelyn Dowd Hall's seminal work *Revolt against Chivalry* for its still-current analysis of the intersection of racial and sexual control embodied in lynching.

23. See Goodman, *Stories of Scottsboro*; Carter, *Scottsboro*; and Rise, *Martins-*

ville Seven. Other works include Davies, *White Lies*, and Smith and Giles, *American Rape*.

24. The accepted belief that all black men paid with their lives and the related assumption that all white women who accused black men of rape were lying function in some ways as does the persistent legend that Dr. Charles Drew died after his car accident because he was refused treatment at a white hospital. Though Drew was not denied treatment because of his race, other blacks were. Thus the legend, even though not true in the particular, expressed a larger truth. See Love, "Noted Physician Fatally Injured," 12.

25. In her insightful analysis of the culture of segregation, Grace Hale (*Making Whiteness*, esp. 335) asserts that segregation was constantly evolving, continually renegotiated, refined, reinforced, and challenged by hundreds of small and not-so-small everyday acts.

26. Other scholars note how the unpredictable nature of lynchings heightened their controlling power. See, for example, Vinikas, "Specters in the Past," 563.

27. The paradigm of "terror-mercy" is familiar to British legal historians. This paradigm suggests that social and political elites used court sentences as a means of inflicting control through terror on peasants. Simultaneously, they used the granting of mercy as a tool to legitimate the legal system and to justify the social order, as well as inspire loyalty among those who generally did not share in society's privileges. See Hay, "Property, Authority, and the Criminal Law," 17–63; Thompson, *Whigs and Hunters*; and Brewer and Styles, *Ungovernable People*.

28. Cleaver, *Soul on Ice*, 14.

29. Over the course of this study, I have been continually baffled by the willingness of scholars, who would, I believe, consider themselves enlightened when it comes to issues of gender to immediately assume that most, if not all, white women who accused black men of rape were lying. Their attitude suggests that even today, there is a fear that acknowledging gender oppression will somehow lessen the significance of racial oppression. I argue that it would instead be more fruitful to explore how racial and gender oppression are mutually reinforcing parts of the same system.

30. These records form the basis for Donald H. Partington's statistical analysis of racial discrepancies in punishment for rape. See Partington, "Incidence of the Death Penalty," 43–75.

Chapter One

1. "Appomatox Jail Heavily Guarded," *Richmond Times-Dispatch*, June 28, 1912.

2. Ibid.

3. "Wright Must Die in Electric Chair August 9," *Richmond Times-Dispatch*, June 30, 1912.

4. *Commonwealth v. Alfred Wright*, Bill of Exception 2, Judgments Circuit Court, Commonwealth Cases Drawer M–Z, Circuit Court of Appomattox County, Appomattox, Va. Drysdale's characterization contrasted sharply with Judge Hund-

ley's view of the courtroom. Drysdale may have been exaggerating to improve his client's position, since he provided no documentation, other than his and Wright's testimony, about the atmosphere of the courtroom. The *Richmond Times-Dispatch* did report that there was a plot to lynch Wright immediately after the trial if he did not receive the death penalty ("Wright Must Die in Electric Chair August 9").

5. *Commonwealth v. Alfred Wright*, Bill of Exception 2.

6. *Commonwealth v. Alfred Wright*, written at the bottom of Bill of Exception 2; "Wright Must Die in Electric Chair August 9"; Governor Mann to S. L. Ferguson, August 9, 1912, *Commonwealth v. Alfred Wright*, Petition for Respite of Execution, July 19–August, 1912, EP.

7. *Wright v. Commonwealth*, 114 Va. 872 (1913).

8. See Brundage, *Lynching in the New South*, Appendix A.

9. George W. Hundley, *Commonwealth v. Alfred Wright*, Law Order Book 1, p. 511, Circuit Court of Appomattox County, Appomattox, Virginia.

10. I am indebted to Gail Bederman's analysis of the connection between male power and white supremacy and the role of both restraint and aggression in white constructions of manhood and civilization. See Bederman, *Manliness and Civilization*, 1–76.

11. Bederman's arguments echo those of Virginia's eugenicists. See Gregory Dorr, "Segregation's Science."

12. Suzanne Lebsock finds evidence of this in Virginia as early as 1895. See Lebsock, *Murder in Virginia*, 64–65.

13. W. W. Lee to Governor Swanson, June 4, 1906, *Commonwealth v. Gabriele Battaile*, Petition for Commutation, June 1–July 16, 1906, EP.

14. The historical literature establishing the development of the rape myth in the South is extensive. The hallmark is Jacquelyn Dowd Hall's *Revolt against Chivalry*, which explores lynching as a means of both racial and gender control. There is also extensive scholarship on lynching as a form of political control over African Americans. See, for example, Grace Hale, *Making Whiteness*, 199–226, and Brundage, *Lynching in the New South*. There is also a growing body of work on the changing meaning of interracial rape in the nineteenth century, including, most importantly, the work of Diane Miller Sommerville, Martha Hodes, and Laura Edwards.

15. Stephen Kantrowitz (" 'One Man's Mob Is Another Man's Militia,' " 81) also argues that in the political realm, violence and paternalism were not mutually exclusive approaches to racial control. Instead, what he terms "carrot and stick" approaches were complementary and served as tactics in the larger effort to assert white supremacy.

16. There is a significant body of literature debating whether or not courts represented effective institutions to enforce hegemonic power. Although in this chapter I argue that for white Virginians, trying cases of black-on-white rape in court represented a system of racial control, subsequent chapters make clear that this method was not as effective as it might seem. This assertion echoes the findings of other scholars. See Waldrep, "Substituting Law for the Lash," 1425–51, and Lazarus-Black and Hirsch, *Contested States*.

17. Historian Diane Miller Sommerville ("Rape Myth Reconsidered," 6–70) has

convincingly argued that twentieth-century scholarship has superimposed post-Reconstruction fears of "black beast rapists" onto antebellum white southerners.

18. See, for example, Percy, *Lanterns on the Levee*, 307–8. Lillian Smith criticized white men's obsession with black men as rapists, as did Virginia Durr. See Smith, *Killers of the Dream*, 126, 106, 104, and Durr, *Outside the Magic Circle*, 123, 172, 175.

19. These quotes appear in Litwack, *Trouble in Mind*, 295, 299.

20. Felton's position on lynching and her address to the agricultural society appears in Brundage, *Lynching in the New South*, 198. For an analysis of Felton's beliefs about white men's duty to white women, see Whites, "Love, Hate, Race, and Lynching," 143–62.

21. Terence Finnegan ("At the Hands of Parties Unknown") persuasively demonstrates that most lynchings in South Carolina and Mississippi sprang from labor disputes between white landlords and their black tenants. Lynchings, then, were one measure of the tension created by African Americans' desire for racial and economic equality.

22. Bederman, "Civilization and the Decline of Middle-Class Manliness," 207–49; Brundage, *Lynching in the New South*, 7–8.

23. Grace Hale (*Making Whiteness*, 199–240) cites newspaper reports of the lynching of Sam Hose in which the crowd is described as "orderly" and "cool and went about its work carefully and almost with a system" (213).

24. The account of Page's lynching is taken from "Negro Assailant of Girls Lynched," *Richmond Times-Dispatch*, August 17, 1917. The same account was reprinted word for word in the African American weekly paper: "Colored Man Lynched in the State of Virginia," *Richmond Planet*, August 25, 1917.

25. "Lynching Investigation Fails to Discover Mob," *Richmond Times-Dispatch*, August 19, 1917.

26. Ibid.

27. "Mob Storms Jail, Lynches Man on Street," *Richmond Times-Dispatch*, March 21, 1925.

28. "Negro Fiend Killed by Aubrey Bowie," *Culpeper Exponent*, March 1, 1912; "Kills Negro Who Insults Daughter," *Richmond Times-Dispatch*, March 2, 1912; *Aubrey Bowie v. Commonwealth*, Law Order Book 12, pp. 267, 432, Circuit Court of Culpeper County, Culpeper, Va.

29. "Negro Who Pursued White Woman Shot Dead after Coming Back Second Time," *Danville Register*, March 1, 1921; "Cranford Acquitted of Killing Negro," ibid., March 3, 1921.

30. "Portsmouth Incensed by Two Awful Crimes," *Virginian-Pilot*, August 12, 1908.

31. Ibid.; "Mob Enters County Jail, Negroes It Sought Were Rushed Here for Safety," *Virginian-Pilot*, August 15, 1908; "Negro Held for Trial, Mayor Reed Releases Mob Members on Bail," ibid., August 16, 1908; "Smith Will Go to Electric Chair for Assault," ibid., September 9, 1908; "Smith Is to Die for His Crime This Morning," ibid., October 13, 1908; "Henry Smith Dies in Electric Chair," ibid., October 14, 1908; *Commonwealth v. Henry Smith*, Order Book 21, pp. 401–3, Circuit Court of Norfolk County (now Chesapeake County), Chesapeake, Va.

32. "Smith Is to Die for His Crime This Morning."

33. Woodbridge, "Why the Difference?" 605–6.

34. After 1900, eleven black men were lynched for allegedly assaulting white women, according to Brundage (*Lynching in the New South*, 263, app. A, tab. 3), that number represents a decline from the number of black men lynched for sexual crimes between 1880 and 1900, when twenty-two black men died. My research shows a slightly higher number of men executed by extralegal violence after 1900 because I include several actions by lone vigilantes, which do not fit the standard definition of a lynching and were not included in Brundage's study.

35. See ibid., 161–62, and John Douglas Smith, *Managing White Supremacy*.

36. The best and most comprehensive discussion of Virginia's embrace of eugenics appears in Gregory Dorr, "Segregation's Science." For a discussion of how ideas about gender shaped these policies, see Lisa Dorr, "Arm in Arm." For eugenic ideas about controlling crime, see Nicole Hahn Rafter, *Creating Born Criminals*.

37. McGuire and Lydston, "Sexual Crimes among Southern Negroes."

38. I have found only a handful of cases in which convicted rapists received vasectomies as part of their sentences. Loo Rooster Jarvis in 1931 was arrested for allegedly raping a white woman, though authorities believed the relationship may have been consensual. He was sent to Central State Hospital, sterilized, and released in 1934. One year later he was convicted of raping another white woman and sentenced to life in prison. (*Commonwealth v. Loo Rooster Jarvis*, Petition for Conditional Pardon, January 8–January 12, 1962, EP). Two white men convicted of raping a white child in Charlottesville, Va., in 1944, agreed to be sterilized, perhaps in exchange for a reduced sentence (*Commonwealth v. Lesley Mooney*, *Commonwealth v. Stonewall Sacre*, December Term 1944 Papers, Charlottesville Corporation Court, Charlottesville, Va.).

39. Quoted in Rise, *Martinsville Seven*, 3.

40. "Masked Mob Storms Jail, Kills Negro," *Richmond News-Leader*, August 16, 1926.

41. "The Opinion of the Press," *Roanoke Times*, August 18, 1926.

42. For a discussion of the role of Raymond Byrd's death on antilynching legislation, see Beers, "Wythe County Lynching of Raymond Bird." John Douglas Smith (*Managing White Supremacy*) includes a discussion of antilynching legislation in his larger discussion of Virginia elites' control over race relations in the 1920s and 1930s.

43. "Denies Negro Was Tortured, Lynched," *Harrisonburg Daily News-Record*, September 23, 1932.

44. "Was It Suicide?"

45. Other scholars have noted the connection between the threat of mob violence and conviction at trial. See, for example, Ayers, *Vengeance and Justice*, 246; McMillen, *Dark Journey*, 206–7; and George Wright, "By the Book."

46. On the legislative history of criminal punishment, see Murchison and Schwab, "Capital Punishment in Virginia," and Partington, "Incidence of the Death Penalty."

47. *Hart v. Commonwealth*, 131 Va. 726 (1921), at 746–47.

48. These conclusions are drawn from anecdotal evidence in Virginia's newspapers, as well as the scant historiography of rape in the South. See Bardaglio, *Reconstructing the Household*, 37–78, and Sommerville, "Rape Myth Reconsidered," 255–78.

49. By 1938, only five other states left sentencing in the hands of the jury. They were Arkansas, Illinois, Kentucky, Missouri, and Texas. In 1938, many Virginia judges and the Virginia State Bar Association were beginning to suggest that this provision be removed because of inequities in sentencing. See Gullette, "Should the Jury Fix the Punishment for Crimes?" 462–66.

50. Murchison and Schwab, "Capital Punishment in Virginia," 107.

51. These numbers are taken from Donald Partington's tables charting rape sentencing by race from 1908 to 1963. Unfortunately, he focuses primarily on the race of the defendants and does not address the role of the race of the victims in racial disparities in sentencing. See Partington, "Incidence of the Death Penalty," 43–75.

52. Carter, *Scottsboro*, 348.

53. Michael Klarman ("Racial Origins of Modern Criminal Procedure") argues that southerners agreed that racism was not always incompatible with due-process protections for black defendants, as long as a given case did not challenge white supremacy or result in national condemnation of white justice in the South.

54. "In Henrico Jail," *Richmond Times-Dispatch*, November 10, 1912. Archer Ellis was found guilty of attempted rape and sentenced to seven years in prison.

55. "Claim Prisoner Confesses Crime," *Richmond Times-Dispatch*, February 26, 1925. Carter was found guilty of rape, sentenced to death, and executed.

56. "Officers Avert Lynching of Young Negro," *Richmond Times-Dispatch*, November 14, 1929. Gibbs was found guilty of attempted rape; he was sentenced to death, but his death sentence was commuted to life in prison. He was granted a conditional pardon in 1947.

57. "2 Negroes Rushed Away from Hopewell," *Richmond Times-Dispatch*, September 1, 1927. Nelson was convicted, sentenced to death, and executed.

58. *Commonwealth v. Lee Archer*, Petition for Change of Venue, September 8, 1913, Princess Anne Circuit Court Papers 1913, LOVA.

59. *Commonwealth v. Lee Archer*, Circuit Court of Princess Anne County, 1913, Princess Anne County Records, LOVA.

60. *Commonwealth v. Arthur Neale*, Law Order Book 4, pp. 182, 183, 203, Circuit Court of King William County, King William Courthouse, Va.; "Negro at West Point Attacks White Girl," *Richmond Times-Dispatch*, October 13, 1914.

61. *Commonwealth v. Sam Pannell*, Common Law Book 22, pp. 566, 567, Circuit Court of Halifax County, Halifax, Va. Warrants for both men's arrests, as well as George Pannell's acquittal, are in the Warrants File for 1932. Pannell was sentenced to death and executed.

62. "Little Girl Is Victim of Assault by Negroes," *Richmond Times-Dispatch*, March 23, 1915; "Militia to Guard Negro during Trial on Friday," ibid., April 28, 1915; "Soldiers Will Guard Negro from Violence," ibid., April 30, 1915.

63. "Little Girl Is Victim of Assault by Negroes"; "Tom Coles Confesses Assaulting Girl," *Richmond Times-Dispatch*, March 24, 1915; "Rumors of Lynching

Prove Groundless," ibid., March 25, 1915; "Militia to Guard Negro during Trial on Friday"; "Soldiers Will Guard Negro from Violence"; "Coles Sentenced to Die June 4," *Richmond Times-Dispatch*, May 1, 1915. Mecklenburg County order books and case files are not available for this period. Though these legal records might indicate that Carter was tried for his participation, no trial was reported in the press. I believe this is strong evidence that he was never charged since the case received extensive media coverage and newspapers likely would have covered or at least referred to Carter's trial if there had been one.

64. "Mob Threatens to Take Justice in Its Own Hands," *Richmond Times-Dispatch*, April 3, 1916. Report of the Nottoway County citizens' dismay appears in "Negro Is Rushed to Henrico Jail," ibid., April 4, 1916. Williams was found guilty of rape, sentenced to death, and executed.

65. "Escaped Prisoner Captured at Opal," *Fauquier Democrat*, August 14, 1920. Andrew Fields was convicted of attempted rape and sentenced to fifteen years in prison.

66. "Attempted Assaults," *Fairfax Herald*, August 31, 1917.

67. "No Attempt at Lynching," *Fairfax Herald*, August 31, 1917.

68. "Burgess to Die," *Fairfax Herald*, September 21, 1917. *Commonwealth v. William H. Burgess*, Minute Book 9, pp. 176, 188, 192, Circuit Court of Fairfax County, Fairfax, Va.

69. "No Attempt at Lynching"; "Burgess to Die."

70. Petition to Governor Davis, undated, *Commonwealth v. Walter Bowen*, Petition for Conditional Pardon, October 3–October 17, 1920, EP.

71. C. R. McCorkle to Governor Westmoreland Davis, September 15, 1920, *Commonwealth v. Walter Bowen*, Petition for Conditional Pardon, October 3–October 17, 1920. See also *Commonwealth v. Walter Bowen*, Petition for Conditional Pardon, February 13–February 29, 1923, EP.

72. *Commonwealth v. Henry Perman*, Law Order Book 32, pp. 1, 18, 20, 38, 123, Circuit Court of Norfolk County, Chesapeake, Va.; Commonwealth's Attorney's statement in file for Commutation of Sentence, Folder "Peed, Claude-Picott, Henry," Governor Trinkle Papers, Box 65, LOVA.

73. "Arrests Negro Charged with Attacking Woman," *Richmond Times-Dispatch*, August 8, 1920.

74. "Woman Fails to Identify Negro as Her Assailant," *Richmond Times-Dispatch*, August 10, 1920.

75. "Negro Confesses He Attacked White Woman," *Richmond Times-Dispatch*, August 16, 1920. This article did not suggest that Williams's confession might have been coerced, but it did mention that he was removed from the Lynchburg jail because of an approaching mob.

76. *Commonwealth v. Robert Williams*, Petition for Commutation, "Pardon Applications, etc." Folder W 2-2, Governor Davis Papers, Box 48, LOVA.

77. Charles Alexander to Governor Montegue, undated, *Commonwealth v. Doc Bacon*, Petition for Commutation, September–October 1903, EP.

78. Judge's Instructions to the Jury, *Commonwealth v. Henry Moton, aka Palmer*, Case File, April Term, 1929, Norfolk Corporation Court I, Norfolk, Va.

79. Oliver Hill, Report of the Investigation of the Case of the Commonwealth of Virginia vs. Joseph Mickens at Waynesboro, Staunton and Roanoke, Virginia,

addressed to Thurgood Marshall, Leon A. Ransom, Dr. J. M. Tinsley, Madison S. Jones, and Albert Simms, undated, PNAACP, Part 8, Series B, Reel 25, Frames 425, 426.

80. Oliver W. Hill to Thurgood Marshall, January 9, 1941, p. 3, PNAACP, Part 8, Series B, Reel 25, Frames 395, 396, 397.

81. Nellie Lloyd to NAACP, April 11, 1925, PNAACP, Part 8, Series A, Reel 12, Frames 314, 315. Bell's case was never brought to trial.

82. *Commonwealth v. Richard Daniel Brown*, Order Book 13, pp. 53, 54, Circuit Court of Amelia County, Amelia, Va. Brown was convicted and sentenced to life in prison.

83. *Commonwealth v. William Gee*, Common Law Order Book 7, pp. 367, 369, 373, 401, Circuit Court of Warwick County, Newport News, Va. Warwick County was absorbed into the city of Newport News. Records for the Warwick County Court reside in the Newport News Courthouse Archives. See also "Negro Attacks Aged Woman," *Richmond Times-Dispatch*, November 3, 1926; "Sentenced to Die in Electric Chair," ibid., November 10, 1926. Gee was convicted, sentenced to death, and executed.

84. *Commonwealth v. John Wade*, Common Law Order Book 44, pp. 358, 415, 416, Roanoke Corporation Court, Roanoke, Va.

85. *Commonwealth v. John Lewis Rollins and George Matthews, aka Rollins*, Law Order Book 7, pp. 264, 265, 266, Circuit Court of Carolina County, Caroline, Va. Accounts of the assault appear in "Two Women Victims of Brutal Attack," *Richmond Times-Dispatch*, July 13, 1915. Quote appears in "Quick Justice Meted out to Two Negroes," ibid., July 16, 1915.

86. Several other black men faced trial for crimes against white women without the benefit of legal counsel, though why their judges were unable to appoint lawyers to represent them is unknown. These men are Wilson Allen, Lee Williams, and Lemis Barnes.

87. "Finney to Die in Electric Chair," *Roanoke Times*, August 1, 1908; *Commonwealth v. Will Finney*, Common Law Order Book 18, pp. 70, 75, 77, Circuit Court of Franklin County, Rocky Mount, Va.; *Commonwealth v. Will Finney*, Petition for Commutation, September 1–October 22, 1908, EP.

88. *Commonwealth v. Solomon Douglas*, Petition for Conditional Pardon, May 22–June 10, 1923, EP.

89. *Commonwealth v. Charlie Brown*, Law Order Book 9, pp. 234, 236, 238, 253, Case File 833, Circuit Court of Isle of Wight County, Isle of Wight, Va.

90. W. L. Parker to Governor Price, June 14, 1941, *Commonwealth v. Charlie Brown*, Petition for Commutation, August 8–August 28, 1941, EP. Brown's petition for commutation was denied, and he was executed.

91. R. R. Farr to Governor Mann, *Commonwealth v. Ernest McKnight*, March 30, 1912, March 20–April 15, 1912, EP.

92. Walter Christian to T. R. Kemper, June 20, 1910, *Commonwealth v. James White*, Petition for Conditional Pardon, December 11–December 18, 1914, EP. White petitioned for pardon in 1910 and 1914 and was rejected both times.

93. Alexander Forward to O. B. Wright, September 20, 1917, *Commonwealth v. John Will Bond*, Petition for Conditional Pardon, September 21–October 10, 1917, EP.

94. Governor Swanson to Harrison and Long, attorneys for John Roberson, December 14, 1910, *Commonwealth v. John Roberson*, Petition for Conditional Pardon, September 1–October 7, 1912, EP.

95. *Commonwealth v. John Anderson*, Common Law Book 16, pp. 308, 309, 314, Case File, December Term 1938, Circuit Court of Loudoun County, Leesburg, Va.

96. *Commonwealth v. Richard Daniel Brown*, Order Book 13, pp. 53, 54, 65, Case File, File Drawer 3448, Circuit Court Papers 1948 March–1950 June, Circuit Court of Amelia County, Amelia, Va.

Chapter Two

1. "Girl Raped; 4 Men Held by Police," *Richmond Times-Dispatch*, August 14, 1939; "Four Jailed in North Side Girl's Case," ibid., October 14, 1939; "3 Deny Attack on White Girl," *Richmond Afro-American*, August 19, 1939; "Charges of Attack Flop, 3 Post Bond," ibid., October 21, 1939.

2. *Commonwealth v. Robert W. Miller, Arthur Lee Harvey, Tom W. Johnson*, Common Law Order Book 96, pp. 2, 37, and *Commonwealth v. George W. Shinault, Jr.*, Common Law Order Book 96, pp. 37, 358, Richmond Hustings Court I, Richmond, Va.

3. "Charges of Attack Flop; 3 Post Bond."

4. Hale, *Making Whiteness*, 182–97.

5. "You couldn't smile at a white woman," a Jones County, Mississippi, black man believed. "If you did you'd be hung from a limb" (Leon Litwack, *Trouble in Mind*, 307). Litwack mentions other minor infractions that led to lynchings, including "paying undue or improper attention to a white woman." While undoubtedly true in some contexts, seemingly innocent or ambiguous actions did not lead inevitably to violence. African American men's fear that it might is testimony to, and an artifact of, the spectacular, though imperfect, power of lynching to control behavior.

6. See Fredrickson, *Black Image*, 256–82, and Williamson, *Crucible of Race*, 306–10. For primary sources describing this ideology, see Cash, *Mind of the South*, and Lillian Smith, *Killers of the Dream*.

7. Philip A. Bruce, a Virginian, described his belief that black men found white women strangely alluring in his *Plantation Negro as Freeman*, 83–84, 129–30. Few white women in Virginia have left records attesting to their fear of black men. There are some sources from women in other southern states. "I lived in Florida ten years and was never free from fear of the negro one moment," a Florida woman recounted. "And if it were only death to be feared, that we could endure. But the thought of outrage is worse than that of a thousand deaths." A Georgian once recounted to a northern journalist, "You don't know and you can't know what it means down here to live in constant fear lest your wife or daughter be attacked on the road, or even in her home. Many women in the city of Statesboro dare not go into their backyards after dark. Every white planter knows that there is always danger for his daughters to visit even the nearest neighbor, or for his wife to go to church without a man to protect her" (Litwack, *Trouble in Mind*, 304, 305). Margaret Jarman Hagood (*Mothers of the South*, 178)

also noted that several white women in her study of tenant farming women in North Carolina in the 1930s refused to be left alone on their family's farm because of their fears of black men. Hagood called this fear part of the "traditional pattern" of race relations.

8. Manly Barnes to Alexander Forward, August 17, 1915, *Commonwealth v. Charles Wilson*, Petition for Conditional Pardon, September 1–September 28, 1915, EP.

9. Form sent to Judge Frank P. Christian, undated, *Commonwealth v. Walter Jones*, Petition for Conditional Pardon, November 1–November 12, 1919, EP.

10. "Special Grand Jury May Be Ordered Today," *Roanoke World News*, June 9, 1914.

11. R. W. Kime to Governor Davis, September 2, 1920, *Commonwealth v. Walter Moore*, Petition for Conditional Pardon, October 3–October 17, 1920, EP.

12. By 1924, Sarah Patterson had died. I argue in Chapter 3 that the victim's subsequent death, among other factors, freed her from the need of white men's protection, thereby making the convicted assailant's release more likely. See R. T. Hubbard to Governor Trinkle, July 23, 1923, *Commonwealth v. Walter Moore*, Petition for Conditional Pardon, December 24, 1923–January 4, 1924, EP.

13. In the trial of the Martinsville Seven in 1949, defense attorneys motioned that the trial be moved to a more neutral location, claiming, among other things, that news coverage of the rape in the Martinsville *Bulletin* had inflamed local opinion against the defendants. The editor of the *Bulletin*, Kay Thompson, defended the paper's coverage and credited it with preventing more open expressions of hysteria. Thompson, somewhat disingenuously, argued that local hysteria had been alleviated partly because the paper had used the term "criminal assault" instead of "rape" to describe the crime. Since Virginia newspapers had been making this semantic switch since the beginning of the twentieth century, it is hardly likely that any white Virginians were confused by the term, and the actions of the editor probably did not contribute to maintaining social order. See Rise, *Martinsville Seven*, 34.

14. "Negroes Attack Woman in Street," *Richmond Times-Dispatch*, November 27, 1910. Other examples from the *Richmond Times-Dispatch* include "Negro Attacks Woman in Park," June 7, 1909; "Vicious Negro Attacks Woman," November 20, 1910; "Little Girl Attacked and Injured by Negro," January 27, 1915; and "Two White Women Victims of Attacks by Danville Blacks," February 26, 1921.

15. "Holds up Woman at Pistol's Point," *Richmond Times-Dispatch*, August 4, 1913.

16. These nonsexual crimes include breaking and entering, insulting or annoying a white woman, simple assault, assault and battery, malicious wounding, robbery, and peeping. They do not include the nine cases, all in Richmond, of black men convicted of being "of ill-fame."

17. "Two Young Ladies Victim of Attack," *Danville Register*, September 12, 1916; *Commonwealth v. Linwood Womack*, *Commonwealth v. Tim Brooks*, Common Law Order Book V, pp. 310, 346, 352, Danville Corporation Court, Danville, Va.

18. "Sent to Grand Jury," *Richmond Times-Dispatch*, September 17, 1916.

19. "2 Negroes Rushed Away from Hopewell"; "Identifies Negro As Her

Assailant," *Richmond Times-Dispatch*, September 2, 1927; "Indict Negro for Alleged Attack," ibid., September 7, 1927; "Death Sentence for Negro in Hopewell," ibid., September, 18, 1927. The *Richmond News-Leader* also carried information about the crime.

20. *Commonwealth v. William Nelson*, Law Order Book 5, pp. 382, 388, 431, Hopewell Corporation Circuit Court, Hopewell, Va.

21. "Attempts Attack on White Woman," *Richmond Times-Dispatch*, October 2, 1927.

22. Ibid.

23. *Commonwealth v. William Dance*, Law Order Book 5, pp. 398, 401, 527, 546, Hopewell Corporation Court, Hopewell, Va.; "Hopewell Man Is Declared Insane," *Richmond News-Leader*, October 19, 1927.

24. "Negro Attacks Woman in Home," *Richmond Times-Dispatch*, December 29, 1910; *Commonwealth v. Junius Robinson*, Common Law Order Book 52, pp. 157, 159, Richmond Hustings Court I, Richmond, Va.

25. *Commonwealth v. William Harrison*, Common Law Order Book Y, pp. 142, 143, Danville Corporation Court, Danville, Va.; *Commonwealth v. William Harrison*, Petition for Conditional Pardon, August 25–September 23, 1924, EP; "Negro Caught under Bed of Woman Given 9 Years," *Richmond Times-Dispatch*, March 8, 1921. The *Danville Register,* in contrast to the Richmond paper, merely noted that a "Dangerous Negro" was found under the bed in a white home. See "Dangerous Negro Found Hidden Underneath Bed in Jefferson Street Home," *Danville Register*, February 27, 1921, and "Negro Caught Hiding under Bed Is Held for Grand Jury," ibid., March 1, 1921. The case of John Wade was similar. The *Roanoke Times* reported an attack on a girl by a black man in 1922. John Wade received two years in prison for his conviction of attempted robbery. See "Girl Attacked; Negro Arrested," *Roanoke Times*, December 22, 1922; *Commonwealth v. John Wade*, Common Law Order Book 44, pp. 358, 415, 416, Roanoke Corporation Court, Roanoke, Va.; and *Commonwealth v. John Wade*, Roanoke Corporation Court Records, Case File 3725, LOVA.

26. "Police Report More Attacks by Negro Men," *Richmond Times-Dispatch*, October 18, 1924; "Faces Grand Jury in Assault Case," ibid., October 19, 1924; *Commonwealth v. Albert Swinson*, Common Law Order Book 78, pp. 152, 367. Richmond Hustings Court I, Richmond, Va.; Indictment, *Commonwealth v. Albert Swinson*, Ended Causes 1924–50, Box 1025, Richmond Hustings Court I Records, LOVA.

27. "Police Report More Attacks by Negro Men."

28. *Commonwealth v. William Thomas*, Law Order Book 8, pp. 160, 163, Circuit Court of Madison County, Madison, Va.; "Outrage Stirs Orange People," *Richmond Times-Dispatch*, January 27, 1927; "Say Negro Admits Charge," ibid., February 22, 1927; "William Thomas Indicted March 7," ibid., March 8, 1927; "Two Colored Men's Pleas," *Richmond Planet*, April 23, 1927. W. Fitzhugh Brundage and Edward Ayers also point out that communities were more willing to punish "outsiders" than their own members. See Brundage, *Lynching in the New South*, 81–82, and Ayers, *Promise of the New South*, 156–57.

29. Many historians have offered analyses of conflicts over racial privilege and the use of public space and their role in hardening segregation and white

supremacy. See Dailey, *Before Jim Crow*, 103-31; Kelley, " 'We Are Not What We Seem,' " 35-54; Gilmore, *Gender and Jim Crow*, 91-118; Gilmore, "Murder, Memory, and the Flight of the Incubus," 73-94; and Simon, "Race Reactions."

30. "Insolent Negro Cuts a Woman," *Richmond Times-Dispatch*, May 16, 1910; *Commonwealth v. Wilson M. Tucker, Commonwealth v. Albert Williams*, Law Order Book 21, p. 460, Lynchburg Corporation Court, Lynchburg, Va. Ten of the twelve jurors served on both juries.

31. "Negro Attacks White Woman," *Richmond Times-Dispatch*, June 27, 1910.

32. Ibid.

33. *Commonwealth v. Junius Booker*, Common Law Order Book 51, pp. 350, 356, Richmond Hustings Court I, Richmond, Va.; *Commonwealth v. Junius Booker*, Case File, Ended Causes 1868-1918, Box 258, Richmond Hustings Court I Records, LOVA.

34. Appeals cases in the higher courts in other southern states reveal that Virginia was not alone in facing this complicated process. In Mississippi, in 1935, for example, the Supreme Court reversed a black man's conviction for attempted rape. The defendant, a fourteen-year-old youth, allegedly grabbed a white woman by the throat. When she screamed, he ran. The justices wrote in their decision to reverse his conviction that "[a]ffirming the conviction in this case—springing perhaps from an instinctive racial feeling—would be tantamount to declaring that because of the audacity of the accused, a member of the colored race, in laying violent hands upon the throat and neck of the prosecution witness, a white woman, attempt to rape might be inferred; and that the mere probability that the act was committed with intent to rape will be sufficient to support a verdict of guilty." Such assumptions, they ruled, could not be made (*Pew v. State*, 172 Miss. 885 [1935]). South Carolina's high court displayed more ambivalence over the matter. In 1909, a black janitor was convicted of assault and battery with the intent to ravish for putting his hands on the shoulders of a white woman while she was playing the piano in an otherwise empty school. The conviction was affirmed; the justices ruled that "[w]hen the great social chasm that exists between the white and colored races, and especially between white women and negro men, is considered, it cannot be said that the facts and circumstances above detailed do not warrant a reasonable inference of a guilty intent on the part of the defendant. . . . He had no business touching her" (*State v. Johnson*, 84 SC 45 [1909]). Three years later, the court reversed the conviction of a black man for assault with intent to ravish. The defendant had approached a white woman while her husband was away and requested sexual relations. She shot at him with a pistol. The court argued that there was no evidence that he intended to use force to gratify his sexual desire (*State v. Sanders*, 92 SC 427 [1912]). I explore similar Virginia cases later in this chapter. North Carolina, despite its reputation as a more racially "liberal" state, seemed more willing to assign sexual motives to black men's actions. In a 1901 case, despite the defense's contention that there was no evidence of rape, the North Carolina Supreme Court upheld the conviction of attempted rape after the defendant was accused of following a fourteen-year-old white girl to her home. The court concluded that "[h]is conduct while walking in front of the girl indicates a flirtation not warranted by the social or racial relations of the parties" and thus

was sufficient evidence of intent. That this case occurred during a particularly turbulent time in North Carolina's racial history might account for its decision (*State v. Garner*, 129 NC 536 [1901]).

35. *Commonwealth v. Joseph Mickens*, 187 Va. 273 (1941), "Evidence Produced on Behalf of the Commonwealth," 46; *Legions v. Commonwealth*, 181 Va. 89 (1943), "Proceedings, Transactions, and Testimony," 57.

36. In 1924, the Virginia General Assembly extended the maximum prison term to life for both rape and attempted rape.

37. "Negro Brute in Franklin Jail," *Roanoke Times*, July 17, 1908; "Finney to Die in the Chair," ibid., August 1, 1908; *Commonwealth v. William Finney*, Common Law Order Book 18, pp. 70, 75, 77, Circuit Court of Franklin County, Rocky Mount, Va. The indictment states that Finney "did throw her to the ground, did pull up her clothing, and place himself upon the body of Nannie Jamison with his male organ exposed" (*Commonwealth v. Will Finney*, Franklin County Court Determined Papers, Box 107, LOVA).

38. *Commonwealth v. Stanfield Sherman*, Common Law Order Book 17, pp. 163, 169, 176, 177, Circuit Court of Pittsylvania County, Chatham, Va.

39. "Negro Is Held for Gross Crime Near Martinsville," *Richmond Times-Dispatch*, October 9, 1919; "Paul Hairston Will Face Jury Today for His Crime," ibid., October 10, 1919; "Paul Hairston to Die in Electric Chair," ibid., October 11, 1919; *Commonwealth v. Paul Hairston*, Order Book 1, pp. 371, 373, Circuit Court of Henry County, Martinsville, Va.

40. Legal officials occasionally noted that young girls often did not know what constituted sexual penetration and thus could not articulate it. See the case of James Smith discussed in Chapter 3.

41. "Attack Girl Going Alone to Early Mass," *Richmond Times-Dispatch*, January 11, 1909; "Gillespie Ordered to Death Chair," ibid., January 17, 1909; *Commonwealth v. Charles Gillespie*, Common Law Order Book 49, pp. 57, 58, 64, 148, Richmond Hustings Court I, Richmond, Va. The indictment describes Gillespie's alleged actions. See *Commonwealth v. Charles Gillespie*, Case File, Ended Causes 1868–1918, Box 245, Richmond Hustings Court I Records, LOVA.

42. *Commonwealth v. Jasper Morrison*, Petition for Conditional Pardon, April 1– April 11, 1928, EP.

43. *Commonwealth v. Robert Sims*, Common Law Order Book 21, pp. 253, 255, 259, Circuit Court of Halifax County, Halifax, Va.; Justice Edward W. Hudgins to Governor John Pollard, October 28, 1932, *Commonwealth v. Robert Sims*, Petition for Conditional Pardon, October 22–November 2, 1932, EP.

44. Information Sheet, July 22, 1957, *Commonwealth v. Louis Riddick*, Petition for Conditional Pardon, November 22–December 19, 1957, EP.

45. Form sent to Judge W. R. Barksdale, April 6, 1916, *Commonwealth v. Harrison Waller*, Petition for Conditional Pardon, May 20–June 28, 1916, EP.

46. *Commonwealth v. Frank Baylor*, Common Law Order Book 6, pp. 107, 114, 120, 121, Circuit Court of Caroline County, Bowling Green, Va.; "Negro Attacks White Woman," *Richmond Times-Dispatch*, December 8, 1908.

47. *Commonwealth v. Ralph Green*, Common Law Order Book 74, pp. 292, 297, 328, 331, Richmond Hustings Court I, Richmond, Va.; "Reported Attack on Small Girl Stirs City," *Richmond Times-Dispatch*, June 16, 1922.

48. Charles M. Wallace, Brief of Argument by Counsel, *Commonwealth v. James Acree*, Petition for Conditional Pardon, May 4–May 18, 1939, EP.

49. *Commonwealth v. Raymond Alsberry*, Common Law Book 11, p. 187, Winchester Corporation Court, Winchester, Va.; "Special Grand Jury Will Indict Negro," *Richmond Times-Dispatch*, January 26, 1930.

50. *Commonwealth v. Theodore Roosevelt Wilson*, Common Law Order Book 6, p. 510, Case File 177, Circuit Court of Isle of Wight County, Isle of Wight, Va.

51. *Commonwealth v. Charles Harris*, Common Law Order Book 57, pp. 183, 201, Richmond Hustings Court I, Richmond, Va.; "Woman Attacked in Broad Street," *Richmond Times-Dispatch*, January 16, 1914.

52. "Woman's Screams Summoned Help," *Richmond Times-Dispatch*, October 20, 1909.

53. *Commonwealth v. Tom Williams*, Franklin County Determined Papers, Box 107, LOVA.

54. "Woman Accuses Negro," *Richmond Times-Dispatch*, August 3, 1924; "To Reduce Charge in Halifax Case," ibid., August 5, 1924; *Commonwealth v. Coleman Crews*, Warrant for Arrest, Circuit Court of Halifax County, Halifax, Va. The only papers remaining regarding Crews's case are the warrant for his arrest and the letter from the governor granting him pardon. I suspect that because Crews's offense was classified as a misdemeanor, he was tried in police court rather than circuit court.

55. *Commonwealth v. Percy Forby*, Common Law Order Book 36, pp. 271, 283, Case File, Ended Cause File February / March 1910, Norfolk Corporation Court, Norfolk, Va.

56. *Henry Hart v. Commonwealth*, "Certificate of Facts," Case File, Box 236, Circuit Court of Augusta County, Staunton, Va.

57. *Hart v. Commonwealth*, 131 Va. 726 (1921), at 749.

58. "Norfolk Woman Victim of Attack," *Richmond Times-Dispatch*, January 24, 1910; "Young Lady Attacked and Choked in Ghent," *Portsmouth Star*, January 24, 1910; "Assault on Lady Points Need of More Policemen," ibid., January 25, 1910.

59. *Commonwealth v. Percy Forby*, Common Law Order Book 36, pp. 271, 283, Instructions to Jury, Case File, Ended Cause File February / March 1910, Norfolk Corporation Court, Norfolk, Va.

60. "Annoyed White Woman," *Richmond Times-Dispatch*, October 27, 1918.

61. Statement of Clarence Brown, September 24, 1939, *Commonwealth v. Clarence Brown*, Petition for Conditional Pardon, September 17–September 30, 1941, EP.

62. C. Carter Lee to Governor Price, July 25, 1941, *Commonwealth v. Clarence Brown*, Petition for Executive Clemency, September 17–September 30, 1941, EP.

63. See Brundage, *Lynching in the New South*, and Finnegan, "Who Were the Victims of Lynching?"

64. The only surviving record of Lynch's case is the judgment regarding his appeal. Montgomery County Circuit Court in Christiansburg, Virginia, destroyed all criminal files from before 1950, including the order books. Consequently, Lynch's precise sentence and the content of the case testimony are unknown.

65. *Lynch v. Commonwealth*, 131 Va. 762 (1920), at 766.

66. *Commonwealth v. Lucius Jackson aka Rufus*, Order Book 14, pp. 279, 291, 305, Richmond Hustings Court II, Richmond, Va.; "Say He Attacked Three Women on Mayo Bridge," *Richmond Times-Dispatch*, December 29, 1918.

67. *Commonwealth v. Martin Wiley*, Order Book 36, pp. 430, 439, Circuit Court of Henry County, Martinsville, Va.; *Commonwealth v. Martin Wiley*, Case File, Henry County Court Determined Papers, 1921–23, LOVA; "Woman Is Insulted on Road by Negro," *Richmond Times-Dispatch*, September 20, 1921.

68. "Prisoner Sent Away," *Culpeper Exponent*, September 21, 1906.

69. C. M. Waite to Governor Stuart, February 2, 1916, *Commonwealth v. George Griffin*, Petition for Conditional Pardon, August 1–August 31, 1916, EP.

70. Letter from Edwin Gibson to Alex Forward, Secretary to Governor Stuart, January 28, 1916, *Commonwealth v. George Griffin*, Petition for Conditional Pardon, August 1–August 31, 1916, Box 274, EP.

71. *Commonwealth v. James Acree*, Petition for Commutation, June 11–June 21, 1923, EP.

72. Charles M. Wallace, Brief of Argument by Counsel, *Commonwealth v. James Acree*, Petition for Conditional Pardon, May 4–May 18, 1939, EP.

73. James Acree to Governor Pollard, June 1, 1930, *Commonwealth v. James Acree*, Petition for Conditional Pardon, May 4–May 18, 1939, EP.

74. James S. Easley to Governor James H. Price, March 24, 1939, *Commonwealth v. James Acree*, Petition for Conditional Pardon, May 4–May 18, 1939, EP.

Chapter Three

1. Richmond and Charlottesville newspapers covered the case extensively. Accounts of the case can be found there and in Wood's appeal, as well as in the file concerning his petition for commutation. See *John Wood v. Commonwealth*, 146 Va. 296 (1926); *Commonwealth v. John Wood*, Petition for Commutation, January 1–January 20, 1928, EP; and *Commonwealth v. John Wood*, Case File, Ended Causes File February 1927, Circuit Court of Albemarle County, Charlottesville, Va.

2. Frank Bane to Governor Byrd, September 13, 1927, *Commonwealth v. John Wood*, Petition for Commutation, January 1–January 20, 1928, EP.

3. Charles G. Maphis to Governor Byrd, August 25 and November 15, 1927, *Commonwealth v. John Wood*, Petition for Commutation, January 1–January 20, 1928, EP.

4. John A. Hornsby to Governor Byrd, August 6, 1927, *Commonwealth v. John Wood*, Petition for Commutation, January 1–January 20, 1928, EP.

5. Folder, *Commonwealth v. John Wood*, Petition for Conditional Pardon, October 1–October 19, 1943, EP.

6. Petition by Counsel, September 22, 1927, *Commonwealth v. Jasper Morrison*, Petition for Conditional Pardon, April 1–April 11, 1928, EP.

7. R. L. Lindsay to Governor Trinkle, August 14, 1925, and John Buford to Governor Trinkle, May 16, 20, 1925, *Commonwealth v. Jasper Morrison*, Folder "Moore, Alice-Murphy, Cota," Governor Trinkle Papers, Box 64, LOVA.

8. John Buford to Governor Trinkle, May 16, 20, 1925, *Commonwealth v. Jasper*

Morrison, Folder "Moore, Alice-Murphy, Cota," Governor Trinkle Papers, Box 64, LOVA.

9. R. L. Lindsay to Governor Trinkle, August 14, 1925, *Commonwealth v. Jasper Morrison*, Folder "Moore, Alice-Murphy, Cota," Governor Trinkle Papers, Box 64, LOVA.

10. Judge Jesse F. West to Governor Davis, November 15, 1919, *Commonwealth v. Lee Williams*, Petition for Conditional Pardon, December 8–December 22, 1919, EP. The minimum term for attempted rape, contrary to the judge's assertion, was three years not five, implying that Williams may have pled guilty to rape. But at the beginning of his letter to the governor, Judge West insisted that Williams only pled guilty to attempted rape.

11. Ibid.

12. "Woman Battles Young Assailant," *Richmond Times-Dispatch*, August 17, 1927; "Arrest Follows All-Day Search," ibid., August 18, 1927.

13. *Commonwealth v. Robert Sims*, Common Law Order Book 21, pp. 253, 255, 259, Circuit Court of Halifax County, Halifax, Va.

14. Judge Edward W. Hudgins to Governor Pollard, October 28, 1932, *Commonwealth v. Robert Sims*, Petition for Conditional Pardon, October 22–November 2, 1932, EP.

15. Judge Frank P. Christian to Governor Mann, undated, and Commonwealth's Attorney Robert D. Yancey to Governor Mann, December 8, 1910, *Commonwealth v. John Roberson*, Petition for Conditional Pardon, September–October 7, 1912, EP.

16. Christopher Waldrep comes to similar conclusions about antebellum southern courts. See *Roots of Disorder*, 37–58.

17. "Negro 'Peeping Toms' Fined Fifty Dollars," *Roanoke Times*, February 12, 1925; "Two Negroes Fined on Peeping Charge," *Richmond Times-Dispatch*, February 12, 1925.

18. Accounts of the murder are taken from the *Virginia Pilot and Norfolk Landmark* and the *Richmond Times-Dispatch*. Testimony of witnesses is taken from a transcript found in the case papers at Isle of Wight Courthouse. See *Commonwealth v. Shirley Winnegan*, Case File, Circuit Court of Isle of Wight County, Isle of Wight, Va. John Douglas Smith also discusses this case in *Managing White Supremacy*, 172–74.

19. "Mob out to Lynch Negro Suspected in Girl's Murder," *Virginia Pilot–Norfolk Landmark*, October 16, 1927.

20. "Mob Disperses after Negro, Sought as Slayer of Girl, Is Taken to Richmond Jail," *Virginia Pilot–Norfolk Landmark*, October 17, 1927.

21. Though the events in Isle of Wight County, especially in terms of the political ramifications, were reported in many papers, the most detailed description of the mass meeting was in "Two Isle of Wight Men under Fire as Result of Murder," *Virginia Pilot and Norfolk Landmark*, October 25, 1927. My discussion of that meeting is largely taken from that account.

22. "Murder Suspect Declared Sane, Faces Trial Soon," *Virginia-Pilot and Norfolk Landmark*, November 5, 1927.

23. Henry O. Humphreys to Governor Mann, June 19, 1913, *Commonwealth v. Owen Goggin*, Petition for Commutation, June 14–July 18, 1913, EP.

24. Petition to the Governor, undated, *Commonwealth v. Owen Goggin*, Petition for Commutation, June 14–July 18, 1913, EP.

25. A. W. James to Frank Bane, March 12, 1929, *Commonwealth v. Henry Jones*, Petition for Commutation, Governor Byrd Papers, Box 90, LOVA.

26. Petition to Governor Davis, undated, *Commonwealth v. John Spencer*, November 10–November 31, 1920, EP.

27. Governor Trinkle to Coleman Crews et al., May 26, 1925, *Commonwealth v. Coleman Crews*, Warrants File, Circuit Court of Halifax County, Halifax, Va.

28. Lemuel F. Smith, Commonwealth's Attorney, to Governor Byrd, June 27, 1927, *Commonwealth v. John Wood*, Petition for Commutation, January 1–January 20, 1928, EP.

29. G. Johnson to Governor Harry Byrd, May 28, 1926, *Commonwealth v. James Smith*, Petition for Conditional Pardon, May 27–June 13, 1926, EP.

30. It is interesting to note that when officials considered the pardons of mentally disabled black men they apparently did not consider whether these men might commit similar crimes in the future. Presumably, they would still be unable to understand the need to avoid white women. The fact that officials did not take this into consideration suggests that rape itself was not a severe crime. It merited the death penalty only when it could be connected to larger issues of racial control.

31. "Negro Shot Down by Brave Woman," *Richmond Times-Dispatch*, May 24, 1912.

32. S. A. Brown, J. A. Brown, W. L. Ransome to Governor Swanson, May 30, 1906, *Commonwealth v. Gabriele Battaile*, Petition for Commutation, June–July 16, 1906, EP.

33. J. R. McGavock to Governor Byrd, April 25, 1928, *Commonwealth v. Jasper Morrison*, Folder "Moore, Alice-Murphy, Cota," Governor Byrd Papers, Box 93, LOVA.

34. *Commonwealth v. Allen Ball*, Common Law Order Book 17, pp. 520, 530, Circuit Court of Frederick County, Winchester, Va.

35. *Commonwealth v. Jacob Jefferson*, Common Law Order Book 9, pp. 362, 369, Circuit Court of Chesterfield County, Chesterfield, Va.

36. Keve, *History of Corrections in Virginia*, 162–64.

37. Judge Latham Fletcher to Governor Davis, December 23, 1918, and Cecil Connor, prosecuting attorney, to Governor Davis, December 20, 1918, *Commonwealth v. Powell H. Smith*, Pardon Applications Etc., Folder "S 3–2," Governor Davis Papers, Box 47, LOVA.

38. Neither sterilization nor incarceration at Central State Hospital (CSH) were common punishments for sexual assault. Reform school was the most common punishment beside prison.

39. Department of Welfare and Institutions/Division of Corrections Classification Report, December 22, 1961, *Commonwealth v. Loo Rooster Jarvis*, Petition for Conditional Pardon, January 8–January 12, 1962, EP. Jarvis's age at his incarceration in CSH is given as either thirteen or seventeen at various times in his pardon papers. Most reports place him at nineteen years of age when he was sentenced to life in 1935, making him fifteen at the time of his incarceration in CSH.

40. See, for example, Paul, *Controlling Human Heredity*, and Kevles, *In the Name of Eugenics*. On the acceptance of eugenics in Virginia, see Gregory Dorr, "'Assuring America's Place in the Sun.'"

41. James, *State Becomes a Social Worker*, 332–33.

42. Frank L. McKinney to Ralph E. Wilkins, April 10, 1945, *Commonwealth v. Willie Lewis Younger*, Petition for Conditional Pardon, April 2–April 24, 1945, EP.

43. Frank Bane to Governor Byrd, September 13, 1927, *Commonwealth v. John Wood*, Petition for Commutation, January 1–January 20, 1928, EP.

44. Judge Moffat, December 19, 1923, *Commonwealth v. Walter Moore*, Petition for Conditional Pardon, December 24, 1923–January 4, 1924, EP.

45. Governor Pollard to Charles M. Wallace et al., August 22, 1930, *Commonwealth v. Albert Cogbill*, Petition for Conditional Pardon, August 20–August 27, 1930, EP.

46. W. Potter Sterne to Governor Price, April 19, 1940, *Commonwealth v. Albert Clark*, Petition for Conditional Pardon, April 23–May 10, 1940, EP. Clark's petition was refused.

47. Letter to Governor Swanson, November 16, 1907, last page with signature missing, *Commonwealth v. William Hundley*, Petition for Conditional Pardon, December 14, 1908–January 16, 1909, EP.

48. Editor of Conyers, Georgia, *Times*, quoted in Hall, *Revolt against Chivalry*, 146.

49. The fact that Lizzie Skiles developed venereal disease after she was raped and that Clarence Nixon showed signs of the disease in jail was important evidence that he assaulted her, even though she was initially unsure he was guilty. See Statement of Testimony, *Commonwealth v. Clarence Nixon*, Petition for Commutation of Sentence, April 16–May 31, 1912, EP.

50. "Woman, Raped Here, Out of Job and Home," *Richmond News-Leader*, September 14, 1940.

51. Thomas Clark, *Southern Country Editor*, 242.

52. Raine, *After Silence*, 190–91. For a more comprehensive analysis of the effects of trauma, see Herman, *Trauma and Recovery*; for more on the trauma of rape, see Rose, "Worse than Death."

53. "Negro Attacks Woman in Home," *Richmond Times-Dispatch*, December 29, 1910. Booker was convicted of robbery and received a sentence of five years in prison.

54. "Given Eighteen Years for Assault on Child," *Richmond Times-Dispatch*, September 25, 1914. Ellett was acquitted of rape but convicted of attempted rape and sentenced to eighteen years in prison. He was refused a conditional pardon in 1920 and again in 1924.

55. *Commonwealth v. John Henry McCann*, 174 Va. 429 (1939). Petition for Writ of Error and *Supersedes*, 12, 14.

56. G. Johnson to Governor Davis, May 28, 1919, *Commonwealth v. James Smith*, Petition for Conditional Pardon, May 27–June 13, 1926, EP.

57. Judge Martin M. Frank, "The Ladykiller," *Cosmopolitan* 143 (October 1957): 75.

58. Pardon Report, June 20, 1952, *Commonwealth v. Bernard Fleming*, Petition for Conditional Pardon, May 12–June 21, 1955, EP.

59. Handwritten, unsigned note, April 3, 1953, *Commonwealth v. Loo Rooster*

Jarvis, Petition for Conditional Pardon, January 8, 1962–January 12, 1962, EP. Jarvis was convicted in 1935 for a second time of raping a white woman. He received a pardon in 1962.

60. Several recent histories of southern women also touch on the power granted women because of their whiteness. See Feimster, "Ladies and Lynching," 45–107; Gilmore, *Gender and Jim Crow*, 91–118; MacLean, *Behind the Mask of Chivalry*, 98–124; and MacLean, "White Women and Klan Violence," 285–303.

61. "Assailant Twice Escapes Officer," *Richmond Times-Dispatch*, August 2, 1927.

62. "Woman Drives off Negro Robber," *Richmond Times-Dispatch*, May 1, 1922.

63. "Woman, 61, Attacked, Robbed in Hanover," *Richmond News-Leader*, July 23, 1956.

64. "Plucky Lady," *Richmond Times-Dispatch*, November 30, 1908. The article recounted how a Birmingham, Alabama, woman met a black man she suspected of criminal intent at her door with a gun and shot him when he tried to flee.

65. "Attacks Woman in Her Kitchen," *Richmond Times-Dispatch*, January 16, 1909.

66. "Mob Threatens Jail," *Richmond Times-Dispatch*, October 27, 1925.

67. "Woman Shot down Battling Assailant," *Richmond Times-Dispatch*, March 2, 1930.

68. *Legions v. Commonwealth*, 181 Va. 89 (1943), at 92.

69. A dissenting opinion in a case from South Carolina in 1934 also insisted that a white man's presence should represent adequate protection. Arguing that Clarence Floyd's conviction should be overturned, one justice wrote, "I am not willing to believe that any white man, however weak and cowardly he may be, would have acted as the male prosecuting witness in this case swore he did. It is impossible to believe that he could stand by and see the woman who was in his care subjected to the foul embraces of a negro . . . without making an effort to defend her though he died in the attempt." Because the male witness did not act as white men were supposed to, the justice argued, his account of his companion's rape raised sufficient reasonable doubt to justify the acquittal of her alleged attacker. In this case, his view remained the minority opinion. See *State v. Floyd*, 174 SC 288 (1934), at 332.

70. "Negro Assailant of Girls Lynched," *Richmond Times-Dispatch*, August 17, 1917.

71. "Finney Is Found Guilty," *Richmond Times-Dispatch*, August 1, 1908; "Negro Brute in Franklin Jail," *Roanoke Times*, July 17, 1908.

72. Robert Price was convicted of "insulting a white lady" in December 1917 and received a sentence of twelve months (B. Theodore Griffin of Griffin Bros. Wood and Coal, to Governor Davis, June 4, 1918, *Commonwealth v. Robert Price*, Petition for Conditional Pardon, Pardon Applications Etc. Folder P201, Box 46, Governor Davis Papers, LOVA). Alexander Garrison was convicted of housebreaking and assault for attacking a "white deaf and dumb girl." He received a sentence of five years in prison (J. C. Sweet to Governor Davis, undated, *Commonwealth v. Alexander Garrison*, Petition for Conditional Pardon, Folder "Pardons-G," Box 44, Governor Davis Papers, LOVA).

73. "Woman Struck by Robber in Home," *Richmond Times-Dispatch*, March 2, 1909.

74. Historians have examined white women's responses to what they believed to be white men's failure to adequately protect white women. See, for example, Whites, "Rebecca Latimer Felton," 41–61. See also Edwards, *Gendered Strife*, 184–217.

75. *Legions v. Commonwealth*, 181 Va. 89 (1943), at 91–92.

76. Crystal Feimster ("Ladies and Lynching," 126) also notes that punishing black offenders restored white women's honor.

77. "On His Deathbed, Negro Asserts His Innocence," *Richmond Times-Dispatch*, May 12, 1914; "Attended Church Day after Crime," *Richmond Evening Journal*, May 12, 1914; "Girl Testifies at Thompson Inquest," *Richmond News-Leader*, May 13, 1914; "Miss Chenault's Description Puzzling," *Richmond Evening Journal*, May 14, 1914. For a full discussion of the Fannie Chenault case, see Lisa Dorr, "Messin' White Women," 239–51.

78. Affidavit by R. H. Bagby, February 9, 1912, *Commonwealth v. Clarence Nixon*, Petition for Commutation, April 16–May, 1912, EP.

79. Lizzie Skiles to Governor Mann, May 21, 1912, *Commonwealth v. Clarence Nixon*, Petition for Commutation, April 16–May, 1912, EP.

80. Governor Mann to R. H. Bagby, May 24, 1912, *Commonwealth v. Clarence Nixon*, Petition for Commutation, April 16–May, 1912, EP.

81. *Commonwealth v. Robert Williams*, Petition for Commutation, "Pardon Applications etc. W 2-2," Governor Davis Papers, Box 48, LOVA.

82. *Commonwealth v. Doc Bacon*, Petition for Commutation, September 1–October 31, 1903, EP.

83. *Commonwealth v. Luther Tyler*, Common Law Order Book 4, p. 624, Circuit Court of Goochland County, Goochland, Va.

84. Defense statements regarding the innocence of Tyler are taken from P. A. L. Smith, "Note of Points," *Commonwealth v. Luther Tyler*, Petition for Commutation, April 16–May 20, 1914, EP.

85. The sequence of events is found in the summary of testimony included with Tyler's petition (*Commonwealth v. Luther Tyler*, Petition for Commutation, April 16–May 20, 1914, EP).

86. Affidavit signed by John Tyler and William Taylor, May 14, 1914, *Commonwealth v. Luther Tyler*, Petition for Commutation, April 16–May 20, 1914, EP.

87. P. A. L. Smith, "Note of Points," *Commonwealth v. Luther Tyler*, Petition for Commutation, April 16–May 20, 1914, EP.

88. Summary of Testimony, *Commonwealth v. Luther Tyler*, Petition for Commutation, April 16–May 20, 1914, EP.

89. P. A. L. Smith, "Note of Points," *Commonwealth v. Luther Tyler*, Petition for Commutation, April 16–May 20, 1914, EP.

90. Alexander Forward to Governor Stuart, undated, *Commonwealth v. Luther Tyler*, Petition for Commutation, April 16–May 20, 1914, EP.

91. "Luther Tyler, in Prison for Criminal Assault, Escapes from Jail," *Richmond Times-Dispatch*, October 7, 1920. References to Tyler's petition for pardon appear in Governor Byrd Papers, Box 98, LOVA. There is no record for Tyler in Byrd's pardon petitions files and no evidence his petition was refused or granted (ibid., Box 114).

Chapter Four

1. There is a growing body of literature on the historiography of rape, all of which demonstrates the unwillingness of Western legal systems to convict men accused of rape. See Merril Smith, *Sex without Consent*; Odem, "Cultural Representations"; Haag, *Consent*; D'Cruze, *Crimes of Outrage*; Dubinsky, *Improper Advances*; Anna Clark, *Women's Silence, Men's Violence*; Chaytor, "Husband(ry)"; Bardaglio, "Rape and the Law"; and Lindemann, "'To Ravish and Carnally Know.'" Examinations of modern prosecutions of rape also demonstrate the obstacles victims of rape face in obtaining redress through the courts. See Odem and Clay-Warner, *Confronting Rape and Sexual Assault*; Taslitz, *Rape and the Culture of the Courtroom*; Schulofer, *Unwanted Sex*; Sanday, *Woman Scorned*; Searles and Berger, *Rape and Society*; Matoesian, *Reproducing Rape*; and Estrich, *Real Rape*, to name a few. Most scholars note that efforts to reform rape law in the 1970s resulted in only modest improvements in conviction rates and in the treatment of rape victims.

2. See Estrich, *Real Rape*, 32–37. Estrich also notes that in her own case, the fact that the man who raped her was black virtually guaranteed acknowledgment both by authorities and by people in general that she was "really raped" (1–3). See also Edwards, "Sexual Violence," 252, and Dubinsky, *Improper Advances*, 82–83, 164.

3. See Hodes, *White Women, Black Men*, 176–208; Sommerville, "Rape Myth in the Old South," 517–18; Edwards, "Disappearance of Susan Daniel," 363–86. Scholarship on other societies in which racial subordination structured colonial power also demonstrates that the prosecution of cross-racial sexual crimes buttressed systems of racial oppression. See McCulloch, *Black Peril, White Virtue*, and Pamela Scully, "Rape, Race, and Colonial Culture."

4. Vivien Miller, in her analysis of executive clemency in Florida between 1880 and 1923, confirms the importance of the victim's character in the deliberations over convicted rapists' pardons, though she confines her analysis to cases of intraracial rape. See Miller, *Crime, Sexual Violence, and Clemency*, 175–216.

5. See Fox, "'Nice Girl,'" 70–75; see also Ayers, *Vengeance and Justice*, and Bertram Wyatt-Brown, *Honor and Violence in the Old South*.

6. I am indebted to Ariela Gross for her analysis of race as performance. Gross argues that in nineteenth-century trials litigating ambiguous racial identity, racial performance could be one factor courts used to determine litigants' status as black or white. Mixed-race women who behaved according to middle-class standards of white womanhood could find that courts upheld their status as white women. See Gross, "Litigating Whiteness." For discussions of courts as sites of performance, see Merry, "Courts as Performances," 35–58, and Hirsch and Lazarus-Black, Introduction to *Contested States*.

7. The accounts of the attack, the investigation, and the subsequent trial are taken from the *Richmond Times-Dispatch*, the *Richmond News-Leader*, the *Richmond Evening Journal*, and the *Richmond Virginian*. The *Richmond News-Leader* and the *Richmond Evening Journal* covered the case extensively and printed lengthy excerpts from trial testimony, as well as statements by the participants. The *Richmond Times-Dispatch* covered the case slightly less completely, usually

printing one article per day, generally on the back page. The *Richmond Virginian* provided very little coverage. Though this case attracted more attention in the Richmond area than any other case I have found for this period, few other Virginia papers outside Richmond paid any attention. Newspapers provide the primary source for this case because Henrico County, the county in which the case was tried, has long since destroyed its old criminal case files. All that remain are the entries in the Order Books.

8. "Negro Brute Assaults Miss Fannie Chenault," *Richmond Virginian*, May 10, 1914; "Girl Attacked by Negro Fiend," *Richmond Times-Dispatch*, May 10, 1914; "Said to Have Confessed," *Richmond Evening Journal*, May 11, 1914.

9. "Negro Brute Assaults Miss Fannie Chenault."

10. Ibid.; "One Suspect Shot and Six Others Arrested for Chenault Assault," *Richmond Virginian*, May 11, 1914.

11. "Negro Did Not Have Marked Features," *Richmond Evening Journal*, May 15, 1914.

12. "Seven Negroes Held As Suspects," *Richmond Times-Dispatch*, May 11, 1914.

13. "Said to Have Confessed"; "One Suspect Shot and Six Others Arrested for Chenault Assault."

14. Despite the importance of the statement made by Chenault and frequent references to it in news reports, no newspaper printed the content of that statement. Consequently, the exact "vulgar" words Chenault allegedly used are lost to the historical record.

15. Accounts of the police taking this statement and the subsequent controversy over the substitution of vulgar words are taken from "Trying to Prove Alibi for Negro," *Richmond News-Leader*, June 19, 1914; "Tells of Finding Handkerchief at Scene of Attack," ibid., June 20, 1914; "M'Mahon Called," *Richmond Evening Journal*, June 19, 1914; "Officer to Upset Alibi," ibid., June 20, 1914; "End Testimony in Chenault Case," ibid., June 22, 1914; "Defense Scores in Clements Case," *Richmond Times-Dispatch*, June 20, 1914; and "Chenault Case Will Be Resumed Tomorrow," ibid., June 21, 1914.

16. "Trying to Prove Alibi for Negro"; "M'Mahon Called."

17. "Officer to Upset Alibi"; "Proven Points in Henrico Assault," *Richmond Evening Journal*, June 22, 1914.

18. "Officer to Upset Alibi."

19. "Clements Set Free after One Man Had Hung Jury Eighteen Hours," *Richmond Evening Journal*, October 30, 1914; "Clements Acquitted by Jury in Henrico," *Richmond News-Leader*, October 30, 1914. All Richmond newspapers reported that the reading of the statement to the jury was of great advantage to the defense.

20. "Clements Set Free after One Man Had Hung Jury Eighteen Hours."

21. "Clements Acquitted by Jury in Henrico."

22. These statements appear in many reports of John Clements's trial. See "Miss Chenault Is Called to Stand against Clements," *Richmond Virginian*, June 18, 1914; "Miss Chenault a Witness; Sticks to Story," *Richmond Evening Journal*, June 18, 1914; "Miss Chenault to Resume Her Testimony Tomorrow," *Richmond News-Leader*, June 18, 1914; "Negro Clements Is on Trial Today," *Richmond Eve-*

ning Journal, June 17, 1914; and "Negro Indicted in Henrico Case," *Richmond News-Leader*, July 6, 1914.

23. William B. Sanders to Governor Byrd, February 20, 1929, *Commonwealth v. Wilson Allen*, Petition for Conditional Pardon, March 1–March 15, 1929, EP.

24. E. A. Edwards to Governor Stuart, October 1, 1917, *Commonwealth v. John Will Bond*, Petition for Conditional Pardon, September 21–October 10, 1917, EP.

25. O. B. Wright to Governor Stuart, September 28, 1917, *Commonwealth v. John Will Bond*, Petition for Conditional Pardon, September 21–October 10, 1917, EP.

26. H. O. Humphreys to Governor Davis, April 5, 1920, *Commonwealth v. John Will Bond*, Petition for Conditional Pardon, April 23–April 30, 1920, EP; emphasis in original.

27. *Commonwealth v. James Yager*, Law Order Book 15, pp. 128, 130, Circuit Court of Culpeper County, Culpeper, Va.; *Commonwealth v. James Yager*, Law Orders 1921 to 1925, pp. 68, 69, 70, Judgment File, Circuit Court of Louisa County, Louisa, Va.

28. T. E. Grimsley to Governor Byrd, November 9, 1926, *Commonwealth v. James Yager*, Petition for Conditional Pardon, March 8–March 23, 1927, EP.

29. William C. Bibb to Governor Byrd, January 13, 1927, *Commonwealth v. James Yager*, Petition for Conditional Pardon, March 8–March 23, 1927, EP.

30. Folder, *Commonwealth v. James Yager*, Petition for Conditional Pardon, March 8–March 23, 1927, EP.

31. "Family Is Aroused," *Richmond Evening Journal*, May 29, 1914.

32. "Trial Not to End Chenault Case," *Richmond Evening Journal*, May 30, 1914.

33. "Officer to Upset Alibi"; "Would Retain Counsel to Protect Her Name," *Richmond Times-Dispatch*, June 28, 1914; "Smith May Be in Chenault Case," *Richmond News-Leader*, June 29, 1914; "Henrico County People Aroused by Treatment of Miss Chenault," *Richmond Evening Journal*, June 29, 1914.

34. "Negro Clements Is on Trial Today."

35. Newspapers reported the addition of a second doctor and the purpose of his testimony in "Clements Case Continued to October 27," *Richmond Evening Journal*, July 20, 1914. Report of his trial testimony is found in "Miss Chenault Says Clements Is Right Man," *Richmond Times-Dispatch*, October 28, 1914.

36. "Rape of Waitress by Four Negroes," *Richmond Times-Dispatch*, October 8, 1940; "Raped by Trio, Girl Reports," *Richmond News-Leader*, September 12, 1940.

37. "Astute Sleuth Work Lauded in Rape Case," *Richmond News-Leader*, September 13, 1940; details of the four men's claims of innocence appear in "Four Men Deny Attack Charge," *Richmond Afro-American*, September 21, 1940, and "Lawyers Drop Case, 4 Attack Suspects Held," ibid., September 28, 1940.

38. Beth Bailey (*From Front Porch to Back Seat*, 90) argues that control over sexual conduct frequently fell on women's shoulders, to the extent that unwilling women were blamed when men took advantage of them. If a man "even tried [to take advantage of her]," she writes, "the woman must not have really been a lady. She must have, somehow, invited or encouraged him."

39. "Negro Is Charged with Criminal Assault," *Richmond Times-Dispatch*, October 5, 1915; "Winston Dismissed," ibid., October 12, 1915.

40. L. L. Stanard to Walter White, April 22, 1925, PNAACP, Part 8, Series A, Reel 12, Frames 00313–00319.

41. "Doctor Swears Miss Chenault Was Unharmed by Negro," *Richmond News-Leader*, June 17, 1914; "Negro Clements Is on Trial Today."

42. Deposition of O. S. Mayberry, *Commonwealth v. Vander Lee Gibson*, Petition for Conditional Pardon, December 20–December 31, 1957, EP. Gibson was convicted of rape in 1945 and sentenced to life in prison.

43. S. L. Ferguson to Governor Mann, August 9, 1912, *Commonwealth v. Alfred Wright*, Petition for Commutation, July 9–August 31, 1912, EP.

44. Accounts of the assault and Yager's arrest are found in "Fear Lynching of Negro Identified by Woman Victim," *Richmond Times-Dispatch*, May 1, 1922, and "Yager Negro Removed to Charlottesville," ibid., May 2, 1922. Information on Beahm's identification of Yager and her medical condition are found in "Miss Annie Beahm, 35, Brutally Attacked," *Culpeper Exponent*, May 4, 1922.

45. "Attended Church Day after Crime," *Richmond Evening Journal*, May 12, 1914; "Miss Chenault's Description Puzzling," ibid., May 14, 1914; "Negro Did Not Have Marked Features," ibid., May 15, 1914.

46. Reports that her clothing was torn appear in "Negro Brute Assaults Miss Fannie Chenault," *Richmond Virginian*, May 10, 1914, and "Said to Have Confessed," *Richmond Evening Journal*, May 11, 1914. "Brutal assault" was used in "Girl Attacked by Negro Fiend," *Richmond Times-Dispatch*, May 10, 1914; "Inquest Will Be Held This Morning," ibid., May 13, 1914; and "Confession Is Doubted by Police," *Richmond News-Leader*, May 11, 1914. The term "horrible" appeared in "One Suspect Shot and Six Others Arrested for Chenault Assault" and "Said to Have Confessed," *Richmond Evening Journal*, May 11, 1914. The *Richmond Evening Journal* reported that the attacker "mistreated" her in "Coroner Places Miss Chenault on the Stand at Inquest," May 13, 1914, and referred to her "revolting experience." The *Richmond Evening Journal* referred to the "capital crime" in "Charge Is Made," May 22, 1914.

47. "Negro Assailant Foiled in Object," *Richmond Evening Journal*, May 25, 1914; "To Take Negro to Scene of Crime," *Richmond News-Leader*, May 26, 1914; "Positively Identifies Clements As Assailant," *Richmond Times-Dispatch*, May 26, 1914. The *Evening Journal* also suggested that the revelation by her doctor implied that the charge against Clements would have to be changed.

48. "Chenault Case Continued to June 17," *Richmond News-Leader*, May 28, 1914.

49. "Sticks to Story," *Richmond Evening Journal*, June 18, 1914.

50. "Negro Assailant Foiled in Object."

51. This statement was found in both the *Richmond Evening Journal* and the *Richmond News-Leader*, July 6, 1914.

52. "Negro Clements Is on Trial Today."

53. "M'Mahon Called." Virtually every article covering the case noted the crowds of onlookers who filled the courtroom at every opportunity.

54. "Chenault Case Begins in Henrico," *Richmond News-Leader*, October 27, 1914.

55. "Miss Chenault Says Clements Is Right Man."

56. "John Clements Not Guilty He Declares on Eve of His Trial," *Richmond Evening Journal*, October 27, 1914.

57. I borrow the term "folk pornography" from Hall, *Revolt against Chivalry*, 151.

58. William B. Sanders to Governor Byrd, February 20, 1929, *Commonwealth v. Wilson Allen*, Petition for Conditional Pardon, March 1–March 15, 1929, EP.

59. Gilmor S. Kendall and Thomas F. Wears to Governor Swanson, October 30, 1906, *Commonwealth v. Joseph Boone*, Petition for Conditional Pardon, November 20, 1906–January 31, 1907, EP.

60. "Their Victims Were Women," *Richmond News-Leader*, April 4, 1903; "Bailey to Face Sussex Jury," ibid., May 7, 1903; "Got Off Easy; Eighteen Years," ibid., May 9, 1903.

61. Judge J. F. West to Governor Stuart, August 1, 1914, and William Cocke to Governor Stuart, February 18, 1915, *Commonwealth v. John Bailey*, Petition for Conditional Pardon, April 21–April 30, 1915, EP.

62. "Negro 'Peeping Toms' Fined Fifty Dollars," *Roanoke Times*, February 12, 1925; "Two Negroes Fined on Peeping Charge," *Richmond Times-Dispatch*, February 12, 1925.

63. "Negro Who Pursued White Woman Shot Dead after Coming Back Second Time," *Danville Register*, March 1, 1921; "Cranford Acquitted of Killing Negro," ibid., March 3, 1921,.

64. "Three Negroes Held on Serious Charge," *Virginian Pilot and Norfolk Landmark*, October 11, 1914; "Negroes Convicted of Attacking White Girl," ibid., October 21, 1914,.

65. S. V. Southall to Governor Davis, November 19, 1920, *Commonwealth v. Lewis Hardy*, *Commonwealth v. Mort Hill*, "Pardon Application, Etc H 2-1" Governor Davis Papers, Box 44, LOVA.

66. "Young Negro Is Held in Attempted Attack," *Richmond Times-Dispatch*, April 24, 1932.

67. Cyrus Hotchkiss to Governor Price, November 2, 1938, and Secretary of Governor Price to Potter Sterne, May 5, 1939, *Commonwealth v. Albert Clark*, Petition for Conditional Pardon, April 23–May 10, 1940, EP.

68. W. Potter Sterne to Governor Price, April 19, 1940, *Commonwealth v. Albert Clark*, Petition for Conditional Pardon, April 23–May 10, 1940, EP. No evidence of his conviction, other than a request for a mental evaluation, remains at the courthouse. See H. C. Henry, MD, to Judge Edwin P. Cox, July 23, 1932, *Commonwealth v. Albert Clark*, Dinwiddie County Case File 437, Commonwealth 1928: 311–557 Drawer, Circuit Court of Dinwiddie County, Dinwiddie, Va.

69. Accounts of the case are taken from *Broaddus v. Commonwealth*, 126 Va. 733 (1918), and "Summary of Testimony" *Commonwealth v. John Broaddus*, Case File, November Term 1918, Circuit Court of Page County, Luray, Va.

70. There is evidence that white officials were concerned enough about the numerous consensual sexual relationships occurring between low-status white women and black men to strengthen legal prohibitions against interracial marriage. See Lisa Lindquist Dorr, "Arm in Arm."

71. E. W. Hudgins to Governor Byrd, March 2, 1929, *Commonwealth v. Henry Jones*, Governor Byrd Papers, Box 90, LOVA.

72. Marybeth Arnold ("The Life of a Citizen in the Hands of a Woman," 38–40) argues not only that poor women were not endowed with "ladyhood" but

that their very poverty made them more vulnerable to unwanted sexual attention. For assumptions about poor women's innate depravity, see Stansell, *City of Women*, 63–101.

73. "Three Negroes Held," *Richmond Times-Dispatch*, December 31, 1915; "Woman Assaulted," *Fredericksburg Daily Star*, December 29, 1915; "Negroes Sent to Grand Jury," ibid., December 30, 1915.

74. Indictment of Ad Armistead, *Commonwealth v. Ad Armistead*, Case File, Circuit Court of Spotsylvania County, Spotsylvania, Va. Carl T. Rowan (*South of Freedom*, 32–33) recounts an example of a white woman crying rape when she feared the discovery of consensual sexual relations. Rowan told of an experience in his youth when he went to spy on his friend having sex with a white woman. When she heard Rowan's approach, she reportedly cried, "Get up! Stop, you black sonofabitch. Jesus, he's raping me." Both the woman and Rowan's friend were relieved to discover it was only Rowan who had discovered them, and she did not repeat her panicked accusation.

75. Marriage information is from Spotsylvania County Marriage Register, Spotsylvania Courthouse, Spotsylvania, Va. Lucy Powell was born Lucy White in 1898. Her mother, Dora White, did not marry James Powell until 1903. Their marriage certificate indicates that Dora White was single, eliminating the possibility that Lucy was the product of a previous marriage that had ended in divorce or widowhood. Moreover, on her marriage license, Dora White listed her mother as Eliza White and her father as unknown, revealing that she was illegitimate. James Powell apparently adopted Lucy; at some point, she became known as Lucy Powell.

76. *Commonwealth v. Ad Armistead*, *Commonwealth v. Arthur Lewis*, Law Order Book C, pp. 93, 100, 105, 106, Circuit Court of Spotsylvania County, Spotsylvania, Va. Instructions to the jury, *Commonwealth v. Ad Armistead* Case File, Circuit Court of Spotsylvania County, Spotsylvania, Va. The case file contains two notes that were the agreements between the parties: Lucy Powell would not charge the men with rape if they each paid her five dollars. The notes also say that "this talk is got to be stopped," suggesting that the agreement was intended to quell rumors about the Powells in the community. William Clark died in prison of unknown causes before he could be tried for attempting to poison Lucy Powell.

77. Microfilm of 1920 Census for Spotsylvania County, Alderman Library, University of Virginia, Charlottesville, Va.

78. Thomas Wright Read to Governor Pollard, December 22, 1931, *Commonwealth v. West Jones*, Petition for Conditional Pardon, July 16–July 20, 1932, EP; emphasis in original.

79. R. W. Kime to Governor Davis, September 2, 1920, *Commonwealth v. Walter Moore*, Petition for Conditional Pardon, October 3–October 17, 1920, EP; note from Judge Moffett at bottom of letter from Governor Davis dated December 19, 1923, *Commonwealth v. Walter Moore*, Petition for Conditional Pardon, December 24, 1923–January 4, 1924, EP.

80. George T. Rison to Governor Trinkle, undated, *Commonwealth v. Solomon Douglas*, Petition for Conditional Pardon, May 22–June 10, 1922, EP.

81. See Paul, *Controlling Human Heredity*. On the acceptance of eugenics in

Virginia, see Gregory Dorr, "'Assuring America's Place in the Sun,'" and Gregory Dorr, "Segregation's Science." Laughlin's quote appears in Kevles, *In the Name of Eugenics*, 110.

82. Micajah Woods to Governor Swanson, December 20, 1909, *Commonwealth v. Daniel Johnson*, Petition for Conditional Pardon, December 14, 1908–January 16, 1909, EP; emphasis in original. Woods makes similar comments about the victim's compromised character in a letter to Governor Swanson, November 30, 1907, ibid.

83. Woods originally petitioned Governor Swanson for Johnson's release in 1906, after he had served only three years. Swanson would have granted his petition had not Johnson committed numerous prison violations including sodomy, fighting, and stealing. Woods instructed Johnson to improve his behavior, and satisfied that he had committed no additional infractions, the governor released him in 1909. Quotations are from Woods to Governor Swanson, December 20, 1909, *Commonwealth v. Daniel Johnson*, Petition for Conditional Pardon, December 14, 1908–January 16, 1909, EP.

84. O. B. Wright to Governor Stuart, September 28, 1917, *Commonwealth v. John Will Bond*, Petition for Conditional Pardon, September 21–October 10, 1917, EP.

85. "Blackstone Girl Brutally Beaten," *Richmond Times-Dispatch*, August 18, 1925; "Negro Boy Alleged to Have Confessed," ibid., August 23, 1925.

86. *Commonwealth v. James Holmes*, Common Law Order Book 5, p. 444, Common Law Causes File June Term to September Term 1925, Circuit Court of Nottoway County, Nottoway, Va. There were allegations that Lassiter had arranged a meeting with James Holmes on a country lane. In this scenario, she cried rape when she feared Laura Crawley might report their rendezvous. Her failure to identify Holmes may have been an effort to save him from arrest and trial.

87. W. R. Jones to Governor Pollard, September 20, 1930, *Commonwealth v. James Holmes*, Petition for Conditional Pardon, February 26–March 3, 1931, EP.

88. Ibid. Legal records for Nottoway County indicate that Mrs. Lassiter was acquitted of a second prohibition offense in 1930, though there is no record of her first offense. There is also no indication that she was ever indicted for murder. See *Commonwealth v. Mrs. N. L. Lassiter*, June 3, 1930, Common Law Order Book 6, p. 355, Circuit Court of Nottoway County, Nottoway, Va.

89. "White Girl and Negro Are Sought," *Roanoke Times*, November 23, 1923; "Will Place Alleged Abductor in Roanoke for Safe Keeping," ibid., November 24, 1923; "Johnson Faces Trial upon Serious Charge," ibid., December 4, 1923; *Commonwealth v. John Johnson*, Criminal Orders [beginning] 1921, pp. 118, 119, Circuit Court of Montgomery County, Christiansburg, Va.

90. John Johnson to Governor Pollard, October 26, 1931, December 20, 1931, and December 10, 1933; and John Johnson to Governor George C. Peery, March 31, 1934, *Commonwealth v. John Johnson*, Petition for Conditional Pardon, December 4–December 18, 1934, EP.

91. Mrs. Reagan S. Wyatt to Governor Pollard, December 12, 1933, Redmond I. Roop to Governor Peery, November 3, 1934, and H. B. Gregory to Governor Peery, November 26, 1934, *Commonwealth v. John Johnson*, Petition for Conditional Pardon, December 4–December 18, 1934, EP.

Chapter Five

1. Accounts of the assault on Mabel Risley are taken from *Thomas, alias Wright, v. Commonwealth*, 106 Va. 855 (1906), at 857–59.

2. *Thomas, alias Wright, v. Commonwealth*, at 862–72. Quote appears on p. 872. Justice J. Whittle agreed with Cardwell's conclusions but added in his own dissent that the jury was influenced by "incompetent evidence."

3. Crandall Mackey to Governor Davis, December 2, 1919, *Commonwealth v. Joe Thomas*, Petition for Conditional Pardon, January 29–February 6, 1920, EP.

4. Crandall Mackey to Governor Lee Trinkle, undated (though in response to a letter from Trinkle, May 23, 1922), *Commonwealth v. Joe Thomas*, Petition for Conditional Pardon, June 27–July 11, 1922, EP. Risley and Gooding's marriage was reported in "Victims of Negro Assailant Wed," *Richmond News-Leader*, October 15, 1906.

5. P. A. L. Smith, "Note of Points," *Commonwealth v. Luther Tyler*, Petition for Commutation, April 16–May 20, 1914, EP.

6. The Harper/Skaggs case was covered extensively in all newspapers in the Portsmouth-Norfolk area. Many articles included long excerpts of trial testimony and closely followed every twist and turn in the case, from Skaggs's first charges of rape on January 7, 1931, to her final acquittal on a perjury charge on September 19, 1931. See also, *Commonwealth v. Dorothy Skaggs*, Order Book 62, pp. 94, 112, 151, 203, 205, 222, 224, 227, 228, 241, 288, 359, 374, 375, 376, 377, 379, 395, Norfolk Corporation Court I, Norfolk, Va. Mysteriously, the case files are missing.

7. My discussion is based on these reports. The editorial on women's ability to charge rape appeared in "A Very Disquieting Case," *Richmond News-Leader*, March 7, 1931.

8. "Westmoreland Today Scene of Taylor Trial," *Richmond Times-Dispatch*, June 25, 1931.

9. Reply to Commonwealth's Attorney's motion to have Henry L. Taylor sent to Western State Hospital for observation, *Commonwealth v. Henry Taylor*, Court Papers, 1932 File, Circuit Court of Westmoreland County, Montross, Va.

10. *Commonwealth v. Henry L. Taylor*, Orders at Law Book 5, pp. 175, 183, 185, 186, 192, 193, 197, 199, 201, 202, 203, 206, 242, Circuit Court of Westmoreland County, Montross, Va.

11. C. Anderson Davis to the New York NAACP, February 22, 1945, PNAACP, Part 8, Series B, Reel 24, Frames 00107–00108.

12. "Negro Is Outwitted by Danville Woman," *Richmond Times-Dispatch*, December 27, 1921; "Negro Sent on to Grand Jury," ibid., December 28, 1921,.

13. *Commonwealth v. Solomon Douglas*, Common Law Order Book 20, pp. 97, 203, 223, 281, 359, 374, 389, 488, 590, and Common Law Order Book 21, pp. 149, 287, 315, 345, 363, Circuit Court of Pittsylvania County, Chatham, Va.

14. Information on the other criminal charges lodged against Douglas are found in Common Law Order Book 15, pp. 533, 534, Common Law Order Book 16, pp. 11, 211, and Common Law Order Book 24, p. 469, Circuit Court of Pittsylvania County, Chatham, Va.

15. R. Irvine Overbey to Governor Trinkle, January 28, 1923, *Commonwealth v. Solomon Douglas*, Petition for Conditional Pardon, May 22–June 10, 1923, EP.

16. Petition for Writ of Error, Record 957, R. I. Overbey for Solomon Douglas, p. 2, *Commonwealth v. Solomon Douglas*, Petition for Conditional Pardon, May 22–June 10, 1923, EP.

17. Judge Richard Ker to Governor Trinkle, May 21, 1923; George T. Rison to Governor Trinkle, undated; Governor E. Lee Trinkle to R. Irvine Overbey, Judge Richard Ker, and George T. Rison, May 28, 1923, *Commonwealth v. Solomon Douglas*, Petition for Conditional Pardon, May 22–June 10, 1923, EP.

18. Grace Hale (*Making Whiteness*, 121–98) explores the role of consumption in the development of the culture of segregation. Kevin Mumford (*Interzones*) explores interracial socializing that occurred around the illegal production, sale, and consumption of alcohol during Prohibition. Though Mumford confines his analysis to the black-and-tan social clubs of Chicago and New York, cases like that of Solomon Douglas suggest that similar cultures existed even in rural Virginia. Other cases appealed to Virginia's high court demonstrate that interracial socializing took place around the consumption of alcohol. In 1921, John Pope was convicted of running a disorderly house in Norfolk. Testimony in that case revealed that both blacks and whites frequented his "cabaret," though they sat on opposite sides of the room. Though the seating was racially segregated, the entertainment was not. White women patrons performed sexually suggestive dances on the club's central stage. See *Pope v. Commonwealth*, 131 Va. 776 (1921).

19. *Commonwealth v. Solomon Douglas*, Common Law Order Book 24, p. 469, Circuit Court of Pittsylvania County, Chatham, Va.

20. Ida B. Wells, editorial, *Free Speech*, May 21, 1892.

21. *Legions v. Commonwealth*, 181 Va. 89 (1943), Brief on Behalf of the Commonwealth, 8.

22. S. L. Ferguson to Governor Mann, August 9, 1912, *Commonwealth v. Alfred Wright*, Petition for Commutation, July 19–August 31, 1912, EP.

23. J. E. Thrift to Governor Swanson, August 7, 1908, *Commonwealth v. Lee Strother*, Petition for Commutation, July 1–August 31, 1908, EP.

24. Most courts have required evidence of bruises or other injury, torn clothing, or the presence of a weapon to demonstrate that force was used and that the victim attempted to resist it. Courts historically have been reluctant to accept verbal statements, even screams, of nonconsent as sufficient evidence of the use of force and have defined what the law sees as adequate resistance by male standards. A woman's failure to resist vigorously at any point in an assault, according to the law in practice, constituted consent to the entire assault. Despite the 1970s' reform of rape laws that attempted to make evidence of women's resistance less central to proving rape, many juries remain unwilling to convict men accused of rape without evidence that he used physical force to overcome the victim's resistance. Juries' reluctance to convict men of rape solely on the testimony of the victim betrays the still-pervasive social belief that women accuse men of rape for their own nefarious purposes. The end result is that although rape laws allegedly serve to preserve women's sexual autonomy

and their ability to choose sexual partners freely, in practice, they ensure men's sexual access to all women, as long as men can compel intercourse without causing women obvious physical injury. More alarming is that some accused men have claimed that injuries women received in the course of a rape resulted from the woman's desire for kinky, violent sex, making her even more suspect in the eyes of the jury. For more complete discussions of rape and resistance, as well as efforts to reform rape law, see Estrich, *Real Rape*; MacKinnon, *Toward a Feminist Theory of the State*; Roberts, "Rape, Violence, and Women's Autonomy"; Dripps, "Beyond Rape"; and Torrey, "When Will We Be Believed?" Historical analyses bear out these theories in practice. See Dubinsky, *Improper Advances*; Block, "Coerced Sex"; Parker, "Law, Culture, and Sexual Censure"; and Dayton, *Women before the Bar*, 231–84.

25. *Commonwealth v. Joe Gibbs*, Case File, Criminal Cases Ended 740, Circuit Court of Prince George County, Prince George, Va. Gibbs was convicted and sentenced to death. His death sentence was commuted at the request of the jury, and he was pardoned in 1947.

26. *Commonwealth v. Charlie Brown*, Case File 833, Circuit Court of Isle of Wight County, Isle of Wight, Va. Brown was convicted, sentenced to death, and executed. In his petition for a stay of execution, Brown's lawyer questioned the authenticity of Brown's alleged confession, claiming its language was not that of an illiterate man.

27. *Commonwealth v. John Anderson*, Case File, December Term 1938, Circuit Court of Loudoun County, Leesburg, Va. Anderson was convicted, sentenced to death, and executed.

28. *Commonwealth v. Paul Hairston*, Order Book 336, pp. 371, 373, Circuit Court of Henry County, Martinsville, Va.; *Commonwealth v. Paul Hairston*, Henry County Determined Court Papers, October 1919, LOVA. Hairston was convicted and sentenced to death. His sentence was commuted to life in prison because of his mental disability.

29. "Special Grand Jury for Assault Case," *Loudoun Times-Mirror*, June 7, 1928; "James Washington Sentenced to Be Killed in the Electric Chair," ibid., June 21, 1928; *Commonwealth v. James Washington*, Common Law Order Book 13, pp. 222, 250, Circuit Court of Loudoun County, Leesburg, Va.; Alexander to Governor Byrd, July 20, 1928, Governor Byrd Papers, Box 98, LOVA.

30. Washington's father (no name given) to Governor Byrd, July 15, 1928, Governor Byrd Papers, Box 98, LOVA. Washington was executed one week after Alexander wrote the governor.

31. J. M. Harvey, parole officer to Charles P. Chew, Va. Parole Board, November 3, 1947, *Commonwealth v. Randolph Hockaday*, Hockaday Folder, Governor Tuck Papers, Box 99, LOVA. I have found no evidence that Clarence Branch applied for or received a pardon for his role in the crime.

32. "Redhead Says Hubby, Helper Attacked Her," *Richmond Afro-American*, October 11, 1952; "Redhead Alters Story Is Fined, Jailed," ibid., October 25, 1952. A white man charged with a similar crime in Georgia appealed his conviction in 1949, though the court affirmed the jury's verdict. The fate of the black accomplice is unknown since he did not appeal his case. See *Williams v. State*, 206 Ga. 107 (1949).

33. These cases echo a famous case in Britain in 1975 in which a man encouraged three other men to have sex with his wife, telling them she was "kinky" and "likely to struggle to get 'turned on.'" The men were convicted, but they appealed their conviction on the grounds that they believed she had consented because her husband said she had. The court upheld their convictions but also ruled that "where a man honestly believed that a woman consented to sex, he was not guilty; and his view did not have to be reasonable." Their ruling created considerable public protest, resulting in an act of Parliament that imposed a requirement of reasonableness on claims of mistaken consent. See DPP v. Morgan 2 All ER 347 (1975). The case is discussed in Lees, *Carnal Knowledge*, xvii. It is doubtful that a black man's claims of "mistaken consent" would have been believed by any southern jury, as few white men could conceive of a white man offering his wife or daughter to a black man. Cases reveal, however, that this did occur, even in the South.

34. Brown and Kimball, "Mapping the Terrain of Black Richmond," 335.

35. *Story v. State*, 178 Al. 98 (1912), at 104; Dittmer, *Black Georgia*, 124.

36. McLaurin, *Separate Pasts*, 65–66.

37. For a discussion of these fears and how white activists sought to use the law to prevent interracial relationships, see Lisa Dorr, "Arm in Arm."

38. *Commonwealth v. Loo Rooster Jarvis*, Petition for Conditional Pardon, EP, January 8–12, 1962, LOVA; *Commonwealth v. Leewood Ashby*, Petition for Conditional Pardon, EP, April 21–May 10, 1943, LOVA.

39. "Danville Negro Held on Serious Charges," *Richmond Times-Dispatch*, August 14, 1927.

40. "Negro Is Lodged in Lynchburg Jail for Safekeeping," *Danville Register*, August 14, 1927. The age of consent in Virginia at this point was sixteen.

41. "Danville Negro Held on Serious Charges"; "Negro Is Lodged in Lynchburg Jail for Safekeeping." The *Danville Register* article stated that at the police station, the girl "made admissions that pointed to a revolting crime on the part of the Negro."

42. *Commonwealth v. Jacob (aka John) Duncan*, Common Law Order Book 30, pp. 206, 233, 235, Danville Corporation Court, Danville, Va. Duncan's plea and sentence appear in "Negroes Given Eighteen Years for Felony," *Danville Register*, September 22, 1927.

43. Nettie Duncan to Governor Pollard, January 22, 1933, *Commonwealth v. Jacob Duncan*, Petition for Conditional Pardon, March 21–April 9, 1933, EP.

44. J. W. Carter to V. E. McDougall, March 29, 1933, *Commonwealth v. Jacob Duncan*, Petition for Conditional Pardon, March 21–April 9, 1933, EP.

45. J. H. Martin to Governor Pollard, March 18, 1933, *Commonwealth v. Jacob Duncan*, Petition for Conditional Pardon, March 21–April 9, 1933, EP; emphasis added.

46. The potential for a white woman to lose her honor frequently appeared in white rhetoric. Nevertheless, for many whites, warnings about white women's potential loss of honor demonstrated the effectiveness of prohibitions on white women's sexual relations with black men. Lillian Smith wryly noted that a "nice white girl" could casually sip a Coke in the drugstore with a member of a lynch mob, "but she would have been run out of town or perhaps killed had she drunk

a Coke with the young Negro doctor who was devoting his life in service to his people" (*Killers of the Dream*, 82). William Alexander Percy (*Lanterns on the Levee*, 308–9) makes a similar claim: "The whites make outcasts of their white women who have violated the taboo [of sexual relations with black men], sometimes punishing them as grossly as they punish the offending Negro. Never are they accepted into even the lowest stratum of white society." See also Hall, *Revolt against Chivalry*, 153–54. Crystal Feimster also examines white women who were physically attacked by mobs as a means of protecting the social order, though the extent of this activity in Virginia is unclear. See Feimster, "Ladies and Lynching," 276–304, and MacLean, *Behind the Mask of Chivalry*, 98–124.

47. Manly H. Barnes to Governor Stuart, August 17, 1915, *Commonwealth v. Charles Wilson*, Petition for Conditional Pardon, September 1–September 28, 1915, EP.

48. Judge B. G. Tyler to Governor Stuart, August 19, 1915, *Commonwealth v. Charles Wilson*, Petition for Conditional Pardon, September 1–September 28, 1915, EP; emphasis in the original.

49. I am indebted to Jacquelyn Dowd Hall's analysis of sex and lynching in *Revolt against Chivalry*. I also acknowledge that I am accepting legal officials' assertions that the relationship between the victim and Wilson was consensual. I concede the possibility that the incident in question was indeed attempted rape and that the victim's reputation led authorities to see *any* sexual interaction on her part as consensual. Either way, white authorities' beliefs about her relations across racial lines in general justified Wilson's release.

50. "Man Jailed on Charge of Attacking Woman," *Richmond Times-Dispatch*, August 17, 1925.

51. *Commonwealth v. Paul Washington*, Common Law Order Book 11, pp. 230, 252, 264, 293, 294, 295, 300, 342, Circuit Court of Allegheny County, Covington, Va.

52. R. E. Dyche to Paul Washington, undated, *Commonwealth v. Paul Washington*, Petition for Conditional Pardon, April 10–April 22, 1933, EP.

53. R. E. Dyche to Miss V. E. McDougall, Executive Secretary to Governor Pollard, October 27, 1932, *Commonwealth v. Paul Washington*, Petition for Conditional Pardon, April 10–April 22, 1933, EP.

54. Benjamin Haden to Governor Pollard, January 30, 1933, *Commonwealth v. Paul Washington*, Petition for Conditional Pardon, April 10–April 22, 1933, EP.

55. Dyche to McDougall.

56. Ibid.

57. Ibid.

58. Ibid.

59. R. B. Stephenson to Miss V. E. McDougall, December 17, 1932, *Commonwealth v. Paul Washington*, Petition for Conditional Pardon, April 10–April 22, 1933, EP.

60. Benjamin Haden, Clerk of the Circuit Court of Allegheny County, to Governor Pollard, January 30, 1933, *Commonwealth v. Paul Washington*, Petition for Conditional Pardon, April 10–April 22, 1933, EP.

61. *Commonwealth v. John Spencer*, Common Law Order Book 10, pp. 246, 256, Judgments Circuit Court 1919 File, Circuit Court of Page County, Luray, Va.

62. Everett M. Berrey et al. Petition to Governor Davis, undated, *Common-*

wealth v. John Spencer, Petition for Conditional Pardon, November 10–November 31, 1920, EP. In Virginia, adultery, like fornication, remains a misdemeanor to this day, though the two acts were rarely prosecuted in the twentieth century.

63. R. S. Parks to Governor Davis, November 8, 1920, *Commonwealth v. John Spencer*, Petition for Conditional Pardon, November 10–November 31, 1920, EP.

64. Everett M. Berrey et al. Petition to Governor Davis.

65. Parks to Davis.

66. O. B. Wright to Governor Stuart, September 28, 1917, *Commonwealth v. John Will Bond*, Petition for Conditional Pardon, September 21–October 10, 1917, EP.

67. "Sensational Drama Is Unfolding in Second Trial of Harper Case," *Portsmouth Star*, March 5, 1931.

68. Unsigned letter to Governor Tuck, undated, "Virginia Board of Corrections–The Penitentiary" Folder, Governor Tuck Papers, Box 69, LOVA. It appears that Governor Tuck took no action in the case at that time. In Virginia, governors did not usually consider pardons of men serving life sentences until they had been incarcerated for twelve years. Butler was pardoned in 1959, after serving fourteen years of a life sentence. See *Commonwealth v. Fred Q. Butler*, Petition for Conditional Pardon, January 16–February 5, 1959, EP.

69. "Not Decided on Question of Perjury," *Portsmouth Star*, March 8, 1931.

70. "A Very Disquieting Case," *Richmond News-Leader*, March 7, 1931.

71. Hall, *Revolt against Chivalry*, 151.

Chapter Six

1. See Shapiro, *White Violence and Black Response*. Robin D. G. Kelley has pioneered analysis of the hidden forms of resistance African Americans practiced in their daily lives. See Kelley, " 'We Are Not What We Seem,' " and Kelley, *Race Rebels*, 1–76. W. Fitzhugh Brundage examines resistance to lynching specifically in his essay "Roar on the Other Side of Silence."

2. See Hodes, *White Women, Black Men*, 147–75.

3. Cash, *Mind of the South*, 414; Percy, *Lanterns on the Levee*, 300.

4. Bruce, *Plantation Negro as Freeman*, 83–84, 129–30.

5. King, *Race Problems of the South*, 162–63. Quoted in Litwack, *Trouble in Mind*, 212. Assertions that the rape of women represents a weapon used in conflicts among men are explored in detail by Susan Brownmiller. She argues that conquered women have historically been considered legitimate "booty" of war and that raping a woman may be an act aimed to demonstrate male powerlessness. See Brownmiller, *Against Her Will*, 23–149. The use of rape as a weapon of war and of genocide was particularly prominent in the recent conflicts in the Balkans.

6. Smith, *Killers of the Dream*, 55.

7. Du Bois, *Darkwater*, 172.

8. Dollard, *Caste and Class in a Southern Town*, 163–64.

9. Myrdal, *American Dilemma*, 591.

10. See, for example, Richard Wright, *Native Son*, and Himes, *If He Hollers Let Him Go*.

11. See Murray, "Beyond Macho."

12. Hernton, *Sex and Racism in America*, 67–69.

13. Cleaver, *Soul on Ice*, 14. Cleaver cites LeRoi Jones's work, *The Dead Lecturer*, offering another iteration of rape as revenge. Frantz Fanon also discusses raping white women as a form of resistance in *Black Skin, White Masks*, 63–82.

14. Guttmacher and Weihofen, *Psychiatry and the Law*; Kopp, "Character Structure of Sex Offenders," 64–70; Pacht, Halleck, and Ehrmann, "Diagnosis and Treatment of the Sex Offender," 802–8.

15. "Morton Found Guilty, Given Death for Rape," *Danville Register*, July 25, 1947.

16. Perhaps the two best-known and earliest examples of feminist analyses of rape as a crime of power and social control are Griffin, *Rape*, and Brownmiller, *Against Her Will*. Many early feminist scholars, however, have been rightly criticized for accepting racial stereotypes in their analyses. Angela Davis angrily criticizes Susan Brownmiller and others for assuming that most rapists were black men and for ignoring the sexual violence committed by white men against black women. See Davis, "Rape, Racism, and the Myth."

17. Herman, "Considering Sex Offenders," 74.

18. Burgess and Holmstrom, *Rape Crisis and Recovery*, 24. See also Davis, "Rape, Racism, and the Myth."

19. Scully, *Understanding Sexual Violence*. Because her interviewees were anonymous, it is impossible to determine if any of the forty-one black men convicted of assaulting white women she interviewed are included in my study. Many of the men I discuss in Chapter 7 would probably still have been in prison at the time she conducted her interviews, making their presence in her study possible.

20. Ibid., 162.

21. Ibid., 147–48. Her results concur with those of Gary LaFree in his "Male Power and Female Victimization," 311–28, and *Rape and Criminal Justice*.

22. See Finnegan, "Who Were the Victims of Lynching?"

23. For a discussion of the relationship between masculinity and racial domination, see Bederman, *Manliness and Civilization*, 1–44.

24. See, for example, Painter, " 'Social Equality,' " and Fredrickson, *Black Image*, 282.

25. I thank Reginald Butler and Gregory Dorr for helping me develop and refine this analytic concept. The distinction between leverage and resistance is similar to the distinction made by historians of slavery between insurrection and the everyday forms of resistance to the master's power. Insurrections like those of Nat Turner and Denmark Vesey were rare, but slaves also protested their condition in less spectacular ways, such as working slowly and inefficiently or damaging the equipment they needed to do their work. See Genovese, *Roll Jordan Roll*, 597–660.

26. Gilmore, *Gender and Jim Crow*, 151–52, 175. Gilmore's use of the term "invisibility" is reminiscent of Ralph Ellison's use of the term.

27. "Two Colored Men's Pleas," *Richmond Planet*, April 23, 1927.

28. "Four Men Deny Attack Charge," *Richmond Afro-American*, September 21, 1940; "Lawyers Drop Case, 4 Attack Suspects Held," ibid., September 28, 1940; "Four Men in Attack Case Get 10 Years," November 16, 1940, ibid.

29. *Commonwealth v. John Henry Williams*, Common Law Order Book 4, pp. 43, 44, Circuit Court of Nottoway County, Nottoway, Va. Accounts of the assault are taken from "After All Day Pursuit Negro Is Surrounded," *Richmond Times-Dispatch*, March 31, 1916. Williams's arrest was reported in "Mob Threatens to Take Justice in Its Own Hands," ibid., April 3, 1916; the picture of the men who caught him appeared in "Negro Is Rushed to Henrico Jail," ibid., April 4, 1916.

30. In several cases, evidence that an accused man had not tried to escape, even though he had every opportunity, became evidence in white eyes that he might be innocent of the crime. See the cases of Luther Tyler in 1914 (Chapter 3) and John Mays Jr. in 1924 and Leon Fry in 1932 (below).

31. *Commonwealth v. Richard "Reds" Jackson*, Minute Book 10, p. 446, and Minute Book 11, pp. 226, 251, 252, 290, 334, 337, 338, Circuit Court of Fairfax County, Fairfax, Va.

32. Accounts of the assault and the search for assailants appear in "Man Not Caught," *Fairfax Herald*, March 31, 1922; "Not Caught Yet," ibid., April 7, 1922; "Still Working," ibid., April 14, 1922; "Extradition Held Up," ibid., May 5, 1922; "Coming Court Term," ibid., May 12, 1922; and "Reds Jackson Indicted," ibid., May 19, 1922.

33. Preston Waters to Governor Pollard, August 17, 1931, *Commonwealth v. Preston Waters*, Petition for Conditional Pardon, November 23–December 8, 1932, EP; R. A. Bickers to Governor Pollard, November 10, 1932, ibid., December 19, 1933–January 9, 1934.

34. Preston Waters to Governor Pollard, August 17, 1931, *Commonwealth v. Preston Waters*, Petition for Conditional Pardon, November 23–December 8, 1932, EP.

35. "Chesterfield Mob Foiled in Search for Negro," *Richmond Times-Dispatch*, May 15, 1921.

36. *Commonwealth v. Charles Green*, Common Law Book 10, pp. 363, 364, 373, Circuit Court of Chesterfield County, Chesterfield, Va. Quotations appear on p. 373.

37. See Carter, *Scottsboro*, 322–24. Even after the Supreme Court's ruling in *Norris v. Alabama*, alleging discrimination in the selection of the jury in cases of black-on-white rape remained an ineffective means of obtaining new trials. Many southern courts of appeals continued to refuse to reverse convictions on that ground. See *Avery v. State*, 209 Ga. 116 (1952); *Heard v. State*, 210 Ga. 524 (1953); *Johnson v. State*, 223 Miss. 56 (1955); and *State v. Middleton*, 207 SC 478 (1944). Only North Carolina appears to have reversed a conviction based on discrimination in jury selection. Raleigh Speller's conviction of rape was overturned once because blacks were excluded from the grand jury and once because blacks were excluded from the petit jury. He was convicted at a third trial, and the North Carolina Supreme Court upheld his conviction. See *State v. Speller*, 229 NC 67 (1948); *State v. Speller*, 230 NC 345 (1949); and *State v. Speller*, 231 NC 549 (1950).

38. *Green v. Commonwealth*, 133 Va. 695 (1922), at 696.

39. Unsigned copy of letter from Assistant Secretary to Nellie Lloyd, April 15, 1925, *Commonwealth v. Lee Ernest Bell*, PNAACP, Part 8, Series A, Reel 12, Frame 00313.

40. Sohn Chang Moon ("Principle and Expediency in Judicial Review," 146) specifically states that this strategy shaped the NAACP's approach to miscegenation cases. See also Kluger, *Simple Justice*.

41. Anne Moody (*Coming of Age in Mississippi*, 126–28) recalled being instructed by adults not to mention the NAACP or acknowledge its existence for fear of antagonizing whites in Mississippi.

42. *Commonwealth v. Lee Ernest Bell*, PNAACP, Part 8, Series A, Reel 12, Frame 00313.

43. *Commonwealth v. Philip Jones*, Common Law Order Book 15, p. 72, Circuit Court of Allegheny County, Covington, Va.; *Commonwealth v. Philip Jones*, Common Law Order Book 1934, pp. 56, 62, 63, 68, Case Files 1934, Circuit Court of Botetourt County, Fincastle, Va.

44. *Commonwealth v. Philip Jones*, PNAACP, Part 7, Series A, Reel 19, Frames 00799–00832.

45. "Behind the Scenes in the 'Jones Case,'" *Richmond Planet*, January 19, 1935.

46. "Winnegan Case Appealed," *Richmond Planet*, December 31, 1927; Petition to Governor Byrd from Citizens of Portsmouth, undated, *Commonwealth v. Shirley Winnegan*, Governor Byrd Papers, Box 100, LOVA.

47. There are numerous examples of articles protesting the seven black men's convictions and promoting the fund-raising efforts on their behalf in both the *Richmond Afro-American* and the *Norfolk Journal and Guide*.

48. For a discussion of defense arguments of racial disparity in punishment, see Rise, *Martinsville Seven*.

49. Clements's employment at a dairy is first noted in "Charge Is Made," *Richmond Evening Journal*, May 22, 1914. Announcement of his defense team appeared in "Chenault Case Continued to June 17," *Richmond News-Leader*, May 28, 1914.

50. "Clarence Howard Convicted of Rape of a White Woman Near Farmville," *Richmond Times-Dispatch*, March 3, 1949.

51. References to the work of the black community appear in Howard's petition to the Virginia Supreme Court of Appeals, *Commonwealth v. Clarence Howard*, Record 2177, p. 19, *Records and Briefs of the Virginia Court of Appeals*, 1949, Arthur J. Morris Law Library, University of Virginia School of Law. Governor Tuck's justification for pardon appears in "Lifer, Convicted of Rape, Pardoned after 10 Years," *Richmond Afro-American*, March 12, 1949. Howard's pardon caused considerable controversy in Prince Edward County. The governor received several letters urging him to refuse Howard's request for pardon, citing little local doubt as to his guilt and fears that his pardon might lead to future extralegal violence. One letter specifically cited fears that Howard might attempt to exact revenge on the elderly mother of the victim who remained in the area. See *Commonwealth v. Clarence Howard*, Folder "C," Governor Tuck Papers, Box 98, and *Commonwealth v. Clarence Howard*, "Virginia Board of Pardons and Reprieves," Governor Tuck Papers, Boxes 69 and 114, LOVA. Judgments about Howard's guilt or innocence are difficult to make. The existing record does not indicate why he was identified as a suspect in West Virginia in the first place. He claimed he had never been to Farmville, yet eight local witnesses identified him

as having been in the area. While researching the case in the Prince Edward County Courthouse, I met William F. Watkins Jr., commonwealth's attorney for Prince Edward County from 1960 to 1990, whose grandfather and uncle had also served long terms as commonwealth's attorneys. Watkins's uncle prosecuted Howard, and he remembered the case from when he was a boy. Watkins told me that when his uncle heard that Howard had been pardoned, he phoned the governor—an old friend—and told him that if Howard ever came through Prince Edward County, he would hang Howard himself. Neither the prosecuting attorney, nor his nephew more than fifty years later, had any doubts about Howard's guilt.

52. "Jail Terms and Fines Imposed on Eight Negroes after Clash over Alleged Insult to Woman," *Virginian Pilot and Norfolk Landmark*, May 3, 1929; "Eight Negroes Jailed after Night Parade," *Richmond Times-Dispatch*, May 3, 1929.

53. Grace Elizabeth Hale (*Making Whiteness*, 199–239) argues that lynching not only limited "black political activity and achieve[ed] significant control of black labor"; it was also central to white identity. See also Massey, "Ideology of Lynch Law."

54. See Zangrando, *NAACP's Campaign against Lynching*; Bederman, *Manliness and Civilization*, 45–76.

55. "Negro Assailant of Girls Lynched," *Richmond Times-Dispatch*, August 17, 1917.

56. Ibid.

57. "Lynched Negro's Family Refuses to Handle Body," *Richmond Times-Dispatch*, August 18, 1917.

58. *Alexandria Gazette*, April 26, 1897, quoted in Brundage, "Roar on the Other Side of Silence," 274.

59. "Colored Man Lynched in the State of Virginia," *Richmond Planet*, August 25, 1917.

60. "Lynching Investigation Fails to Discover Mob," *Richmond Times-Dispatch*, August 19, 1917.

61. "Indication of Trouble from Heathsville Negroes," *Richmond Times-Dispatch*, September 30, 1917.

62. "A Mob Leader Is Boycotted," *Norfolk Journal and Guide*, October 6, 1917. See also Brundage, "Roar on the Other Side of Silence," 275.

63. In 1916, thirteen-year-old Jacob Jefferson was sent to a reform school when he was accused of assaulting a white child. Allen Ball received a similar penalty in 1909. Claude Miles in 1925 was sent to Central State Hospital for five years in lieu of trial, as was Loo Rooster Jarvis after his first "affair" with a white woman in 1931. Informal agreements to spirit a black man out of the state are mostly anecdotal. However, governors throughout the period of this study agreed to pardon some black men provided they left either the state of Virginia or the county in which the assault took place. Preston Waters's pardon included this provision, as did James Yager's, among others. But this provision was not included in every conditional pardon. Exile as punishment continued into the 1950s and 1960s in cases of interracial sex. The Lovings, whose case eventually overturned legal prohibitions on interracial marriage, were initially banished from Virginia rather than sent to the penitentiary.

64. "Sent to Grand Jury on Assault Charge," *Richmond Times-Dispatch*, June 18, 1922; *Commonwealth v. Ralph Green*, Common Law Book 74, pp. 292, 297, 328, 331, Richmond Hustings Court I, Richmond, Va.

65. Superintendent Youell to Governor Pollard, September 10, 1930, and Petition from Carrie L. Hill to Governor Pollard, July 30, 1930, *Commonwealth v. Ralph Green*, Petition for Conditional Pardon, April 10–April 30, 1931, EP.

66. Fitzhugh Brundage (*Lynching in the New South*, 81–82) discusses whites' fear of "floaters"—itinerant black laborers—and its connection to lynchings. Edward Ayers (*Promise of the New South*, 156–57) also notes that itinerant black men were more likely to become targets of lynch mobs. Terence Finnegan ("Who Were the Victims of Lynching?" 79–80), however, disagrees that floaters were a significant target of white mobs, arguing that most lynchings stemmed from labor disputes between black agricultural workers and their landlords, though he concedes that itinerant laborers had little regard for racial etiquette, which often caused whites to fear them. Diane Miller Sommerville notes in her study of black-on-white rape in the nineteenth century ("Rape Myth in the Old South," 84, 170–73, 214–15) that a black man accused of assaulting a relative of his master faced swifter, more extreme punishment.

67. Testimony of L. W. Lane cited in Bill of Exception 2, *Commonwealth v. Lee Archer*, Princess Anne Circuit Court Papers 1913, LOVA.

68. *Commonwealth v. Alex Hatton*, Petition for Conditional Pardon, April 14–April 27, 1922, EP.

69. "Citizens Seize Negro," *Richmond Times-Dispatch*, May 10, 1914; "Mrs. Adams Identifies Brown As Her Assailant," ibid., May 12, 1914; "Negro's Hearing To-morrow," ibid., May 14, 1914; "Secures Discharge When He Proves Alibi," ibid., May 16, 1914; "Henrico Assault Case Hearing Is Delayed," *Richmond News-Leader*, May 13, 1914.

70. "Girl Choked by Negro Robber," *Richmond Times-Dispatch*, October 16, 1912; "Arrest Negro on Serious Charge," ibid., October 17, 1912; "Bring True Bill against Officer," ibid., January 7, 1913; "Tried for Capital Crime," ibid., January 8, 1913; "Acquit Debero," ibid., January 9, 1913,.

71. Mary Frances Berry (*Pig Farmer's Daughter*, 207–10) argues that whites interfered with the legal process primarily to protect their labor force or to shelter "good Negroes." I would certainly not dispute that there was an element of self-interest in the actions of white patrons. Nevertheless, the testimony about relationships between white patrons and black accused men and their families suggests that Berry's characterization is too simplistic.

72. Accounts of the assault and capture of Leon Fry appear in the *Harrisonburg Daily News-Record* and the *Richmond Times-Dispatch* beginning April 28, 1932.

73. Coverage of law enforcement precautions to protect Fry is in "Mob Is Feared; Jail Garrisoned in Valley Town," *Richmond Times-Dispatch*, April 30, 1932; "Militia Guards Valley Prison against Mob," ibid., May 1, 1932; "Troops Still on Guard at Harrisonburg Jail," ibid., May 2, 1932; "Armed Guards Are Placed around Jail to Protect Negro," *Harrisonburg Daily News-Record*, April 30, 1932; "State Militia Now Guard Jail against Possible Mob," ibid., May 2, 1932; and "Militia Withdrawn as Jail Guards," ibid., May 3, 1932.

74. "Militia Withdrawn as Jail Guards"; "Feeling Is Growing Fry Is Inno-

cent," *Harrisonburg Daily News-Record*, May 7, 1932. Details about evidence are scattered throughout the coverage of the case.

75. Lucas's relationship to the sheriff is reported in "Leon Fry Is Held for Grand Jury," *Harrisonburg Daily News-Record*, May 19, 1932. "Senator Weaver Probes Into Fry Case," ibid., May 20, 1932, reports Weaver's interest in the case. "Page Grand Jury Indicts Leon Fry," ibid., May 25, 1932, reports Weaver's conviction of Fry's innocence.

76. "Leon Fry's Trial Will Start Today," *Harrisonburg Daily News-Record*, July 25, 1932.

77. "Fry's Second Trial Opens at Luray," *Harrisonburg Daily News-Record*, July 26, 1932.

78. "Leon Fry Acquitted of Assault Charge," *Harrisonburg Daily News-Record*, July 27, 1932; "Page County Jury Acquits Leon Fry," *Richmond Times-Dispatch*, July 27, 1932; *Commonwealth v. Leon Fry*, Order Book 14, pp. 40, 47, 59, 61, Judgments Circuit Court 1932 May–November Term File, Circuit Court of Page County, Luray, Va.

79. It is difficult to determine whether accused black men and their families requested the help of white allies or whether whites acted on their own initiative. I consciously use language that allows for black agency, and that reflects the obligation and deference that characterized many of these relationships.

80. *Commonwealth v. William Rose*, Common Law Order Book 14, pp. 257, 259, Circuit Court of Hanover County, Hanover, Va.; William Rose to Governor Trinkle, October 5, 1923, *Commonwealth v. William Rose*, Petition for Conditional Pardon, November 15–November 30, 1923, EP.

81. S. B. Whitehead to Governor Pollard, November 6, 1930, *Commonwealth v. John Mays, Jr.*, Petition for Conditional Pardon, December 22–December 24, 1930, EP.

82. Dr. and Mrs. A. A. Sizer to Governor Pollard, November 4, 1930, and December 9, 1929, *Commonwealth v. John Mays, Jr.*, December 22–December 24, 1930, EP.

83. Lombardo, "Three Generations."

84. See Gregory Dorr, "Segregation's Science."

85. Dr. A. A. Sizer to Governor Pollard, November 4, 1930, *Commonwealth v. John Mays, Jr.*, December 22–December 24, 1930, EP.

86. Ibid., December 9, 1929.

87. Ibid., November 4, 1930.

88. Petition, undated, *Commonwealth v. William Finney*, Petition for Commutation, September 1–October 22, 1908, EP.

89. *Commonwealth v. Preston Byrd*, Petition for Conditional Pardon, May 3–May 21, 1923, EP.

90. "Negro Is Electrocuted for Assaulting Girl," *Richmond Times-Dispatch*, May 26, 1916.

91. W. W. Lee to Governor Swanson, June 4, 1906, *Commonwealth v. Gabriele Battaile*, Petition for Commutation, June 1–July 16, 1906, EP.

92. Revs. S. A. Brown, J. A. Brown, and W. L. Ransome to Governor Swanson, May 30, 1906, *Commonwealth v. Gabriele Battaile*, Petition for Commutation, EP, June 1–July 16, 1906, EP.

93. Sarah Ellett to Miss Slater, Assistant Secretary to Governor Davis, October 19, 1920, *Commonwealth v. Russell Ellett*, Petition for Conditional Pardon, October 18–November 9, 1920, EP; *Commonwealth v. Russell Ellett*, Petition for Conditional Pardon, February 17–March 6, 1924, EP.

94. *Commonwealth v. Beverly Carr*, Petition for Conditional Pardon, May 31–June 17, 1935, EP. Carr began petitioning yearly for early release in 1930 and was rejected every time.

95. Susie Smith to Governor Swanson, October 8, 1908; R. H. Bagby to Governor Swanson. Both letters are enclosed mistakenly in the folder containing Winston Greene's request for commutation, September–October 22, 1908, EP.

96. Evidence indicates that in rape cases white men's appeals for clemency based on the needs of their families were generally more successful. Perry B. Pruitt was convicted of rape in 1939 and received a twelve-year sentence. His wife and his mother requested his release in 1941, saying they needed his support. However, they also stated that the victim had consented to sex with him and was of bad character. He was pardoned (*Commonwealth v. Perry B. Pruitt*, Petition for Conditional Pardon, December 22–27, 1941, EP). In 1940, the wife of Aught Tiller, who was convicted of attempted rape in 1939 and sentenced to seven years in prison, requested his release because she needed his support. The governor refused until he received a letter on Tiller's behalf sent on the stationery of the U.S. House of Representative's Agricultural Subcommittee. Tiller received a conditional pardon in June 1941 (*Commonwealth v. Aught Tiller*, Petition for Conditional Pardon, June 21–30, 1941, EP). Earl R. Cregger's wife, on the other hand, was unsuccessful in her petition for her husband's release, despite having no work and being in poor health (*Commonwealth v. Earl R. Trigger*, Petition for Conditional Pardon, September 2–29, 1943, EP).

97. Virginia Abbott to Governor Stanley, April 5 and December 20, 1957, *Commonwealth v. Fred Q. Butler*, Petition for Conditional Pardon, January 16–February 5, 1959, EP.

98. Virginia Abbott to Governor Almond, January 12, 195[9], *Commonwealth v. Fred Q. Butler*, Petition for Conditional Pardon, January 16–February 5, 1959, EP. She wrote 1958 at the top of the letter, but considering the contents, I believe she merely forgot that it was a new year.

99. Governor Almond to Virginia Abbott, February 10, 1959, *Commonwealth v. Fred Q. Butler*, Petition for Conditional Pardon, January 16–February 5, 1959, EP.

Chapter Seven

1. Wilbur A. Hamman, M.D., December 29, 1959, to Judge Mitchell, *Commonwealth v. Sam G. Townes*, Case File, Circuit Court of Mecklenburg County, Boydton, Va.

2. *Commonwealth v. Sam G. Townes*, Common Law Order Book 27, pp. 219, 244, 289, 315, 320, 337, Circuit Court of Mecklenburg County, Boydton, Va.

3. Waller H. Horsley to Governor Godwin Jr., August 22, 1969, *Commonwealth v. Sam Townes*, Petition for Conditional Pardon, September 1969, EP. Townes was granted a conditional pardon and released in 1969 because he was suffering from a terminal kidney disease. He died shortly thereafter.

4. Partington, "Incidence of the Death Penalty."

5. "Cross Burned at Home of Rape Suspect," *Norfolk Journal and Guide*, September 17, 1949. Cupid Diggs was eventually convicted of rape and received a life sentence (*Commonwealth v. Cupid Diggs*, General Index of Judgments A–L, pp. 150, 153, 179, 181, Circuit Court of Warwick County [now Newport News], Newport News, Va.).

6. Between 1908 and 1909, 11.3 percent of the African Americans convicted of rape in Virginia received the death penalty; between 1940 and 1950, only 1.8 percent ended up on death row (Rise, *Martinsville Seven*, 184 n. 58).

7. "Another Negro-Did-It Crime Flops," *Norfolk Journal and Guide*, October 26, 1946.

8. O'Brien, *Color of the Law*, 97–108. See also Motley, *Invisible Soldier*, and Graham Smith, *When Jim Crow Met John Bull*.

9. See *Nixon v. Condon* (1931); *Morgan v. Virginia* (1946); *Boynton v. Virginia* (1961); *Shelley v. Kramer* (1948); *Sweatt v. Painter* (1950); *McLaurin v. Oklahoma* (1950); and *Brown v. Board of Education of Topeka* (1954).

10. See Sullivan, *Days of Hope*; McCoy and Ruetten, *Quest and Response*. Richard Kluger (*Simple Justice*) provides the best analysis of the NAACP Legal Defense Fund's quest for civil rights in the courts. Harvard Sitkoff, *Struggle for Black Equality*, 11–18) argues that the New Deal and the Second World War provided an important foundation for the civil rights movement of the 1950s and 1960s. Gail William O'Brien (*Color of the Law*) uses an averted lynching in Tennessee in 1946 as the lens through which she explores the impact of World War II, postwar prosperity, and changing local and national political agendas on race relations, white supremacy, and black agency.

11. "Another Negro-Did-It Crime Flops"; "Negro-Did-It Crime Is Implausible," *Norfolk Journal and Guide*, December 13, 1947.

12. "Men Freed of Assault Charges Filed by Two Frightened Women," *Norfolk Journal and Guide*, October 12, 1946.

13. Rise, *Martinsville Seven*, 1–4.

14. According to several of the men, they had been unable to obtain an erection and thus could not fully penetrate the victim. Virginia law did not then and does not now require full penetration or emission to prove rape. Penetration, "however slight," is sufficient to charge rape.

15. Eric Rise analyzes the Martinsville Seven lawyer's briefs extensively in *Martinsville Seven*, 102.

16. Ibid., 102. These statistics became the basis for Donald H. Partington's article on rape and the death penalty in Virginia, which appeared in the *Washington and Lee Law Review* in 1965. My research largely supports these statistics; the slightly higher number of executed men includes men charged with both rape and murder. Most courts tried defendants on murder charges first and, after handing down a death sentence, declined to prosecute on the rape charge. These men were not included in Partington's numbers.

17. Franklin Williams, "Death Penalty and the Negro," 501–12; Florida Civil Liberties Union, "Rape"; Koeninger, "Capital Punishment in Texas"; Wolfgang and Riedel, "Race, Judicial Discretion, and the Death Penalty." Later scholars continued to examine racial discrimination in the death penalty. See Banner,

Death Penalty, 123, 289–90; Kleck, "Racial Discrimination"; Phillips, "Social Structure and Social Control"; Baldus, Woodworth, and Pulaski, *Equal Justice and the Death Penalty*, 250–51; George Wright, "Executions of Afro-Americans"; and Hunter, Ralph, and Marquart, "Death Sentencing of Rapists."

18. See Meltsner, *Cruel and Unusual*, 106–8; Acker, "Social Science," 431–33; Muller, "Legal Defense Fund's Capital Punishment Campaign," 168–70.

19. Rise makes this point specifically in *Martinsville Seven*, 4.

20. *Commonwealth v. Kenneth Weatherspoon*, Common Law Order Book 75, pp. 504, 573, Norfolk Corporation Court I, Norfolk, Va.; "Weatherspoon Given Life Term for Rape of Fifteen-Year-Old Girl," *Norfolk Virginian Pilot*, July 23, 1949. Similar sentiments appear in "Sailor Gets Life; Declined to Talk at Risk of Death," *Norfolk Journal and Guide*, July 30, 1949.

21. *Commonwealth v. Lloyd Junius Dobie*, Common Law Order Book 18, pp. 39, 51, 52, 63, 72, 108, 110, 113, 234, 337, 346, 377, Circuit Court of Southampton, Courtland, Va.

22. *Commonwealth v. Albert Jackson, Jr.*, Case File "Criminal Cases," Charlottesville Corporation Court, Charlottesville, Va.; *Jackson v. Commonwealth*, 193 Va. 664 (1952).

23. "Shed No Tears for Me," *Richmond Afro-American*, August 30, 1952; "How the Courts Cause the Crime of Rape," ibid., May 26, 1951; "Death Penalty Is Upheld in Criminal Attack Case," ibid., April 26, 1952; "God Stayed Execution, Says Doomed Man," ibid., August 2, 1952.

24. "Ex-GI, 15 Years for Keeping a 'Date,'" *Norfolk Journal and Guide*, July 31, 1954. Dixon was tried in Danville Corporation Court. Mack Ingram's case in 1952 received extensive attention in the black press. See "Leering Case," *Norfolk Journal and Guide*, November 8, 1952; "Court Frees Farmer in 'Looking' Case," ibid., February 28, 1953; "Never Laid Eyes on Her, Says Ingram," *Richmond Afro-American*, November 15, 1952; and "Discrimination Charged in 'Look Attack,'" ibid., December 20, 1952.

25. For an analysis of white beliefs that all blacks were infected with syphilis, see James Jones, *Bad Blood*, 16–29.

26. "McGuire Hospital Clerk, White Girl Arrested in Auto," *Richmond Afro-American*, July 26, 1952.

27. "Charley Wallace Arrested with Blonde in Car," *Richmond Afro-American*, December 12, 1953. The *Afro-American* frequently referred to whites as blondes.

28. "Man Gets Six Months in Romance," *Richmond Afro-American*, September 6, 1958.

29. *Commonwealth v. Ernest Harris, Jr.*, Pre-Sentence Investigation Report, Case File, Circuit Court of New Kent County, New Kent, Va. News of Harris's arrest appeared in "Scout Leader Pleads Not Guilty to Woman's Charge," *Richmond Afro-American*, March 30, 1957.

30. Ibid.

31. *Commonwealth v. Ernest Harris, Jr.*, Common Law Order Book 7, pp. 136, 137, 144, 146, Circuit Court of New Kent County, New Kent, Va.

32. "Jones Acquitted of Assault and Battery Charge," *Norfolk Journal and Guide*, November 11, 1950; *Commonwealth v. Fletcher Jones*, Common Law Order Book 45, p. 4, Portsmouth Hustings Court, Portsmouth, Va.

33. "Peeping Tom Sentenced to Twelve Months," *Richmond Afro-American*, June 27, 1953.

34. The *Norfolk Journal and Guide* happily announced this decision in an editorial on December 13, 1947.

35. See *Avery v. State*, 209 Ga. 116 (1952); *Heard v. State*, 210 Ga. 524 (1953); *Johnson v. State*, 223 Miss. 56 (1955); and *State v. Middleton*, 207 SC 478 (1944). In all of these cases, black men were accused of raping or attempting to rape white women and the defense appealed the jury's guilty verdict, arguing that racial minorities had been excluded from jury service. In each case, the respective state appeals panel upheld the verdict.

36. "Seven Negroes Serve on Norfolk Jury," *Norfolk Virginian-Pilot*, January 18, 1946.

37. "Five Colored on Jury in Corporation Court," *Norfolk Journal and Guide*, January 12, 1946.

38. "Justice Knows No Color Line in Portsmouth Hustings Court," *Norfolk Journal and Guide*, December 21, 1946.

39. "Frasker Young, 18-Year-Old Negro Confessed to Rape of 26-Year-Old Wife in Henrico County," *Richmond News-Leader*, June 28, 1949.

40. "Attacker Held Moron, Meted 15 More Years," *Richmond Afro-American*, March 31, 1951. A year and a half later, Young was tried before a judge for the earlier rape of a young black girl. He received an additional fifteen-year sentence. The black press criticized police for initiating a manhunt only after a white woman was raped; the rape of the black girl occurred first. Young's first trial occurred in Henrico County. See *Commonwealth v. Frasker Young*, Order Book 107, pp. 285, 344, 402, 461, and Order Book 108, pp. 7, 60, 229, 317, 318, 379, 411, 476, 477, Circuit Court of Henrico County, Richmond, Va. His second trial occurred in downtown Richmond (*Commonwealth v. Frasker Young*, Common Law Order Book 109, pp. 37, 234, Richmond Hustings Court I, Richmond, Va.).

41. "Woman Raped in Her Home Near Suffolk," *Norfolk Virginian-Pilot*, March 28, 1957; "Police Get Many Tips on Rapist," ibid., March 29, 1957; "New Trial Offers Hope for Once Condemned Man," *Norfolk Journal and Guide*, January 11, 1958; "3rd Trial Ordered Man in Suffolk Rape Case," ibid., January 18, 1958; "Appeal May Be Noted in Third Palmer Trial," ibid., February 8, 1958; "Palmer Defense Committee Seeking Ways for Appeal," ibid., March 15, 1958. The African American community raised funds for Palmer's defense.

42. "Hung Jury for Marine in Baby-Sitter Rape Trial," *Norfolk Journal and Guide*, September 20, 1952; "Hung Jury," *Richmond Afro-American*, September 20, 1952; "Virginia Judge Frees Attack Suspect," *Norfolk Journal and Guide*, March 21, 1953; "Irate Citizens Protest Dropping of Attack Case," *Richmond Afro-American*, March 21, 1953.

43. "Man Rescued from Mob Attack Denies Criminal Attack," *Norfolk Journal and Guide*, February 21, 1953. See also "Taxi Fleet Owner Denies Attack Guilt," *Richmond Afro-American*, February 21, 1953.

44. *Skipper v. Commonwealth*, 195 Va. 870 (1952), at 874.

45. Ibid., 878.

46. Ibid., 196 Va. 1057.

47. "Police Brutality Charged in Lynchburg, Probe Asked," *Norfolk Journal and Guide*, July 26, 1952; "Beatings Charged by Youth, 19," ibid., August 23, 1952; "Youth Seeks $100,000 in Rights Case," ibid., August 30, 1952.

48. "New Charge Filed Against Skipper, Man Suing Police," *Lynchburg Daily Advance*, October 3, 1952. This article announcing Skipper's arrest for burglary is the first mention in the white press of Skipper's civil suit and the Justice Department probe.

49. "Hearing for Skipper Scheduled Oct. 21; Denies Raping Woman," *Lynchburg Daily Advance*, October 14, 1952; "Skipper Hearing Postponed on Rape Count, Defendant Held for Jury in Burglary Cases," ibid., October 21, 1952; "Skipper Ordered Committed to Hospital for Observation," ibid., November 10, 1952.

50. *Commonwealth v. Bernard Skipper*, Law Orders Book 37, pp. 424, 425, 430, 431, 484, 486, 494, 497, 502, 504, 505, and Law Orders Book 38, pp. 91, 92, 234, 249, 257, 274, 277, 285, 286, 398, Lynchburg Corporation Court, Lynchburg, Va.

51. "Man Slain and Woman Raped on Road in Princess Anne; Killer Believed Sex Maniac," *Norfolk Virginian-Pilot*, June 7, 1953; "Bloody Slacks Found at Rape Killing Scene," ibid., June 8, 1953; "Rape-Slaying Suspect Freed after Quizzing," ibid., June 9, 1953; "Murder-Rapist Moved Auto between Crimes, Police Learn," ibid., June 10, 1953. The *Norfolk Virginian-Pilot* covered the case extensively, from the crime, to Selby's arrest, through his trial.

52. "Rape-Murder Arrest Made, After Hours of Grilling; Robbery Charge Also Filed," *Norfolk Virginian-Pilot*, June 22, 1953; "Truck Driver Sticks by Denial of Princess Anne Rape Killing," ibid., June 23, 1953.

53. "First Outsiders See Rape-Murder Suspect," *Norfolk Journal and Guide*, June 27, 1953.

54. "Selby Defense Fund $1,048," *Norfolk Journal and Guide*, July 25, 1953.

55. "Princess Anne County Adds $200 to Selby Fund," *Norfolk Journal and Guide*, August 15, 1953; "More Donations Boost Selby Defense Fund," ibid., August 22, 1953.

56. "Selby Fund Saved Life of Defendant," *Norfolk Journal and Guide*, December 5, 1953.

57. "Grand Jury Next for Selby," *Norfolk Journal and Guide*, August 1, 1953.

58. "Escape . . . ! From Shadow of Electric Chair," *Norfolk Journal and Guide*, July 25, 1953.

59. *Commonwealth v. Ruffin Junior Selby*, Common Law Order Book 25, pp. 11, 12, 22, Circuit Court of Princess Anne County, Princess Anne, Va. See also "Selby Acquitted of Rape; Verdict Brings Applause," *Norfolk Virginian-Pilot*, October 2, 1953; "Jury Quickly Frees Selby," *Norfolk Journal and Guide*, October 3, 1953; "Free Truck Driver of Attack Charge," *Richmond Afro-American*, October 17, 1953.

60. "Selby Fund Saved Life of Defendant."

61. Rise, *Martinsville Seven*, 184 n. 58.

62. Sanday, *Woman Scorned*, 131. Freud came to this conclusion after pondering the case of Dora, a girl who claimed she had been sexually abused by her father. Freud initially posited that such abuse caused later neuroses, but his theories were scoffed at by the likes of Richard von Krafft-Ebing. He eventually abandoned that theory in favor of fantasies of seduction. See Freud, *Dora*.

63. Deutsch, *Psychology of Women*. Many other disciples of Freud disagreed with Deutsch's analysis. Susan Brownmiller criticized Deutsch in *Against Her Will* for offering all men an ironclad defense for rape, that all women, deep down, wanted to be raped regardless of their verbal and physical resistance.

64. Forrester, "Rape, Seduction, and Psychoanalysis," 58–66.

65. Wigmore, *Treatise*, 744, 737.

66. Glanville Williams, "Corroboration—Sexual Cases," 662–71.

67. "Corroborating Charges of Rape," *Columbia Law Review* 67 (1967): 1137–38.

68. "The Resistance Standard in Rape Legislation," *Stanford Law Review* 18 (February 1966): 682.

69. "Forcible and Statutory Rape," *Yale Law Journal* 62 (December 1952): 52–68.

70. *Barker v. Commonwealth* 198 Va. 500 (1956); *Young v. Commonwealth*, 185 Va. 1032 (1947).

71. Chakejian's case did not appear in Charlottesville newspapers, though the *Richmond Times-Dispatch* covered his trial since the victim was from Richmond. A summary of the trial appeared in "Ex-Student of University Acquitted of Rape Charge," ibid., March 1, 1957. See also, *Commonwealth v. Richard N. Chakejian*, Law Order Book 24, p. 197, February Term 1957, Charlottesville Corporation Court, Charlottesville, Va.

72. See, for example, Estrich, *Real Rape*, 32–33.

73. Deutsch, *Psychology of Women*, quoted in Brownmiller, *Against Her Will*, 252.

74. There is a growing body of scholarship on women in the 1950s. See, for example, May, *Homeward Bound*; Breines, *Young, White and Miserable*; and Meyerowitz, *Not June Cleaver*. Rickie Solinger addresses unmarried motherhood in *Wake up Little Susie*. Beth Bailey examines courtship practices in *From Front Porch to Back Seat*.

75. Being raped while "parked" became a new and powerful narrative of sexual danger for white women. Joan Cordle, who came of age in Alabama in the 1960s, recalls being told not to park with white boys not because it would harm her reputation or result in an unwanted pregnancy but because she might be raped by roving gangs of black youth. When a white girl in her community was raped this way, there was an unspoken judgment that her decision to park with her date made her at least partially responsible for her assault (Jackie Cordle Paper, May 2002 [in possession of author]).

76. "Sailor's Tie Is Only Lead in Rape Try," *Norfolk Virginian-Pilot*, May 12, 1949.

77. Ibid.; "Sailor Confesses Rape after Being Identified by Blair Student Victim," *Norfolk Virginian-Pilot*, May 13, 1949; "Weatherspoon Given Life Term for Rape of 15-Year-Old Girl."

78. "Woman, 23, Is Raped, Companion Beaten," *Richmond Times-Dispatch*, March 25, 1957; *Commonwealth v. Matthew Mack Callahan*, Common Law Order Book 18, pp. 259, 405, 408, 431, Richmond Hustings Court I, Richmond, Va. Callahan's wife insisted he was innocent and that he had been home with her at the time of the assault ("Made A Mistake," *Richmond Afro-American*, June 1, 1957).

79. "Taxi Drivers, Police, and Sailor Trap Fugitive in Park after Alleged Attempt to Attack Woman," *Norfolk Virginian-Pilot*, November 9, 1952; "Bricklayer, 26, Is Convicted of Attempted Rape," ibid., December 18, 1952; *Commonwealth v. Lester Sawyer*, Common Law Order Book 79, pp. 74, 110, 187, 246, Case File, Ended Law Causes December Term 1952, Pre-Sentencing Report, Norfolk Corporation Court I, Norfolk, Va.

80. *Commonwealth v. Garland Warren Marshall*, Case 8097, 8098, 8099, 8100; *Commonwealth v. Dan L. Thomas, Jr.*, Case 8101, 8102, 8103, 8104; *Commonwealth v. William Robinson*, Case 8105, 8106, 8107, 8108; *Commonwealth v. John Camillous Smith*, Case 8109, 8110, 8111, 8112, Circuit Court of Fairfax County, Fairfax, Va. The four were also charged with a similar assault on a black woman parked with her black companion. They received twenty years for the second rape count, to be served concurrently. The charge against the black couple suggests that the four went out specifically seeking women in compromising circumstances on lover's lanes.

81. "Police Hold Woman; Doubt Story of Rape," *Richmond Afro-American*, August 4, 1951; "Woman Tells Police 5 'Men' Assaulted Her," ibid., August 11, 1951; "1 of Richmond Five Freed of Attack Count," ibid., August 18, 1951; "Woman Not Sure; Free 5 in Attack," ibid., September 1, 1951; "One of 5 Negroes Acquitted of Rape of 25-Year-Old White Woman in Field," *Richmond News-Leader*, August 10, 1951; "Four Negro Boys Won Outright Acquittals in Charges of Raping 25-Year-Old White Woman," ibid., August 23, 1951.

82. Sam Legions's conviction for rape was overturned by the Virginia Supreme Court of Appeals in 1943 after the court ruled that the victim's husband's feeble attempts to protect his wife were laughable and thus made his account and his wife's account of rape unbelievable. See *Legions v. Commonwealth*, 181 Va. 89 (1943). A judge made a similar comment concerning a case in South Carolina in 1933. See *State v. Floyd*, 174 SC 288 (1934).

83. See Pre-Sentence Investigation, John Camillous Smith, March 23, 1956, p. 2, *Commonwealth v. John Camillous Smith*, Felonious Assault No. 8110, Circuit Court of Fairfax County, Fairfax, Va.

84. "Redhead Says Hubby, Helper Attacked Her"; "Redhead Alters Story Is Fined, Jailed"; *Commonwealth v. Raymond Matthews, Commonwealth v. Floyd Jewett*, Common Law Order Book 111, pp. 106, 151, Richmond Hustings Court I, Richmond, Va. A similar case in Georgia resulted in a conviction of the white man, and the Georgia Supreme Court upheld his conviction. See *Williams v. State*, 206 Ga. 107 (1949). The decision does not state Williams's sentence, nor does it indicate whether or not the black man, James Dunn, was also convicted, since he did not appeal his case.

85. "Blond Accused," *Richmond Afro-American*, December 19, 1959.

86. *Commonwealth v. George Washington*, Proceedings from Police Court, September 22, 1959, Transcript, 8–9, Criminal Section Files, 1952–63, Box "1959 A–Y" Richmond Hustings Court Papers, LOVA. The defense also asked the witness if her husband had accused her of being unfaithful. She answered that though he never accused her outright, he was extremely jealous, to the point that he refused to allow her to talk with bill collectors (Transcript, 14).

87. "Portsmouth Attack Case Gets Another Hung Jury," *Richmond Afro-*

American, June 20, 1953; "Two Rape Juries Hung," *Norfolk Journal and Guide,* June 20, 1953; *Commonwealth v. Leon Woodley,* Common Law Order Book 47, pp. 34, 92, 105, 242, 292, Portsmouth Hustings Court, Portsmouth, Va.

88. "Bi-Racial Rape Trial Enters Second Day," *Norfolk Virginian-Pilot,* December 8, 1959; "Rape Trial Ends with Hung Jury," ibid., December 9, 1959; "Co-Defendant on Charge of Rape of County Woman Goes on Trial," ibid., January 16, 1959; "Man Acquitted by Hustings Jury in Rape of Norfolk County Woman," *Portsmouth Star,* January 17, 1960; "Two Men Deny White Woman's Charges; Jury Is Deadlocked," *Norfolk Journal and Guide,* December 12, 1959; *Commonwealth v. Philip Holley,* Common Law Order Book 54, pp. 354, 418, 421, 502, and *Commonwealth v. Drexel Williams,* Common Law Order Book 54, pp. 355, 410, 493, 494, Portsmouth Hustings Court, Portsmouth, Va.

89. Rise, *Martinsville Seven,* 16. The quote appeared in Taylor's statement to police (ibid., 169 n. 28).

90. This analysis focuses primarily on cases in which black men were acquitted or received lenient sentences. I suspect that, similar to cases between 1900 and 1945, many more men (in addition to those whose case records I was able to review) were released long before they completed their sentences, and part of the justifications for those releases likely included allegations about the victim's sexual behavior. By the 1950s, most decisions regarding early release were made by a parole board rather than the governor, and because parole board records are closed to the public, I cannot draw conclusions from these additional cases.

91. See Partington, "Incidence of the Death Penalty," 64–67, table 1.

92. *King v. Commonwealth,* 165 Va. 843 (1936).

93. The court tried approximately fifty-one cases of rape, attempted rape, or statutory rape. Races of the participants were determined through marriage records, if available, or through newspaper accounts. The one white-on-black case in Charlottesville I discovered was tried in the Albemarle County Circuit Court.

94. See Egemonye, "Treat Her Like a Lady"; Edwards, *Gendered Strife,* 184–217; Edwards, "Sexual Violence"; Jennings, "Us Colored Women"; Giddings, *When and Where I Enter,* 321–22; D'Emilio and Freedman, *Intimate Matters,* 215–21; Wolfe, *Daughters of Canaan,* 77–79; Jacqueline Jones, *Labor of Love,* 37–38, 94–95, 149, 150; and Hunter, *To 'Joy My Freedom,* 11–12, 33–34.

95. *Commonwealth v. Allen Gammon,* Petition for Conditional Pardon, Probation and Parole Report, December 15, 1947, EP.

96. "White Man Charged with Rape on Feebleminded Woman Gets Fine of $20," *Norfolk Journal and Guide,* October 16, 1948.

97. "Rape of Expectant Mother by White Farmer Draws $350 Fine," *Norfolk Journal and Guide,* October 16, 1948.

98. Accounts of the assault are taken from Probation and Parole Office Report, W. R. Banton, March 30, 1948, *Commonwealth v. Carl R. Burleson,* "Parole Board" Folder, Governor Battle Papers, Box 88, LOVA; and *Davis v. Commonwealth,* 186 Va. 936 (1948); as well as articles in both the *Norfolk Journal and Guide* and the *Richmond Afro-American.*

99. Probation and Parole Office Report, W. R. Banton, March 30, 1948, *Commonwealth v. Leonard Davis,* "Parole Board" Folder, Governor Battle Papers, Box 88, LOVA.

100. "State Opposes Appeal of Richmond Policemen Convicted of Rape," *Norfolk Journal and Guide*, October 18, 1947.

101. *Davis v. Commonwealth*, 186 Va. 936 (1948).

102. "Two Richmond Officers Convicted in Rape Case," *Norfolk Journal and Guide*, January 25, 1947.

103. Ibid. The *Guide's* complaints about the legal system's treatment of black women who accused black men also held true for white men accused by white women. When race was not a factor, most courts did not severely punish men convicted of rape, if they punished them at all.

104. Petition, undated, *Commonwealth v. Burleson* and *Commonwealth v. Davis*, "Parole Board" Folder, Governor Battle Papers, Box 88, LOVA.

105. Resolution from the Association for Justice in Virginia and America, September 2, 1949, *Commonwealth v. Burleson* and *Commonwealth v. Davis*, Folder B-2, Governor Tuck Papers, Box 97, LOVA.

106. Virginia's parole board records are not open to the public; consequently, it is impossible to determine who received parole and when.

107. "White Man Held on $7,500 Bond on Rape Charge," *Norfolk Journal and Guide*, November 23, 1946; "White Seaman Held on Attempted Rape Charge," ibid., August 21, 1948.

108. "Brutal Attack on Matron, 30," *Richmond Afro-American*, April 28, 1951; "Red-Haired Cabbie Held without Bail in Attack," ibid., May 5, 1951; "Cabbie Beats Assault Rap but Gets Ten Years," ibid., June 23, 1951.

109. "2 Virginia Men Get 3 Years for Abducting Housewife," *Richmond Afro-American*, December 19, 1953. The third white man involved in the attack had yet to face trial when the article appeared.

110. "Maid Reports Assault Case 5 Days Late," *Richmond Afro-American*, August 25, 1953; "Charge Blond with Attack on Housemaid," ibid., September 5, 1953.

111. "Suffolk Blond 'Not Guilty,'" *Richmond Afro-American*, February 20, 1954.

112. "Farmville Girl, 12, Attacked in Woods, White Man, 29, Held," *Richmond Afro-American*, June 2, 1951; "Accused Farmville Attacker Indicted," ibid., June 16, 1951; "Judge Okays Mental Exam for Man Held in Attack of Girls," ibid., June 30, 1951; "Molester of Girl Guilty," ibid., November 10, 1951.

113. "Attack Charged by Babysitter," *Richmond Afro-American*, August 19, 1950; "Rape Charge Placed against Local Man," *Charlottesville Daily Progress*, July 26, 1950; "Alleged Rapist Bound to Jury," ibid., August 11, 1950; "Rape Evidence Heard Here," ibid., February 26, 1951; "Elkins Acquitted of Rape Charge," ibid., February 27, 1951; *Commonwealth v. Thomas Elkins, Jr.*, Law Orders Book 2, pp. 377, 380, 410, 419, Circuit Court of Albemarle County, Charlottesville, Va. An account of Dr. Ralph Brown's testimony appeared in "Elkins Acquitted of Rape Charge."

114. L. B. West to Governor Trinkle, October 26, 1923, *Commonwealth v. William Griffin*, Petition for Conditional Pardon, November 15–November 30, 1923, EP.

115. W. C. Bibb to Governor Trinkle, August 25, 1922, *Commonwealth v. Tom Desper*, August 24–September 17, 1922, EP.

116. "Two Whites Accused of Savage Rape Freed on Minor Bond," *Norfolk Journal and Guide*, July 22, 1950. The paper did not report the disposition of the two men's case.

117. "Free White Soldier of Rape Attempt," *Norfolk Journal and Guide*, January 5, 1946.

118. "Teen-Agers Say White Men Molested Them," *Richmond Afro-American*, August 25, 1951; "Jury to Sift Attack Count," ibid., September 8, 1951; "Free Ashland Man of Attack Count," ibid., September 29, 1951.

119. "White Youth Accused of Attack Is Free 48 Hours," *Richmond Afro-American*, August 4, 1951; "State's Attorney Called Lax on Girl's Rape Report," ibid., August 11, 1951; "Goochland Citizens to Press for Action on Attack Attempt," ibid., August 18, 1951; "White Lad Indicted in Attack on Girl," ibid., October 27, 1951.

120. *Commonwealth v. Harold Parrish*, Common Law Order Book 9, pp. 155, 165, Circuit Court of Goochland County, Goochland, Va.

121. "White Man, 25, Held in Attack of Girl, 16," *Richmond Afro-American*, September 16, 1950.

122. "Disrobed Her at Point of Gun, Girl, 16, Says," *Richmond Afro-American*, November 25, 1950; "Mill Worker Clear in Virginia Attack Case," ibid., November 21, 1950. Quotation is from ibid., November 25, 1950.

123. "7 Colored to Die; 1 White Reprieve," *Richmond Afro-American*, January 13, 1951.

124. "Two Blondes Fined for Attempted Criminal Attack on 23-Year-Old Woman," *Richmond Afro-American*, August 31, 1957; Ellerson's quote appeared in "Assault Case Fines Draw Hot Criticism," *Richmond Afro-American*, September 7, 1957.

125. "No Crime to Rape Negro Women in the Southland," *Norfolk Journal and Guide*, September 29, 1951.

126. "Wish I Had a Nickel for Every Man Who Said 'Hello Baby,' " *Richmond Afro-American*, November 10, 1956.

127. "Search for Women Starts Near Riot," *Richmond Afro-American*, September 22, 1956; "Seven Men Are Convicted for Disorder in Culpeper Riot," ibid., October 6, 1956.

128. "Husband Slays Wolf Whistler," *Richmond Afro-American*, September 1, 1956; "Handyman Guilty of 'Wolf Whistle' Slaying," ibid., October 27, 1956; "Freed in Wolf Whistle Death," ibid., November 17, 1956.

129. "Mashers Molest Women, Police Look Other Way," *Richmond Afro-American*, September 1, 1956.

130. "Girl Held for Slaying White Man," *Norfolk Journal and Guide*, May 16, 1959; "Jury Refuses to Indict Girl for Slaying Nottoway White Man," ibid., June 6, 1959. Why the two couples were together is unclear. The articles described the group together on a "tryst." Since the charges of statutory rape were brought by the thirteen-year-old's mother, it is possible that the sexual relations were not forcible rape. The black girl's age, however, should have made her consent irrelevant.

131. John A. Hornsby to Governor Byrd, August 6, 1927, *Commonwealth v. John Wood*, Petition for Commutation, January 1–January 20, 1928, EP.

132. "Assault Warrant Sworn against Hospital Worker," *Charlottesville Daily Progress*, January 1, 1948; "Authorities Probe Alleged Hospital Assault Attempts," ibid., January 9, 1948; *Commonwealth v. Lewis Washington*, Law Orders Book 2, pp. 167, 170, 186, Circuit Court of Albemarle County, Charlottesville, Va.

Conclusion

1. *Commonwealth v. Alfred Wright*, Law Order Book 1, p. 511, Circuit Court of Appomattox County, Appomattox, Va.

2. "Charley Crumley Charged with Attack on Miss Newell Saved from Mob," *Richmond Times-Dispatch*, February 12, 1909.

3. "Mob Threatens Jail," *Richmond Times-Dispatch*, October 27, 1925; "Negro Is Freed, Trouble Feared," ibid., November 8, 1925.

4. "Taylor Found Guilty, Given 3 Years," *Richmond Times-Dispatch*, September 28, 1931.

5. See *Spurlock v. Mississippi*, 158 Miss. 281 (1930), and *Clark v. Alabama*, 239 Ala. 380 (1940).

6. See *North Carolina v. Garner*, 129 NC 537 (1901), and *Walker v. Georgia*, 194 Ga. 727 (1942).

7. See *Milton v. Mississippi*, 142 Miss. 364 (1926), and *Pew v. Mississippi*, 172 Miss. 885 (1935).

8. See *Wright v. Georgia*, 184 Ga. 63 (1937); *Thomas v. Georgia*, 213 Ga. 237 (1957); *State v. Finger*, 131 NC 781 (1902); *Harper v. Georgia*, 210 Ga. 10 (1946); *Rider v. Georgia*, 195 Ga. 656 (1943); *Milton v. Mississippi*, 142 Miss. 364 (1926); *Richardson v. Mississippi*, 196 Miss. 560 (1944); *South Carolina v. Floyd*, 174 SC 288 (1934); *South Carolina v. Sanders*, 92 SC 427 (1912); *Spurlock v. Mississippi*, 158 Miss. 281 (1930); and *Pew v. Mississippi*, 172 Miss. 885 (1935). These cases are discussed more fully in Lisa Dorr, "Messin' White Women," 426–33.

9. LaFree, "Male Power and Female Victimization," 311–28.

10. "Imprisoned 15 Months on a Lie, Culpeper Man Now Hopes for Freedom," *Washington Post*, December 20, 1995.

Courthouse Archives

Albemarle County Circuit Court, Charlottesville, Va.
Allegheny County Circuit Court, Covington, Va.
Amelia County Circuit Court, Amelia Court House, Va.
Amherst County Circuit Court, Amherst, Va.
Appomattox County Circuit Court, Appomattox, Va.
Augusta County Circuit Court, Staunton, Va.
Bedford County Circuit Court, Bedford, Va.
Botetourt County Circuit Court, Fincastle, Va.
Buckingham County Circuit Court, Buckingham, Va.
Caroline County Circuit Court, Bowling Green, Va.
Charles City County Circuit Court, Charles City, Va.
Charlottesville Corporation Court, Charlottesville, Va.
Chesterfield County Circuit Court, Chesterfield, Va.
Culpeper County Circuit Court, Culpeper, Va.
Danville Corporation Court, Danville, Va.
Dinwiddie County Circuit Court, Dinwiddie, Va.
Elizabeth City County Circuit Court (now Hampton Corporation Court),
    Hampton, Va.
Fairfax County Circuit Court, Fairfax, Va,
Fluvanna County Circuit Court, Palmyra, Va.
Franklin County Circuit Court, Rocky Mount, Va.
Frederick County Circuit Court, Winchester, Va.
Goochland County Circuit Court, Goochland, Va.
Halifax County Circuit Court, Halifax, Va.
Hampton Corporation Court, Hampton, Va.
Hanover County Circuit Court, Hanover, Va.
Henrico County Circuit Court, Richmond, Va.
Henry County Circuit Court, Martinsville, Va.
Hopewell Corporation Court, Hopewell, Va.
Isle of Wight County Circuit Court, Isle of Wight, Va.
James City County Circuit Court, Williamsburg, Va.

King William County Circuit Court, King William, Va.
Loudoun County Circuit Court, Leesburg, Va.
Louisa County Circuit Court, Louisa, Va.
Lynchburg Corporation Court, Lynchburg, Va.
Madison County Circuit Court, Madison, Va.
Mecklenburg County Circuit Court, Boydton, Va.
Montgomery County Circuit Court, Christiansburg, Va.
Nelson County Circuit Court, Lovingston, Va.
New Kent County Circuit Court, New Kent, Va.
Newport News Corporation Court, Newport News, Va.
Norfolk Corporation Court, Parts I and II, Norfolk, Va.
Norfolk County Circuit Court (now Chesapeake County), Chesapeake, Va.
Northumberland County Circuit Court, Heathsville, Va.
Nottoway County Circuit Court, Nottoway, Va.
Page County Circuit Court, Luray, Va.
Petersburg Corporation Court, Petersburg, Va.
Pittsylvania County Circuit Court, Chatham, Va.
Portsmouth Hustings Court, Portsmouth, Va.
Powhatan County Circuit Court, Powhatan, Va.
Prince Edward County Circuit Court, Farmville, Va.
Prince George County Circuit Court, Prince George, Va.
Princess Anne County Circuit Court, Princess Anne, Va.
Richmond Hustings Court, Parts I and II, Richmond, Va.
Roanoke Corporation Court, Roanoke, Va.
Roanoke County Circuit Court, Salem, Va.
Southampton County Circuit Court, Courtland, Va.
Spotsylvania County Circuit Court, Spotsylvania, Va.
Suffolk County Circuit Court, Suffolk, Va.
Sussex County Circuit Court, Sussex, Va.
Warwick County Circuit Court (now part of Newport News Corporation
    Court), Newport News, Va.
Westmoreland County Circuit Court, Montross, Va.
Winchester Corporation Court, Winchester, Va.
Winchester County Circuit Court, Winchester, Va.

Manuscript Collections

Alderman Library, the University of Virginia, Charlottesville, Va.
    Papers of the NAACP on Microfilm
Library of Virginia Archives, Richmond, Va.
    Papers of Governor J. Lindsay Almond Jr.
    Papers of Governor John S. Battle
    Papers of Governor Harry F. Byrd
    Papers of Governor Colgate Darden
    Papers of Westmoreland Davis
    Ended Causes, Richmond Hustings Court I
    Franklin County Court Determined Papers

Henry County Court Determined Papers
Papers of William Hodges Mann
Papers of Governor Andrew Jackson Montague
Papers of John Garland Pollard
Papers of James H. Price
Roanoke Corporation Court Records
Secretary of the Commonwealth, Executive Papers, Accession 35196
Papers of Governor Thomas B. Stanley
Papers of Governor Claude A. Swanson
Papers of Governor E. Lee Trinkle
Papers of Governor William M. Tuck

Newspapers

Charlottesville Daily Progress
Christiansburg Messenger
Culpeper Exponent
Danville Register
Fairfax Herald
Fauquier Democrat
Fredericksburg Daily Star
Harrisonburg Daily News-Record
Loudoun Times-Mirror
Lynchburg Daily Advance
Norfolk Journal and Guide
Portsmouth Star
Richmond Afro-American
Richmond Evening Journal
Richmond News-Leader
Richmond Planet
Richmond Times-Dispatch
Richmond Virginian
Roanoke Times and World News
Virginian Pilot and Norfolk Landmark

Published Sources

Acker, James R. "Social Science in Supreme Court Death Penalty Cases: Citation Practices and their Implications." *Justice Quarterly* 8 (December 1991): 431–33.

Arnold, Marybeth Hamilton. " 'The Life of a Citizen in the Hands of a Woman': Sexual Assault in New York City, 1790 to 1820." In *Passion and Power: Sexuality in History*, edited by Kathy Peiss and Christina Simmons, 35–56. Philadelphia: Temple University Press, 1989.

Avary, Myrta Lockett. *Dixie after the War*. New York, 1906.

Ayers, Edward L. *Promise of the New South*. New York: Oxford University Press, 1993.

——. *Vengeance and Justice: Crime and Punishment in the Nineteenth-Century American South*. New York: Oxford University Press, 1984.

Bailey, Beth. *From Front Porch to Back Seat: Courtship in Twentieth-Century America*. Baltimore: Johns Hopkins University Press, 1989.

Baldus, David C., George Woodworth, and Charles A. Pulaski Jr. *Equal Justice and the Death Penalty: A Legal and Empirical Analysis*. Boston: Northeastern University Press, 1990.

Banner, Stuart. *The Death Penalty: An American History*. Cambridge: Harvard University Press, 2002.

Bardaglio, Peter. "Rape and the Law in the Old South: 'Calculated to Excite Indignation in Every Heart.'" *Journal of Southern History* 60 (November 1994): 749–72.

——. *Reconstructing the Household: Families, Sex, and the Law in the Nineteenth-Century South*. Chapel Hill: University of North Carolina Press, 1995.

Bederman, Gail. "Civilization and the Decline of Middle-Class Manliness: Ida B. Wells's Anti-Lynching Campaign, 1892–1894." In *Gender and American History since 1890*, edited by Barbara Melosh, 207–39. London: Routledge Press, 1993.

——. *Manliness and Civilization: A Cultural History of Gender and Race in the United States, 1880–1917*. Chicago: University of Chicago Press, 1995.

Beers, Paul G. "The Wythe County Lynching of Raymond Bird: Progressivism vs. Mob Violence in the '20s." *Appalachian Journal* 21 (Fall 1994): 34–59.

Bellesiles, Michael A., ed. *Lethal Imagination: Violence and Brutality in American History*. New York: New York University Press, 1999.

Bennett, W. Lance. *Reconstructing Reality in the Courtroom: Justice and Judgement in American Culture*. New Brunswick: Rutgers University Press, 1981.

Berry, Mary Frances. "Judging Morality: Sexual Behavior and Legal Consequences in the Late-Nineteenth-Century South." *Journal of American History* 78 (December 1991): 835–56.

——. *The Pig Farmer's Daughter and Other Tales of American Justice*. New York: Knopf, 1999.

Block, Sharon. "Coerced Sex in British North America, 1700–1820." Ph.D. diss., Princeton University, 1995.

——. "Rape without Women: Print Culture and the Politicization of Rape, 1765–1815." *Journal of American History* 89 (December 2002): 849–68.

Boris, Eileen. "'You Wouldn't Want One of 'Em Dancing with Your Wife': Racialized Bodies on the Job in World War II." *American Quarterly* 50 (March 1998): 77–108.

Breines, Wini. *Young, White, and Miserable: Growing up Female in the Fifties*. Boston: Beacon Press, 1992.

Brewer, Jon, and John Styles, eds. *An Ungovernable People: The English and their Law in the Seventeenth and Eighteenth Centuries*. New Brunswick: Rutgers University Press, 1980.

Brown, Elsa Barkley, and Gregg D. Kimball. "Mapping the Terrain of Black Richmond." *Journal of Urban History* 21 (March 1995): 296–346.

Brownmiller, Susan. *Against Her Will: Men, Women, and Rape*. New York: Bantam Books, 1975.

Bruce, Philip Alexander. *The Plantation Negro as Freeman: Observations on His Character, Condition, and Prospects in Virginia*. New York: G. P. Putnam, 1889.

Brundage, W. Fitzhugh. *Lynching in the New South: Georgia and Virginia, 1880–1930*. Urbana: University of Illinois Press, 1993.

——. "The Roar on the Other Side of Silence: Black Resistance and White Violence in the American South." In *Under Sentence of Death: Lynching in the New South*, edited by W. Fitzhugh Brundage, 271–91. Chapel Hill: University of North Carolina Press, 1997.

——. "The Varn Mill Riot of 1891: Lynchings, Attempted Lynchings, and Justice in Ware County, Georgia." *Georgia Historical Quarterly* 78 (1994): 257–80.

——, ed. *Under the Sentence of Death: Lynching in the New South*. Chapel Hill: University of North Carolina Press, 1997.

Buckley, Thomas E. "Unfixing Race: Class, Power, and Identity in an Interracial Family." *Virginia Magazine of History and Biography* 102 (July 1994): 349–80.

Burgess, Ann, and Lynda Holmstrom. *Rape Crisis and Recovery*. Bowie, Md.: Robert Brady, 1979.

Bynum, Victoria. *Unruly Women: The Politics of Social and Sexual Control in the Old South*. Chapel Hill: University of North Carolina Press, 1992.

Capeci, Dominic J., Jr. *The Lynching of Cleo Wright*. Lexington: University of Kentucky Press, 1998.

Carter, Dan T. *Scottsboro: A Tragedy of the American South*. Baton Rouge: Louisiana State University Press, 1969.

Cash, W. J. *The Mind of the South*. 1941. Reprint, New York: Vintage, 1991.

Cecelski, David S., and Timothy B. Tyson, eds. *Democracy Betrayed: The Wilmington Race Riot of 1898 and Its Legacy*. Chapel Hill: University of North Carolina Press, 1998.

Chamberlain, Bernard Peyton. *The Negro and Crime in Virginia*. Charlottesville: Publication of the University of Virginia Phelps-Stokes Fellowship Papers, 1936.

Chaytor, Miranda. "Husband(ry): Narratives of Rape in the Seventeenth Century." *Gender and History* 7 (November 1995): 378–407.

Clark, Anna. *Women's Silence, Men's Violence: Sexual Assault in England, 1770–1845*. London: Pandora, 1987.

Clark, Thomas D. *Southern Country Editor*. Indianapolis, Ind.: Bobbs-Merrill Co., 1948.

Cleaver, Eldridge. *Soul on Ice*. New York: Delta Books, 1968.

Clinton, Catherine, and Michele Gillespie, eds. *The Devil's Lane: Sex and Race in the Early South*. New York: Oxford University Press, 1997.

Collins, Patricia Hill. "The Tie that Binds: Race, Gender, and U.S. Violence." *Ethnic and Racial Studies* 21 (September 1998): 917–38.

Coughlin, Anne M. "Sex and Guilt." *Virginia Law Review* 84 (February 1998): 1–46.

Dailey, Jane. *Before Jim Crow: The Politics of Race in Post-Emancipation Virginia*. Chapel Hill: University of North Carolina Press, 2000.

Dailey, Jane, Glenda Gilmore, and Bryant Simon, eds. *Jumping Jim Crow: South-*

ern Politics from Civil War to Civil Rights. Princeton: Princeton University Press, 2000.

Daniels, Jessie. *White Lies: Race, Class, Gender, and Sexuality in White Supremacist Discourse.* London: Routledge Press, 1995.

Davies, Nick. *White Lies: Rape, Murder, and Justice Texas Style.* New York: Pantheon, 1991.

Davis, Angela Y. "Rape, Racism, and the Myth of the Black Rapist." In *Women Race and Class*, by Angela Y. Davis, 172–201. New York: Vintage Books, 1981.

——. *Women, Race, and Class.* New York: Vintage Books, 1981.

Dayton, Cornelia Hughes. *Women before the Bar: Gender, Law, and Society in Connecticut, 1710–1790.* Chapel Hill: University of North Carolina Press, 1995.

D'Cruze, Shani. *Crimes of Outrage: Sex, Violence, and Victorian Working Women.* DeKalb, Ill.: Northern Illinois University Press, 1998.

D'Emilio, John, and Estelle Freedman. *Intimate Matters: A History of Sexuality in America.* New York: Harper and Row, 1988.

Deutsch, Helene. *Psychology of Women: A Psychoanalytic Interpretation.* New York: Grune and Stratton, 1940.

Dittmer, John. *Black Georgia in the Progressive Era, 1900–1920.* Urbana: University of Illinois Press, 1977.

Dollard, John. *Caste and Class in a Southern Town.* New York: Anchor Books, 1937.

Dorin, Dennis D. "Two Different Worlds: Criminologists, Justice, and Racial Discrimination in the Imposition of Capital Punishment in Rape Cases." *Journal of Criminal Law and Criminology* 72 (1981): 1667–98.

Dorr, Gregory Michael. " 'Assuring America's Place in the Sun': Ivey Foreman Lewis and the Teaching of Eugenics at the University of Virginia." *Journal of Southern History* 66 (May 2000): 257–96.

——. "Segregation's Science: The American Eugenics Movement and Virginia, 1900–1980." Ph.D. diss., University of Virginia, 2000.

Dorr, Lisa Lindquist. " 'Another Negro-Did-It Crime': Black-on-White Rape and Protest in Virginia, 1945–1960." In *Sex Without Consent: Sexual Coercion in America*, edited by Merril D. Smith, 247–64. New York: New York University Press, 2001.

——. "Arm in Arm: Gender, Eugenics, and Virginia's Racial Integrity Acts of the 1920s." *Journal of Women's History* 11 (Spring 1999): 143–66.

——. " 'Messin' White Women': White Women, Black Men, and Rape in Virginia, 1900–1960." Ph.D. diss., University of Virginia, 2000.

——. "Victims of Assault and Unkind Opinion: Rape, the Legal System, and Public Opinion." *IRIS: A Journal for Women* 41 (Fall 2000): 32–35.

Dripps, Donald A. "Beyond Rape: An Essay on the Difference between the Presence of Force and the Absence of Consent." *Columbia Law Review* 92 (1992): 1780–1809.

Dubinsky, Karen. *Improper Advances: Rape and Heterosexual Conflict in Ontario, 1880–1929.* Chicago: University of Chicago Press, 1993.

Du Bois, W. E. B. *Darkwater.* New York: Harcourt, Brace, and Company, 1921.

Dunlap, Leslie K. "The Reform of Rape Law and the Problem of White Men: Age-of-Consent Campaigns in the South, 1880–1910." In *Love, Sex, Race: Crossing Boundaries in North American History*, edited by Martha Hodes, 352–72. New York: New York University Press, 1999.

Durr, Virginia Foster. *Outside the Magic Circle*. New York: Simon and Schuster, 1985.

Edwards, Laura F. "The Disappearance of Susan Daniel and Henderson Cooper: Gender and Narratives of Political Conflict in the Reconstruction-Era U.S. South." *Feminist Studies* 22 (Summer 1996): 363–86.

——. *Gendered Strife and Confusion: The Political Culture of Reconstruction*. Urbana: University of Illinois Press, 1997.

——. "Sexual Violence, Gender, Reconstruction, and the Extension of Patriarchy in Granville County, North Carolina." *North Carolina Historical Review* 68 (July 1991): 237–60.

Egemonye, Uche. "Treat Her Like a Lady: Judicial Paternalism and the Justification for Assaults on Black Women." In *Lethal Imagination: Violence and Brutality in American History*, edited by Michael Bellesiles, 283–94. New York: New York University Press, 1999.

Estrich, Susan. *Real Rape*. Cambridge: Harvard University Press, 1986.

Fanon, Frantz. *Black Skin, White Masks*. New York: Grove Press, 1967.

Feimster, Crystal Nicole. "Ladies and Lynching: The Gendered Discourse of Mob Violence in the New South, 1880–1930." Ph.D, diss., Princeton University, 2000.

Fields, Barbara. "Race and Ideology in American History." In *Race, Region, and Reconstruction: Essays in Honor of C. Vann Woodward*, edited by J. Morgan Kousser, 143–78. New York: Oxford University Press, 1982.

Finnegan, Terence. " 'At the Hands of Parties Unknown': Lynching in Mississippi and South Carolina, 1881–1940." Ph.D. diss., University of Illinois at Urbana Champaign, 1993.

——. "Who Were the Victims of Lynching?: Evidence from Mississippi and South Carolina, 1881–1940." In *Varieties of Southern History: New Essays on a Region and Its People*, edited by Bruce Clayton and John A. Salmond, 79–98. Westport: Greenwood Press, 1996.

Florida Civil Liberties Union. "Rape: Selective Electrocution Based on Race." 1965 Microfiche. Glen Rock, N.J.: Microfilming Corporation of America, 1976.

Forrester, John. "Rape, Seduction, and Psychoanalysis." In *Rape*, edited by Sylvana Tomaselli and Roy Porter, 57–83. Oxford: Basil Blackwell, 1986.

Fout, John C., and Maura Shaw Tantillo, eds. *American Sexual Politics: Sex, Gender, and Race since the Civil War*. Chicago: University of Chicago Press, 1993.

Fox, Greer Litton. " 'Nice Girl': The Social Control of Women through a Value Construct." *Signs* 2 (Summer 1977): 70–75.

Francisco, Patricia Weaver. *Telling: A Memoir of Rape and Recovery*. New York: Harper Collins, 1999.

Frank, Martin M. "The Ladykiller." *Cosmopolitan* 143 (October 1957): 68–83.

Frankenberg, Ruth. *White Women, Race Matters: The Social Construction of Whiteness*. Minneapolis: University of Minnesota Press, 1993.

Fredrickson, George. *The Black Image in the White Mind: The Debate on African American Character and Destiny, 1817–1914*. New York: Harper and Row, 1971.

Friedman, Lawrence M. *Crime and Punishment in American History*. New York: Basic Books, 1993.

——. "Law, Lawyers, and Popular Culture." *Yale Law Journal* 98 (1989): 1579–1606.

Fuller, Hugh N. *Criminal Justice in Virginia*. New York: The Century Co., 1931.

Genovese, Eugene. *Roll Jordan Roll: The World the Slaves Made*. New York: Vintage Books, 1972.

Giddings, Paula. *When and Where I Enter: The Impact of Black Women on Race and Sex in America*. New York: Bantam Books, 1984.

Gilmore, Glenda. *Gender and Jim Crow: Women and the Politics of White Supremacy in North Carolina*. Chapel Hill: University of North Carolina Press, 1996.

——. "Murder, Memory, and the Flight of the Incubus." In *Democracy Betrayed: The Wilmington Race Riot of 1898 and Its Legacy*, edited by David S. Cecelski and Timothy B. Tyson, 73–94. Chapel Hill: University of North Carolina Press, 1998.

Goffman, Erving. *The Presentation of the Self in Everyday Life*. Garden City: Doubleday Books, 1959.

Goodman, James. *Stories of Scottsboro: The Rape Case that Shocked 1930s America and Revived the Struggle for Equality*. New York: Pantheon Books, 1994.

Greenhalgh, Paul. *Ephemeral Vistas: The Expositions Universelles, Great Exhibitions, and World Fairs, 1851–1939*. Manchester: Manchester University Press, 1988.

Griffin, Susan. *Rape: The Politics of Consciousness*. San Francisco: Harper and Row, 1986.

Grimes, Ruth-Ellen Marie Jacqueline. "Race, Rape, and the Death Penalty: Revisited." Ph.D. diss., University of Toronto, 1993.

Gross, Ariela J. "Litigating Whiteness: Trials of Racial Determination in the Nineteenth-Century South." *Yale Law Journal* 108 (1998): 109–88.

Gullette, G. L. "Should Juries Fix the Punishment for Crimes?" *Virginia Law Review* 24 (February 1938): 462–66.

Guttmacher, Manfred, and Henry Weihofen. *Psychiatry and the Law*. New York: Norton, 1952.

Haag, Pamela. *Consent: Sexual Rights and the Transformation of American Liberalism*. Ithaca: Cornell University Press, 1999.

Hagood, Margaret Jarman. *Mothers of the South: Portraiture of the White Tenant Farm Woman*. 1939. Reprint, Charlottesville: University Press of Virginia, 1996.

Hale, Grace Elizabeth. "Deadly Amusements: Spectacle Lynchings and Southern Whiteness." In *Varieties of Southern History: New Essays on a Region and Its People*, edited by Bruce Clayton and John Salmond, 63–78. Westport, Conn.: Greenwood Press, 1996.

———. *Making Whiteness: The Culture of Segregation in the South, 1880–1940.* New York: Pantheon, 1998.

Hale, Sir Matthew. *The History of Pleas to the Crown I.* London: Professional Books, 1971.

Hall, Jacquelyn Dowd. *Revolt against Chivalry: Jessie Daniel Ames and the Women's Campaign against Lynching.* New York: Columbia University Press, 1974.

Hariman, Robert. "Performing the Laws: Popular Trials and Social Culture." In *Popular Trials: Rhetoric, Mass Media, and the Law,* edited by Robert Hariman, 17–30. Tuscaloosa: University of Alabama Press, 1990.

———. *Popular Trials: Rhetoric, Mass Media, and the Law.* Tuscaloosa: University of Alabama Press, 1990.

Hay, Douglas, et al., eds. *Albion's Fatal Tree: Crime and Society in Eighteenth-Century England.* London: Penguin Books, 1975.

———. "Property, Authority, and Criminal Law." In *Albion's Fatal Tree: Crime and Society in Eighteenth-Century England,* edited by Douglas Hay et al., 17–63. London: Penguin Books, 1975.

Herman, Judith Lewis. "Considering Sex Offenders: A Model of Addiction." In *Rape and Society: Readings on the Problem of Sexual Assault,* edited by Patricia Searles and Ronald J. Berger, 74–98. Boulder: Westview Press, 1995.

———. *Trauma and Recovery.* New York: Basic Books, 1992.

Hernton, Calvin C. *Sex and Racism in America.* New York: Doubleday, 1965.

Hewitt, Nancy A., and Suzanne Lebsock, eds. *Visible Women: New Essays on American Activism.* Urbana: University of Illinois Press, 1993.

Himes, Chester. *If He Hollers Let Him Go.* London: Sphere Books, 1945.

Hirsch, Susan F., and Mindie Lazarus-Black. Introduction to *Contested States: Law, Hegemony, and Resistance,* edited by Mindie Lazarus-Black and Susan F. Hirsch, 1–31. New York: Routledge, 1994.

Hodes, Martha. *White Women, Black Men: Illicit Sex in the Nineteenth-Century South.* New Haven: Yale University Press, 1997.

———, ed. *Love, Sex, Race: Crossing Boundaries in North American History.* New York: New York University Press, 1999.

———. "Sex across the Color Line: White Women and Black Men in the Nineteenth-Century American South." Ph.D. diss., Princeton University, 1991.

———. "The Sexualization of Reconstruction Politics: White Women and Black Men in the South after the Civil War." In *American Sexual Politics: Sex, Gender, and Race since the Civil War,* edited by John C. Fout and Maura Shaw Tantillo, 59–74. Chicago: University of Chicago Press, 1993.

Horowitz, Helen Lefkowitz, and Kathy Peiss, eds. *Love across the Color Line: The Letters of Alice Hanley to Channing Lewis.* Amherst: University of Massachusetts Press, 1996.

Howard, Walter T. *Lynchings: Extralegal Violence in Florida during the 1930s.* Selinsgrove: Susquehanna University Press, 1995.

Hunter, Robert J., Paige Heather Ralph, and James Marquart. "The Death Sentencing of Rapists in Pre-Furman Texas (1942–1971)." *American Journal of Criminal Law* 20 (Spring 1993): 313–37.

Hunter, Tera W. *To 'Joy My Freedom: Southern Black Women's Lives and Labors after the Civil War.* Cambridge: Harvard University Press, 1997.

James, Arthur W. *The State Becomes a Social Worker: An Administrative Interpretation.* Richmond: Garrett and Massey, 1942.

Jennings, Thelma. " 'Us Colored Women Had to Go through A Plenty': The Sexual Exploitation of African-American Slave Women." *Journal of Women's History* 1 (Winter 1991): 45–74.

Jones, Jacqueline. *Labor of Love, Labor of Sorrow: Black Women, Work, and Family from Slavery to the Present.* New York: Vintage, 1985.

Jones, James H. *Bad Blood: The Tuskegee Syphilis Experiment.* New York: Free Press, 1981.

Kantrowitz, Stephen. " 'One Man's Mob is Another Man's Militia': Violence, Manhood, and Authority in Reconstruction South Carolina." In *Jumping Jim Crow: Southern Politics from Civil War to Civil Rights*, edited by Jane Dailey, Glenda Gilmore, and Bryant Simon, 67–87. Princeton: Princeton University Press, 2000.

Kelley, Robin D. G. *Race Rebels: Culture, Politics, and the Black Working Class.* New York: The Free Press, 1994.

———. " 'We Are Not What We Seem': Rethinking Black Working-Class Opposition in the Jim Crow South." *Journal of American History* 80 (June 1993): 75–112.

Keve, Paul W. *The History of Corrections in Virginia.* Charlottesville: University Press of Virginia, 1986.

Kevles, Daniel. *In the Name of Eugenics: Genetics and the Uses of Human Heredity.* New York: Knopf, 1985.

King, Alexander. *Race Problems of the South: Proceedings of the First Annual Conference Held under the Auspices of the Southern Society for the Promotion of the Study of Race Conditions and Problems of the South.* Richmond, Va.: B. F. Johnson Publishing Co, 1900.

Klarman, Michael. "Is the Supreme Court Sometimes Irrelevant? Race and the Southern Criminal Justice System in the 1940s." *Journal of American History* 89 (June 2002): 119–53.

———. "The Racial Origins of Modern Criminal Procedure." *Michigan Law Review* 99 (October 2000): 48–97.

Kleck, Gary. "Racial Discrimination in Criminal Sentencing: A Critical Evaluation of the Evidence with Additional Evidence on the Death Penalty." *American Sociological Review* 46 (1981): 783–804.

Kluger, Richard. *Simple Justice: The Story of Brown v. Board of Education and Black America's Struggle for Equality.* New York: Vintage, 1977.

Kneedler, H. Lane. "Sexual Assault Law Reform in Virginia: A Legislative History." *Virginia Law Review* 68 (March 1982): 459–505.

Koeninger, Rupert C. "Capital Punishment in Texas, 1924–1968." *Crime and Delinquency* 15 (1969): 132–41.

Kopp, Sheldon B. "The Character Structure of Sex Offenders." *American Journal of Psychotherapy* 16 (1962): 64–70.

LaFree, Gary B. "The Effect of Sexual Stratification by Race on Official Reactions to Rape." *American Sociological Review* 45 (October 1982): 842–54.

——. "Male Power and Female Victimization: Towards a Theory of Interracial Rape." *American Journal of Sociology* 88 (1982): 311–28.

——. *Rape and Criminal Justice: The Social Construction of Sexual Assault*. Belmont, Calif.: Wadsworth, 1989.

Langum, David J. *Crossing over the Line: Legislating Morality and the Mann Act*. Chicago: University of Chicago Press, 1994.

Lazarus-Black, Mindie, and Susan F. Hirsch, eds., *Contested States: Law, Hegemony, and Resistance*. New York: Routledge, 1994.

Lebsock, Suzanne. *A Murder in Virginia: Southern Justice on Trial*. New York: Norton, 2003.

Lee, Harper. *To Kill a Mockingbird*. New York: J. B. Lippincott, 1960.

Lees, Susan. *Carnal Knowledge: Rape on Trial*. London: Hamish Hamilton, 1996.

Lindemann, Barbara S. " 'To Ravish and Carnally Know': Rape in Eighteenth-Century Massachusetts." *Signs* 10 (Autumn 1984): 63–83.

Litwack, Leon. *Trouble in Mind: Black Southerners in the Age of Jim Crow*. New York: Knopf, 1998.

Lockley, Timothy J. "Crossing the Race Divide: Interracial Sex in Antebellum Savannah." *Slavery and Abolition* 18 (December 1997): 159–73.

Lombardo, Paul M. "Three Generations, No Imbeciles: New Light on *Buck v. Bell*." *New York University Law Review* 60 (April 1985): 30–62.

Love, Spencie. " 'Noted Physician Fatally Injured': Charles Drew and the Legend that Will Not Die." *Washington History* (Fall / Winter 1992–93): 5–19.

MacCannell, Dean. *The Tourist: A New Theory of the Leisure Class*. 1976. Reprint, New York: Schocken Books, 1989.

MacKinnon, Catharine A. *Toward a Feminist Theory of the State*. Cambridge: Harvard University Press, 1989.

MacLean, Nancy. *Behind the Mask of Chivalry: The Making of the Second Ku Klux Klan*. New York: Oxford University Press, 1994.

——. "White Women and Klan Violence in the 1920s." *Gender and History* 3 (Autumn 1991): 285–303.

Massey, James L. "The Ideology of Lynch Law: A Case Study of Southern Editorial Opinion." *Quarterly Journal of Ideology* 18 (June 1995): 65–85.

Matoesian, Gregory M. *Reproducing Rape: Domination through Talk in the Courtroom*. Chicago: University of Chicago Press, 1993.

May, Elaine Tyler. *Homeward Bound: American Families in the Cold War Era*. New York: Basic Books, 1988.

McCoy, Donald R., and Richard Ruetten. *Quest and Response: Minority Rights and the Truman Administration*. Lawrence, Kans.: University of Kansas Press, 1973.

McCulloch, Jock. *Black Peril, White Virtue: Sexual Crime in Southern Rhodesia, 1902–1935*. Bloomington: University of Indiana Press, 2000.

McGovern, James R. *Anatomy of a Lynching: The Killing of Claude Neal*. Baton Rouge: Louisiana State University Press, 1982.

McGuire, Hunter, and G. Frank Lydston. "Sexual Crimes among Southern Negroes." *Virginia Medical Monthly* 20 (May 1893): 105–25.

McLaurin, Melton. *Separate Pasts: Growing up White in the Segregated South*. 1987. Reprint, Athens: University of Georgia Press, 1998.

McMillen, Neil R. *Dark Journey: Black Mississippians in the Age of Jim Crow*. Urbana: University of Illinois Press, 1989.

Meier, August, and Elliott Rudwick. "Attorneys Black and White: A Case Study of Race Relations within the NAACP." *Journal of American History* 62 (March 1976): 913–46.

Meltsner, Michael. *Cruel and Unusual: The Supreme Court and Capital Punishment*. New York: Random House, 1993.

Merry, Sally Engle. "Courts as Performances: Domestic Violence Hearings in a Hawai'i Family Court." *Contested States: Law, Hegemony, and Resistance*, edited by Mindie Lazarus-Black and Susan F. Hirsch, 35–58. New York: Routledge, 1994.

Meyerowitz, Joanne, ed. *Not June Cleaver: Women and Gender in Postwar America*. Philadelphia: Temple University Press, 1994.

Miller, Vivian M. L. *Crime, Sexual Violence, and Clemency: Florida's Pardon Board and Penal System in the Progressive Era*. Gainesville: University Press of Florida, 2000.

Mills, Gary B. "Miscegenation and the Free Negro in Antebellum 'Anglo' Alabama: A Reexamination of Southern Race Relations." *Journal of American History* 68 (June 1981): 16–34.

Mitchell, Timothy. *Colonizing Egypt*. Berkeley: University of California Press, 1988.

Moody, Anne. *Coming of Age in Mississippi*. New York: Dell, 1968.

Motley, Mary Penick, ed. *The Invisible Soldier: The Experience of the Black Soldier, World War II*. Detroit: Wayne State University Press, 1975.

Muller, Eric L. "The Legal Defense Fund's Capital Punishment Campaign: The Distorting Influence of Death." *Yale Law and Policy Review* 4 (1985): 159–87.

Mumford, Kevin J. *Interzones: Black/White Sex Districts in Chicago and New York in the Early Twentieth Century*. New York: Columbia University Press, 1997.

Murchison, Kenneth, and Arthur J. Schwab. "Capital Punishment in Virginia." *Virginia Law Review* 58 (January 1972): 97–142.

Murray, Rolland Dante. "Beyond Macho: Literature, Masculinity, and Black Power." Ph.D. diss., University of Chicago, 2000.

Myers, Martha. *Race, Labor, and Punishment in the New South*. Columbus: Ohio State University Press, 1998.

Myrdal, Gunnar. *An American Dilemma: The Negro Problem and Modern Democracy*. 1944. Reprint, New York: Harper Torchbooks, 1962.

O'Brien, Gail Williams. *The Color of the Law: Race, Violence, and Justice in the Post–World War II South*. Chapel Hill: University of North Carolina Press, 1999.

Odem, Mary. "Cultural Representations and Social Contexts of Rape in the Early Twentieth Century." *Lethal Imagination: Violence and Brutality in American History*, edited by Michael Bellesiles, 353–72. New York: New York University Press, 1999.

Odem, Mary E., and Jody Clay-Warner, eds. *Confronting Rape and Sexual Assault*. Wilmington, Del.: SR Books, 1998.

Oshinsky, David. *Worse than Slavery: Parchman Farm and the Ordeal of Jim Crow Justice*. New York: Free Press, 1996.

Pacht, Asher, Seymour Halleck, and John C. Ehrmann. "Diagnosis and Treatment of the Sex Offender: Nine Year Study." *American Journal of Psychiatry* 118 (1962): 802–8.

Painter, Nell Irvin. " 'Social Equality,' Miscegenation, Labor, and Power." In *The Evolution of Southern Culture*, edited by Numan V. Bartley, 47–67. Athens: University of Georgia Press, 1988.

Parker, Kathleen Ruth. "Law, Culture, and Sexual Censure: Sex Crimes Prosecution in a Midwest County Circuit Court." Ph.D. diss., Michigan State University, 1993.

Partington, Donald H. "The Incidence of the Death Penalty for Rape in Virginia." *Washington and Lee Law Review* 22 (Spring 1965): 43–75.

Pascoe, Peggy. "Miscegenation Law, Court Cases, and Ideologies of 'Race' in Twentieth-Century America." In *Love, Sex, Race: Crossing Boundaries in North American History*, edited by Martha Hodes, 464–90. New York: New York University Press, 1999.

Paul, Diane B. *Controlling Human Heredity: 1865 to the Present*. Atlantic Highlands, N.J.: Humanities Press, 1995.

Peiss, Kathy, and Christina Simmons, eds. *Passion and Power: Sexuality in History*. Philadelphia: Temple University Press, 1989.

Percy, William Alexander. *Lanterns on the Levee*. New York: Knopf, 1941.

Phillips, Charles David. "Social Structure and Social Control: Modeling Discriminatory Execution of Blacks in Georgia and North Carolina, 1925–1935." *Social Forces* 65 (December 1986): 458–75.

Radelet, Michael L., and Ronald L. Akers. "Deterrence and the Death Penalty: The View of Experts." *The Journal of Criminal Law and Criminology* 87 (1996): 1–11.

Rafter, Nicole Hahn. *Creating Born Criminals*. Urbana: University of Illinois Press, 1997.

Raine, Nancy Venable. *After Silence: Rape and My Journey Back*. New York: Crown Publishers, 1998.

Raper, Arthur. *The Tragedy of Lynching*. 1933. Reprint, Montclair, N.J.: Patterson Smith, 1969.

Rise, Eric W. *The Martinsville Seven: Race, Rape, and Capital Punishment*. Charlottesville: University Press of Virginia, 1995.

Roberts, Dorothy E. "Rape, Violence, and Women's Autonomy." *Chicago-Kent Law Review* 69 (1993): 359–88.

Robertson, Stephen. "Signs, Marks, and Private Parts: Doctors, Legal Discourses, and Evidence of Rape in the United States, 1823–1930." *Journal of the History of Sexuality* 8 (1998): 345–88.

Roediger, David. *Towards the Abolition of Whiteness: Essays on Race, Politics, and Working-Class History*. London: Verso, 1994.

Rose, Deborah. " 'Worse than Death': Psychodynamics of Rape Victims and the Need for Psychotherapy." *American Journal of Psychiatry* 143 (1986): 817–24.

Rothman, Joshua D. *Notorious in the Neighborhood: Sex and Families across the*

Color Line in Virginia, 1787–1861. Chapel Hill: University of North Carolina Press, 2003.

——. " 'To Be Free from Thate Curs and Let at Liberty': Interracial Adultery and Divorce in Antebellum Virginia." *Virginia Magazine of History and Biography* 106 (Autumn 1998): 443–81.

Rowan, Carl T. *South of Freedom*. 1952. Reprint, Baton Rouge: Louisiana State University Press, 1997.

Sanday, Peggy Reeves. *A Woman Scorned: Acquaintance Rape in Trial*. New York: Doubleday, 1996.

Scherer, Migael. *Still Loved by the Sun: A Rape Survivor's Journal*. New York: Simon and Schuster, 1992.

Schulofer, Stephen J. *Unwanted Sex: The Culture of Intimidation and the Failure of Law*. Cambridge: Harvard University Press, 1998.

Scully, Diana. *Understanding Sexual Violence: A Study of Convicted Rapists*. Boston: Unwin Hyman, 1990.

Scully, Pamela. "Rape, Race, and Colonial Culture: The Sexual Politics of Identity in the Nineteenth-Century Cape Colony, South Africa." *American Historical Review* 100 (April 1995): 335–59.

Searles, Patricia, and Ronald J. Berger, eds. *Rape and Society: Readings on the Problem of Sexual Assault*. Boulder, Colo.: Westview Press, 1995.

Shapiro, Herbert. *White Violence and Black Response: From Reconstruction to Montgomery*. Amherst: University of Massachusetts Press, 1988.

Simon, Bryant. "Race Relations: African-American Organizing, Liberalism, and White Working-Class Politics in Postwar South Carolina." *Jumping Jim Crow: Southern Politics from Civil War to Civil Rights*, edited by Jane Dailey, Glenda Gilmore, and Bryant Simon, 239–59. Princeton: Princeton University Press, 2000.

——. "The Appeal of Cole Blease of South Carolina: Race, Class, and Sex in the New South." *Journal of Southern History* 62 (1996): 57–86.

Sitkoff, Harvard. *The Struggle for Black Equality, 1954–1992*. New York: Hill and Wang, 1993.

Smead, Howard. *Blood Justice: The Lynching of Mack Charles Parker*. New York: Oxford University Press, 1986.

Smith, Graham. *When Jim Crow Met John Bull: Black American Soldiers in World War II Britain*. New York: St. Marten's Press, 1987.

Smith, John Douglas. "Managing White Supremacy: Politics and Culture in Virginia, 1919–1929." Ph.D. diss., University of Virginia, 1998.

——. *Managing White Supremacy: Race, Politics, and Citizenship in Jim Crow, Virginia*. Chapel Hill: University of North Carolina Press, 2002.

Smith, Lillian. *Killers of the Dream*. New York: Anchor, 1963.

Smith, Merril D., ed. *Sex without Consent: Rape and Sexual Coercion in America*. New York: New York University Press, 2001.

Smith, Robert A., and James V. Giles. *An American Rape: A True Account of the Giles-Johnson Case*. Washington, D.C.: New Republic Book Company, 1975.

Sohn Chang Moon. "Principle and Expediency in Judicial Review: Miscegenation Cases in the Supreme Court." Ph.D. diss., Columbia University, 1970.

Solinger, Rickie. *Wake up Little Susie: Single Pregnancy and Race before* Roe v. Wade. New York: Routledge Press, 1992.

Sommerville, Diane Miller. " 'I Was Very Much Wounded': Rape Law, Children, and the Antebellum South." In *Sex without Consent: Rape and Sexual Coercion in America*, edited by Merril D. Smith, 136–77. New York: New York University Press, 2001.

——. "The Rape Myth in the Old South Reconsidered." *Journal of Southern History* 61 (August 1995): 481–518.

——. "The Rape Myth Reconsidered: The Intersection of Race, Class, and Gender in the American South, 1800–1877." Ph.D. diss., Rutgers University, 1995.

——."Rape, Race, and Castration in Slave Law in the Colonial and Early South." In *The Devil's Lane: Sex and Race in the Early South*, edited by Catherine Clinton and Michele Gillespie, 74–89. New York: Oxford University Press, 1997.

Stansell, Christina. *City of Women: Sex and Class in New York, 1789–1860*. Urbana: University of Illinois Press, 1986.

Sullivan, Patricia. *Days of Hope: Race and Democracy in the New Deal Era*. Chapel Hill: University of North Carolina Press, 1996.

Taslitz, Andrew E. *Rape and the Culture of the Courtroom*. New York: New York University Press, 1999.

Thompson, E. P. *Whigs and Hunters: The Origins of the Black Act*. London: Penguin Books, 1976.

Tomaselli, Sylvana, and Roy Porter, eds. *Rape*. Oxford: Basil Blackwell, 1986.

Torrey, Morrison. "When Will We Be Believed?: Rape Myths and the Idea of a Fair Trial in Rape Prosecutions." *UC Davis Law Review* 24 (1991): 1013–71.

Vinikas, Vincent. "Specters in the Past: The Saint Charles, Arkansas, Lynching of 1904 and the Limits of Historical Inquiry." *Journal of Southern History* 65 (August 1999): 535–64.

Waldrep, Christopher. *Roots of Disorder: Race and Criminal Justice in the American South, 1817–1880*. Champagne-Urbana: University of Illinois Press, 1998.

——. "Substituting the Law for the Lash: Emancipation and Legal Formalism in a Mississippi County Court." *Journal of American History* 82 (March 1996): 1425–51.

——. "Word and Deed: The Language of Lynching, 1820–1953." In *Lethal Imagination: Violence and Brutality in American History*, edited by Michael A. Bellesiles, 229–60. New York: New York University Press, 1999.

Whites, LeeAnn. "Love, Hate, Race, and Lynching: Rebecca Latimer Felton and the Gender Politics of Racial Violence." In *Democracy Betrayed: The Wilmington Race Riot of 1898 and Its Legacy*, edited by David S. Cecelski and Timothy B. Tyson, 143–62. Chapel Hill: University of North Carolina Press, 1998.

——. "Rebecca Latimer Felton and the Problem of 'Protection' in the New South." In *Visible Women: New Essays on American Activism*, edited by Nancy Hewitt, 41–61. Urbana: University of Illinois Press, 1993.

Whitfield, Stephen J. *A Death in the Delta: The Story of Emmett Till*. Baltimore: Johns Hopkins University Press, 1988.

Wigmore, John Henry. *A Treatise on the Anglo-American System of Evidence in Trials at Common Law, Vol IIIA*. Boston: Little, Brown, 1970.

Williams, Blanville. "Corroboration—Sexual Cases." *Criminal Law Review* (October 1962): 662–71.

Williams, Franklin H. "The Death Penalty and the Negro." *The Crisis* 67 (October 1960): 501–12.

Williamson, Joel. *The Crucible of Race: Black-White Relations in the American South since Emancipation*. New York: Oxford University Press, 1984.

Wolfe, Margaret Ripley. *Daughters of Canaan: A Saga of Southern Women*. Louisville: University of Kentucky Press, 1995.

Wolfgang, Marvin E., and Marc Riedel. "Race, Judicial Discretion, and the Death Penalty." *The Annals of the American Academy of Political and Social Science* 407 (1973): 119–33.

Woodbridge, W. A. "Why the Difference?" *The Independent* 65 (1908): 605–6.

Wriggins, Jennifer. "Rape, Racism, and the Law." *Harvard Women's Law Journal* 6 (1983): 103–41.

Wright, George C. "By the Book: The Legal Executions of Kentucky Blacks." In *Under Sentence of Death: Lynching in the South*, edited by W. Fitzbugh Brundage, 250–70. Chapel Hill: University of North Carolina Press, 1997.

——. "Executions of Afro-Americans in Kentucky, 1870–1940." *Georgia Journal of Southern Legal History* 1 (Fall / Winter 1991): 321–55.

Wright, Richard. *Native Son*. New York: Harper, 1940.

Wyatt-Brown, Bertram. *Honor and Violence in the Old South*. New York: Oxford University Press, 1986.

Zangrando, Robert L. *The NAACP's Campaign against Lynching*. Philadelphia: Temple University Press, 1980.

Ziegenmeyer, Nancy. *Taking Back My Life*. New York: Summit Books, 1992.

Jewitt, Floyd, 229
Johnson, Andrew, 71
Johnson, B. D., 108–10
Johnson, Daniel, 135
Johnson, Eliza, 109
Johnson, Guy, 211
Johnson, John
Johnson, Pearl, 108–10
Johnson, Sarah, 235
Johnson, William, 48–49
Jones, Fletcher, 215
Jones, Henry, 92, 131
Jones, LeRoi (Amiri Baraka), 172
Jones, Philip, 183–84
Jones, Walter, 54
Jones, West, 133
Juries: race of, 32; and sentencing, 32, 67; as part of white community, 32–33; and public opinion, 38; instructions to, 45, 68, 70, 132; exclusion of African Americans, 181; inclusion of African Americans, 207, 215–17

Ker, Richard, 149
Kime, R. W., 55, 133
King, Alexander C., 171
King, James, 232
Kirkendorfer, Dean L., 220–21

Lancaster, Freddie, 235
Lane, L. W., 192
Lassiter, Swannie, 136
Laughlin, Harry, 134
Law enforcement. See Confessions
Lee, Carter, 72
Lee, John P., 42
"Legal lynching," 17
Legal officials: control over punishment, 28, 87–88, 114, 164
Legal system: legitimacy of, 10, 18, 81, 143–44, 168; and potential extralegal violence, 16–18, 37–39; racial prejudice in, 17, 21, 181, 206, 234, 249; and racial control, 20–21, 29, 73–74, 80; skepticism of women's charges, 52–53, 59, 113, 131, 153–54, 165, 207, 209, 213; limiting access to white privilege, 81; power of white women in, 101, 140, 142, 143; and class hierarchy, 108–10, 146; and chastity of victim, 121–22, 138, 142; influence of African Americans on, 170, 215–17, 238–39, 245; and African American women's charges of rape, 207. See also Trials

Legions, Samuel, 64, 103, 105, 151
Leverage, 175–78, 190–99, 204
Lewis, Arthur, 132–33
Lindsay, R. L., 85
Louisa County, 237
"Lover's lanes": assaults in, 214, 227
Lucas, Lynn, 194
Lynch, Frank, 74–75
Lynchburg, Va., 38, 54, 61, 156, 219
Lynching, 5; as historical focus for discussion of interracial relationships, 8; as form of racial control, 8, 10, 186, 253 (n. 22); and white solidarity; 8, 23; justifications for, 8, 175, 187; and charges of sexual assault, 8, 257 (n. 34), 261 (n. 5); and racial injustice, 8–9; decrease in, 20; national opinion of, 20, 29; of William Page, 23–24, 187–90; of James Jordan, 24–25; of Harry Davis, 25; of Adam Howard, 25; of Raymond Byrd, 29–30; and African American community, 186–90. See also Extralegal violence

Mackey, Crandall, 142–43
Madison, J. Hugo, 221
Madison County, 60
Malicious wounding, 64
Mann, William Hodges, 44
Mann Act, 1, 3
Maphis, Charles, 83
Marriage: of victim, 100–101, 143
Martin, J. H., 156
Martin, Martin A., 238
Martin, Mary, 74–75
Martinsville, Va., 185, 206, 210–11, 240
Martinsville Seven, 185, 206, 210–11, 231, 242, 262 (n. 13)
Massenburg Public Assemblage Act, 27
Massive resistance, 202–3
Matthews, George, 41
Matthews, Raymond, 229
Mayo, John Henry, 216
Mays, John, Jr., 196–99
McCann, John Henry, 99
McGavock, Jim, 85–86
McGuire Hospital, 214
McKnight, Ernest, 44
McLaurin, Melton, 155
Mecklenburg County, 35, 206
Menefield, James, 214
Mental ability of accused assailant, 6, 83–85, 93–94, 119, 184, 199–200, 213